PUBLIC EDUCATION, NEOLIBERALISM, AND TEACHERS

New York, Mexico City, Toronto

PAUL BOCKING

Public Education, Neoliberalism, and Teachers

New York, Mexico City, Toronto

UNIVERSITY OF TORONTO PRESS
Toronto Buffalo London

Toronto Buffalo London
utorontopress.com

ISBN 978-1-4875-0660-5 (cloth) ISBN 978-1-4875-3251-6 (ePUB)
ISBN 978-1-4875-3450-9 (PDF)

Library and Archives Canada Cataloguing in Publication

Title: Public education, neoliberalism, and teachers : New York, Mexico City, Toronto / Paul Bocking.
Names: Bocking, Paul, 1984– author.
Description: Includes bibliographical references and index.
Identifiers: Canadiana (print) 20200176234 | Canadiana (ebook) 20200176269 | ISBN 9781487506605 (cloth) | ISBN 9781487534516 (PDF) | ISBN 9781487532512 (ePUB)
Subjects: LCSH: Public schools – New York (State) – New York. | LCSH: Public schools – Mexico – Mexico City. | LCSH: Public schools – Ontario – Toronto. | LCSH: Education and state – New York (State) – New York. | LCSH: Education and state – Mexico – Mexico City. | LCSH: Education and state – Ontario – Toronto. | LCSH: Teaching – New York (State) – New York. | LCSH: Teaching – Mexico – Mexico City. | LCSH: Teaching – Ontario – Toronto. | LCSH: Neoliberalism.
Classification: LCC LC59 .B63 2020 | DDC 371.01 – dc23

This book has been published with the help of a grant from the Federation for the Humanities and Social Sciences, through the Awards to Scholarly Publications Program, using funds provided by the Social Sciences and Humanities Research Council of Canada.

University of Toronto Press acknowledges the financial assistance to its publishing program of the Canada Council for the Arts and the Ontario Arts Council, an agency of the Government of Ontario.

Canada Council for the Arts Conseil des Arts du Canada

Funded by the Government of Canada Financé par le gouvernement du Canada

For all teachers who cultivate wisdom and struggle for social justice

Contents

Preface xi

Abbreviations xv

1 **Introduction** 3
- 1.1 What Is Teachers' Professional Autonomy? Why Is It Important for Public Education? 3
- 1.2 Key Dimensions for Assessing Challenges to Professional Autonomy 6
- 1.3 A Geography of Teachers' Professional Autonomy 11
- 1.4 Challenging Professional Autonomy 15
- 1.5 Methodology 19
- 1.6 Book Overview 26

2 **Geographies of Professional Autonomy and Neoliberalism in North America** 30
- Preface: Día del Trabajo 30
- 2.1 The Emergence of Public Education, Teachers' Unions, and Professionalism 34
- 2.2 The Postwar Consolidation of Public Education Systems and Teachers' Unions 37
- 2.3 The Neoliberalization of Education: Teacher Unionism on the Defensive 44
- 2.4 Transnational Elite Policy 53
- 2.5 Counter-Hegemonic Continental Networks 61

3 **New York City** 68
- Preface: Visiting a Small High School on the Upper West Side 68
- 3.1 Structural Changes I: Centralizing Power to Facilitate Neoliberal Fast Policy 74
- 3.2 Structural Changes II: Transforming Workplace Culture 81

3.3 Teacher Precariousness and the Weakening of the School Site Union and Professional Autonomy 89
3.4 Scaling-Up: Initiative in Neoliberal Policy Shifts from New York City to Albany 100
3.5 Cuomo's Expansion of Standardized Testing into Teacher Evaluation: Undermining Professional Autonomy 105
3.6 State of Our Union, State of Our Schools 114

4 **Mexico City** 126
Preface: Día del Maestro 126
4.1 Transitions in State Power, Decentralization, and the Emergence of Elba Esther Gordillo's SNTE as a Key Neoliberal Actor 129
4.2 Re-centralized Governance through School-Based Competition 135
4.3 From Clientelism to a Neoliberalized Teaching Profession 143
4.4 Enrique Peña Nieto and Fast Policy 150
4.5 What Makes a Teacher? Marginalizing the Normales and Teacher Education 154
4.6 Testing Teachers 158
4.7 Precarious Employment and Professional Autonomy 163
4.8 Acquiescence, Resistance, and the Challenges of Scaling-Up: The CNTE in the City and the Countryside 171

5 **Toronto** 181
Preface: School Workroom Cultures 181
5.1 Centralizing Governance: Increasing Ontario Ministry of Education Control of the Toronto District School Board 184
5.2 Quantifying Student Achievement: Policy from the Centre 188
5.3 Quantifying Student Achievement: The Impact on the Classroom and Professional Autonomy 202
5.4 Quantifying Student Achievement: Intersection of Race, Class, and School Choice on Teachers' Work 213
5.5 Scaling-Up: The Centralization of Bargaining and the Negotiation of Professional Autonomy 221

6 **Conclusion** 235
Preface: Confronting the Neoliberalization of Education 235
6.1 The Centrality of Teachers' Professional Autonomy in the Struggle against the Neoliberalization of Education 237
6.2 Teachers' Unions as Champions of Professional Autonomy 244
6.3 A Multi-Scalar Geography of Teachers' Professional Autonomy 246

Appendix: List of Interviews 251
Notes 253
References 273
Index 293

Preface

At some point in training to become a teacher, we are asked to describe our inspirations for entering the profession. Extolling the virtues of her job to all who would listen, scavenging ideas and materials for her classes from any context, an endless stream of staffroom gossip and anecdotes of her students, "teacher-ness" permeated my mother's being from my earliest memories to her recent retirement. A great joy of teaching was the ability to create, to devise engaging assignments and find novels that gripped her students and inspired reflection. This was predicated on a way with banter that informed a familiarity with each of her students and demonstrated concern and compassion. Students would never describe her with a knowing grin as an "easy teacher." One of my lazier friends in high school described her as "that bitch" after serving another detention. She was not an easy adopter of new technology, comparing herself with the young teacher across the hall who dressed like his students and was always using the latest gadget with his class. She insisted that writing on the blackboard was sometimes the most direct way to teach grammar. Though she usually respected principals, she relished standing up in staff meetings to refute policies passed down from the education ministry, which she believed were wrong or lacking in substance. For my mom, being a union member was an inseparable element of a teacher's identity. I learned that education was politically contested from childhood visits to picket lines in the 1990s and saw the stresses that governmental policies can create in the personal lives of teachers. She provided me with limitless encouragement, alleviating my introversion and my pessimism over the hiring prospects for history and politics teachers in Toronto.

The final years of my undergraduate studies and teacher training were defined in large part by interwoven personal and political relationships that saw me taking the Greyhound bus from Toronto to Mexico

City whenever the opportunity provided itself. On one trip in October 2006, venturing south of the capital to the state of Oaxaca, I witnessed the "commune" of teachers and their allies who had rebelled against a repressive government. Thousands of educators, dressed according to the paragon of middle-class respectability, many middle-aged, erected barricades and occupied city squares and buildings, demanding the resignation of the governor, who had sent police to burn down their strike encampments and shot several of their colleagues. Compared with the prospects of our calm teacher lives in Toronto, the scene greatly affected me. I became familiar with the powerful radical current among Mexican teachers, the National Coordination of Education Workers (CNTE).

After graduating from the Ontario Institute for Studies in Education, I began teaching with the Toronto District School Board.[1] With a dearth of permanent positions available, I obtained semester- and year-long contracts, taking me to schools across the city. I worked in both struggling and affluent neighbourhoods, mostly in the former, with many newcomer families. When I arrived in the department work room, the Curriculum Leader[2] would present me with the syllabus for each course I would teach, consisting of a list of units aligned with education ministry guidelines. They then familiarized me with unit plans and handouts compiled by previous teachers of these courses. I usually felt most comfortable with my own materials. As a new teacher I depended on the advice of my experienced colleagues for feedback on constructing workable assignments and dealing with wayward students.

In the classroom, I was unprepared for the extent that many of my students were unmoved by learning for learning's sake. Building rapport was all-important, and I often felt I lacked the ability to do so, especially compared with what I imagined my mother would do. Some days were good; some days were full of self-doubt. Without knowing, I was learning the importance of space and place – geography – that later I would base my PhD on. Neither my students nor I were the same once we were in a classroom. Each classroom was a unique territory where we all tried to know each other better. I had substantial freedom in devising my day-to-day classroom activities, and I wasn't tied to a scripted plan, though this fact often kept me at my desk well into the evening trying to figure out what would work best the next morning. I gradually developed my planning abilities and a sense of what worked in a given classroom.

My union, the Ontario Secondary School Teachers Federation (OSSTF), whose members were at far less risk of state violence than Mexican teachers, engaged in a more institutionalized labour relations regime. I was a regular attendee at the biennial Labor Notes conferences of union activists from across North America. I was deeply impressed by the insurgent Chicago Caucus of Rank and File Educators (CORE), who in 2010 were elected to the leadership of their union. Like many, I was inspired by CORE's intensive organization of teachers, open approach to alliances with parents, and frontal ideological counter-attack against the neoliberalization of education. I saw lessons for my own union and political context, but I also thought it would be revealing to understand why, in the far more prevalent and representative cases, activism does not take off, often despite similarly provocative conditions. This led to my interest in learning more about the situation of teachers in New York City, a group of whom who were striving to organize themselves on a basis similar to that of CORE and who faced many of the same challenges, but within a very different institutional context.

As a representative of my union, I became active with the Trinational Coalition in Defence of Public Education, whose major impetus has been Mexican teachers and students. While speaking at a solidarity conference with Mexican teachers in November 2013, I was introduced to a group of Mexico City high school teachers. I struck up relationships that enabled me to visit secondary schools and interview their colleagues and administrators and witness the conditions under which they teach. Their passion, political commitment, and vast energy helped sustain my own commitments as a union activist under usually far less dramatic circumstances in Canada, though here too I could see a continuum rather than a divergence of shared issues.

I compared the experiences of teachers from Mexico City and New York with my own emerging experience in Toronto and those of my colleagues, alongside literature on education policy and governance, and concluded that many of the debates and conflicts over contemporary education reform could be understood as struggles over the professional autonomy of teachers. Standardized testing and its use in facilitating "school choice" and sometimes defining the quality of schools and even individual teachers constrained the space for educators to define their own pedagogy and draw on their expertise to meet the specific needs of their classes. A key to understanding how these policies unfolded and have been contested has been the varied responses of teachers' unions and movements.

Abbreviations

ACE	Alianza Por la Calidad Educativa (Alliance for Quality Education)
AFT	American Federation of Teachers
AFSEDF	Administración Federal de Servicios Educativos en el DF (Federal Administration of Education Services in the Federal District)
ANMEB	Acuerdo Nacional para la Modernización de la Educación Basica (National Accord for the Modernization of Basic Education)
APPR	Annual Professional Performance Review
ATR	Absent Teacher Reserve
BCTF	British Columbia Teachers Federation
BOE	Board of Education (NYC)
CEA	Confederación de Educadores Americanos (Confederation of American Educators)
CNTE	Coordinadora Nacional de los Trabajadores de la Educación (National Coordination of Education Workers)
CORE	Caucus of Rank and File Educators
CSD	Community School District
CTF	Canadian Teachers Federation
DF	Distrito Federal (Federal District)
EQAO	Education Quality and Accountability Office
ETFO	Elementary Teachers' Federation of Ontario
GDP	Gross Domestic Product
INEE	Instituto Nacional por la Evaluación Educativa (National Institute for the Evaluation of Education)
ISSSTE	Instituto de Seguro Social de Trabajadores al Servicio del Estado (Public Sector Social Security Institute)
MORE	Movement of Rank and File Educators
Morena	Movimento Regeneración Nacional (National Regeneration Movement)

MOSL	Measures of Student Learning
NCLB	No Child Left Behind
NEA	National Education Association
NDP	New Democratic Party
NTIP	New Teacher Induction Program
NYC DOE	New York City Department of Education
NYSED	New York State Education Department
NYSUT	New York State United Teachers
OCT	Ontario College of Teachers
OECD	Organisation for Economic Cooperation and Development
OECTA	Ontario English Catholic Teachers' Association
PAN	Partido de la Acción Nacional (National Action Party)
PC	Progressive Conservative
PDT	Provincial Discussion Table
PEC	Programa de Escuelas de Calidad (Quality Schools Program)
PEP	Panel for Education Policy
PISA	Program for International Student Assessment
PRD	Partido de la Revolución Democratica (Party of the Democratic Revolution)
PRI	Partido Revolucionario Institucional (Institutional Revolutionary Party)
OISE	Ontario Institute for Studies in Education
OPSBA	Ontario Public School Boards Association
OSSTF	Ontario Secondary School Teachers Federation
RTTT	Race To The Top
SBM	School Based Management
SEP	Secretaria de la Educación Publica (Secretary of Public Education)
SNTE	Sindicato Nacional de los Trabajadores de la Educación (National Union of Education Workers)
TDSB	Toronto District School Board
TFA	Teach For America
TPA	Teacher Performance Appraisal
UCORE	United Caucus of Rank and File Educators
UFT	United Federation of Teachers
UNAM	Universidad Nacional Autonoma de México (National Autonomous University of Mexico)
UNESCO	United Nations Educational Scientific and Cultural Organization
UPN	Universidad Nacional Pedagogica (National Pedagogical University)
US DOE	United States Department of Education

PUBLIC EDUCATION, NEOLIBERALISM, AND TEACHERS

1 Introduction

1.1. What Is Teachers' Professional Autonomy? Why Is It Important for Public Education?

What it means to be a teacher or a student within public education is undergoing a transformation. In recent years public primary and secondary schools in New York City, Mexico City, and increasingly in Toronto, which serve vastly divergent students and communities, have been subject to strikingly similar waves of policy proposals. Many of these initiatives can be characterized within a neoliberal rationality (Klees 2008; Aboites 2012; Weiner 2012; Hernandez Navarro 2013) that seeks to expand market relations into ever further realms of human activity and, while doing so, reinforce the political power of the economic elite (Harvey 2007). A key outcome has been the de-professionalization or deskilling of teachers.

Although highly uneven in terms of the resources dedicated by the state, mass schooling emerged through the twentieth century in North America to a large extent defined by humanist ideals of relative equality and the intrinsic worth of education, at least in theory (Manzer 2003; Levinson 2001; Pinto 2015). Through waves of organizing and strikes, teachers both won a substantial degree of security and increased their professional status. The neoliberal shift in education in the twenty-first century confronts the universal public service model, striving to realign its form and content to for-profit rationalities. Within a broader labour market context of the retrenchment of workers' power in the workplace and the precariousness of employment and weakened unions, a key dimension of the neoliberalization of education has been the undermining of teachers' control over their work. The "quality" of an education system is increasingly defined by quantitative metrics administered from the top-down. With their purported objectivity, they negate the need for teachers with the autonomy and expertise to adapt broad curriculum guidelines to the specific needs of their students. Instead, deskilled teachers and their schools compete on the basis of standardized test scores both for increased student enrolment and to keep their own jobs. This model is limited by the continued existence of the classroom as a space of labour autonomy, run by experienced and highly educated teachers.

This book uses case studies situated in New York City, Mexico City, and Toronto to explore why teachers' professional autonomy is under assault in the United States, Mexico, and Canada, to varying degrees and with commonalities and differences. Despite the considerable social, political, and economic differences between these "global cities," a surprisingly high degree of common experience exists in terms of how contemporary policy is affecting professional autonomy. Using these three case studies, this book argues for the importance of understanding neoliberal education policy as a dominant trend that transcends the realities of local school districts, municipalities, states, or national governments. At the same time, it will also show the significance of local contexts to explain variations in education governance, especially for understanding the role of resistance, most often led by teachers' unions.

Professional autonomy means the capacity and freedom of teachers to exercise their judgment in interpreting broad curriculum guidelines established by the state into their day-to-day classroom activities. Teachers exercise their autonomy by making pedagogical decisions (methodologies of instruction and evaluation), determining the relative emphasis to place on these general objectives, choosing many of the resources used, and striving to build rapport with students and effectively run the class. The capacity for judgment teachers exercise in these areas derives principally from professional training and years of experience and peer support. The objective of exercising professional autonomy or judgment is to most effectively meet the specific needs of each unique group of students. Teachers' professional knowledge could be organized into three areas: subject area knowledge, pedagogy, and the less tangible emotional intelligence for supporting child and adolescent development. While important in all schools, the latter is especially critical in contexts where students experience severe deprivation of social supports, often for reasons associated with high levels of poverty. These parameters place the professional autonomy of teachers within broad boundaries, more limited than the academic freedom of tenured university faculty. Professional autonomy is essential for teachers to be able to interpret policies and curriculum originating from distant authorities in a way that is meaningful for their students. There are also justifiable limits to this autonomy.

Of the many factors determining teachers' job satisfaction, professional autonomy may be the most significant (Strong and Yoshida 2014). A concise, though not exhaustive definition of "teachers' professional judgment," is provided by the Ontario Ministry of Education's *Growing Success*, an official document intended to guide teachers in assessing and evaluating student's work:

> Judgement that is informed by professional knowledge of curriculum expectations, context, evidence of learning, methods of instruction and assessment, and the criteria and standards that indicate success in student learning. In professional practice, judgement involves a purposeful and systematic thinking process that evolves in terms of accuracy and insight with ongoing reflection and self-correction. (2010, 152)

Concerned by member reports of school administrators unilaterally ordering changes to student grades or dictating preparation methods for standardized exams, the OSSTF distributed a brochure to its members defining professional judgment. In addition to the above quote, there is a "not exhaustive" list of examples of exercising professional judgment, that includes:

- choosing the order and emphasis of specific expectations when delivering the curriculum
- identifying the instructional strategies to deliver the curriculum
- determining the format and content of your lesson plans
- selecting methods for differentiating instruction and assessments for students
- deciding what resources are used to support the curriculum and outcomes and whether or not to use ministry approved textbooks
- choosing the frequency, timing, methods and types of assessment and evaluation used to measure student learning (OSSTF 2015a)

The brochure was introduced in the monthly union newspaper in an article titled "Professionalism = Autonomy" (OSSTF 2016). As is suggested by this example, teachers' unions have been decisive in supporting and defending professional autonomy, particularly to the extent that they have been able to push back on the various challenges outlined below.

1.2. Key Dimensions for Assessing Challenges to Professional Autonomy

I assess challenges to teachers' professional autonomy in my case studies across five dimensions of comparison on governmental policy and teacher responses. First, I will be looking at changes in governance, namely, the centralization of authority to higher levels, often legitimized by mobilizing policies from elsewhere. A weakening of local democratic control often ensues. Citing the recent experience of Chicago, in 2002 former New York City (NYC) Mayor Michael Bloomberg was given mayoral control over the New York City Department of Education (NYC DOE) by the state legislature. The locally elected board of trustees was replaced with an advisory panel, a majority appointed by the mayor and a minority appointed by borough leaders. Both supporters and critics of Bloomberg's subsequent education policies affecting teachers' work have attributed his ability to rapidly push through major, often controversial, changes to this concentration of power in the mayor and his appointed education "CEO." While Bloomberg generally enjoyed the support of the state government, which shared many of his ideological stances on education, this common interest was not shared by Bloomberg's centre-left successor, Bill de Blasio. The state government under Governor Andrew Cuomo has repeatedly exercised its greater power over municipal policymaking by thwarting many of de Blasio's more progressive education proposals. During the George W. Bush and Barack Obama administrations, which covered most of the 2000 to 2017 period studied in his book, the federal government was also a significant actor in education policy, passing legislation that included No Child Left Behind (NCLB) in 2002, setting mandates for states, and Race to the Top (RTTT) in 2009, which provided financial incentives for state compliance.

In contrast to New York City's periods of decentralized education governance, Mexico City's education system has been highly centralized throughout its modern existence. While there is generally no equivalent to locally elected school trustees in the country, Mexico City's education system is subject to central control more than elsewhere. Because of the city's special status as the Federal District, without the powers of a state until 2016, the local school authority has been appointed by the federal Secretary of Public Education (SEP). In relation to the effect of neoliberal education policy on teachers' professional autonomy, the most important centralizing shift affecting Mexico City's teachers was the codification in the national constitution that their employment would be subject to standardized evaluation. By placing this policy in the constitution, teachers in Mexico City and elsewhere in the country would not be able to negotiate a legal exemption at a subnational level.

Meanwhile in Toronto, the trend that began in the late 1990s of the provincial government taking power over education policy from local school boards (through the transfer of budgetary powers) continued. Using the premise of local scandals, the government diminished the capacity of trustees to advocate in local and provincial politics. During this period, the Ministry of Education increased its role in setting policies for the province and monitoring their implementation by school boards. Following this centralization of power with the provincial government, legislation in 2014 codified the creation of a two-tier central/local split in negotiations, the most consequential issues generally being addressed directly between the provincial leadership of the unions and the government itself, thus reducing the importance of local-level negotiations with school boards.

Second, I will consider how contemporary policies have shifted workplace power relations between principals and teachers from a collegial model to a manager-employee hierarchy. "School-Based Management" (SBM) programs download budgetary, teacher-hiring, discipline, and dismissal practices to school administrators. The role of principals in all three sites has increasingly shifted to responsibility for the implementation at their school of policies passed down from the school district and, especially, from state, provincial, and national governments. While principals in New York never have been part of the existing teachers' union, they were removed by the governments in Mexico and Ontario in 2017 and 1997, respectively. In Mexico, the requirement of graduating from a university faculty of education or a teachers' college (the normales) was replaced with a standardized exam of "teaching knowledge." Many educators and union leaders believe that without formal training in pedagogy and classroom management, these teachers will be ill-prepared to exercise their autonomy and will also lack an integral experience in the construction of their professional identity as teachers. At the same time, it became more difficult and time-consuming to obtain permanent (so-called tenured) status as a teacher in New York City and Mexico City. This trouble affects worksite power dynamics when combined with rising turnover rates and the fact that a growing proportion of the teaching staff in many schools does not have recourse to union protections, including "just cause" for discipline.

As a result, these teachers are poorly positioned to defend their professional autonomy when it is challenged by school administrators, for example, through directives to "teach to the (standardized) test," as discussed below.

Third, I look at the effect of standardized testing of students and teachers on the latter's capacity to exercise professional judgment in the classroom through designing appropriate and unique lesson plans, pedagogy, and forms of evaluation. In all three case studies, the imperative to produce rising test scores has been an important premise for the intervention of administrators into teachers' work, pushing them to teach to the test, particularly in struggling schools, in order to meet official mandates of showing steadily improving results. In addition to raising results on standardized literacy and math tests, in some cases teachers in Toronto have also been pushed to ensure their evaluation policies contribute to an overall increase in graduation rates. In New York City, and in Mexico City from 2006 to 2013, pressure on teachers to align their teaching with test preparation was considerably compounded by the tying of their student's test scores to criteria for their continued employment and annual salary increases. From 2013 to 2016, the primary issue of contention for Mexican teachers was making their continued employment conditional on the passing of a standardized competencies exam, which many viewed as being ill-equipped to assess their teaching capabilities and/or as a "punitive" test that would be used as a premise to fire dissidents.

Fourth, and particularly relevant in New York City and Toronto, I assess "school choice" or the competition of schools for enrolment and thereby funding, based on publicly available standardized test scores. In both cities to varying degrees, schools with high scores, which are overwhelmingly attended by students from the most privileged demographics, are flooded with applicants. Low-score schools, attended by lower-income students, more often struggle for enrolment. The ensuing segregation of easy-to-teach students and students with greater needs considerably affects teachers' work and, more broadly, equity. Particularly among more affluent and mobile families, school choice has also propagated a "student/parent as customer" discourse in which the teachers' professional judgment is increasingly questioned.

Finally, in each case study site I consider the trajectories of teachers' unions towards accommodation and resistance. These paths encompass their ability to enact a multi-scalar strategy with a strong school-site presence while challenging higher levels of government and their capacity to construct broad alliances with parents, community groups, and other sectors of labour. In New York City, the union struggled to confront the Bloomberg administration's significant revisions to the conditions of teachers' employment, pushed through under mayoral control. Although the union had a legal collective bargaining agreement with the municipal government, it lacked a legal basis for negotiations with the state government (which held legal authority over the city); thus, the union was arguably even more vulnerable when an unfriendly governor began to actively intervene, despite the presence of a new, friendlier mayor. A relatively hierarchical union, with a general preference for political lobbying over member organizing and mobilization, contributed to a generally cautious approach to confronting key authorities. As a result, the union leadership lacked connections to grass-roots, parent-led movements that gathered force in 2015 (and continued in subsequent years) against what was seen as excessive testing of students. Many rank-and-file teachers were active supporters.

In Mexico City, the teachers' movement was greatly disadvantaged by the legal inability to obtain a local exemptions from national policies affecting professional autonomy as had been previously done, after key reforms were embedded in the national constitution. On the whole during this period, the Mexico City teachers' movement depended on the strength of the broader national movement to overturn the standardized teacher evaluation, which was tentatively achieved in the summer of 2016. Important factors in this context were both the relatively stronger administrative apparatus of the Mexico City education authorities, compared with that of many other states, and the weaker connections of Mexico City teachers with potential organized allies of parents and other groups than existed in states such as Oaxaca and Chiapas, where the movement was particularly strong.

The Toronto secondary school teachers' union and, by extension, the provincial-level union enjoyed a stronger institutional standing than did the other two cases studied. It ostensibly benefited from a mutually negotiated shift in the focus of collective bargaining from the local to the provincial level, to follow the previous movement of power, in contrast to New York City and Mexico City, where no such accommodation occurred. Moreover, to a greater extent than in New York City, or even in Mexico City, the Toronto and Ontario secondary school teachers' unions explicitly identified professional autonomy as a key area to be defended. A key weakness of the union in Toronto and in Ontario as a whole was, as in New York, a lack of organic linkages to organized civil society groups, which were so important to the successes of the Mexican movement.

Table 1.1 Summary of Key Commonalities across Case Studies: Teachers' Professional Autonomy in New York City, Mexico City, and Toronto

Dimension	New York	Mexico City	Toronto
Centralization of governance and weakening of local democratic control	Mayoral control since 2002; abolition of elected school board; overarching federal policy guides local parameters till 2015; overarching state policy continues to set local parameters	No elected school board; education policy changes codified in national constitution, overruling state policies in 2013; centralization of human resources from state to federal government in 2014	Weakening of elected school board, control of education finance moved from municipal to provincial in 1997; centralization of collective bargaining in 2014; overarching provincial policy sets local parameters
Shift in workplace power relations	Principals: not in union, enhanced power to hire and fire since 2001, oversee implementation of top-down policy; lengthened probationary period and more difficult to obtain permanent status for teachers	Principals: removed from union (2017), oversee implementation of top-down policy; lengthened probationary period and more difficult to obtain permanent status for teachers; education degree not required for teaching	Principals: removed from union (1997), oversee implementation of top-down policy; no major changes for teachers obtaining permanent status
Effect of standardized testing and "quantitative metrics" on professional judgment	Publicized results of standardized student exams, linked to teacher evaluation	Publicized results of standardized student exams, linked to teacher evaluation and additional school funding until 2013; education degree replaced with exam as teaching prerequisite; continued employment linked to standardized exam	Publicized results of standardized student exams, no link to teacher evaluation
School choice/ school markets	Heightened competition between public schools, and with charter schools for enrolment, use of standardized test scores, teacher imperative to raise scores	Not as evident at primary/secondary levels	Heightened competition between public schools for enrolment, use of standardized test scores, teacher imperative to raise scores

Dimension	New York	Mexico City	Toronto
Union responses: acquiescence or resistance, use of scalar strategies	UFT moderately oppositional, strongest at municipal level especially with favourable administration, weak influence over state or national policy; limited grass-roots community networks	CNTE strongly oppositional; limited local negotiations on primary schools, little power in secondary schools; power at federal level during peak national mobilizations; strong grass-roots community networks	OSSTF strongly oppositional, strong in negotiations at local and provincial level; limited grass-roots community networks

1.3. A Geography of Teachers' Professional Autonomy

New York City, Mexico City, and Toronto share the characteristics of "global cities." They comprise the dominant metropolitan area of their nation and a high-profile site for policy development and implementation, owing to a critical degree of international interconnectedness through the presence of major universities, think-tanks, media, and policymakers (Sassen 2012). Each is also the home of teachers' unions with complex histories of dissent, collaboration, and acquiescence by educators to waves of reforms. A tremendous diversity and unevenness of political culture, economics, and history exist between and within the countries in which these cities are situated (especially between Mexico and its northern neighbours). A North American study is a useful lens for understanding contemporary education policy and teachers' work for what it can tell us about policy mobility within such a diverse region and because actors are increasingly conscious of and influenced by developments elsewhere on this continent. Of course, these reforms also exist and derive their logic (as do sometimes resistant teachers) from definitions of "common sense" in education that are increasingly global in scale (Verger, Altinyelken, and de Konig 2013; Weiner and Compton 2008).

As the populations of the three cities vary widely, so do their teachers' union membership numbers.[1] In 2018, approximately 22,000 teachers (including substitutes) were employed by the Toronto District School Board (TDSB), affiliated with two unions, the Elementary Teachers Federation of Ontario (ETFO) and the Ontario Secondary School Teachers Federation (OSSTF).[2] The New York City Department of Education reports 77,000 active teachers affiliated with the United Federation of Teachers (UFT). In Mexico City, the key subnational unit in the education system is at the state level, which is paralleled by the National Union of Education Workers (SNTE)'s structure of local union sections. As the nation's capital, Mexico City has a special administrative status and its own education authority. It was titled the Federal District until 2016, when it achieved the full status of a state and is known since simply as Mexico City. The SNTE has three Mexico City sections, representing elementary and secondary teachers (Sections 9 and 10) and support staff (Section 11), totalling nearly 200,000 members. I focus on the teacher locals.

Governments often implement scalar strategies to optimize their capacity to implement policies, frequently in these cases with the objective of overcoming a critical weight of organized teachers at a particular scale. Teachers respond with their own strategies that, with varying effectiveness, try to make scale work for them too. Across all three cases in this book, the tendency is towards a scaling-up of governance, usually from the municipal scale – the basic institutional level of union organization – to the state/provincial or even national level. In all cases, the primary state actors leading these initiatives constitute a relatively small group around the executive, with the elected legislature playing a less significant role. The centralization of labour relations for teachers in North America provides an interesting contrast with contemporary trends in decentralization for significant sectors of unionized workers in the private sector (Sweeney, McWilliams, and Hickey 2012). Nevertheless, while assessing these scalar shifts, since this book argues that the agency of teachers is vital for understanding the success or failure of how such policies impact their work, the case studies take place primarily at the local scale. This is the level at which ordinary teachers live and work and where I employ field observation at schools and interviews with classroom teachers.

It is important to recognize the diversity of teachers' experience at the subnational level. In Canada, it is evident through the provincial administration of K–12 education. Although the characteristics of the systems share strong similarities in terms of policies and governance, the dynamics of distinct provincial governments lead to a divergence between the experiences of the British Columbia Teachers' Federation (BCTF), which engaged in a major strike in 2005, and the Ontario teachers who practised a relative labour peace during this period. Similarly, the experience of teachers' work varies dramatically across the United States. Despite the challenges described in chapter 3, New York City remains a relative bastion of professional stability in comparison with the context of education in Florida, Arizona, North Carolina, and elsewhere in the mostly poorer and socially conservative "Right to Work" South. In Mexico, the principal divisions are between the predominantly rural and Indigenous south and the urban, more affluent Mestizo centre and north and, within these

Figure 1.1. Scales of Education Authority and Teachers' Organization

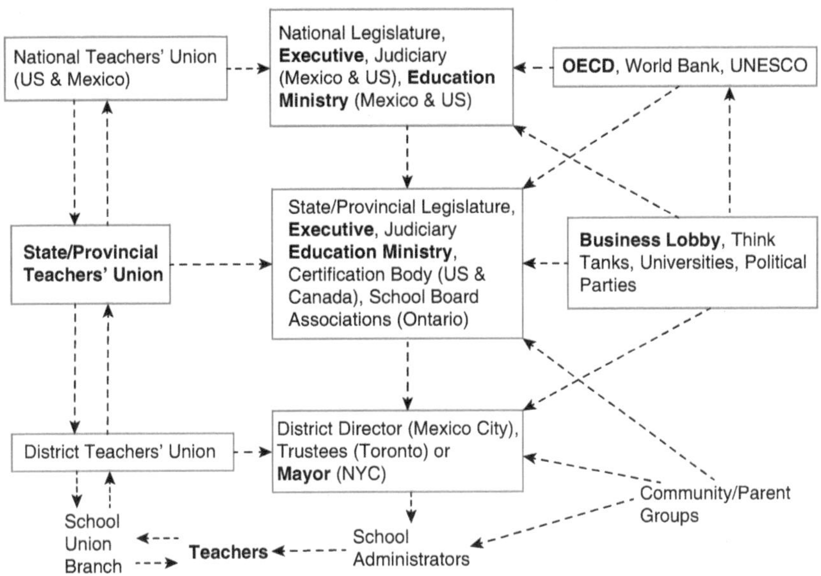

Ascending Levels of Authority. More powerful groups in bold, institutional organizations in boxes, flows of influence shown with arrows.

regions, between cities and the countryside. The former is the bastion of the democratic teachers' movement; teachers' union locals in the latter are mostly presided over by the official national union. Many studies of Mexican teachers have focused on high-profile struggles in Chiapas, Guerrero, or Oaxaca. Part of the purpose of this study is to understand the conditions that have led to a less militant response in Mexico City, as well as in New York City and Toronto, while colleagues elsewhere have more assertively contested similar policies.

How teachers' organizations, state authorities, and various policy advocates utilize scalar strategies in their efforts to shape public education in North America is visually represented in Figure 1.1. This is a very general schema for understanding scalar structures and flows of influence within public education across North America. For example, in the extremely hierarchical official union structures of the Mexican SNTE, there are fewer spaces for grass-roots influence on the direction of the national executive than there are through the delegate assemblies of the dissident National Coordination of Education Workers (CNTE) movement or other unions such as Ontario's OSSTF. Likewise, in many specific local contexts in the case studies of this book, teachers have made meaningful connections with parent leaders, as did the standardized testing Opt Out activists associated with the Movement of Rank and File Educators (MORE) caucus of New York's UFT, discussed below in chapter 3. However, Figure 1.1 indicates that a disconnect exists in typical conditions.

Figure 1.1 shows that the scales of institutional structures within which teachers' professional autonomy and education policy in general exist and are developed in North America. Four scales of power relations are shown here, from the classroom to the national level. While these scales depict an overall hierarchy of authority, more horizontal relations also exist between different levels of unions and governments as well as spaces for bottom-up contestation as exercised by some community and parent groups. Despite the global reach of their activities, I placed powerful, multilateral, non-governmental agencies such as the Organisation for Economic Cooperation and Development (OECD) in a tier alongside national governments to illustrate how the authority of the former is contingent on the recognition and endorsement by state authorities. At least within the context of Canada, the United States, and Mexico, these global policy developers and advocates derive their primary importance from their usage by domestic elites to validate their own policy agendas.[3]

One of the most important case study distinctions within Figure 1.1 is the virtual absence of a national-level tier for education policy in Canada. What is more difficult to clearly depict here are differences between the United States and Mexico in the degree of centralization. Whereas US federal intervention in education policy, alongside an increase in funding, grew substantially with the passage of No Child Left Behind (NCLB) in 2001 and Race to the Top in 2009, much of this national authority was relinquished to the state level with the Every Student Succeeds Act of 2015. However, the latter law only codified widespread state exemptions and modifications from NCLB policies that had existed in practice almost since its enactment. The federal level remains important in the United States for its role as a high-profile bully pulpit to set a national agenda and define the "common sense" of education policy, which is subsequently articulated and rolled out to a large extent by state governments. The institution of mayoral control in New York and other big US cities represents a different scalar approach to place power in the hands of a local executive. By contrast, education policy in Mexico was steadily centralized over the 2000s, particularly through the constitutional amendments of 2012–13 that prohibit state-level exemptions from national evaluation programs and the uploading from states of responsibility for SEP employee salaries.[4] In Ontario, the key scalar shift since the turn of the twenty-first century has been the uploading of collective bargaining from school districts to the provincial level, following the course of British Columbia and other provinces (Slinn and Sweetman 2012). In both Mexico and Canada, the primary objective appears to be to exert greater executive control over labour negotiations, though mayoral control appears to have accomplished this goal as well.

1.4. Challenging Professional Autonomy

Workplace power relations are a critical factor determining the professional autonomy of teachers. As such, a focus is placed on how contemporary neoliberal reforms in all three cities have changed the way that teachers and school administrators work with each other. In the literature of many policy advocates and academics, there is a tendency to view administrators as the primary resource for educational expertise and as those on the frontline implementing reforms who need to be liberated from contractual restrictions in order to effectively manage teachers. Historically in the United States, since 1997 in Ontario, and since 2017 in Mexico, school principals have been formally classified as management and ineligible for membership in the teachers' union.[5] Prior to the most recent change in Mexico, school directors intervened less to regulate teachers' work, though, as will be discussed in the Mexico City case study, this situation has changed with the onset of new forms of standardized evaluation for students and teachers.

The James Keegstra case, concerning an Alberta teacher who fought up to the Supreme Court of Canada his dismissal for expounding anti-Semitic views in his classroom in the 1980s, serves as an infamous reminder of why some limits on professional autonomy are justified. I do not use professional autonomy to advocate for a pure individualism, where teachers do their own thing in their own classroom. With the improvements it can bring to teaching as well as facilitating school-wide initiatives, collegial collaboration and mentoring are increasingly viewed as integral parts of autonomy that embrace the capacity of teachers as professionals to draw on each other's expertise (Vangrieken et al. 2017). In some sense, the issue here is of supporting and defending a collective notion of "professionalism." Within a larger context of a democratically accountable public education system, teachers as a group, particularly through their unions, should have the autonomy, but also the responsibility, to self-regulate.

Another issue complicating professional autonomy, is the extent to which teachers defer to or accommodate the concerns of parents and, especially at the secondary level, students. These relationships occur within structural power dynamics, where middle-class teachers often hold considerably more social capital than low-income, racialized, or new-immigrant parents. As chapter 5 shows, the reverse may be true in affluent communities. The ability of a student or a parent to appeal a grade assigned by a teacher may be important for accountability and equity, or it may facilitate grade inflation by families comfortable with working the system. In Mexico, poverty and state repression, traditions of collective action including peasant and Indigenous organizing, and socialist currents among teachers have frequently led educators to socially and politically identify closely with the communities in which they live and work, especially in rural areas. As employees of the national government, they remain beholden to its curricular policy, which can clash with the priorities of local communities, for example, instruction in regional Indigenous languages. In Ontario, alternatively, progressive ministry reforms to the health and physical education curriculum, endorsed by the teachers' federations, to instruct students about gender diversity, healthy relationships, and consent, among other issues, became a defining issue for socially conservative communities in the 2018 provincial election. Opponents of the so-called sex-ed curriculum claimed it encouraged sexual activity and homosexuality. They rallied behind the victorious Progressive Conservative (PC) Party, which vowed to "listen to parents" and revoke the teaching guide. Thousands of Ontario teachers responded by pledging to exercise their professional judgment and "teach best practices in physical and health education," opposing any regressive changes. These forces shape the extent of teachers' professional autonomy. The challenge of balancing the power of a central government, the will of local communities, and teachers' professional autonomy is a fundamental question for democracy.

Teacher claims to professional autonomy have sometimes exacerbated divisions between them and the communities they serve. Mark Ginsburg argues that pursuing professional status and placing their practice above popular critique can isolate teachers from parents and other workers, making them vulnerable in times of struggle. Teachers "may succeed for a while in their struggle with economic and state elites but perhaps only as long as the educators are perceived to be serving the elites' interests" (Ginsburg 1991b, 385). In 1968, less than a decade after its founding, New York City's United Federation of Teachers embroiled itself in a series of ugly, racially divisive, citywide strikes against an experimental "community-controlled" school district in the predominantly African-American Ocean Hill / Brownsville neighbourhoods of Brooklyn. Led by Black Power activists, the district demanded the right to circumvent disciplinary due process rights and seniority to transfer (and later fire) teachers deemed to be poorly serving African-American students and to hire preferable replacements. The strikes dragged on, cumulatively, for months. They acquired a strong racial dimension of black parents and students versus overwhelmingly white (mostly Jewish) teachers, rupturing previous relationships the union had had with black community organizations in the city and alienating many of its small minority of African-American members.[6] Marjorie Murphy (1992), Susan Robertson (2000), and Lois Weiner (2012) argue that the UFT under the leadership of Al Shanker bore considerable responsibility for the conflict. While flexing its power to solidify the professional rights of its members, the union had neglected the needs and concerns of the most marginalized, racialized communities that they served. The conflict had profound political ramifications. Murphy (1992) and New York labour historian Joshua Freeman (2000) argue it contributed to the breakup of the broader US civil rights movement and killed the idealism of the 1960s public sector union movement. While professional autonomy is crucial to teachers' work because of the socially vital role of educators particularly in marginalized communities, the pursuit of occupational interests must be entrenched within a larger vision of being responsive and accountable to the communities in which teachers work.

Particularly in the United States, struggles over teachers' professional autonomy continue to be racialized. NYC charter schools, particularly the Success Academy chain led by the high-profile Eva Moskowitz, have widely touted a highly scripted model of teaching. She argues that a relentless focus on drills, rote learning, and strict discipline is necessary for their black and Latinx pupils from predominantly low-income families to excel, as measured on the basis of their standardized test results. Conversely, allowing teachers to interpret the specific needs of their students and using more open-ended forms of instruction is associated with perpetuating the existing dismal results for poor, racialized children. The significance of the socio-economic context in educational inequity is dismissed by Moskowitz and others as tantamount to harbouring low academic expectations. One of the greatest challenges of New York State's parent-led standardized testing Opt Out movement, whose success is described in chapter 3, is to build alliances with working-class racialized parents. Then secretary of education, Arne Duncan, dismissed the movement in 2014 as "white suburban moms who – all of a sudden – their child isn't as brilliant as they thought they were, and their school isn't quite as good as they thought" (*Rethinking Schools* 2014). In Chicago, activists in the predominantly African-American South Side have linked the usage of standardized test scores that label their schools as failures, to a drive to racially gentrify their neighbourhoods by replacing these schools with charters that can exclude local students from enrolment (ibid.; Lipman 2017). This work is ongoing in NYC, where members of the Movement of Rank and File Educators caucus within the UFT have led public campaigns to increase the number of funded sports and extra-curricular activities offered in the small high schools that replaced large institutions in Latinx and black communities in Harlem, the South Bronx, and central-eastern Brooklyn. In doing so, they confront the argument of many neoliberal advocates that the well-being of students is primarily measured by test scores, and they reassert the role of teachers as activists for the interests of their students.

Larry Cuban (2009, 2013) takes a stance distinct from the more direct critics of neoliberal education policy cited here. He alternately critiques or supports various aspects of what he describes as the "dominant reform agenda" since the early 1980s in the United States. Cuban eschews the term "corporate reform movement," arguing that it implies more unity of motivation and strategy among its participants than really exists. He does not utilize the concept of neoliberalization to describe the shift in education politics, though he notes the increasing shift towards market-style models and discourses in education alongside other public institutions. However, he demonstrates that, despite various waves of top-down reforms in recent decades such as mandating new curriculum guidelines, pedagogical practices, or technology, what teachers do in their classrooms has not changed radically (2013). In this sense, Cuban is arguing that a greater degree of resilience exists among teachers in determining how they work in the face of externally imposed policies than is typically acknowledged by the advocates of these policies or their opponents. He explains in an earlier book based on similar studies of teachers' work:

> Teachers use (and have used) their limited discretion in classrooms to construct practical blends of teaching traditions to manage efficiently 25 or more students while addressing the abiding expectations of a community with long-standing beliefs about what schools ought to do. In addition, they teach content and skills tailored to both shifting currents in the larger society and their sense of what will work best with the students they see daily -regardless of what policy makers and administrators cajole or demand from teachers. Most top-down policies ignore this slender autonomy that teachers possess and use. (2009, 63)

Cuban does argue that some recent policies, such as student standardized testing and its linkage to teacher evaluations through Value Added Metrics (discussed in chapter 3 concerning their use in New York), have demonstrably changed teaching – for the worse and in ways contrary to the goals claimed by their proponents, since rote learning and drills on test questions push aside student-centred inquiry. Cuban is significant as a high-profile mainstream voice within North American education policy; he argues that teaching would most likely change for the better if would-be reformers attempted to overcome their inability to see schools and the classroom from a teachers' perspective and focused on meaningful engagement through professional development programs. I am inclined to agree with outspoken Texan school superintendent and anti-standardized testing activist John Kuhn (2014), that some advocates of neoliberal education reforms may indeed have good intentions, but that the end for most others is profit-making through privatization and weakening teachers' unions. Cuban's efforts to understand the practical effects of contemporary education policy on teachers' work are very valuable.

Particularly in Mexico and the United States, in the face of a much more severe political attack than was generally the case in Canada, the national AFT, NEA, SNTE, and many local leaders began varying forms of accommodations in the 1990s with the neoliberal drive for "teacher accountability" (Riegel 2003; Peterson 1999). These leaders and academics, such as Kerchner, Koppich, and Weeres (1997), argued for a turn away from militancy and the defence of contractual rights, to embrace new forms of teacher evaluation as a mark of "professionalism," alongside teacher voice in school budgeting, teacher evaluation, and hiring and firing decisions, thus implicating union members in managerial decision-making. By the early 2010s, some concluded that high-stakes standardized exams and their use to facilitate "school choice" were irresistible (Weiner 2012), though they fundamentally undermined professional autonomy. Forms of this approach to professionalism have been pursued by the UFT in New York City, as I show in chapter 3. Canadian teachers' unions have largely avoided falling into this false dichotomy of choosing between (a diminishing) professional responsibility versus upholding salaries and working conditions. Nevertheless, all North American teachers' unions should place greater emphasis on defending the professional autonomy of their members from incursions by neoliberal policy. Some thoughts on overcoming the existing institutional barriers will be discussed in the Conclusion.

1.5. Methodology

Part of the effort by critical researchers to have a political impact beyond academia involves socially situating themselves as authors (Jensen and Glasmeier 2010). Haraway (1991) developed the concept of "situated knowledge," by which, in contrast to positivist claims to objectivity, ideas are shaped by the social context of the researcher and the relationship of the researcher with the subject of study. Addressing the key questions of this book – how teachers' work and professional autonomy have been transformed by contemporary neoliberal policy – necessitates prioritizing research among those directly affected: the educators. In doing so I address the absence of classroom teacher voices in much of qualitative education policy research. This shortcoming can often be associated with an ideological orientation that sees teachers categorically as a key part of problems facing education, as noted in Bruns and Luque's report for the World Bank (2014) on Latin American and Caribbean teachers, Viteritti's edited collections about US schools (2000 [with Ravitch], 2009b), and most publications of the Brookings Institution, such as Manna and McGuinn (2013). Teachers are seen as interested parties who must be acted upon, as the objects rather than the subjects of education policy (Rezai-Rashti 2009). Sometimes, as in the People for Education's annual survey of Ontario schools or in Laura Pinto's (2015) research on the province's education policy, principals are enlisted where a "ground-level" perspective is needed. Alternatively, the format of the research itself precludes the inclusion of teacher voices, as in the annual *Education at a Glance* comparative study of national education statistics (456 pp. in 2017) compiled by the OECD. Influenced by my background as a teacher, I have strived to remedy this deficit of teachers talking about their own work. I used a combination of formal, semi-structured, recorded interviews from fifty to ninety minutes in length, which, following Cresswell (2013), utilized phenomenological questioning on how policies impacted their experiences and the contexts of these occurrences and ethnographic study through participating in teachers' organizations and working alongside other educators. During the course of my research, I solidified my understanding of what became the five common dynamics[7] of the neoliberalization of teachers' work through their de-professionalization that I consider across my three case studies. I benefited in this way from what McDowell (2010) describes as the importance of flexibility and allowing the focus of one's research to evolve through interviews.

For my Toronto case study, I focused my qualitative research around interviews with English teachers in two high schools. Because of their widely divergent student demographics, I hoped to capture my first-hand observation as a teacher that working in a school whose students are predominantly from poor and working-class families makes the job fundamentally different from the experience of teaching children from affluent families. These interviews were conducted between August

2014 and July 2015. One school is located in an affluent, predominantly white, Anglo, west-end neighbourhood. The other is in Scarborough, one of Toronto's "inner suburbs" populated by young, first-generation families from south Asia and east Africa. I taught from six months to a year in the English departments at both of these schools. I was able to recruit former colleagues to participate in interviews; they represented a fairly typical cross-section of years of teaching experience, participation in school activities (including leading departments[8]), age, gender, political views, and union involvement. All eight of the teachers interviewed at these two schools were white, which is close to representative of their departments, which were 80–90 per cent white. The entire teaching staff of their schools was perhaps 70–80 per cent white in 2014–15, in line with demographics across schools under the Toronto District School Board (which are attended by the majority of students of colour). Using a combination of snowball and purposive sampling (Babbie and Benaquisto 2002), it was a priority for me to recruit a cross-section of participants who would represent the "average" sentiment of teachers about how their work has changed over the course of their careers, how they conceive of teacher-principal power relations, the role of the union, and the impact of standardized testing and curriculum changes on their work, among other issues. In addition to these representative participants, I interviewed self-identified union activists and elected OSSTF leaders at the local and the provincial level. I also spoke with academics and leading policy activists in the Ontario education sector. Unfortunately, I was unable to meet with officials from the provincial Ministry of Education or the Toronto District School Board. A total of fourteen individuals were formally interviewed in Toronto, including ten teachers (listed anonymously) and four other key informants.

My interviews in Mexico were more extensive, in part to compensate for less initial familiarity. In Mexico City in November 2013, I participated in an international conference of teachers and union leaders from Canada, the United States, and Mexico. With the help of secondary teachers in the audience from Mexico City, I obtained contact information and offers of introductions to school principals. These initial contacts were made based on my legitimacy established by speaking at the conference and being introduced by others as a known union activist and teacher and therefore as somebody likely to be sympathetic to their struggles. Being a graduate student at the time was of secondary importance. I ultimately worked with two teachers who facilitated visits to their two schools throughout 2015, the winter and fall of 2016, and the spring 2017. Using a combination of snowball and purposive sampling, I interviewed in Spanish (and translated into English; reproduced as extracts included in this book) a sample of their colleagues who were broadly representative in terms of experience, subject area, age, gender, school involvement, and political views. I also interviewed administrators and principals at both schools and, at one, the official SNTE school representative. I chose not to pursue official endorsement or assistance from a higher level of education authorities, owing to the suspicion in which I knew they were held by many teachers.

In these visits I also observed the ambience of both their overall conditions of teaching, specifically the ways in which they interacted with each other and what was said between colleagues in the staffroom or the corridor. I was frequently invited into classrooms to speak to students and participate in lessons. Following Kearns (2004), I saw these informal observations as an important, often non-verbal supplement of information to my interviews. I would write my observations in my notebook in the evening on the bus and Metro rides back to my apartment. Though the range of the Mexico research did not come close to my years in Toronto high school classrooms, I wanted to gain a first-hand idea of what it was like to teach in a Mexico City secondary school. Both of these schools were located in the massive borough of Iztapalapa in southeastern Mexico City, with over 2 million residents, the largest of the city's sixteen delegations. Predominantly working class, the neighbourhoods in which these two schools are located are representative of this urban region. In contrast to the method used in Toronto, I decided to base my interviews in two schools serving demographically similar communities. While it would not be as useful in distinguishing the differences of teaching in an affluent versus a working-class neighbourhood, the approach recognized that the latter represented the characteristics of the vast majority of the city's schools, in comparison with Toronto's far larger middle and upper classes as a proportion of the population. Controlling for socio-economic status would help me to identify other causes for divergent experiences of teachers in these schools.

In Mexico City, I also interviewed a selection of activists with the CNTE and its elected officers, who were invaluable for providing explanations for the development of the movement since the publication of Maria Lorena Cook's key study in 1996. I especially wanted to understand the context of the movement in the city, as so much journalistic and activist coverage focuses on more visible CNTE contingents in Oaxaca, Michoacan, and Guerrero. I always asked why the movement in the capital had seldom reached the strength of these predominantly rural states. I also benefited from substantial interviews with several of Mexico's most engaged academics on labour and education policy. Mexican policymakers were far more receptive to meeting with me than their equivalents in Toronto and New York City. I interviewed senior officials of both the Mexico City SEP and the national administration, from whom I gained some valuable insights into how their government interacted with multilateral agencies such as the OECD and UNESCO. Unfortunately, I was unable to obtain a response from the official leaders of Sections 9 and 10 of the Mexico City SNTE, its national office, or its research centre, the Institute for Education and Union Studies of the Americas.[9] A total of twenty-two people were formally interviewed in Mexico City, including twelve teachers (listed anonymously).

In New York City I employed a snowball approach to obtaining interviews. This included contacting teachers I became aware of through their online blogs and essays on their experiences in New York's school system. My teacher interview base in New York was therefore skewed towards the politically active, specifically those involved in the Movement of Rank and File Educators (MORE), a dissident left caucus within the UFT. Despite this limitation, I benefited from articulate, highly critical perspectives on the experience of education under mayors Bloomberg and de Blasio and Governor Cuomo. These teachers worked in a diverse range of subject areas and responsibilities (two were department leaders) and were representative in terms of age and gender, years of experience, employment status, and union involvement (a few led their school's union chapters). As in Toronto, they were predominantly white. They tended to teach in struggling inner-city schools, but with a fairly even dispersal across the city, though a disproportionate number taught in alternative schools that had some exemptions from the state's standardized student evaluations. The interviews were conducted during visits in December 2014, in January and April 2015, and in follow-up conversations later that year in October.

I received recognition from the NYC Department of Education's Institutional Review Board, but this did not assist me in obtaining responses to interview requests from central office administrators. Despite a letter of introduction from the president of OSSTF, I also did not receive a response from the offices of the UFT. Social networks ultimately connected me to two former union officials. Where I lacked access to institutional settings, I was able to engage in a limited ethnographic study of the organizing of the MORE caucus by attending meetings, conferences, socials, and a rally at the state capitol in Albany in January 2015. Attending the major international conferences of union activists in Chicago organized by Labor Notes in 2016 and 2018 was particularly valuable. The event included hundreds of teachers from Canada, Mexico, and the United States, many of the latter with the United Caucus of Rank and File Educators, which has emerged as a significant network for dissidents in AFT- and NEA-affiliated unions (see chapter 2). A total of sixteen people were formally interviewed in New York, including thirteen teachers (listed anonymously).

Insider research presents the challenge of bias. However, in addition to providing me with easier access to informants, insider status gave me a considerable advantage in understanding both the practical functions and the official jargon of education policy. Most important, my own teaching experience gave me a reference point to help me formulate relevant questions within interviews and read social contexts within schools (Merriam et al. 2010). Despite the vast differences between experiences in Toronto and in New York City or Mexico City, the overall contours of teachers' work remained familiar.

I draw inspiration from Rosemary Hennessy's phrase, "rigorous but not disinterested scholarship," which she used to describe her study of the sexual politics of queer organizers in Mexico's Maquiladora factory districts (2013). Hennessy's ethnographic research made her a witness to crowded meetings of women workers in small living rooms and spirited protest camps of fired activists outside the gates of windswept, sterile, industrial parks, some of whom confided their personal stories to her on the basis of trust in a woman who was in solidarity with their struggles and their lives. A key challenge emerges in balancing one's sense of loyalty to and solidarity with a movement or group with the necessity of maintaining one's academic integrity – especially when it is necessary to make a critique. I grappled with this issue while analysing the union of which I am an active part: the OSSTF. Perhaps it was even more challenging in relation to the Mexican teachers' movement, given the stakes in which their struggle unfolds.

Taking a clear political stance may have cost me opportunities to meet and interview those who oppose my views. Those views are easy to triangulate from an internet search. On the other hand, by conveying an insider stance of being pro-teacher and pro-union, I built trust with individuals, encouraging them to be more candid than they likely would be if I came across as an impartial academic (Greene 2014). Along with establishing a basis of trust in the context of the hierarchical worker-boss power relations of the workplace, I may not have been considered worth the time of my informants to accompany to a colleague's school on their day off or to shuttle around to talk with teachers on their breaks between classes amid the chaos and cacophony of hundreds of adolescents, or to confide a critique of their principal or their school's union representative if it wasn't in the service of a project that strives to assist in creating a better public education system and better working conditions for teachers.

I focused on the city scale of union organization to conduct my intensive case study research, as I believe that despite uneven degrees of regional-federal centralization across the three national contexts,[10] this scale is still the most critical for determining the results of collective bargaining. It is so through the intersection of the union local's capacities and political culture with the resources and political direction of both the municipal school board and the varying levels of senior government in each country. Further, the city-level local is optimal for studying the political culture of each union, as it is the scale at which rank-and-file education workers are most likely to engage meaningfully with their union. As Herbert (2010) contends, locally situated case studies add depth to our research by understanding the context of a specific place. Then we can assess whether our case study confirms broader trends and dynamics on the bases of comparability or is in fact an aberration, opening up further discussion. The "extended case method" (Peck and Theodore 2015) is not to be confused with a pure, comparative approach.

I focus on secondary schools, owing to my personal experience as a teacher and a corresponding higher degree of access. Some important differences exist between the distribution of grade levels and institutions in these sites. Toronto and New York City have similar arrangements, students attending primary schools (junior kindergarten to 4th grade), middle schools (5th–8th grades; some elementary schools in Toronto encompass both), and high schools (9th–12th grades). The system in Mexico City is the most distinct. The city-state's administration of the national SEP operates three-year kindergartens, primary schools that are six years in duration and secondary schools that last for three years (corresponding to grades 7 through 9). Upper-level high school, which became compulsory nationwide in the early 2000s and is not fully enforced, is divided in Mexico City between preparatory feeder schools operated by the city's public universities and technical colleges and the Instituto de Educación Media Superior (Institute of Mid-Superior Education) operated by the municipal government.[11] Owing to this complex system of governance, I made the grades 7 to 9 secondary schools my basis of comparison in Mexico City. They are administered directly by the SEP, and its teachers are affiliated with the SNTE, allowing for an easier basis of comparison with Toronto and New York City.

Since the 2008 recession, teachers' unions in each country have fought high-profile battles. The character of these struggles grew beyond contesting specific government policies associated with austerity, curtailing union rights, or de-professionalization, to take on a larger public ideological significance of defending education as a social good, upholding workers' rights, and opposing privatization. A brief survey includes the continuous battles of the British Columbia teachers with the provincial Liberal government from 2001 to 2017, the Chicago teachers' strikes of 2012 and 2016, and the protests and strikes of the teachers of southern Mexico in 2008–9, 2013, and 2016. My choices of New York City, Mexico City, and Toronto are also guided by an interest in why greater levels of protest did not emerge so close to policymaking centres. In contrast with each country's "hot spots" in which militant unions resist aggressive governments, the experiences of the teachers and unions in my case studies may be more typical of the status quo in their countries and therefore perhaps more useful for understanding it.

1.6. Book Overview

Historical context is important to avoid the portrayal of contemporary education politics as somehow unique or without precedent. Mary Kay Vaughan's *The State, Education, and Social Class in Mexico, 1880–1928* reveals that the privileging of the nation's capital and the north over the south in the distribution of education resources is an old pattern, as are conflicts between humanist versus utilitarian, "labour ready" visions of the purpose of education; or the usage of scalar strategies by actors whose bases of political power is concentrated at the state, regional, or national level; or fears by the authorities that teachers will organize communities against the ruling party (1982, 143–8). Chapter 2 begins by describing the importance of New York City, Mexico City, and Toronto as centres of education policy. It then provides an overview of the emergence of professional autonomy within the context of twentieth-century teacher unionism in Toronto, New York City, and Mexico City and its later challenge by the neoliberalization of education. I then explore some international organizations that have produced a teachers' policy mobility. They range from the institutional – Education International and collaboration between the leaders of the SNTE of Mexico and the American Federation of Teachers – to the grass roots, including the United Caucus of Rank and File Educators and the Trinational Coalition in Defence of Public Education. The chapter concludes with a baseline of the commonalities and differences between professional autonomy in New York City, Mexico City, and Toronto as the twenty-first century begins and the case studies pick up.

The first case study, New York City, is presented in chapter 3. I begin by explaining the context of structural reforms to the governance and operations of the city's schools at the outset of the twenty-first century, which created the context for policies that have greatly undermined the professional autonomy of teachers. The implementation of mayoral control, under former Mayor Michael Bloomberg, was crucial for concentrating power in the hands of him and his appointed executives and for subsequently facilitating the implementation of his neoliberal "fast policy" (Peck and Theodore 2015). A key example was an extreme acceleration of earlier initiatives to break up large high schools into smaller institutions within the same building, with over a hundred schools created in one year at its peak. The small size of these schools comprising a few hundred students intersected with an increased emphasis on high-stakes Regents exams;[12] the result was a narrowing of the curriculum and pressure on faculty to teach to the test. The default neighbourhood school was also eliminated in order to increase competition for enrolment through "school choice," assessed on the basis of test score results. The most prestigious, established, exclusive entrance requirements tend to perpetuate class and racial segregation. Changes in school finance intersected increased powers for principals under mayoral control, creating an incentive to save money in the budgets of individual schools by hiring low-seniority teachers. The sum of these and other policies, such as changes to tenure rules and higher turnover, dramatically shifted the balance of power in schools from teachers to administrators. Bloomberg's avalanche of neoliberal reforms was challenged by his left-leaning successor. Mayor Bill de Blasio's administration attempted to alleviate the effects of high-stakes testing, to curb the expansion of charter schools, and to make some improvements in working conditions for teachers. Governor Andrew Cuomo's considerable success in stymieing de Blasio's efforts, through state policies to increase the punitiveness of teacher evaluations and high-stakes standardized tests, provides an important case of scalar struggle. This example also demonstrates the weakness of the municipally bound United Federation of Teachers (UFT) in effectively confronting the governor. I conclude with a look at the successful mobilization of the parent-led Opt Out movement in 2015, which succeeded in reducing the weight of these tests, and the 2016 campaign of UFT union office for the dissident Movement of Rank and File Educators (MORE) for what can be learned for multi scalar teacher-community solidarity.

Chapter 4 brings us to Mexico City. I begin by explaining the attempts at neoliberal education reform under the National Action Party (PAN) presidents Vicente Fox (2001–6) and Felipe Calderon (2007–12). In this era in which the influence of most other official unions declined, SNTE leader Elba Esther Gordillo consolidated her power base both within the union and in national politics. She collaborated with Fox and Calderon in the creation of the National Institute for Education Evaluation (INEE), and the roll-out of the nationwide, standardized ENLACE exam in 2006. This exam ranked schools and when combined with the "Alliance for Quality Education' initiative in 2008, purported to provide a basis for evaluating teachers on the basis of their students' test scores. The CNTE and other dissident movements provided steady opposition, exempting the application of these national programs in states where their presence was strongest. An important turning point was the election of Enrique Peña Nieto and the return of the Institutional Revolutionary Party (PRI) to the presidency from 2012 to 2018. In another textbook case of "fast policy," he worked closely with his compatriot José Ángel Gurria, general secretary of the OECD, and business lobby group Mexicanos Primero, to make major constitutional amendments governing education within months of his inauguration. These changes facilitated the Professional Teaching Service Law (Ley de Servicio Profesional Docente) with far-reaching effects on teachers' professional autonomy. One key element was eliminating a university degree in education as a prerequisite for K–12 teaching. This amendment undermined both the distinct pedagogical knowledge base obtained by attending a teachers' college[13] and the shared professional identity of teachers. Most crucial was a standardized national exam to be taken by teachers every three years as a condition for maintaining their employment. Peña Nieto's reforms were built upon a scalar strategy in which policies entrenched in the national constitution would be more difficult for state governments to exempt themselves from under pressure from the CNTE. Administrative functions that had been decentralized in the 1980s and 1990s and that had given the CNTE influence in states where it was powerful also were reversed. Meanwhile, funding for school facilities was decentralized to the municipal level and in many cases to parents. I explain the factors that impeded the mass participation of Mexico City teachers in the CNTE's militant protests and strikes, despite the sentiment expressed by many educators that their profession was being undermined. I conclude with evaluating the changes in local and national politics that facilitated the participation of thousands of teachers from the nation's capital in the wave of strikes in the summer of 2016 that ultimately helped force a compromise from Peña Nieto's government.

I discuss my home city of Toronto in chapter 5. The contemporary scaling-up of education governance in the province of Ontario began during the tenure of the Mike Harris led PC Party from 1995 to 2002 and was continued by the Liberal Party under premiers Dalton McGuinty and Kathleen Wynne from 2003 to 2018. The shifting of taxing powers from the school district to the provincial government under Harris significantly undermined the autonomy of the Toronto District School Board. Budget shortfalls led to regular threats by the provincial government to suspend its elected board of trustees. The most important event shaping teacher and principal power relations was the removal of the latter from the teachers' federations and their reclassification as management in the late 1990s. Along with discussing the workplace dynamics that ensued, I explain how the Ontario Public School Board Association strongly advocated at the provincial level for increased management rights over the work of teachers. Standardized testing of students is present in Ontario, though with less punitive power against teachers and schools than was current in the United States and Mexico. Nevertheless, Toronto teachers explain how they are subjected to pressure, passed from the Ontario Ministry of Education to the TDSB, to produce steadily rising scores, which has an effect on classroom instruction, felt differently in schools with high or low results. In a demographic context of declining student enrolment and fiscal austerity, Toronto also has dynamics of school choice, if not as defining as in New York, with specialty magnet programs; while competing for students, these programs have increased racial and class segregation between and within schools. Finally, I look at how collective bargaining followed the scaling-up of finance, with province-wide negotiations taking precedence over local agreements. This process led to an imposed province-wide contract in 2012 and confusing, protracted struggles over 2015–16, where much of the conflict centred on professional autonomy. Despite, in contrast to the UFT, having institutional mechanisms to engage in scaled-up negotiations, OSSTF has not yet successfully navigated these multi-scalar structures of bargaining, especially in the case of Toronto.

I end this book by making some comparisons across my case studies, drawing some larger conclusions of what the experience of teachers in New York City, Mexico City, and Toronto means for understanding the contemporary trajectory of neoliberal education policy. To take back the initiative from pro-privatization reformers who seek to degrade the basis of professionalism in order to take control of teachers' work, I contend that teachers' unions should be more proactive and assertive in defining professional autonomy. This means developing a clearer vision among its members of what constitutes good pedagogy and classroom practice. By elevating professional autonomy to the prominence of traditionally negotiated issues of salary and class sizes, teachers may collectively be able to shape the public schools and classrooms of the future.

2 Geographies of Professional Autonomy and Neoliberalism in North America

Preface: Día del Trabajo

One of the most visible symbols of the resistance of Mexican teachers to the education policies of President Enrique Peña Nieto was the occupation of the plaza surrounding the historic Monumento a la Revolución in the heart of Mexico City. From September 2013, when teachers were forcibly evicted by police from the central Zocalo, to late 2015, when the movement reached a lull and the city government pressured it to disperse, it was at times occupied by hundreds of tents. Over 1,000 teachers slept here at its peak. The largest contingents were from Veracruz, Michoacan, Guerrero, Chiapas, and Oaxaca, the latter four states being the traditional bastion of the movement. Teachers would rotate for two weeks at a time before returning home to their schools and communities. The Veracruz contingent operated the collective kitchen, using a system of water tanks for drinking or washing, and jerry-rigged light bulbs strung under a sea of tarps. Smelly porta-potties across the street lined half a city block. Near the centre of the camp were tents housing teachers from Mexico City. I was invited to their meetings when I first visited in November 2013, just after the peak of the initial protests. Some offered to bring me to their schools and introduce me to their colleagues to facilitate my research.

Squads of riot police were still deployed at major intersections on the streets between the Monumento a la Revolución, and the Zocalo, two kilometres away, to prevent the return of the teachers. For both teachers and the broader public, bringing protest power to bear on the national government in the capital was a familiar ritual, practised for decades as a primary way of exercising dissent in a system that provided limited institutional channels for doing so. I wondered if my teacher colleagues in Toronto would endure this discomfort, risk losing their careers, and even experience violence to struggle for what these teachers believed was the defence of their profession.

A year and a half later, I asked Isabel,[1] who had brought me several times to visit her secondary school in the borough of Iztapalapa, if there were any interesting plans for Labour Day (1 May), a public holiday, which, as in Canada and the United States, traditionally features parades and rallies. She and several colleagues were travelling to the city of Puebla, two hours away, to participate in a march at the urging of a radical street vendor's union that feared police repression because of its dissident history. I met them at 11:30 p.m. at a Metro station near the outskirts of the city, to wait for an overnight ride. An hour passed. The Metro was by then closed, and I was feeling quite stuck there as we sat on the curb under a streetlight. My companions bantered amiably, not showing their tiredness after the workday. They were still clad in the classic teacher outfit: sweater vests and dress pants for men, generic blouses and slacks for women. A rickety old pickup truck pulled up. "Wouldn't it be funny if that was our ride?" I half-joked to Isabel. The five of us soon crawled onto the flatbed and lay down; the driver tied a tarpaulin over us. Another piece of rope served as the tailgate. We drove along the highway, the tarp billowing furiously above my nose. I thought about the year's worth of interview audio recordings, which I had not backed up anywhere, stored on a USB key in a backpack under my head as we drove over speed bumps. The teacher next to me snored contentedly. Around 3 a.m. we arrived at the offices of the vendor's union in Puebla and were ushered into an empty room where we could rest for a few hours. I spread out my jacket beneath me as we lay down on some cardboard that we stacked on the floor. Next door was a large room containing around forty women from a *campesino* (farmer and rural labourer) group that had also come for the march. I was grouchy and sore when dawn came; I wandered outside into a vast square where marchers were assembling. Murals of Marx, Lenin, and Mexican revolutionaries covered the surrounding buildings. A fresh coffee and pastry from the market in which we found ourselves cheered me up, and we joined the thousands marching.

Teachers with this degree of commitment to struggle were the minority in Mexico. However, they have collectively succeeded over the decades in repeatedly challenging the dictums of powerful political actors, despite not having the institutional resources enjoyed by their Canadian or US colleagues. The passion and degree of self-sacrifice with few prospects for personal gain of these ordinary classroom teachers, clearly driven by a broader vision of social justice, left a strong impression on me.

This chapter provides an overview of key historic developments in the geographies of neoliberal education policy in North America up to the twenty-first century, providing the necessary background to the city-specific case studies in the following chapters. With a brief overview of twentieth-century teacher unionism here, I will make my case for why the issue of professional autonomy and the question of who controls teachers' work has been so integral in this movement's development. While doing so, I will also show how the three global cities at the heart of my case studies – New York City, Mexico City, and Toronto – have been significant sites for the development of education policy, which progressed in particular ways because of to their specific political, social, and economic contexts. I begin in section 2.1 with the parallel emergence of public education systems and teacher unions in the early twentieth century and continue in section 2.2 with their rapid expansion and institutionalization in the postwar era demographic boom. Section 2.3 focuses on the early neoliberalization of education from the late 1970s and 1980s and its impacts on professional autonomy and teacher unions.

The final sections of this chapter, 2.4 and 2.5, will look in turn at contemporary continental linkages in education policy mobility by elite actors as well as at teachers' unions and dissident movements. The latter include diverse tendencies from conservative to radical unionism and forms from top-level meetings of leaders to horizontal networks with more bottom-up participation. While this book is structured around a case-study method of exploring the impact of contemporary policy on professional autonomy in three cities, it does not follow a formal comparative approach. Nevertheless, I will further demonstrate the value of assessing education policy at the continental scale by demonstrating the existence of a specific community of neoliberal education policy mobility and resistance in North America within the larger global flows of ideas and governance networks.

New York is influential with by far the largest school district in the United States, whose students represent a socio-economic polarization that is racially and spatially organized, dynamics that are present in large urban centres across the country. It is home to the nation's largest cluster of media, some of the most important faculties of education in terms of the number of its teacher graduates and prominent academics, and major think-tanks on education policy. From the 1930s through the 1950s it was a national policy-setter with a reputation for having the "best schools" (Ravitch 2000, 142). It is home to arguably the most prestigious teachers' faculty, Teachers' College at Columbia University, known primarily for its research, while City University of New York's Queens College became the largest conventional producer of teachers in the United States.

Mexico City is home to the nation's second-largest school authority (following Mexico State, which encompasses its suburbs). Given Mexico's heavy institutional centralization in the nation's capital, the city enjoys an even greater relative concentration of important faculties of education, media, think-tanks, and offices for multinational policy centres, including UNESCO, the OECD, and the World Bank. The history of Mexico's post-revolutionary public education system up to the neoliberal era has been dominated by a handful of elite, cosmopolitan intellectuals based in Mexico City. Jose Vasconcelos, the founder of modern Mexico's education system, was strongly influenced by his secretary, Moises Saenz, who studied under the progressive educator John Dewey at Columbia University in New York City. Saenz brought back ideas for dynamic pedagogy and the use of schools to meet popular needs and demands in a mostly rural system, with teachers as "moral, social, and technical 'apostles' of modernity … guiding their communities to practical and spiritual liberation – and integration into national life" (Levinson 2001, 21).

Canada's largest school district is located in Toronto. It is the capital of Ontario, the largest province (by population). Under the federal system, provinces hold sole jurisdiction over the governance of primary and secondary education, giving the city important scope for education policymaking. Like New York City and Mexico City, it is the most important national site for media, such that conflicts over education in Toronto are more likely to have further reverberations than those elsewhere, a significant factor in teachers' struggles and education policy province-wide. The Ontario Institute for Studies in Education (OISE) opened in Toronto in 1965 to conduct research on behalf of the provincial Ministry of Education. It was created in the context of elementary and secondary teachers' colleges merging with university departments of education and the requirement of a bachelor's degree for elementary teachers. In the mid-1990s OISE merged with the University of Toronto (Gidney 1999, 54–5). Its academics have been the most prominent scholars in shaping the province's education trajectory, despite their marginalization during the Progressive Conservative (PC) governments of 1995 to 2003 (Gidney 1999). Its most prominent professors on education policy – Michael Fullan, Charles Pascal, and Andy Hargreaves – served as special advisors to the premier and deputy ministers of education under the Liberal governments of Dalton McGuinty and Kathleen Wynne (Sue Winton, interview Dec. 2015).

This chapter will introduce the importance of both structural factors informing distinctive local, regional, and national contexts, and the agency of significant organizations and individuals in creating the North American geographies of neoliberal education policy, out of which important common developments can be identified. It will move up and down geographical scales, analysing developments in teacher unions and education systems from the case-study cities to the state/provincial and national levels. While these cities are arguably the most significant sites for education policy development and rollout in their respective countries, the specific nature of their prominence varies. An important factor is the distinctive federal structures of government in each country, shaping how policy moves from the centre to other regions and its ease in doing so. Needless to say, there are vast differences between the political, social, and economic histories of these cities and the countries in which they are situated, particularly between Mexico and the United States and Canada. Some of the ways these differences have shaped the evolution of teachers' work at each site will be explored below. They are being studied together because of their shared commonality as global cities, where significant precedents are set for education governance within their countries, across North America, and around the world. This chapter concludes with a relative baseline of professional autonomy at each of the case-study sites at the opening of the twenty-first century, where the three subsequent chapters pick up.

2.1. The Emergence of Public Education, Teachers' Unions, and Professionalism

At its origins in the late nineteenth century, mass public education in Canada and the United States typically gave little recognition to the capacity of teachers, many of whom had limited or no professional training, to interpret the needs of their students. As documented by Ravitch (2000), in New York City's early schools methods frequently consisted of rote learning using standard texts in large, crowded classrooms. Few students were expected to achieve more than basic literacy and numeracy. While New York's and Ontario's secondary schools were growing in the 1920s, Mexico's system of middle schools (equivalent to grades 7–9) was only officially established in 1923. Public education in Mexico expanded rapidly in the 1920s, following the end of the country's revolution. Article 3 of the Mexican Constitution, ratified in 1917 in the midst of the violent upheaval, specified that the new public education system would be "free, secular and scientific,"[2] emphasizing a drive at the time to inculcate a humanistic vision of education as an important pillar of national development. It also served to demarcate the autonomy of teachers from the influence of still powerful clerical authorities and local *caciques* (traditional, clientelistic, political bosses). Teachers were important actors for the post-revolutionary state. In terms of furthering social development, they were among the few federal employees located in every community. They perpetuated official ideology by cultivating a national identity (Torres 1991).

The professional prestige of teachers was heightened by their status, particularly in rural communities, as intellectuals and leaders. As a function of the vast ambitions of the post-revolutionary Secretary of Public Education under Jose Vasconcelos that public education would be the medium for social transformation, combined with the limited resources of the state, teachers were given a broad mandate within which they had considerable autonomy.[3] They were not only to establish schools in rural communities, but to serve as local leaders and organizers. Their formal training followed after the fact. These were the origins of the foundational myths of the Mexican education system of dedicated teachers rooted in communities. They are alternately described as "the martyrs," willing to acquiesce to abysmal salaries and working conditions (Martin 1994). Reflecting the predominantly rural population of Mexico through the first half of the twentieth century and the government's priority of establishing federal authority across its vast geography, the first teachers' colleges in the 1920s opened in Michoacan, Hidalgo, Guerrero, Guanajuato, and Puebla, with an emphasis on agricultural training. Rural teachers led many peasant and Indigenous movements and, in the case of Lucio Cabañas, a graduate of the Ayotzinapa teachers' college in Guerrero in the 1970s, leftist guerrilla movements[4] (Padilla 2013; Cook 1996, 243). Because education authorities lacked the capacity to regularly surveil schools, a significant degree of de facto professional autonomy existed in many regions of Mexico until the introduction of the first national standardized testing system in 1992 (Aboites 2012, 16).

The mass expansion of public education in Canada, the United States, and Mexico was followed by varying approaches to grouping teachers. In Canada and the United States the dominant trajectory was the establishment of professional associations to regulate teachers, represented by the National Education Association (NEA) in the United States (founded in 1857), which included principals and superintendents. The American Federation of Teachers (AFT) established in 1916, defined itself as a union and affiliated with the American Federation of Labor. It remained a minor presence outside of its stronghold in Chicago and non-majority unions in New York and a handful of other cities. K–12 public education in the United States was the responsibility of local school boards, directed by state governments. Financing was divided roughly evenly between local and state taxes. The Great Society program of Lyndon Johnson in 1964 established a precedent for additional funding from the federal government. However, Washington's intervention in education policy would not be significant until decades later (Murphy 1992, 225; Vergari 2013).

In Canada, K–12 education is constitutionally established as a provincial responsibility without federal intervention, while the balance of finance and governance powers between local and provincial governments was similar until centralization towards the latter in the 1990s (Wallner 2014; Vergari 2013, 232). Teachers' federations had emerged in every province but Ontario by 1917, where the Federation of Women Teachers' Association was formed in 1918[5] representing elementary teachers, followed by the Ontario Secondary School Teachers' Federation (OSSTF) in 1919 and the Ontario Public School Men Teachers' Federation in 1920. Unlike most provinces, where teachers formed one unified federation, in Ontario teachers were divided between five organizations, including the Catholic Teachers' Association for those employed in the publicly funded Catholic school boards and an association for the French-language public system. None affiliated to provincial or national labour federations.[6] The Ontario Teachers' Federation (est. 1944) coordinated provincial lobbying and represented its five affiliates in pension discussions, but it held no formal role in collective bargaining. The Canadian Teachers' Federation (est. 1920) had less power, as an umbrella organization tasked with international liaisons and limited forms of interprovincial cooperation. Ontario's federations, relatively weak in relation to the provincial government, were strengthened institutionally by the Teaching Profession Act in 1944. This act made membership in the corresponding affiliate and the payment of dues mandatory for all publicly employed teachers. Having no provisions for certification, decertification, or contestation by another union, it represented some of the strongest institutional language in Canadian law (Spagnuolo and Glassford 2008, 58–9; Shilton 2012, 224). Decades would pass before the federations would take collective action as unions and strengthen the autonomy of the profession.

In Mexico, at the urging of President Manuel Avila Camacho and with the assistance of the government-aligned Confederation of Mexican Workers (CTM), an array of regional teachers' unions merged into the National Union of Education Workers (SNTE) in 1943. Like the CTM and the rest of organized labour in Mexico, the SNTE was rapidly absorbed into the corporatist political structure of the ruling Institutional Revolutionary Party (PRI), which through its predecessor parties had governed Mexico since the 1920s. The takeover of the SNTE in 1948 by PRI-aligned groups led by Jesús Robles Martinez, extinguished democracy within the union. Robles and other bosses imposed by the state on unions were known as the *charros* (cowboys), for the fashion preferences of the newly installed leader of the railroad workers' union (Rincones 2008, 217–18; Foweraker 1993, 45–50; Torres 1991, 118–19; Monsiváis 1987).

2.2. The Postwar Consolidation of Public Education Systems and Teachers' Unions

The career of Mexico's Education Secretary Jaime Torres Bodet from 1943 to 1946 and 1958 to 1964 provides an example of the Mexico City-based system's early international vision. After overseeing the expansion of the SEP with its budget increasing from 76 million pesos in 1940 to over 200 million by 1946, he served as the second director of UNESCO from 1948 to 1952. When he returned to Mexico, he oversaw the continued expansion of the system, standardized teacher training, and worked with UNESCO to organize conferences on comparative Latin American education policy with a focus on progressive pedagogy and benchmarks for eliminating illiteracy. UNESCO's Mexican offices were housed in SEP headquarters from the 1970s through 1980s, a symbol of the multilateral agency's prominence.[7] Torres Bordet unsuccessfully urged the members of the Organization of American States to increase the percentage of GDP dedicated to education to 15 per cent through the United States's Alliance for Progress funding (Caballero and Medrano 1982, 395–402; SEP Officials 1 and 2, interview June 2015).

As late as 1958, while NYC high schools enjoyed a reputation as among the best in the country (prior to mass expansion in the 1960s), the reappointed secretary of education, Jaime Torres Bordet, reported that of every 1,000 entrants to primary schools, only 114 graduated (an 88.6 per cent dropout rate). Of these 114, 59 enrolled in secondary school, of which only 27 graduated. One in 1,000 obtained a university degree (Curiel Méndez 1982, 152). Under Torres, the SEP focused on retaining students and increasing overall enrolment by funding more schools and teachers (though with miserly salaries) in the 1960s and 1970s. Like the United States and Canada in these decades, Mexico experienced a baby boom, but the profoundly centralized nature of the country's infrastructure and the postwar "economic miracle" in Mexico City, driven by growing manufacturing industries protected by Import-Substitution policies led to the *zona metropolitana* (the contiguous urban area of the Federal District and adjacent municipalities in Mexico State), growing disproportionately from the migration of rural families. Mexico City became the pre-eminent megapolis of the developing world in this period, and its education system expanded apace. Mexico's secondary school enrolment increased 1,000 per cent from 1950 to 1970 (Levinson 2001, 27). It became compulsory in 1993, but enforcement was delayed for nearly a decade, owing to the 1995 peso crisis and an ensuing deep recession (ibid.). Citing government statistics for 2008, David Marquez Ayala places the secondary attendance rate at 72 per cent (2008, 156).

In the early 1950s, the Escuela Nacional de Maestros (National Teachers' School) for primary teachers was founded in the Santa Maria de la Ribera neighbourhood west of Mexico City's centre, and the Escuela Normal Superior de Mexico for secondary teachers was started in the northwest borough of Azcapotzalco (Curiel Méndez 1982, 456–8). Both were four-year, tuition-free programs in which students boarded on campus, which contributed to a collective identity. The location of these large facilities in the capital was consistent with the state's centralizing tendencies and coincided with Mexico City's population explosion and the nation's rapid urbanization. They immediately became centres of activism, where secondary teachers in training protested against initial assignments of only six hours a week, demanding at least twelve hours. Their activism flowed into the teachers' movement of 1956–8, centred in Mexico City (Enrique Enriquez Ibarra, interview, June 2015). They also contributed to the rising movement of university students in the city with their colleagues at the National Autonomous University of Mexico that culminated in 1968 (Curiel Méndez 1982, 442).

There was an upsurge of activist teachers in 1958, centred in Mexico City and led by the Mexican Communist Party, demanding wage increases and control over their own union, in the context of a major national strike by railroad workers over similar issues. Both movements were crushed by police and military units in cooperation with the charro union leadership. Robles controlled the union until 1972, when he in turn was ousted at gunpoint by Jongitud Barrios and his Vanguardia Revolucionaria (Revolutionary Vanguard) group. Barrios had the tacit support of PRI officials, who were concerned that Robles was unable to control his restive members. Nearly from the outset, rather than serving as a legitimate union of educators, the SNTE acted as a mass membership appendage of the state-party (Cook 1996; Rincones 2008, 218). The SNTE seldom advocated assertively on behalf of its membership, and so teacher salaries and working conditions generally followed the will of the governing party in this period. Yet its corporatist status as a political arm of the state mobilized during election periods to support the ruling party, gave it a high degree of influence within the SEP. The union exercised significant influence over administration, often controlling the appointment of school- and state-level officials, as well as the "sale" of teacher jobs. While ruling the union, Barrios amassed considerable power. Through the 1980s he was simultaneously a federal senator, president of the Congress of Labour (the umbrella organization for PRI-aligned unions), and state governor of San Luis Potosi (Foweraker 1993, 50–60; Torres 1991, 123; Monsiváis 1987, 170–2).

The rapid expansion of the SEP during the 1950s–70s created an increasingly unwieldy bureaucracy highly centralized in Mexico City. Fuelled by a short burst of oil wealth in the late 1970s, the system reached its maximum extent for decades, as did teachers' salaries (alongside workers' wages overall) (Brambila 2008, 217). The National Pedagogic University (UPN), founded in 1982 at the height of the oil boom, was also situated in the capital. It was to be the nation's primary centre for research in education policy, responsible with the SEP for defining the teacher education curriculum used in normales across the country, and an important faculty of education in its own right. In these respects its role was similar to that of OISE in Toronto. The UPN was intended to be autonomous of Jongitud Barrio's SNTE leadership, provoking considerable resistance from him and his successor, Elba Esther Gordillo (Brambila 2008; Arnaut 2008, 148)

The defeat of the initial large-scale attempt by Mexico City teachers to organize independently of their corporatist leadership and improve their conditions was superseded by educators in New York City. With the decline of the Cold War era repression that had broken up the Communist-led New York Teachers Union, they benefited from considerably greater freedom of association at a time when municipal workers were beginning to organize and private sector unionism was near its twentieth-century peak of influence (Freeman 2000). The rapid victory between 1961 and 1963 of the AFT-aligned United Federation of Teachers (UFT) in signing up a majority of NYC's teachers, obtaining legal status as their official bargaining agent, and winning significant gains after short, city-wide strikes, had explanations related to far more than a desire to match the salaries of skilled, unionized, private sector workers (Robertson 2000, 101–3; Murphy 1992, 222). Marjorie Murphy refutes claims that it was driven primarily by status-conscious, militant, male high school teachers in spite of docile female elementary teachers, citing the many examples of important female teacher union leaders to this point in New York. She argues that

> teachers were fed up with the centralized bureaucracy of the schools. Teachers complained about oversupervision, increasing bureaucratization, inappropriate assignments, and a lack of control over licensing, training, and assignments. These grievances go back to the beginnings of

> unionization; after tenure laws had been effectively introduced, teachers were willing to strike for those same demands (as well as higher pay) after World War II. (1992, 222)

Alongside the expansion of high school education after the Second World War, teachers in New York State in the 1960s and Ontario in the mid- to late 1970s made substantial gains in defining and protecting their professional autonomy in a wave of union militancy. In his book on the Newark Teachers Union of New Jersey, historian Steve Golin finds that its strikes in the early 1970s, directly inspired by the UFT's victories, were not solely over salaries or learning conditions, as the school board and the union alternatively claimed: "more than anything, striking teachers hoped to end the tyranny of principals and of the Board of Education" (2002, 3–4). Golin quotes a teacher who co-founded the union in the late 1930s: "The personal indignity that you had to undergo as a teacher when I first started teaching – you wouldn't believe it. Being treated like children. Whatever the superiors told you, that was law" (ibid., 10–11).

Success for the UFT in NYC-inspired victories in Detroit and Philadelphia, among twenty-six union elections to represent urban teachers across the United States between 1961 and 1965. Spurred by the upstart AFT, which had quickly grown to 110,000 members, the NEA embraced collective bargaining and began to formally organize as a union, winning fourteen elections during this period, mostly in suburban and rural districts. The NEA's membership at the time stood at 943,000 (Murphy 1992, 224, 227–8). Increasing competition between the two unions led to calls for unity. While unattained at the national level, state-level federations in New York (New York State United Teachers; NYSUT) and California affiliated by 1970. These mergers created electorally focused organizations that partially addressed the obvious limitations of the urban-focused AFT and the suburban/rural NEA, which was structured to negotiate with state governments but had little presence in large cities (ibid., 253). Murphy describes how the union victories of the 1960s and early 1970s transformed and empowered the profession:

> For elementary teachers, collective bargaining meant breaks from the constant pressure of being in front of the classroom for six hours; for high school teachers it meant time to prepare for classes; for junior high school teachers it mean relief from extra lunch guard duties. Teachers were no longer told arbitrarily when they had to appear at school and when they could leave; surprise faculty meetings after school disappeared; and administrators could no longer appear suddenly in a teacher's classroom.

> Teachers still had to report to school at a prescribed time, they still had to attend meetings, they still had to welcome in outsiders to their classes, but what changed was the arbitrariness, the complete absence of control on the job that teachers had incessantly complained of. If the fundamental object of unionism is to give workers dignity on the job, unionization achieved that much for teachers and more. (Ibid., 209)

Frustrations of a loss of professional autonomy within growing, increasingly bureaucratized school boards resonated with teachers in Ontario a decade later, according to Peter Hennessy, who surveyed educators there and in Quebec and New York State on behalf of the Canadian Teachers Federation in 1975 on their motivations for participating in unions. Many teachers in Ontario were estranged from their employers by the consolidation of 1,400 local boards into 77 public and 49 Catholic boards in the early 1970s, "foster[ing] suspicion and hostility" (Hennessy 1975, 9, 10). In an alternative interpretation, the decreased proximity to their supervisors created the space in many communities for teachers to organize. Hennessy describes the union-building effect of the breakdown of paternalist relationships resulting from the amalgamation of small school boards:

> Schools were becoming larger, more highly structured, and more impersonal as management of education increasingly was divorced from teaching. Often, too, teachers did not identify with the community in which they taught – and often enough did not even live there. The result was a progressive sense of alienation from both the school and the community; it was to the group, either the union or association – that teachers turned increasingly for security and support. (1975, 14–15)

An immediate cause of militancy in 1973–5 was the imposition by the provincial government of spending ceilings on school boards in the context of rising inflation, setting a maximum funding level per student and thereby a cap on the salary increases that boards could offer their employees. Boards with the capacity to raise their taxes could not create a greater gulf with poorer, usually rural boards, which led to a fiscal squeeze on the largest urban boards in Toronto and Ottawa, which offered the widest range of programs (Gidney 1999, 114). This policy caused many boards to lay off staff from 1971 onwards (Head and Hutton 2005, 6–13; Hennessy 1975, 11). Not having the right to strike, about 7,800 public and Catholic teachers across sixteen mainly urban boards tendered their resignations in protest in November–December 1973. When the provincial government ruled the resignations out of order,

OSSTF and the other federations conducted a one-day strike on 18 December, featuring a rally of over 20,000 teachers in Toronto (Head and Hutton 2005, 12–16; Hennessy 1975, 5–8). Along with restoring school board control of funding and initiating a wave of local strikes that won improvements in working conditions and wage gains of over 20 per cent for thousands of teachers,[8] the action led to legislation in 1975 awarding full collective bargaining rights to the federations, including grievance and arbitration procedures and the right to strike[9] (Hennessy 1975, 53). Possessing the legal rights of unions and a demonstrated capacity for militancy that had won significant material and professional gains in the mid 1970s, Ontario teachers had arrived at unionism.

Secondary school became a nearly universal institution in Canada and the United States in the 1960s. In Ontario, as elsewhere, this advance coincided with policy struggles over meeting the needs of students who in previous decades would not have attended high school and over sustaining academic rigour. The debate impacted teachers' professional autonomy, as the outcome by the 1980s was a more defined curriculum and greater centralization of its development and oversight in the provincial ministry of education. The OSSTF was particularly vocal where its members' employment and professional integrity were at stake, as when it warned that raising the number of mandatory courses would reduce enrolment in electives and potentially increase student dropout rates. Its advocacy affected public opinion and was taken seriously by the governing PCs (Gidney 1999, 96–103). During this period, OSSTF led the other federations in developing a significant campaign capacity to electorally support or punish politicians and parties. The strategy balanced between pragmatically engaging with the ruling party and assisting the more ideologically aligned labour-endorsed New Democratic Party (NDP) where it was viable.

When the Mexican teachers' movement resurged in 1979 as the Coordinadora Nacional de los Trabajadores de la Educación (National Coordination of Education Workers; CNTE), it was preoccupied by a layer of bread-and-butter issues: better medical facilities for public employees, the regular payment of salaries, and increases to meet rising costs of living. However, beneath all these concerns was the more intractable, far-reaching, and ultimately most challenging demand: control over their own union, the SNTE. Because of the SNTE's power in the education system, union democracy meant professional autonomy (Cook 1996; Foweraker 1993). The eruption of the movement in 1979 occurred at the end of a decade-long surge in workers' organizing and strikes unprecedented since the consolidation of PRI control over unions in the 1940s. The United States and Canada also experienced unprecedented strike waves in the early 1970s, pointing to political and economic developments (a resurgent leftist politics and high working-class expectations combined with economic uncertainty caused by rising inflation and unemployment) that were global, though also shaped by distinctly national and regional contexts (Glyn 2007; Brecher 1997). Its specific origins in Mexico evolved from social ferment and popular dissatisfaction with the government party in the aftermath of the bloody repression of the 1968 pro-democracy student movement. Many Mexican leftists were inspired by revolutionary Cuba and the recently killed Che Guevara's internationalist efforts to foment insurrections among Latin America's oligarchies. Maria Lorena Cook (1996) emphasizes that many future teacher leaders were graduates of the 1968 student movement. Some spent the early to mid-1970s working in central Mexico's expanding and modernizing industrial sectors.[10] They participated in the "Workers' Insurgency," attempting to establish militant, independent unions in place of the corrupt CTM (Robles and Gómez 1997). Others joined Indigenous peasant and rural labour movements in the southern states of Chiapas, Oaxaca, and Guerrero, where they fought for land rights (Cook 1996; Monsiváis 1987). By the time they became teachers, these activists in their late twenties and early thirties possessed considerable experience as organizers. As they subsumed themselves in the particular problems of their new profession, they retained an outward orientation to building broader coalitions.

Triggered by a rapidly rising cost of living and the tepid response of official union leadership aligned with Jongitud Barrios, teachers in Chiapas walked out in 1979, joined by colleagues in neighbouring Oaxaca. Both were states where his Vanguardia Revoluciónaria had a relatively weak hold over the union. Cook (1996) applies to this context an analysis developed by sociologists Charles Tilly and Sidney Tarrow (2007) of how successful social movements leverage strategic political conjunctures such as intra-elite conflicts. Both Cook (1996) and Torres (1991) emphasize the conflict among SEP officials, who resented the SNTE's control over education and so were decentralizing some administration from Mexico City to the state level, where the SNTE's power would be diluted. Negotiating with the CNTE in Oaxaca and Chiapas provided a means of fulfilling this agenda and curbing the influence of the national SNTE, which was subsequently compelled by the federal government to convene transparent elections for the union executives in these states, which the CNTE overwhelmingly won. To apply pressure on the SEP to make these agreements, thousands of teachers from Oaxaca and Chiapas travelled to Mexico City and erected a protest camp outside the SEP headquarters on Avenida Republica de Brasil. They were joined by thousands more from states surrounding Mexico City, including Guerrero, Hidalgo, Mexico State, and Morelos. Cook (1996) explains the failure of the movement in these states to consolidate themselves as due to the far stronger political base held there by Vanguardia Revoluciónaria in the form of patronage networks among the union membership. Allied local PRI officials were also more willing to send police to attack marches. Just as crucial, the teachers of Oaxaca and Chiapas launched their movement on a much stronger base of prior organization and pre-existing alliances with local peasant and Indigenous organizations, factors that, combined with less repression, enabled them to more quickly build up a critical mass of support. When the movement ebbed in 1983, the CNTE weakened in these central states, unable to force their demands for democratic union elections. Most state sections of the SNTE, including its largest one in Mexico City, remained under the control of the charros. Yet the emergence of the CNTE set a precedent for an enduring, independent movement. While not "national" in scope, it established a significant regional base from which it would later expand. In the interim, despite the fact that school systems in Oaxaca and Chiapas (two of Mexico's poorest states) remained grossly underfunded, the CNTE transformed faculty relations, giving classroom teachers a significant voice in their work (Monsiváis 1987, 193–201; Cook 1996, 105–73, 195–6; Foweraker 1993, 50–60). Given the importance of the SNTE in politics at all levels, the CNTE made an impact beyond the schools where their members worked:

> At the local level, dissident teachers broke with clientelistic ties to national union and government officials and created largely autonomous union organizations that forced administrators to abide by teachers' collective decisions concerning their jobs and workplaces. Ambitious local union officials, displaced in those areas where the dissident teachers' movement emerged most strongly, lost their support base and often their political careers, and local PRI politicians could no longer rely on teachers' networks for local electoral campaigns. The success of the dissident teachers' movement in some regions of the country upset the regional balance of power and threatened, where it did not sever, previous ties with state and federal government, party, and union officials. (Cook 1996, 24)

2.3. The Neoliberalization of Education: Teacher Unionism on the Defensive

After common, though distinctly timed, periods of growth and consolidation, teachers' organizations in all three countries confronted firm barriers to further advancement and gains. The timing and strength of these blockages varied, but all related to state fiscal austerity and the emergence of neoliberal education policy. With notable exceptions, a shared outcome was the decline of teacher militancy, reducing opposition to the implementation of neoliberal reforms. From the mid-1970s through the 1990s, teachers' work came under increased scrutiny from the state and the public. During this period, fiscal austerity was followed by policies that undermined professional autonomy, including standardized evaluations of students and teachers, the decline in collegial relations between teachers and school administrators, and the introduction of market-style mechanisms whereby schools and teachers would compete for enrolment.

NYC teachers were the first to experience this shift, within the context of the city's fiscal crisis of 1975. Their public schools were demonized as among the worst "inner-city" schools during the 1970s through the 1980s in the midst of the crisis and its long aftermath for its public education system. Its resolution in the late 1970s was a harbinger of neoliberal policy in the rest of the United States and of structural adjustment programs carried out in Mexico and elsewhere in the global South by the International Monetary Fund and the World Bank in the 1980s and 1990s. When banks refused to lend more money to the city in 1975, the federal government under President Gerald Ford saw an opportunity to use New York City as a disciplinary test case against defaulting by other municipal governments, while drastically scaling down the city's social democratic welfare state (Freeman 2000, 259–63). Among the massive cuts made to New York's public services from 1975 to 1978, over 8,000 teachers and para-professionals were laid off in the summer of 1975 (ibid., 265), 25 per cent of their total numbers. They were disproportionately African-American and Latinx, who were among the most recently hired (ibid., 271). Class sizes rose dramatically. Rank-and-file anger led to a five-day strike, settled by UFT president Albert Shanker[11] in exchange for freezing existing benefits and salaries; however, per pupil funding adjusted for inflation did not recover until 1989 (Ravitch and Viteritti 2000).

The resolution of New York's fiscal crisis through public austerity and the curbing of union militancy was a turning point for organized teachers and the broader labour movement as well as the idea of a "social" or welfare state. It set the stage for subsequent neoliberal showdowns at the municipal level, owing to both its profile and the unusually high degree of organization of New York labour and the UFT as the most prominent teachers' union. Despite later funding increases, NYC schools struggled to meet community needs. As service correspondingly declined, as did that of municipal hospitals and transit, it came to be seen as second-best compared with private alternatives increasingly adopted by those who could afford them. Freeman concludes:

> The fiscal crisis constituted a critical moment in the history of privatization, spreading the belief that the market could better serve the public than government ... Because New York served as the standard-bearer for urban liberalism and the idea of the welfare state, the attacks on its municipal services and their decline helped pave the way for the national conservative hegemony of the 1980s and 1990s. Working-class New York led they way in both the rise and the fall of social democracy in America. (2000, 272)

Increasing popular economic and social conservatism by the late 1970s in New York City, to which racial tension greatly contributed, manifested itself in anti-union sentiment and a cynicism towards public services. A further sign of retreat from a working-class social democratic vision in the aftermath of the fiscal crisis was a change in the basic approach of NYC unions such as the UFT, from strikes to joining corporatist lobby boards pushing for business and income tax cuts and backing publicly funded private developments such as convention centres to create jobs and expand the tax base (ibid.).

New York City's ideological shift to the right was facilitated by the foundation of conservative think-tanks in this period that responded directly to issues facing the city. One of the most significant was the Manhattan Institute, formed in 1975 "in the heart of the beast" in the words of its founders (Peck 2010), to bring the ideological battle to the bastion of the US left. The Manhattan Institute initially saw its role as the provider of more academic neoliberal theory geared towards intellectuals and elites. Future mayor Rudy Giuliani claimed it helped shape his "tough on crime" and workfare policies. His mayoralty was lauded by the Institute (ibid.). The think-tank contributed to NYC, along with other key sites such as Chicago and Washington, DC, becoming key sources of neoliberal policy innovation. By 2016 the Manhattan Institute had become involved in applied forms of policy intervention with a significant focus on education. Its website, www.schoolgrades.org, purported to rate US schools on the basis of their literacy and math exam scores, normed to National Assessment of Education Progress and PISA test scores and the proportion of students receiving subsidized lunches, to offer local and international comparisons. The National Education Policy Centre (NEPC) at the University of Colorado, described the website's methodology as highly flawed, stating that it was unclear how to meaningfully compare the results of various different local, state, and national tests, and that the Institute's method for doing so was not transparent (NEPC 2016).

Teachers' College at Columbia University is much more ideologically heterogeneous. Both its importance and its political variability are embodied in the career of its PhD graduate and sometime lecturer Diane Ravitch. The foremost historian of NYC's education system, she was the author of several books in the 1980s through the early 2000s that aimed to provide "lessons" from the NYC system for the rest of the United States. She promoted the rollout of charter schools and standardized testing, believing that competitive "school choice" market mechanisms would subject teacher professionalism to greater rigour. Ravitch served as the assistant secretary of education in the administration of George H.W. Bush from 1991 to 1993. From there, she became a regular contributor on education policy studies jointly published by Teachers' College and the DC-based Brookings Institution, the latter considered the most influential think-tank in the world (McCann 2016). She also affiliated to the conservative Thomas B. Fordham Institute, the Hoover Institution, and the Manhattan Institute. In the mid-2000s she radically reassessed her beliefs. In *The Death and Life of the Great American School System* published in 2010, she confronted many of the policies she had previously advocated, disassociated herself from earlier collaborators at Brookings and the other right-wing think-tanks, and became arguably the most prominent champion of public education in the United States in the early twenty-first century (Bailey 2015, 327–8; Ravitch 2010, 1–14).

NYC is far from alone among key American urban centres for policy in the early twenty-first century, and states can also be the primary level of policy rollout. Chicago under Arne Duncan and Rahm Emmanuel, DC under Michelle Rhee, and Florida under Governor Jeb Bush come to mind. The criteria for being a key policy-influencing centre seem to be a combination of the national prominence of the city and or state plus a charismatic neoliberal leader with considerable power via legislation and outward influence through media and intellectuals.[12] As policy advocates Michael Fullan and Alan Boyle enthused about the prominence of NYC's Bloomberg era:

> New York City has attracted enormous attention over the past decade for its educational reform efforts for several reasons: It is a large prominent system; it represents an aggressive, relentless attempt by a mayor and his appointed chancellor to pull out all the stops to get successful reform; and it was carried out in a transparent, high-profile manner. Everyone in the school reform community was watching! (2014, 21)

One activist NYC teacher argues that his city is an important centre for neoliberal innovation because of its significance for capitalist accumulation. As a result, it is also an important site for racial and class conflict:

> Here in the city you have Goldman Sachs overseeing a charter school in Harlem. They will drop down in the middle of Harlem a gleaming cube with new everything! ... And throw millions of dollars to prove that resources don't matter. And bring in a few kids by lottery, Willy Wonka style. In order to prove that the public schools suck. And then the kids who act up and won't follow their super strict rules get kicked back to the public schools in order to further prove that the public schools can't do it ... there's this tremendous publicity machine that promotes to the whole world that they are miracle workers in this miracle factory sponsored by Goldman Sachs ... Goldman Sachs doesn't care in the same way about what's happening in Albany or Syracuse. New York City's like a laboratory for this remaking of the cities. As is Chicago ... they really want to reconquer the city centre. It used to be, the geography of American cities was a despised inner city. The phrase "inner city" is practically synonymous with *black*! Now the inner city is where the rich people want to be! ... Get these black people out of here! But to do that, you have to dislodge them from the schools, you've got to dislodge them from the unions ... you've got to break up the connection between the school and the community. (NYC Teacher 1, interview Dec. 2014)

Mexico's 1982 debt crisis was even more drastic than New York's. The value of a worker's wage plummeted. Government spending on public education as a share of the Gross National Product declined from 5.2 per cent in 1982 to 2.45 per cent by 1989, at the end of the deep recession (Torres 1991, 121). Teachers' salaries fell by 62 per cent between 1982 and 1989, reaching the national minimum wage[13] by the end of the decade (Cook 1996, 184). Student dropout rates soared. During this time of reduced teacher demand, authorities upgraded the prerequisite required to become a teacher to the equivalent of a bachelor's degree in education (Brambila 2008, 217). Though limited in its initial effect, as it did not apply to existing teachers, this measure runs contrary to the general trajectory of this period, since it represents a form of increased professionalization. The CNTE was unable to expand significantly during these years. Though it consolidated its base in Oaxaca, manipulations by the national SNTE, which had made peace with the SEP, resulted in the movement's losing control of the Chiapas local in 1987 and the killings of hundreds of teachers, peasants, and other leftists there (Monsiváis 1987, 193–201; Cook 1996, 183–215).

In Ontario, austerity and neoliberal policy hit education in the early 1990s in a recession during the administration of a left-leaning NDP government. While the imposed salary freezes and unpaid days off were relatively mild compared with the austerity measures of future governments, it set an important precedent for undermining free collective bargaining, not least because it was implemented by an avowedly pro-labour government, creating a deep well of cynicism towards electoral participation for many teachers and union activists and contributing to support for future alliances of a much more transactional nature. Though coupled with progressive policies, the NDP government's proposals for far-reaching reforms would be implemented by the subsequent hard-right PC government after 1995. Gidney, Basu, Robertson, and Kerr identify the NDP's 1994 Royal Commission on Learning as an important precedent. Arguing that public confidence in teacher effectiveness needed to be restored, the report proposed a more prescribed provincial curriculum; provincial standardized tests in literacy and math, administered through a new Education Quality and Accountability Office (EQAO); and the creation of the Ontario College of Teachers (OCT). The OCT would be a disciplinary body for teachers, reducing the power of the teachers' federations to self-regulate, while the EQAO used test scores to produce tables of quantified data ranking "good" and "bad" schools. Despite the ideological gap with the social democratic predecessor (NDP), these proposals were adopted by the hard-right PC premier, Mike Harris (Gidney 1999, 232–3; Robertson 2000, 134; Kerr 2006; Basu 2004, 625).

Under the PCs, professional autonomy and working conditions were undermined by drastic reductions in daily preparation time and increases in class sizes, as well as the reclassification of vice-principals and principals as management and their removal from the federations. Ontario's elementary and secondary teachers mounted a vigorous defence, including an illegal two-week strike at all public and Catholic schools in 1997. It garnered popular support, as the unions presented themselves in opposition to nearly $1 billion in proposed cuts to education, rather than only to the specific contractual issues of teachers. Despite militancy and broad support, their struggles remained defensive, defeating some (e.g., a proposal to replace some categories of teachers with uncertified instructors) but not all of Premier Harris's policies. Community-led efforts also pushed the PCs to prevent the closure of 100 schools in Toronto (Gidney 1999, 256–64; Head and Hutton 2005, 54–65; Kerr 2006; Rose 2002; Basu 2004).

Despite being demonized by PC politicians as out-of-touch academics dictating policy from their ivory tower in Toronto (PC Party of Ontario

2013), as noted in the opening section of this chapter, a handful of professors at OISE have wielded disproportionate influence on the trajectory of education far beyond the province. Annie Kidder, the founder and executive director of the Toronto-based People for Education, has a nuanced, critical perspective on the powerful influence exerted on education politics by a small circle of travelling policy superstars. People for Education is a pro-public education research and advocacy group, founded in the mid-1990s as a parent activist network opposing the Harris government's budget cuts. Among Kidder's concerns is a tendency by OISE's high-profile policy advocates to contribute to a narrowing of education policy goals. According to Kidder, one of the most recognizable "brands" of Ontario's policy advocates, and of the "Ontario model" they promote, is the "pressure and support" formula coined by Michael Fullan. "Pressure and support" refers to holding school boards, principals, and teachers to account through quantitative metrics such as standardized test scores administered by the EQAO and overall graduation rates, while also providing additional resources to struggling schools. She contrasts this approach with the punitive agenda of No Child Left Behind (NCLB) in the United States, where schools with low scores are threatened with closure, "Their brand is not to attack teachers" (Annie Kidder, interview Nov. 2015). People for Education has evolved within the context of Ontario's education politics. From its protest roots over the tenure of the McGuinty and Wynne Liberal governments, it increasingly focused on research and has become one of the most influential education advocacy groups in Canada, drawing considerable media coverage to its reports (Winton and Brewer 2014, 1105; Gordon 2017). Its high-profile annual conferences feature academics, many consultants, and prominent officials from the Ministry of Education and school boards. Though comprising around half of the hundreds of attendees, no teachers were among nearly forty "expert" speakers or panelists in 2015; two were included in 2016, along with a representative from a Norwegian teachers' union. This omission is most notable when the session topic is assessment and evaluation practices, an important issue for teachers' professionalism. The teachers' federations are virtually invisible in its work, but People for Education has conducted several research studies with the Ontario Principals' Council.[14]

While the policies put forward by Fullan and others are friendlier to the teaching profession than many of the dominant discourses in the United States, retired Toronto secondary teacher Lindsay Kerr's critique is that these are still top-down reforms. She contends that under Harris and McGuinty, they were implemented with little meaningful consultation with teachers and their federations. She charges that Fullan's and Andy Hargreaves's prescriptions, while claiming to "empower" teachers, in fact facilitate neoliberalism. They intensify teachers' work by not providing additional resources, and leave systemic external factors such as poverty, which would require significant increases in funding, unaddressed (Kerr 2006, 153–7). Nevertheless, the powerful discourses emanating from OISE are part of the explanation why Toronto remains a centre for policy that's divergent from the dominant ideas south of Ontario's borders.

The dominance of these three cities as policy centres persisted through changes in ideology. The distinctive federal structures of government in each country are also an important means for understanding differences in how New York City, Mexico City, and Toronto act as policymaking centres. While power is highly centralized in the capital, Mexico City, it is comparatively far more decentralized through provincial/state administrations in Canada and the United States, in which the influence of Toronto and New York City is more defined by example than by executive fiat. While Ontario and New York State are among the most important subnational entities within their respective countries, their education administrators can give only suggestions to authorities in Vancouver or Los Angeles. What is common among the case studies is the importance of the metropolis as a policy centre, which has both a critical concentration of state power and influential intellectuals, and as a proximate, large-scale site for implementation.

Though the circumstances varied – of New York State in the late 1970s, of Mexico in the mid-late 1980s, and of Ontario in the early 1990s – in each instance an economic downturn facilitated significant cuts to public spending on education, not reversed for years or decades. These "crises" in education facilitated politically subsequent neoliberal policies related to privatization and incursions on teachers' professionalism (Ginsburg 1991b). The ability of states to overturn previous years of union gains had an impact on member morale, diminishing militancy. All of this occurred alongside drastic declines in overall strike rates in all three countries and drops in unionization rates in the United States and Mexico, which left the heavily unionized K–12 public education sector isolated.

An important exception to this general trajectory was the strike of half a million Mexican teachers in 1989, marking a dramatic resurgence of the CNTE (Torres 1991, 130). Sensing the political vulnerability of the new president, Carlos Salinas, widely viewed to have prevailed through electoral fraud over leftist candidate, Cuauhtémoc Cárdenas, and perceiving that his government was not as closely aligned with

Jongitud Barrios, the movement rapidly expanded across the country, demanding the restoration of a living wage for its members. Mexico City's teachers joined the movement in mass numbers, led by the predominantly female elementary teachers of Section 9, the SNTE's largest local. Since the poor response of authorities to the devastating 1985 earthquake, the emergence of independent urban social movements for housing rights, and Cárdenas's 1988 campaign for president, the city had become the nation's new centre of political dissidence towards the ruling PRI. Never before had teachers struck so effectively nationwide, again occupying downtown Mexico City streets surrounding the SEP offices. To head off a political crisis, Salinas deposed Barrios and promoted one of his rising lieutenants from Mexico State, Elba Esther Gordillo. Teachers won a 25 per cent salary increase (the SEP initially had offered 10 per cent), and Gordillo responded to pressure from the CNTE by scheduling free elections for the local union executives of Oaxaca, Chiapas, and Section 9. All were won overwhelmingly by the movement. Teachers in Guerrero and Michoacan were unsuccessful in obtaining open elections, but were recognized as representatives of the union by their state governments (Cook 1996, 266–89; Torres 1991, 131–2; Maria de la luz Arriaga, interview June 2015).

Cook attributes the success of the CNTE to its commitment to participatory, democratic processes that helped maintain the momentum of a mass movement and mitigated the corrosive effects of internal factional conflicts. The development of functioning school- and district-level committees that elect delegates to state assemblies, helped ensure the movement could continue to function were it to lose control of the formal machinery of the union. This is how the CNTE functions in states where it has the support of a critical mass of teachers but lacks institutional control of the local. Also vital to the longevity of the CNTE and its ability to consolidate its bases has been its capacity to effectively address members' day-to-day issues, from transfer requests to resolving payment problems, as well as the marked difference of a greater climate of freedom from interference from the charro union and SEP officials at the school level[15] (Cook 1996, 193–6, 216–65).

The geographic growth of the teachers' movement after the 1989 strike was quickly challenged by Gordillo. Her path to becoming one of the most important neoliberal policy advocates during the National Action Party (PAN) governments of Fox and Calderon (from 2001 to 2012) and mastermind of Mexican politics, began in the early 1990s in the twilight of the PRI's era of uninterrupted national hegemony. Once under her control, the SNTE, Latin America's largest union, was her springboard into national politics, where she became a president maker. First she had to roll back the advances won by the CNTE. In the precarious years following her appointment, the CNTE had obtained a large minority of seats on the national union executive, a majority of the executive of Section 9 representing Mexico City's primary teachers, and roughly half the executive of Section 10 (the city's secondary teachers). According to a CNTE activist elected to Section 10's executive in the 1990s, Gordillo co-opted much of the movement's leadership among secondary teachers and to a lesser extent among those in Section 9, preventing dissidents from maintaining majority control over Section 10. Gordillo welcomed many Mexico City dissident leaders into full-time union positions for Section 10 and at the national office. Others were fast-tracked over the standard career steps into school directorships. Individuals in both were enrolled in the Carrera Magisterial (Teaching Career) program negotiated by Gordillo and the SEP in 1993, which granted salary increases upon completion of courses, examinations, and classroom observations, without having to meet these prerequisites. While Section 9 remained under the leadership of the movement,[16] these measures shifted the balance of power within Section 10 in her favour, winning control of the entire institutional structure by the early 2000s (CNTE Section 10 activist, interview Feb. 2015; Leyva Piña and Rodriguez Lagunas 2012, 544). However, new waves of dissent came quickly in the early twenty-first century in opposition to the neoliberalization of education.

2.4. Transnational Elite Policy

This section provides an overview of how the ideas that became known as neoliberal education policy became the dominant frame of reference for governance in the context of North America. It will show how these particular ideas facilitated a tendency towards both a scaling-up of education policy and increasing cross-border mobility. This discussion will also suggest some reasons for the greater mobility of neoliberal education policy from the United States to Mexico than from either country to Canada.

Many accounts of the emergence of neoliberal education policy begin with the publication of *A Nation at Risk* by the US Department of Education in 1983 (Kuhn 2014; Ravitch 2010). While some of its concerns were historically specific and its prescriptions scarcely mention standardized testing or school choice (Ravitch 2010),[17] its legacy stems from being a high-profile declaration of "the crisis" in public education. Issued by a national authority, this profile served as a precursor of the future scaling-up of education policy to this level in the 2000s. In the meantime, as the neoliberal era emerged, it facilitated a national "discussion" that precipitated rapid policy exchanges at the state and local levels. It soon became international in the scale of its analysis, along with academic Philip Coombs's influential *The World Crisis in Education* (1985), a timely sequel to his *The World Educational Crisis: A Systems Analysis* (1968). Both complain of the "disparity" between education systems and economies and the rising cost of education and propose to replace teachers with technology (Ginsburg 1991a, 13–14; Hernandez Navarro 2013, 71).

Mexican president Carlos Salinas was perhaps the first key importer of neoliberal education policy from the United States to his country.[18] He proposed standardized tests for primary and secondary students and their use to evaluate teachers during his presidential campaign in 1988. According to Hugo Aboites, Mexico's CENEVAL high school and university application exam was designed as a "detailed replica" of that created by the American semi-non-profit corporation, Educational Testing Service, which administers NAEP, SAT, GRE, and TOEFL tests on behalf of universities, school districts, states, and the Department of Education in the United States and the United Kingdom. The CENEVAL exam was initiated at the end of his term in 1994 to coincide with the launch of the North American Free Trade Agreement (NAFTA) (Aboites 2012, 333–6). Aboites contends that Salinas and his peers wilfully ignored substantive evidence available by the early 1990s of the failings of similar tests in the United States (ibid., 329).

Politics, Markets and America's Schools (1990) by John Chubb and Terry Moe, published by the Brookings Institution, was important as an early intellectual argument frequently cited by other academics and policymakers for introducing market mechanisms into public education. It advocates for choice through school vouchers and de-professionalizing teaching by removing certification requirements and eliminating teachers' unions. It represents the fully envisioned, "hard" version of the neoliberal agenda. Chubb and Moe's work gained international influence and bolstered its credibility at home through its endorsement by the World Bank as part of its curated "policy menu":

> The rationale and evidence used by the [World] Bank and other agencies in the 1980s, 1990s, and 2000s to promote the privatisation of primary and secondary schooling in developing countries has often come from the United States. The two studies by Coleman and Chubb and Moe were and still are used to show the benefits of privatising schools, and the small voucher experiments in the United States are used similarly. (Klees 2008, 322)

Joseph P. Viteritti, a former long-time collaborator with Diane Ravitch, is considered by neoliberal education advocates to have made important contributions to developing their narrative beyond Chubb and Moe's market efficiency. A professor at the City University of New York, he previously taught at New York University, Harvard, and Princeton and served as special assistant to the chancellor of schools of New York City, Boston, and San Francisco (American Center for School Choice 2015). According to the American Center for School Choice, which lobbies on behalf of charter schools and voucher programs, his book published by the Brookings Institution, *Choosing Equality: School Choice, the Constitution, and Civil Society* (1999), "helped shift the debate about school choice from a discussion about the efficacy of free markets to a moral argument about how schools might better accommodate the educational needs of poor and under-represented communities" (ibid.). This change in discourse represents one of the most important shifts in political strategy that characterizes how neoliberal education policy transitioned from an initial "rollback" phase that attacked the legitimacy of the public sector to a more sophisticated "rollout" phase in the early twenty-first century (Peck and Tickell 2002). The latter discourse that frames poor and racialized children against self-interested unionized teachers was presented in the high-profile anti-public school documentary, *Waiting for Superman*, released in January 2010 at the Sundance film festival in the United States. Its Mexican clone, *De Panzazo!*, was released in October 2010 at the Morelia International Film Festival in Mexico (Hernandez Navarro 2012, 429–30).

The Washington, DC-based Brookings Institution's status as the most influential think-tank in the world (McCann 2016) is facilitated by its formidable resources, including a large staff of researchers at this "university without students." While it portrays itself as politically "centrist," many of its flagship publications on education policy are themselves associated with conservative free-market think-tanks, academic research centres, and business lobby groups. Its major edited volume, *Education Governance for the Twenty-First Century* (2013), includes contributors affiliated with the American Enterprise Institute, the Center for American Progress, the Thomas B. Fordham Institute, the Hoover Institution, and a NYC charter school management organization. Among the contributors there is scant K–12 classroom teaching experience. None is associated with teachers' unions. Most of the contributors share similar assumptions: the problems of public education have little or nothing to do with funding or social equity and everything to do with unions and school boards that disagree with their prescriptions.[19]

Movement of education policy in Latin America is significantly mediated by (northern led) multilateral agencies such as the World Bank. Graciela Messina (2008) contends that for issues of education governance, of which the dominant policy proposal in Latin America from the 1990s onwards were forms of decentralization (e.g., "school-based management" and federalization), the most significant sources of inspiration for Mexico were experiments by other Latin American nations, particularly Chile, which was the first to implement radical decentralization as part of its neoliberal reforms to education under dictatorship in the late 1970s. Also significant were the Escuela Nueva experiments in Colombia, and projects from the early 1990s in Argentina, Brazil, and Spain, all of which were analysed and promoted by the World Bank. This policy affinity is due to ease of linguistic exchange and shared socio-economic conditions within the region (more so than in developed countries such as the United States or Finland) and pre-existing channels for policy exchange, such as the regional branch of UNESCO (SEP Official 2, interview June 2015). Messina notes a distinction of discourse between the World Bank's "human capital theory" and the more humanist vision of UNESCO, emphasizing rights and equity and professional development for teachers. She acknowledges that some authors see an emerging convergence in ideology between the two, with UNESCO becoming more neoliberalized. It is difficult to measure the extent to which the World Bank drove policy mobility versus national governments, but it appears the Bank was significant as a key broker, shaper, and funder of ideas taken up by sympathetic governments.

From the 1990s, UNESCO's role in Mexico became more a symbolic source of pride for the nation's prominent engagement in international relations. The OECD and the World Bank occupied more influential positions, as their discourses on economic growth and quantitative evaluation resonated more within the neoliberalized policy circles of the day than the well-meaning but "vague" principles of UNESCO's Education for All (SEP Officials 1, 2, 3, interview June 2015). The political synergy between the OECD led by Mexican politician José Ángel Gurría and the government of Enrique Peña Nieto (2012–18) over education policy will be discussed in chapter 4.

According to Messina, the literature on education decentralization was most developed within the Latin-American context, serving as a model for African and Asian countries (2008, 15–20). Decentralization became a "global discourse" through its adoption by UNESCO, the OECD, and the World Bank, though with distinctions among them of what it entails. For the Bank it is primarily about greater efficiency in education disbursements and reducing them where possible through substitution with private sources, whereas for UNESCO it is more about effectively meeting local needs (ibid., 22–4). Brambila concludes:

> This expected common education agenda, in Latin America's case, consists of a limited number of general ideas that are elaborated daily in the multilateral organizations and in many other agencies, such as governmental offices, universities, foundations, academic associations, and specialized journals. They are part of an *education discourse* from which it is practically impossible to escape ... Decentralization, educational quality and coverage, privatization and social participation, acquire tones, and various and even opposed meanings according to the particular features of each nation. (2008, 222)

However, it will be demonstrated that while decentralization discourse (e.g., school-based management and autonomy) has been retained in Mexico, over the early twenty-first century the most significant trend in education governance has been centralization of policy in the executive of the national government, as in the United States, and at the provincial level in Canada. This was the means to attempt to implement an array of neoliberal policies, which provoked resistance from teachers' unions, a reaction most effective at lower levels (i.e., municipal or regional).

One method of measuring the World Bank's influence on Mexico's education policy is by the size of its loans and grants, which peaked in 2010 at $6.4 billion, dropped to $2.8 billion the following year, and declined to $500 million in 2016 (World Bank 2016). Meanwhile, the OECD has increased its influence over education policy, arguably eclipsing UNESCO in Mexico (Sellar and Lingard 2013, 716; SEP Officials 1, 2, 3, interview June 2015). A senior official in Mexico's SEP credits the OECD with creating awareness of its own qualitative deficiencies:

> It was the OECD that came and said, "Yes you have many schools but they [students] are not understanding what they're learning, they don't understand what they're reading and in some cases can't even complete basic mathematical equations." But this was the OECD that opened our eyes, not UNESCO. (SEP Official 1, interview June 2015; author's translation)

Their colleague continues:

> It's not as if the government says, "from this moment on, I'm going to work more with the OECD than with the United Nations." No, we were working on a series of programs that we wanted to strengthen. The OECD

> has more interest in evaluation, and so we've asked for their studies. (SEP Official 3, interview June 2015; author's translation)

A tangible means of measuring this influence can be found in the publications issued by the OECD and directed towards Mexico's education system, which are endorsed or republished by the SEP, such as the 250-page *OECD Review of Evaluation and Assessment in Education: Mexico 2012.* It is also found in the biographies of key policymakers such as Mexican academic Sylvia Schmelkes, a researcher with the OECD before becoming president of the National Institute for the Evaluation of Education (INEE), the governmental authority responsible for overseeing Mexico's testing systems of students and teachers. Beyond Mexico's particular political dynamics, the OECD, like the World Bank, gained importance among its members as the purveyor of internationally comparable education statistics, particularly its Program for International Student Assessment (PISA) of the performance of fifteen-year old students in reading and math since 2000 (Sellar and Lingard 2013, 716–17). For Winton, the PISA is

> organizing behaviour all over the world and definitely in Ontario. And it's very effective. A lot of policy isn't effective. But this policy linked to economics, it's really taken hold as a dominant discourse. Last year our math test scores were lower. A lot of people said they actually weren't lower; there were more people in the game, so our overall ranking fell, but that set off a lot of dialogue and movement around where our math education should be and what we should be doing. (Sue Winton, interview December 2015)

According to the World Bank's report, *Great Teachers: How to Raise Student Learning in Latin America and the Caribbean*:

> Hard data on education system results are a crucial political tool. Especially powerful are data on student learning outcomes, results that are internationally benchmarked ... Political leaders' use of these to build the case for reform has been a factor in all successful strategies to date. Of all international tests, the OECD's PISA seems to resonate most strongly with the business community and civil society groups. (Bruns and Luque 2014, 39)

Susan Robertson adds from a critical perspective:

> Given that the OECD represents the interests of powerful member states and the multi-national corporate sector, and, it can be argued convincingly, is ideologically committed to the new global competitive agenda, it is a

> matter of considerable significance how it articulates the issues and trends concerning teachers. In other words, given that the OECD sets important dimensions of the reform agenda for member nations on economic and public sector activity, the assumptions upon which this agenda are framed is very important, even if member nations choose to ignore the agenda. (2000, 206)

Sellar and Lingard (2013) observe that the PISA has also led to the global prominence and celebration of the top-scoring education system of Finland, whose features include a high degree of professional autonomy for teachers and an absence of measures celebrated by neoliberal reform advocates in North America, including high-stakes testing and "school choice." However, policy lessons from Finland are absent from the principal recommendations that the OECD provides to its member nations, as will be seen in its *Getting It Right: Strategic Agenda for Reforms in Mexico* (2013), discussed in chapter 4. This selectiveness suggests the OECD's neoliberal ideological frame described above by Robertson.

A key question is why the most aggressive neoliberal education policies pursued by political leaders in the United States and Mexico, which threaten to seriously undermine the professional autonomy of teachers and privatize public education, have had much more difficulty taking root in Canada. After participating in the 2015 conference of the American Education Research Association[20] in Chicago, Annie Kidder left with the impression that "Americans had just given up on the idea of public education itself" (interview Nov. 2015). Like Sue Winton (interview Dec. 2015), Kidder believes differences in popular ideology and the strength of key political actors are important:

> It's also our core value in Canada about social democracy ... what we also don't have in Canada is huge corporations making lots of money off education, because we still assume, even though less and less, that we'll pay taxes, that the testing systems aren't private, they're a part of our government. So we're still leery about private involvement in government, or even the idea of ... private companies, non-profit or for-profit, running schools. (Ibid.)

However, she notes that that there are gathering voices for similar policies in Ontario, citing a 2014 conference on education she attended hosted by the University of Toronto's Rotman School of Management. The K–12 panel, led by speakers from Teach for America (TFA) and US charter schools, elicited support for bringing their programs to Ontario. Kidder sees emerging forms of "school choice" within the public system, such as Toronto's selective specialty programs, as a worrying step in the direction of the advanced social segregation and privatization that exists in the US system. This topic will be further pursued in chapter 5.

The scaling-up of education policy to the national level in the United States in the early twenty-first century under Presidents George W. Bush and Barack Obama, respectively responsible for NCLB legislation and the Race to the Top (RTTT) program (both discussed in chapter 3), were crucial in accelerating the neoliberalization of education. The absence of similar constitutional means to do so in Canada may have hindered a faster movement of policy across provincial education systems.[21] Sandra Vergari contends that a larger federal role in US education facilitated a stronger and more rapid push to "performance standards" through standardized exams than has been the case in Canada. Both state and provincial test scores are reconciled against PISA, and random sample groups of students participate in the National Assessment of Educational Progress (US) and the Pan-Canadian Assessment Program (Vergari 2013, 241; Wallner 2014, 222–6). However, no structure with equivalent punitive powers exists in Canada compared with those held by the US Department of Education through NCLB (rescinded in 2015) or RTTT. A high degree of interprovincial policy mobility occurs through the Council of Ministers of Education Canada which also represents the country in education discussions at the OECD (Wallner 2014). However, it "lacks enforcement power" held by some initiatives of the US National Governors' Association (Vergari 2013, 239). Distinct roles for education policy at the federal level in Canada and the United States, the differences in political culture cited by Kidder and Winton, and more effective provincial teachers' unions are used by Mindzak (2015) to explain why charter schools have not expanded in Canada beyond their initial beachhead since 1994 of a couple of dozen schools in Alberta. Mindzak concludes, "Canadians do not appear to be interested in such reforms and continue to largely support their systems of public education" (105).[22]

Political momentum for the neoliberalization of education emerged with varying intensities in every province during the period studied here. Yet it could be argued that the absence of a federal mechanism for strengthening the push behind these policies, such as through the engagement of powerful national actors (e.g., Mexicanos Primero in Mexico or myriad similar business-led organizations in the United States) has maintained education policy in Canada on local and provincial levels, where teachers and community groups are more able to exercise political pressure. These ideas will be explored further in the case studies.

2.5. Counter-Hegemonic Continental Networks

Workers and their organizations possess agency and the capacity to intervene in the economic geographies in which they are situated (Herod 2001, 2010). This section considers the engagement of teachers' organizations, both official unions and informal networks, in transnational policy mobility and their relevance to struggles over professional autonomy. An overview is provided of how SNTE leaders Elba Esther Gordillo and her successor, Juan Diaz de la Torre, practised international labour diplomacy to burnish their weak legitimacy at home. Subsequently, a more hopeful presentation is made of the development of the Trinational Coalition in Defence of Public Education, through the leadership of provincial teachers' federations in Canada, Mexican solidarity activists in the United States, and grass-roots groups aligned with and inside the democratic teachers' movement of Mexico. The inspiration and support of Canadian and Mexican teachers for the emergence of "rank-and-file caucuses" in US teachers' unions is another direction in transnational teachers' solidarity.

A measure of Elba Esther Gordillo's trajectory from an authoritarian in the classic corporatist style, who gained some legitimacy by extracting tangible benefits for her members, to an authoritarian reliant on wealth and elite connections can be found in her engagement in international teachers' diplomacy. According to Hernandez Navarro (2013) and Professor Enrique de la Garza Toledo (interview Feb. 2015), the efforts were an extension of her ambitions for leadership apparently unquenched by her power in national politics and control of the teachers' union. Her courting of intellectuals with "dinners in deluxe restaurants, trips, book printings and paid conferences" were to compensate for her "profound lack of prestige in public opinion" (Hernandez Navarro 2013, 129). From 1991 to 2000, with considerable financial assistance provided by the Mexican government, Gordillo's SNTE hosted a series of four international conferences over which she presided on public education, attended by delegations from teachers' unions across the Americas and beyond (Enrique de la Garza Toledo, interview Feb. 2015). The first event gathered academics and union leaders with a significant critical analysis of education policy and its drift towards what would later be described as neoliberalism. Conference papers, reprinted in *Understanding Educational Reform in Global Context: Economy, Ideology, and the State* (Ginsberg 1991), are extensively cited here for their discussion on teachers' professionalism.

Under Gordillo, the SNTE was an active affiliate of the Confederation of American Educators (CEA).[23] The SNTE funded the creation in

Mexico City in 1993 of the Institute for Education and Union Studies of America (Instituto de Estudios Educativos y Sindicales de América; IEESA), following a joint proposal of the SNTE and the CEA. It would be directed by Gordillo's son-in-law. At its peak in the late 1990s, the centre had a full-time staff of sixty academic researchers to pursue its mandate of studying education in the Americas (Enrique de la Garza Toledo, interview Feb. 2015). The resources of the institute have declined considerably since the fall of Gordillo in 2013. Interestingly, while the institute is clearly a branch of the official SNTE, its publications carry a markedly critical analysis of Enrique Peña Nieto's education policies that were lauded by the Juan Diaz de la Torre union leadership. They are described in an online editorial by the institute as neoliberal, business-driven, and resulting in the "devalorization of teachers' labour" (IEESA 2015).

Gordillo's increasingly prominent public reputation in Mexico for political manipulation and corruption likely reduced the prospects for international union collaboration, even if the opposition that she generated among her members was less likely to be heard. After keeping a low profile for a year after Gordillo's arrest, and while teachers grouped around the CNTE waged protests across the country against Peña Nieto's education policies, in 2014 her successor, Juan Diaz de la Torre, initiated an aggressive outreach effort to the highest-profile international education institutions. Through the SNTE's print and online communications as well as the media, de la Torre strove to present to the nation and his own membership the image of an upbeat, positive union whose forward-looking embrace of necessary reforms was endorsed by significant authorities abroad (*El Universal* 2015; *La Jornada* 2015).

Under Juan Diaz de la Torre, a delegation of SNTE leaders was dispatched to the Washington, DC, headquarters of the American Federation of Teachers (AFT) in July 2014 to discuss "social participation, workplace violence, legal issues and union governance including transparency, accounting, training, service unions, and the training and evaluation of teachers" (SNTE 2014a). Several days later, de la Torre met AFT president Randi Weingarten at her union's national convention in Los Angeles. The SNTE also met here with the president of Education International, the global federation of teachers' unions affiliated with the International Trade Union Confederation. A photo of the Education International president and de la Torre embracing was prominently placed on the SNTE website under the title "Education International recognizes leadership of the SNTE." De la Torre responded to a warm endorsement that the "SNTE has transformed itself to work at the side of teachers and give them certainty in their new role and at the same time redefine their relationship with the government, without losing their autonomy" (SNTE 2014b, c). The SNTE reported additional meetings with AFT leaders from Texas, California, and Illinois, where agreements were made for benefits and discount plans accessible to members of both unions (SNTE 2014d). Leaders of the AFT subsequently travelled to Mexico City to meet with the SNTE executive in September 2014 and April 2015, in the latter event holding a press conference at a primary school in the middle-class borough of Benito Juarez (SNTE 2015a).

Having established strong recognition from the AFT and Education International, the SNTE pursued endorsement from UNESCO and the OECD. In contrast to Gordillo's early international activities, de la Torre reached out to elite policymakers and proudly asserted his union's support for their agenda[24] (*El Universal* 2015; *La Jornada* 2015). SNTE leaders praised Peña Nieto's policies in a meeting with a UNESCO delegation studying Mexico's teacher evaluation systems:

> The SNTE is an institution within the Mexican State that has to assume its commitment for the public policies that serve to improve education. If doing so represents the transformation of our profession, we are in agreement. We are very clear that the right of children to a quality education is not opposed to the rights of education workers. (SNTE 2015b; author's translation)

At a later Mexico City meeting in April 2016, the SNTE again reported that "UNESCO recognizes the SNTE for its work in support of teachers" for its collaboration with the government. "The most important thing we value is the quality of the relationship between the Secretary of Public Education and the SNTE," announced a union spokesperson (SNTE 2016b). Turning to the OECD, SNTE representatives flew to the agency's Paris headquarters in January 2016 to meet with senior education policy staff and the president of Education International (SNTE 2016c). The relationship was consolidated at a meeting in Mexico City in October 2016 with OECD general secretary, José Ángel Gurría, where the union's importance was reiterated in administering remedial online courses for teachers who did not pass the standardized exams prescribed by Peña Nieto's government (SNTE 2016d).

The SNTE under Juan Diaz de la Torre has engaged in considerable work to provide endorsements and validations with significant international actors for the policies of Peña Nieto's government. These activities have occurred at a time when Mexican authorities have been threatened not only by ongoing disruptive protests from the teachers' movement in the CNTE, but by a widespread discrediting of Peña Nieto's regime at home and abroad. They include the disappearance of forty-three student teachers from the Ayotzinapa College in September 2014 (see chapter 4) and many other high-profile incidents of violence in a context of state complicity, corruption, and persistent poverty and inequality, despite the promises of neoliberal reforms such as the privatization of energy. This support from de la Torre was surely welcomed by Peña Nieto. It can also be read as a sign of the union's vulnerability and dependence on the state. While engaging in this process, the SNTE is also trying to counter the international reach of critical portrayals put forward by the CNTE of neoliberal reforms, in which the SNTE has invested its credibility and support.

The most important means by which Mexican educators critical of their government's neoliberal reforms have sought international solidarity has been through the Trinational Coalition in Defence of Public Education[25] (Arriaga 2008, 225). Education activists from Canada, Mexico, and to a lesser extent the United States, concerned about the implications of the North American Free Trade Agreement for public education, began a series of meetings in 1993 in Olympia, Washington. At subsequent meetings in Mexico in 1994 and 1995, OSSTF, Quebec federations, and the British Columbia Teachers' Federation (BCTF)[26] formally joined, as did the CNTE and its largest state sections and university workers' unions in Mexico City. Neither the AFT nor the NEA formally participated, owing to their affiliation alongside the SNTE in Education International (Kuehn 2006, 174). An initial unifying concern was around proposals, since dropped, by the US Education Testing Service towards a continental certification scheme for teachers, which could result in de-professionalization (Kuehn 2008, 62–6). The Trinational's biennial conferences, which provide critical analyses of contemporary education, rotate between Canada, the United States, and Mexico; participants include the Chicago Teachers Union, the United Teachers of Los Angeles, and the Professional Staff Congress of the City University of New York after left-leaning caucuses were elected in these unions (Roman and Velasco Arregui 2015, 130–1).

Led by the Mexican section, its most active national contingent, the Trinational organizes international solidarity campaigns when its member organizations are engaged in struggles with their respective state. One of the most significant contributions of the Trinational has been overcoming the international isolation of the CNTE and Mexico's other dissident education unions, by creating direct connections and spaces for support, particularly with the BCTF, OSSTF, and the left-leaning local US teacher unions (Kuehn 2006; Arriaga 2008). While the official SNTE leadership is not known to have publicly commented on the Trinational, the former's aggressive outreach efforts with international unions should also be seen in the context of the Trinational's success in raising concern among teachers in British Columbia, Ontario, and some US cities for struggles of their colleagues in Mexico that were unsupported or opposed by the SNTE. The movement for justice since 2014 for the forty-three missing student teachers of the Ayotzinapa College and the 2013 and 2016 strikes and protests against Peña Nieto's standardized teacher evaluation are recent examples (Potter 2016).

In the early twenty-first century, the proliferation of online social networking applications such as Facebook and Skype, along with lower-cost air travel, has considerably reduced the resource threshold required to participate in international activities for teacher activists across North America, with or without the official endorsement of their union. Leaders of the CNTE in the Mexico City elementary teachers' local post calendars of upcoming events on Facebook which are shared by their online followers. The biennial conferences of leftist rank-and-file labour activists, organized in the United States by Labor Notes, have become an important space for teachers seeking to radicalize their unions.[27] Conferences in 2012, 2014, 2016, and 2018 were sites for networking among teachers inspired by the successes of the Caucus of Rank-and-File Educators (CORE) in winning elections to the executive of the Chicago Teachers Union since 2010 and, as the union, building alliances with parents and community groups that manifested in popular support for strikes in 2012 and 2016. Among the many local US teacher groups inspired by CORE, the most established are the Movement of Rank and File Educators (MORE) within New York City's United Federation of Teachers (discussed in chapter 3), and the Caucus of Working Educators in Philadelphia. Together with many smaller groups, they formed the national United Caucuses of Rank and File Educators (UCORE), which meets at Labor Notes conferences and online over Skype.

Less well known among the many accounts of the emergence of CORE, is its early inspiration from Mexican and Canadian teachers. In a fascinating network ethnography (Ball and Junemann 2012), Jane McAlevey (2016) explains how CORE co-founder Jackson Potter, then on a sabbatical from high school teaching, was encouraged by education professor Pauline Lipman to attend the 2006 conference of the Trinational in Oaxaca, Mexico. By McAlevey's account, after meeting activists with the CNTE and especially Alex Caputo-Pearl, leader of a left caucus within the United Teachers of Los Angeles, who was later elected its president, he was inspired to form a caucus of similar-minded teachers to transform his union. Also influential was Jinny Sims, then president of the BCTF, who delivered an inspirational speech on her union's successful illegal strike in 2005, and the extensive community organization which it required. Potter convinced other early CORE members to pool their money to fly Sims to Chicago for more in-depth strategic discussions. After CORE's union election victory and shortly before Sims's election in 2011 to the Canadian parliament as an NDP member, she returned to speak at a conference gathering US teacher activists seeking to replicate CORE's success. Maria de la Luz Arriaga spoke on behalf of the Trinational and the Mexican teachers' movement.[28]

The experiences of the Trinational Coalition and CORE demonstrate how teachers' movements in North America increasingly consider strategy and build relationships at a transnational, continental level, despite the apparently geographically limited primary sites of their struggle at the municipal and, at most, the national levels. This development is also demonstrated by the prioritization placed by Juan Diaz de la Torre's SNTE on international endorsements in the context of his leadership's weak legitimacy. It suggests a similar concern on the part of Enrique Peña Nieto's government. Nevertheless, for those concerned with making teachers' unions more democratic, effective, and radical, it is heartening to see how cross-border networking is becoming increasingly accessible and widespread.

The development of teacher unionism in North America over the twentieth century demonstrates significant national and subnational divergences on the basis of political, cultural, and economic contexts. It also presents convergences, as happened with the postwar expansion and the institutionalization of teachers unions, the economic downturn of the late 1970s through 1980s, and the emergence of neoliberalism for placing teachers' unions on the defensive. In all three case-study sites, one of the most significant activities of teachers' unions has been negotiating the dynamics of professionalism and the form of their members' work.

As has been suggested here and will be explained in more detail in the case study chapters, a shared hallmark of neoliberal governance has been the centralization and scaling-up of education systems. As global centres of governance, New York City, Mexico City, and Toronto share important similarities as sites for the development and diffusion of education policy, liaising with important multilateral actors such as the OECD and UNESCO. Teachers' networks and unions are also important participants in cross-border continental sharing of ideas and sometimes of strategies for resistance to the neoliberalization of education.

Before continuing to the case studies, I present below a short summation of the context of professional autonomy for teachers in New York City, Mexico City, and Toronto at the opening of the twenty-first century. In all three sites, the official curriculum was becoming increasingly defined and mandated. This change was represented particularly by the recent (1990s) introduction of high-profile standardized tests for students in subject areas prioritized by the government for quantitative measurement, which somewhat diminished an earlier degree of autonomy. However, these test score metrics were not yet used substantially to facilitate school competition for student enrolment ("school choice"). Once hired, the path towards permanent status was relatively direct for the vast majority of teachers. Graduates of Mexico's teacher colleges (the normales) were guaranteed a position, though for many it would take years and sometimes special favours to obtain the equivalent of full-time hours. In all three jurisdictions, the professional knowledge of teachers was formally recognized by the prerequisite of a university degree in education (or graduation from a normale) as well as the subject areas one would teach.

A recent change for teachers in Ontario was the redefinition by the government of principals and vice-principals as management, ineligible for membership in the teachers' federations. This had long been the case in New York City. By contrast, in Mexico City (and throughout the country), school directors remained members of the union. Institutionally strong teachers' unions predominated in all three jurisdictions, representing virtually of their colleagues in the primary and secondary schools and, despite various conflicts particularly in Ontario, acknowledged by the state as their legitimate representative. The local representing Mexico City's primary teachers was led by the dissident movement (CNTE), while pro-"institutional" factions aligned with Gordillo were dominant in the secondary teachers' section. In all three cases, teachers had relatively recent memories of austerity, in which their conditions of work had been rapidly and sometimes drastically undermined by the state. Since at least the 1990s, teachers in all three cities had worked in a context in which a neoliberal "common sense" was gaining legitimacy among both political and economic elites and the public and was beginning to find its expression in education policy. The twenty-first century would bring far greater changes and struggles over the control of teachers' work.

3 New York City

Preface: Visiting a Small High School on the Upper West Side

I met Jen, a history and special education teacher with six years' experience but without permanent status, on her preparation period at the entrance to her high school in Manhattan's Upper West Side.[1] The large building had formerly been one school with an enrolment of over 2,000 students. Citing high crime and low standardized test scores, it was closed in the late 2000s and converted to house four small schools of around 400 students on each of its four floors. "If anyone asks, just say you're a friend of mine from college," she says as we pass by metal detecters and the security desk. In New York's complex "school choice" system, middle-school children must apply to several high schools without recourse to a default "neighbourhood school." Around a third have enrolment prerequisites such as high marks in 8th grade, an entrance exam, or an essay and extensive interviews with the child and their parents. Jen's school requires none of these conditions, giving priority to children whose parents attend an information night and live within Manhattan. Over two-thirds of the students are Latinx, around a quarter are black, and about 1 per cent are white. The students come overwhelmingly from poor families in the Washington Heights area.

She leads me to the drama space, where, according to Jen, our interview will be undisturbed, owing to the lack of any drama classes. "The small school movement ruined everything," she says, citing a program begun by progressive New York educators in the 1980s to convert some of the city's most problematic giant high schools into smaller institutions, where students would be less likely to fall through the cracks and teachers would have a democratic voice in its operations. Beginning under Mayor Rudy Giuliani and accelerating dramatically under

Michael Bloomberg in the 2000s with a new mission, the program closed dozens of large schools and opened hundreds of small schools. She explains:

> [The closed big school] was notoriously bad. There was a lot of crime … But they did have any club you could imagine. They had an award-winning orchestra, a fully developed sports program. They had a huge staff and a huge student body to support these programs. By closing it now, we don't have arts at our school. We have one arts teacher, who was left over and she does a couple classes for two different schools here, but only a few. The kids don't get to choose their classes here either, at all. They have zero input in [where] they get placed. So we've got this dance teacher giving arts credits, arbitrarily getting students assigned to her class. Then they get arts credits through the creative writing English classes because we don't have arts teachers. There's no arts programs. There's a room full of instruments that are just collecting dust and falling into disrepair. Hundreds of instruments and a beautiful auditorium no one ever uses because no school has the resources to support a band program.

Unable to offer a broad curriculum beyond the core subjects that students must study to pass their Regents exams and graduate or even substantial extracurriculars, these small education ecosystems are then subject to varying pedagogical regimes at the behest of their administrators. "This school was maybe started six years ago, by a twenty-nine-year-old principal," Jen continues:

> She just tested all these different radical pedagogical theories one after another. It was just drastically changing every year … it's become a laboratory for different models of teaching. The most recent: last year we had a new principal … who implemented this curriculum model, Learning Cultures, which is school-wide. Every teacher's required to do it in their class. It dictates how classes should run. Very specific guidelines for teachers and for students. It's supposed to be the opposite to a script. The idea behind it is that teachers don't need to teach content, because content is freely available on the internet now. So we're supposed to teach kids strategies of how to learn. So, what it looks like is – I taught history; we basically give the kids a list of what they need to learn, some websites they can use to access it, some textbooks, and we tell them to go work together and learn it. Which is really beautiful in theory, but in practice, it looks like a mess.

Learning Cultures is the product of a professor at a New York university who is seeking to develop and market this pedagogical form, according to Jen. The academic, a friend of the school principal, receives royalties from its use and is paid from the school budget to train the staff on its usage:

> There's no direct instruction: seventy-minute periods, a ten-minute lesson. We're not supposed to teach content in the lesson just, they call them "grass-roots lessons" which is: "I saw this student do this really good strategy yesterday. She used this website and found this video and wrote notes on the video. You all should use this strategy." Just different skills that we see the kids doing. We're not really allowed or supposed to mandate anything really. The idea is the kids are supposed to have autonomy. We don't assign seats. There's a lot of really good things about it, but ... there's a lot of pushback among the students and the staff.

Without sufficient instruction from teachers, the students struggle:

> the lack of structure is overwhelming for them, especially because the students we get are struggling. On average, we have a 3rd grade reading level here. Attendance is an issue. A lot of them don't know what they're supposed to be doing, and then once we tell them what they're supposed to be doing, it's just too much for them to handle without more direct instruction.

According to the 2013–14 "School Quality Snapshot" prepared by the New York City Department of Education (NYC DOE), less than 30 per cent of this school's teachers would recommend their school to parents. The city average is 76 per cent. However, the proportion of parents "satisfied" with the education their child receives here is just below the city average of 94 per cent. By the end of 9th grade, the proportion of students with enough completed course credits to graduate within the standard four-year period was well above the city average of 83 per cent. By the end of 10th grade, it had dropped nearly 30 points, well below the city standard.

> Everything we do has to fit within this rigid mould of Learning Cultures. So, it's not just a "free for all" like it sounds. The cornerstone of the model is what's called unison reading, choral reading, where the kids have to sit in groups for fifteen minutes and read out loud. There are rules about it and the way the teacher should act. So that has to happen in every class. Then the teacher spends their time doing individual conferences with each student. Especially in the history department, we have to prepare them for the Regents exam.

Jen compares her experience at this school with the middle school in the South Bronx where she began her career several years ago. Lessons there were highly scripted and paired with a "very militant" student discipline regime emphasizing quiet and straight lines. She says the commonality in these divergent pedagogies, was an underlying belief by the school administration "that teachers cannot be trusted as professionals to use their professional judgment in how to educate kids." She adds:

> There's been a lot of pushback in the history department because our inclination was to teach the content and lead students in discussion about the content and guide them to interesting things to read about it. But we were told that was too teacher directed. I was in the history department for the first semester. My background is in humanities and I've only ever taught English and history, but because I'm Special Education certified, I'm technically certified to teach anything. So I made my opinions pretty loud about how I felt this was working in history, because our assessments were showing our kids weren't learning anything. It was really painful every day to not be able to do the things we as professionals know work … with two days' notice at the start of the second term, the principal pulled me into her office … she said, "I'm switching your entire program, you're teaching all math classes."

Jen is unequivocal that she was the subject of retaliation by her principal for her outspoken stance on the mandatory teaching structure used at her school. At this point we are joined in the drama space by Jen's colleague Karen, an English teacher for twelve years, with permanent status, who transferred to this school three years ago. Both feel they are being pushed out of the school because they haven't "drunk the Kool-Aid" and bought into the scheme. After having previously received "Satisfactory" ratings under the NYC DOE's former system of "Satisfactory"/"Unsatisfactory" annual evaluations, last year for the first time Karen was rated "Developing" under the new four-level system, and her movement up the pay grid was frozen.

I asked about the school's union chapter and its response to these erosions of teachers' professional autonomy. Both note that less than a quarter of the young staff have the full "tenure" protection of their union, gained after four years and the evaluation by a superintendent of a "portfolio" with samples of student work. Karen has the most years of teaching experience in the school. The only other with more than ten years is the chapter leader, whom Jen describes as "very vocal in defence of teachers' rights." Jen warns that a strong perception exists among the untenured staff that being seen talking with her will result in some form of retaliation from the administration. The school union leader is also the only remaining teacher of colour on the staff of around forty. According to Karen, over the past two years, five other high-seniority black women were fired or forced out after receiving low ratings, despite previously having received good scores. Karen and Jen describe it as racist. The women had refused to adopt disciplinary methods they felt were inappropriate for their students and were generally critical of the administration. Their replacements were young and white and accepted the explanation that they had replaced "bad" teachers. Jen sums up her future prospects:

> I don't have tenure, but I just can't keep my mouth shut. And I'm not going to get it. She [the principal] extended it [probationary status] twice, even though I've got heaps of data which show I know how to do my job. Most people just keep their mouth shut, which is the wise thing to do if you want a career here.

Before her prep period ends, Jen leads me on a quick tour of the rest of the building. Climbing the stairs, we encounter a very different school. Unlike Jen and Karen's, its entrance requirements are difficult and highly competitive. Students come from a wide area, but are overwhelmingly white. A bulletin board in the hallway boasts of the universities that the 12th grade students will attend next year. Another board displays formulas drawn by students in an advanced algebra class. Another floor up we reach an elementary charter school. A class marches by in a silent, orderly column, students wearing formal uniforms, hands in their pockets. Next to each classroom door is a roster of the students, ranked according to their test scores. Students with low scores have red dots beside their names. The classes are named after the alma mater of their teacher and the expected year of graduation of the students. All the teachers look young. The corridors are clean, with shiny new motivational posters on the wall and words on the floor. I feel as if I'm in a school vertically segregated by race and class, with various forms of neoliberal experimentation underway. As I leave, I read a notice on the outside door for the parents of 3rd and 4th grade students taking the New York State math exams over three days that week: "If your scholar arrives after 7:30 am they are late!"

Jen and Karen's school exemplifies the outcomes of neoliberal education reforms in New York City in the early twenty-first century. This chapter demonstrates how contemporary reforms have resulted in the loss of teachers' professional autonomy and the degradation of their work in the city schools and how this process connects to both the mobility of neoliberal policy and shifting scalar struggles over political power. I will first explore structural-institutional changes that have affected teachers' work and that have facilitated subsequent policy changes. The former begin with the implementation of "mayoral control" under Michael Bloomberg in 2002 and the dissolution of elected community school boards (section 3.1). It is followed by the scaling-up of the original "small schools movement," known as the New Century Schools Initiative,[2] which, in conjunction with increased standardized testing, sought to multiply the number of NYC high schools while removing the option of a "default" neighbourhood school, to create a marketplace for school choice (section 3.2). As at Jen and Karen's school, the small size of the faculty made the delivery of curriculum beyond the five core subjects tested under the Regents exams difficult, but because of the emphasis placed on these test scores, the loss of arts, languages, physical education, and other electives apparently has not been deemed a serious shortcoming by education authorities – at least at the state level under Governor Andrew Cuomo. Instead, teachers in these hundreds of small worksites compete through test score results with their colleagues across the city to enrol and retain students. In practice, however, in terms of teachers' work and professional autonomy, small schools have had the most impact where they have increased the importance of standardized testing and by generating a negative institutional influence on union culture.

Failure in this "market" would bear grave professional consequences through subsequent policy changes. Section 3.3 reviews policies that have weakened the school site union presence, facilitating attacks on teacher professionalism. They include the elimination of seniority in 2005 for teachers at closed or downsizing schools and the decentralization of staff budgets to school principals, creating strong incentives for retaining and hiring low-seniority, lower-paid teachers. Procedural changes to the awarding of tenure resulted in an increase in the difficulty and time necessary for new teachers to gain full job security, which, when combined with increasing teacher turnover, quickly led to a rising proportion of untenured faculty in most New York City schools, who lack basic union protections.

Section 3.4 will look at how, since the election of progressive-leaning mayor Bill de Blasio in 2013, the initiative in neoliberal education policy has "scaled up" to Governor Cuomo. The latter has directly confronted and frequently defeated attempts by the mayor to reduce the emphasis on standardized testing for students and teachers, roll back the expansion of charter schools, and otherwise mitigate the education "market."

Section 3.5 focuses on the expansion of student standardized testing, initially under Bloomberg in 2002 within the context of the federal No Child Left Behind (NCLB) legislation. It was subsequently expanded in 2010 under Governor Cuomo to include "value-added assessments" based on student test scores to determine teacher evaluations as part of the state's successful bid for President Obama's Race to the Top (RTTT) funding program. This punitive system created a powerful impetus for "teaching to the test," particularly when combined with changes by the state government to the weighting of annual teacher evaluations in 2015 to give roughly half the value to state test scores. I conclude this section with a brief study of the rising Opt Out Movement since 2015, which, in the face of tepid union opposition to standardized testing and its related reforms, has emerged as the most important form of resistance to the edifice of neoliberal education policy and the degradation of teachers' work in New York.

In the final section of this chapter (3.6), I present the voices of teacher activists on how these policies have cumulatively affected their union at the school level and the impact on their professional autonomy. This discussion introduces the activist left-wing caucus within New York City's United Federation of Teachers (UFT) and the Movement of Rank and File Educators (MORE).

3.1. Structural Changes I: Centralizing Power to Facilitate Neoliberal Fast Policy

Since the founding of the publicly funded, secular "free schools" in the early nineteenth century, New York City public education has been transformed by waves of reform. Irish Catholics, elite reformers, corrupt Tammany Hall politicians, New Dealers, and civil rights activists have sought with greater or lesser success, to decentralize the United States's largest school system into various forms of local boards or to centralize the system into the hands of the mayor and his appointees (Ravitch 2000). Prior to Bloomberg's mayoralty, the structure of the New York City Board of Education (BOE) had been constituted by the state government in 1969, in response to demands by black civil rights activists (and to a lesser extent by pockets of schools where predominantly white parents resisted busing that would lead to integration) for greater "community control" of local schools. The central BOE consisted of seven members appointed jointly by the mayor and the five borough presidents. It appointed the system's chancellor, set overall policy and supervised system operations, and was directly responsible for the city's high schools as well as English as a Second Language (ESL) and Special Education programs. However, thirty-two geographically defined Community School Districts (CSDs) enjoyed substantial autonomy to set budgets and priorities for their elementary schools. They were presided over by locally elected trustees, who appointed their superintendents. Despite strong initial parental involvement in the CSDs, by the late 1990s, Fullan and Boyle describe a third as being well run, a third as mediocre insofar as they did not sufficiently acknowledge and address problems in their schools, and the remaining third as "characterized by patronage and corruption" (2014, 22). The best CSDs, as measured by high school graduation rates and elementary math and literacy test scores as well as by their clean and effective governance, were overwhelmingly located in gentrifying and affluent, mostly white regions of Manhattan, Queens, and Staten Island; with few exceptions, the worst were in the city's low-income, predominantly black and Latinx neighbourhoods in Harlem, the South Bronx, and Central and Eastern Brooklyn (Ravitch 2000; Fullan and Boyle 2014, 22). Where it functioned, however, this structure did provide opportunities for strong parental and, indirectly, teacher voices concerning the operation of their schools.

Near the end of his final term, Giuliani vented his frustration with the BOE's administration by exclaiming that he wanted to "blow up" its headquarters in Brooklyn.[3] For proponents of neoliberal education policy as well as for many exasperated with the status quo, the implementation of mayoral control offered a "shock doctrine" style (Klein 2007) potential for systemic transformation. A strong chancellor, politically backed by a powerful mayor, could respond to a widely perceived institutional crisis by rapidly blasting through bureaucratic obstruction to make the hierarchy accountable – superintendents and principals as well as teachers and, perhaps implicitly, though they were not placed in the same group in the language of reformers, the students themselves.

Mayoral control can also be conceived as an example of fast policy in the sense developed by Peck and Theodore (2015), for its rapid proliferation across the United States by neoliberal "thought leaders" who presented it as an experimental "idea that works" to policymakers looking for "solutions" to the perceived crisis of public education. Chicago is the commonly recognized point of origin for the contemporary form of mayoral control from its implementation in 1995.[4] Then mayor Richard M. Daley widely promoted it as a governance model while he was president of the US Conference of Mayors in 1997, and he was put in the spotlight by President Clinton's State of the Union addresses in 1998 and 1999 (Shipps 2009, 118). From Chicago, mayoral control spread to Boston in 1996, Cleveland in 1998, Detroit in 1999 (subsequently reversed in 2004 amid controversy), Harrisburg in 2000, and New York City in 2002 (Henig 2009, 23). However, alongside Chicago and DC,[5] education policy professor Jeffrey Henig contends, "When new mayors in other cities make a pitch for gaining authority over the schools, they are as likely, or more so, to name New York as their model as the other cities" (ibid., 22). The prominence of these three cities as policy models has much to do with the political and economic importance of their school systems at the national scale, giving experiments in charter schools, standardized high-stakes testing, and reductions in teacher job security a broad audience among would-be emulators and opponents alike. For advocates of neoliberal education policy, implementing mayoral control weakens the capacity of teachers' unions and parents' groups to oppose these subsequent projects by insulating key decision making from popular pressure. Mayoral control facilitates neoliberal fast policy by curtailing the powers of democratically elected school boards, enabling policies from city hall, the state capitol, or the White House to be more easily and rapidly implemented locally.

When Mayors Take Charge: School Governance in the City analysed the first seven years of mayoral control in New York City under Bloomberg and successfully advocated for its renewal in 2009. Editor Joseph P. Viteritti relates:

> Before the 2002 implementation of mayoral control, New York had one of the most ambitious systems of political decentralization in the country. Yet for more than thirty years, turnout rates in community school board elections had not exceeded 10 percent of the eligible voters and were usually much lower. Candidates were largely anonymous.[6] (2009a, 8)

The result, according to Viteritti, was that Community School Districts led by elected trustees did not represent the genuine democratic will of their constituents. In practice, they were easily "captured" by highly organized groups, including anti-poverty activists, resident's associations, and, in particular, the teachers' union.[7] Adhering to a theory of representative democracy that eschews collective organization, Viteritti argues that a strong mayor better represents the popular will, given a mandate by a much higher voter turnout rate and greater media exposure leading to increased accountability (ibid.). Henig contends in the same volume that mayoral control facilitates the enactment of policies that may be locally unpopular or adverse for teachers and other education workers[8]:

> Mayors, chosen citywide in elections that engage a broad array of groups and interests, are structurally less dependent than school board members on teachers unions, which can wield tremendous influence in the generally low-visibility, low-turnout elections that typically select school boards. That, in theory, gives them a freer hand to engage in a range of

> administrative strategies that many believe are conducive to more efficient and effective use of government resources – including closing schools, contracting out for key functions, and bargaining more aggressively to limit teacher work rules and tenure protections. (Ibid., 25)

Kerry Kretchmar contends that mayoral control is driven by an ideology that sees corporate business management principles as applicable to public education (and the public sector more broadly) in order to enact greater "accountability." The opportunities for substantive democratic participation by those who actually work and study within the system are reduced, as their perspectives and desires may contradict those of the top-down reformers (2014, 5).

Kenneth Wong adds in Viteritti's volume that mayoral control can thereby counteract demands for increased education spending and make budget cuts under the pressure of fiscal austerity. He cites the origins of public sector austerity as being in New York City in 1975, which subsequently emerged in other big US cities, and sets it within an ideological convergence that has informed the education policies of urban Democrat and Republican administrations:

> From a broader institutional perspective, city hall is likely to apply fiscal discipline and accountability to the school system in both formal and informal ways. During the late 1970s and the 1980s as well as the early years of the present decade [2000s], when cities faced severe fiscal stress, mayors began to adopt a new governing culture, which may be characterized as the new fiscal culture ... Responsive to concerns of taxpayers, these mayors moved away from policies defined by traditional party labels and organized interest groups. In local governance that adopts this new culture, the traditional party labels become less relevant as the relation between social and fiscal issues weakens. Fiscal responsibility and social conservatism are no longer strongly linked. In reforming management of agencies, mayors who adopt the new fiscal culture accelerate contracting out, hold down taxes, focus on management efficiency, and introduce outcome measures for periodic evaluation. These changes tend to overlap with the policy vision of civic-spirited business leaders and the taxpaying electorate. (2009, 83)

Contributors to *When Mayors Take Charge* agree that organized business interests are among the strongest supporters of mayoral control. Viteritti argues schools need to produce graduates better suited to the labour market, a discourse dominant in education policy since publication of the *Nation at Risk* report in 1983 (Ravitch 2013a; Kuhn 2014).

Wong indicates a strong interest for business elites in obtaining reduced taxes thanks to a friendly mayor running the school board, also crediting the (re)implementation of mayoral control in Chicago in 1995 with improving that city's bond rating (2009, 83).[9] The imperative for "fiscal discipline" to serve "taxpayers" and business leaders implicates an aggressive stance by mayors towards education workers, whose wages and salaries comprise by far the largest component of education budgets:

> Central to this strategy is the notion of fiscal discipline in constraining labor costs. We see this in the inverse relationship between mayoral control and expenditures. Education mayors, while continuing to partner with labor unions, seem able to leverage cooperation (or concessions) from the school employees' unions. (Ibid., 82)

The experience of mayoral control in New York City under Bloomberg largely confirmed this claim.

Fullan and Boyle (2014) divide the education history of Bloomberg's mayoralty into two periods, both dominated by major structural reforms with a significant impact on teachers' work. The first period from 2002 to 2005 at the start of his tenure, is characterized by centralization. After receiving approval from the State Assembly, Bloomberg took control of the city's former Board of Education, now renamed the Department of Education (NYC DOE) in July 2002 (Traver 2006, 502). As happened in Chicago and DC, the other two cities with the highest-profile mayoral control regimes associated with neoliberal education reform, Bloomberg used his new power to appoint the chancellor by selecting a non-educator, Joel Klein, a Department of Justice lawyer and corporate CEO, who, like DC's Michelle Rhee and Chicago's Arne Duncan, became an important policy advocate. The new thirteen-member Panel for Education Policy (PEP) appointed by the mayor plus one individual from each borough president may not appear to be substantially different from its preceding seven-member appointed structure, but the larger PEP included a clear majority of mayoral appointees. Bloomberg intervened to ensure the PEP approved his initiatives (New York Teacher 10, interview Apr. 2015). In a high-profile incident in 2004, he earned the ire of parent activists by removing three panel members who threatened to vote against holding back 3rd grade children who were well below the grade reading level. According to Fullan and Boyle, this move contributed to public opposition that began stalling his initiatives in his third term. During this period, the PEP vowed to raise test scores by forcing through a single, citywide literacy and math curriculum, previously used in Manhattan's District 2. The initiative drew resistance from many teachers, who argued it removed the capacity for professional judgment in assessing the best means to teach their students. Amy Traver (2006) describes the homogenizing initiative as reminiscent of the Scientific Management labour deskilling principles of Taylorism. It was soon abolished after its content received criticism from the US DOE (Fullan and Boyle 2014, 26, 28–9; Traver 2006, 502–7). Bloomberg's and Klein's efforts would have become obsolete a few years later in any case, after the implementation of Common Core.

Another key structural change was the elimination of elected CSDs, which previously had given active parents a degree of power comparable to Chicago's local school councils. They were replaced by Community Education Councils, that lacked the power to appoint principals and district superintendents. Authority over school budgets was increasingly transferred to principals (Traver 2006, 504; New York Teacher 2, interview Dec. 2014). On the operational side, Bloomberg and his chancellors experimented with a range of structures, which from 2005 through to the end of his final term in 2012 had become a highly decentralized system of fifty-two networks, to which schools would affiliate, with a limited association with geography. Despite appearing to be a more horizontal system, in practice schools were increasingly under the direct control of NYC DOE headquarters. The new Office of Accountability kept them under surveillance by monitoring test scores (Fullan and Boyle 2014, 31). The aggregate of these policies was increasing autonomy for school principals in relation to their teaching staff and parents. Journalist Clara Hemphill quotes a parent activist in her chapter for Viteritti's book assessing mayoral control, "In the old days, if a principal got off track, the district superintendent could step in. Now, we live in a world where the principals are kings and queens" (2009, 203). Accompanying the elimination of geographic CSDs and centralization of power under mayoral control was the end of a policy, enacted in 1996, that mandated school leadership teams comprising elected parent and teacher representatives who worked with the principal to collectively establish a school's priorities and budget. Along with empowering parents, it also represented increased recognition and scope for the exercising of teacher professionalism. Its implementation was derided by policy advocates (many of whom were gathered in an earlier volume edited by Ravitch and Viteritti in mobilizing policy, *City Schools: Lessons from New York*, 2000), who claimed it hamstrung principals from making fast decisions unbeholden to "interest groups." Like Viteritti's 2009 work, it is interesting in itself as a collective representation of the ideological orientations of high-profile academics working on education policy. The exhortions of several contributors on what I describe as the "principal as protagonist" concept is one of several ideas from these volumes that would later be realized under Bloomberg. Hemphill, who also contributed to *City Schools*, articulates this belief well when she writes:

> Improving the quality of principals is the single most important thing we can do to improve urban education. It's more important than recent initiatives to decrease class size or to provide universal pre-kindergarten ... It's even more pressing than repairing crumbling schools and buying new equipment such as computers. A good principal will make do in less than perfect conditions. But if the leadership of each building is uninspired, other efforts to improve education will fail. (2000, 59)

She reversed her criticism of school leadership teams following their elimination in 2007, describing it as a loss for meaningful parental engagement in her entry for *When Mayors Take Charge*.

Reflecting on mayoral control under Bloomberg, Hemphill writes about how his community education councils and the new paid position of a school parent liaison are not empowering, as the former lacks any power and the latter reports directly to the principal (2009). Hemphill argues that these policies were driven by a vision of Chancellor Klein (and Bloomberg), in which parents and students exercised their voices as consumers, free to choose and change schools based on test score results, rather than as democratic citizens. Klein explained his opposition to giving organized parents political voice by describing their groups as "biased," middle-class, and predominantly white, not representative of the majority of poor or working-class parents of colour (Hemphill 2009, 203). Despite the pretensions of an equity lens, his discourse remarkably resembles comments quoted above by Viteritti (2009a) and Henig (2009), who praised mayoral control as a means to avoid capture by interest groups. While its proponents embrace a market discourse of "school choice," mayoral control has facilitated New York City's becoming a site for experimentation in neoliberal education policy. In this context, owing to the reduction of electoral means for parents and community groups to voice opposition, systemic barriers for the political participation for parents – the majority racialized and working class – have increased. As one NYC teacher, who contributes to the education website Chalkbeat New York, argues:

> City kids are lab rats for the state to test out new things. The state cares about suburban parents and fights for their votes ... Those parents pay high property taxes. So their teachers are treated better because those

> parents don't want to come into schools where ... they have a new English teacher every year. Neither do parents in the city, but the state doesn't care what parents in the city think. Partly they've frozen them out with mayoral control ... In New York, and this is true in Chicago too, part of the no political power thing is that it's taken for granted that the city's overwhelmingly Democratic, so nobody worries about how that's going to affect voting. (New York Teacher 2, interview Dec. 2014)

These characteristics help explain why NYC, like many other major northern US urban centres but unlike their neighbouring predominantly affluent and white suburban districts, have been particularly susceptible to the rapid rollout of neoliberal education policies.

3.2. Structural Changes II: Transforming Workplace Culture

Mayoral control and a weakened parent voice facilitated the rapid rollout of a program that epitomized Bloomberg and Klein's faith in strong administrators and a marketplace of "school choice": the closures of dozens of struggling large high schools and their replacement with hundreds of small schools with fewer than 500 students and thirty to forty teachers (De Jesus 2012, 63). The balkanization of secondary students has had a profound impact on teachers' work. A small faculty limits the capacity to offer a broad curriculum, while converging with increased emphasis on the five subject areas at the high school level tested in the Regent exams (Shiller 2011). If arts, languages, and other elective courses are no longer important for a student's graduation, then it fits well that every teacher must be timetabled into math, English, science, history, or geography, because enrolment numbers and the accompanying funding do not allow otherwise. Alongside this curricular narrowing, the multiplicity of small schools puts into effect the competitive "market" of school choice, which, through the publishing of test score data, operates as a disciplinary mechanism for teachers.

As Jen described at the start of this chapter, many of the large high schools that were closed had serious problems. Most had four-year graduation rates under 50 per cent.[10] Because of their huge size, they were widely seen as places where their growing populations of at-risk students became anonymous and alienated. Many had significant problems related to crime and violence (Barbanel 1993; Herszenhorn 2005). A majority were built in the early twentieth century, at a time of booming immigration, during which the system struggled to find seats for tens of thousands of new students every year. Because of populations rapidly shifting between neighbourhoods and a desire to save money with economies of scale, New York's high schools were constructed as large campuses several storeys tall, filling most of a city block. These schools housed 2,000 to 5,000 students and a few hundred staff. From the 1920s through to the end of the 1950s, they were widely seen to be functioning effectively and even considered among the best schools in the United States. During this period, less than half of all youth attended secondary school, and fewer graduated (Ravitch 2000). Classrooms and lecture halls were filled with willing students with few special needs. From the 1960s, a high school diploma became a social and an economic necessity, coinciding with major demographic and fiscal shifts for the city.

Aggarwal, Mayorga, and Nevel (2012), Kretchmar (2014), and many others argue that these schools were set up to fail, with a combination of a high-needs population, insufficient resources, and demands for steady improvement on low exam scores and graduation rates mandated under NCLB legislation from 2002 (New York Teacher 2, interview Dec. 2014). New York's large high schools appeared structurally unable to effectively educate their students, necessitating some form of transformation. However, many parents, students, and teachers of these now former schools interviewed by Aggarwal et al. and Kretchmar contend that under mayoral control, they were excluded from these deliberations. According to Shiller (2007, 2009, 2010, 2011), they were replaced with the small school system advocated by Klein and Bloomberg, guided by a neoliberal ideology that many schools competing for student enrolment would inevitably lead to improvements in all, as indolent educators would be forced to work harder to avoid losing their positions from declining funding tied to student attendance. The result has been a narrowing of the curriculum and correspondingly of professional autonomy, as teachers are pressured to raise the averages of Regents exams. For a variety of reasons, principally the limited actual mobility of many racialized poor and working-class students, initial research suggests teachers are more pressured by the test score cut marks than by potential or real exoduses of pupils, thus undercutting the claims to efficacy of the "choice" mechanism. However, the small schools also have an insidious effect on teachers' professional autonomy and working conditions. This follows both from their tendency to segregate the neediest students in certain schools (Fullan and Boyle 2014, 37), bereft of the necessary additional resources to effectively teach them (as indicated in Jen's and Karen's accounts) and from the small size of the faculty, which compounds the tendency towards a narrowed curriculum (Shiller 2010).

This result did not match the original intent of creating small schools in New York. Beginning in the late 1960s, the small schools movement in New York was led by educators, perhaps most famously Deborah Meier, motivated by social justice concerns for poor and racialized youth they saw as ill served by the existing system of giant high schools (Hantzopoulos and Tyner-Mullings 2012; Shiller 2011, 164). Many shared progressive ideas inspired by Kozol (2009) and Postman and Weingartner (1969) on how schools could function democratically and on teachers collectively exercising their professional judgment to determine pedagogy, with more input and relevance for students. Under Meier's leadership, the small Central Park East 1 elementary school opened in 1974, serving predominantly low-income black and Latinx children in East Harlem. Inspired by its success, she opened Central Park East Secondary School in 1985, from which emerged the Coalition for Essential Schools, a network of small high schools with critical pedagogy and an egalitarian structure (Hantzopoulos and Tyner-Mullings 2012, xxviii).[11]

A former UFT official who worked with the movement in the late 1980s describes its origins:

> The kids are still dropping out, and it's no longer something that is acceptable … given the role of race in American society and American education, disproportionate numbers of kids living in poverty are black and brown. By the 1960s, we're saying, at least aspirationally, that that's not acceptable that we would have this situation where these kids would be sent to high schools where there's no chance. So what the small school movement, in its origins, was really saying was that if we organize our schools differently, and if we have schools where we really pay attention to kids, they're not warehouses, but we know the kids well. (Former UFT Official 2, interview Apr. 2015)

For him, scaling schools down offered exciting possibilities for transforming traditional education:

> One of the notions was that in a smaller school, with a smaller number of students, every kid would be well known by at least two or three adults. Another was the notion that the school needed to operate democratically, and so in a small school you can put all of the staff around a big table in one room and they can work out their educational issues. So there's a sense of a kind of democracy. (Ibid.)

The collective decision-making required of teachers participating in a democratic workplace also would lead necessarily to more active union chapters in these schools, he thought. In this context, to facilitate the development of distinct institutional cultures with a committed faculty, he reasoned it would be appropriate to relinquish some clauses of the union contract (e.g., subjecting teacher transfers to approval by a receiving school committee rather than seniority or changing the structure of the school day, including the distribution of teacher preparation time), as long as it was teachers at each school site who were making these decisions. The "School-Based Option" (SBO) was introduced to small schools beginning in the late 1980s, subject to a super-majority 75 per cent vote, later lowered to 66 per cent, of all teaching staff:

> Schools where the adults feel empowered to make important educational decisions, that can change outcomes for poor kids and kids of colour: not only is there a compelling educational justice case for that, but I think that really the sorts of changes that would demand of unions are to my mind challenges. But from the way people are used to having these huge union chapters of 300 people ... where you could have a small number of union activists and therefore have a union chapter. But when you're talking about small schools in a regional division, you're really talking about having to pull all the teachers into the union. If you're going to be making decisions about how you can change parts of the contract or who gets to come to your school, you need to have real teacher involvement. (Ibid.)

For this union leader, the SBO, designed to develop unique, small schools, was the antidote to the excessively homogenizing effects of what he described as "industrial-style unionism." It would also rebuke critics who claimed teacher unions drowned public education in regulation and bureaucracy that did not serve children, a charge the UFT, as the largest and arguably most powerful local education union in the country, frequently faced from anti-union politicians, academics, and pundits (Kuhn 2014, 8). With this understanding, he worked with Deborah Meier and other education activists to close problematic large high schools, notably Julia Richman High School in Manhattan and James Monroe High School in the Bronx, replacing each with several smaller institutions (Barbanel 1993). "What was different about this, than what happened later, was you would do at most one or two schools a year, and they were schools where you had tried everything else before you decided you were going to close them" (former UFT Official 2).

Under Mayor Bloomberg, a breakneck expansion of small schools shared only the concept of replacing big troubled schools. The how and why were completely different.[12] Recognizing the successes of existing small schools for increasing graduation rates, Bloomberg and Klein sought to dramatically scale up the experiment, receiving a $51.2 million grant from the Bill and Melinda Gates Foundation to open sixty-seven of them. From 2002 to 2010, forty-five large and mid-size high schools (all comprising over 1,400 students) that had four-year graduation rates below 45 per cent were closed and replaced with a total of 207 new small schools accommodating up to 500 students, most located in the same buildings, predominantly in poor and working-class black and Latinx communities in Central and Eastern Brooklyn and the South Bronx (Fullan and Boyle 2014, 35; Kretchmar 2014, 4).[13] The dramatic wave of closings and openings were presided over by a new Office of Portfolio Development. However, for the mayor and the DOE, the primary rationale for dividing and multiplying schools was not spreading the advantages of smaller institutions. Many remaining big high schools grew even larger as they took in students who did not fit in the new schools, often those who required more Special Education or ESL services or did not have adult assistance in choosing a specific, specialized small school (Herszenhorn 2005; Hemphill and Nauer 2009, 2–4). Rather, creating a "market" of schools competing for enrolment was a key manifestation of an ideology that held education to be a tradable commodity and thus that anti-monopoly principles from the business world would force schools to compete or perish. Activating this system was a new policy in 2004 stipulating incoming students *must* choose their high school and could not attend their closest school by default (Fullan and Boyle 2014, 35). The neighbourhood high school was to all intents eliminated. As data materialized showing improvements in some new schools, accompanied by declines in old, big high schools that experienced large influxes of leftover students, Klein interpreted the figures by using his sink-or-swim free-market philosophy: "Some of those schools managed the challenges and some are not managing the challenges. And those that aren't, we'll have to reconstitute" (quoted in ibid., 37).

A New York teacher and active member of MORE completing his doctorate in education explains how "school choice" is increasingly applied across the entire K–12 system:

> I'm *shopping* for a kindergarten for my daughter, and the good news is, there are a lot of great kindergartens in my neighbourhood. The problem is, that as soon as a kindergarten gets hot, everybody gets excited about what's going on in that kindergarten, then that school becomes a "choice" school. No longer a "district" school. So just because I live in that district … I can't just march her into one of those. I have to apply and be selected. (New York Teacher 1, interview Dec. 2014)

He charges that "choice" schools further the geographic atomization of communities:

> It's about breaking the solidarity between a community and a school ... In New York City in particular, we had some of the biggest parent movements here in the 1960s and really intense struggles over trying to establish strong community schools and especially for black communities. And I feel like their answer to make sure that never happens again is to rupture the link between community and school. (Ibid.)

For this activist teacher, "school choice" has the outcome of making school-community organizing more difficult. Two other teachers noted the difficulties of convincing parents to be active in their student's school, because their far-flung dispersal across the city discourages face-to-face meetings (New York Teachers 2 and 4, interview, Dec. 2014). Again, we see the importance of New York and other major US cities in setting precedents in neoliberal education policy:

> In New York City this has gone further along ... In small towns where there's *a* high school, you're not going to create this free market. You can do the testing and you can do certain things to weaken the union. But you can't use these market-based reforms. In the big cities, that's what they're trying to do. There's a geography to it. (Ibid.)

Klein boasted of the success of the initiative in a 2008 study indicating a significant 6.8 per cent increase in four-year graduation rates among the new small schools compared with those of the institutions they replaced (Fullan and Boyle 2014, 37). A review a year later revealed this initial increase had rapidly reversed (Hemphill and Nauer 2009, 2). An intensive qualitative study by Shiller (2010) of three new small schools in the Bronx questioned the extent to which higher graduation rates actually indicated an improved quality of education. From observing classes and staff meetings and interviews with teachers and students, she determined that the school's predominantly low-income, racialized students were ill served by a relentless focus on preparation for the five Regents exams (Shiller 2010). The pressure to either teach to the test or receive a poor school rating was compounded by the relative inexperience of the teachers, aggravated by higher turnover rates. As Fullan and Boyle explain, "their inherent characteristic, being small, makes them more fragile than larger schools because they inevitably have less professional capacity. Their success is often dependent on a small, highly committed faculty, and normal turnover is more threatening than it would be in a larger faculty" (2014, 37).

These characteristics of Bloomberg's small schools also tended to create weak union chapters. Two teachers working in small high schools contended that the SBO, praised by the former UFT official for creating greater worker control, had actually weakened union culture at their schools. One, employed at a small school with a progressive mandate distinguished outcomes of the new small schools from the intentions of the original movement:

> In these small schools, the union contract doesn't actually work for you … everyone's supposed to have … this many hours of this duty, but when you have a school of fifteen teachers you don't have that! … I feel like the Small School Movement, as taken by the DOE itself, as opposed to the radical educators who worked to do it for really positive reasons, was co-opted and used as a union-busting technique. Because in all these small schools, you have to hire a lot of new teachers … Over the course of the week, it all sort of evens out and it's sort of fine. But … the contract isn't so present because you have to do all these things to make it happen, so you have these new teachers coming in who don't really understand how a union is anyway, because union density in America is so low, most people don't even know what the hell that means. (New York Teacher 5, interview Dec. 2014)

New teachers do not see the direct role of the union in enforcing daily standards. For this teacher, despite her colleagues' remaining dues-paying union members as before (as statutorily required in New York State), the reduced role of the union in determining daily working conditions distances it from their awareness. Another teacher contends that SBOs, in combination with schools overwhelmingly staffed by untenured teachers, who because of their employment status are unable to challenge their principals (or, as the prior teacher suggests, by their inexperience may not even see a reason to do so), have become a means for administrators to increase the workload of their staff:

> in this environment, where the majority of teachers are untenured in many schools, probably at this point hundreds of schools throughout the city … and there's just such a high rate of turnover. So, like the school I worked at which was a very typical new, small school with some sort of concept behind it, you know it'd have great funding; bells and whistles come with these new schools. The union chapter leader there was always telling us not to – they'd bring this School-Based Option up. We'd have this crazy schedule with only

> thirty minutes for lunch; we had something like four staff meetings a week. We had one that was all faculty, two before school and then one after school. Which totally was a violation of the contract. It's great for the principals, because they'd use that time to do administrative work, essentially. So all the School Based Option in this case was used as a way to push administrative work on to the teachers, give us longer working hours, have us work this insane schedule. (New York Teacher 2, interview Dec. 2014)

The result was an intensification and extension of the teachers' workday:

> The kids still got there at 8:15; we got there at 7:30, which is normally when I'd like to get there to set up, so it meant it was taking away from our teaching time when we'd be writing on the board – our prep time was gone! There's been a proliferation of schools operating on these weird schedules. And the idea is that it's all for the students, but what it really is, the city's getting around the contract. (Ibid.)

He explained the role of the chapter leader, echoing the experience described by Jen and Karen of the socially isolated union representative at their school, who had limited influence over a new staff eager to please the administration and ambivalent towards unionism:

> The person who is the chapter leader for the union is not often, but sometimes, doing the principal's bidding. Or, is sometimes totally isolated in the building because they're the only tenured teacher or one of a few, and the principal will pack that vote on the School-Based Option with the teachers that are in their corner. That's what happened at the school where I worked. (Ibid.)

According to the former UFT official, the SBO was subsequently negotiated in the early 2000s into being available for all high schools. One can speculate that the extent to which SBOs are implemented varies according to the diverse workplace dynamics of each school. Mayoral control created the context in which the work spaces of New York City teachers (and the learning spaces of their students) could be transformed through the rapid rollout of small schools, operating outside union work rules, within a competitive school choice system regulated by test score results (this topic is dealt with further in section 3.5). How these changes impacted the composition of New York City teachers will be explored next in the context of policy and union contract changes under Bloomberg, which all have contributed to shifting power relations in schools across the city away from teachers and towards increasingly managerial principals.

3.3. Teacher Precariousness and the Weakening of the School Site Union and Professional Autonomy

"You cannot go after more than one or two teachers at once. There simply isn't time," a principal complains to economics Professor Dale Ballou in "Contractual Constraints on School Management: Principal's Perspectives on the Teacher Contract," his contribution to *City Schools* (2000, 100). Another principal gripes about the difficulties of firing teachers through the system's disciplinary process: "I need fifteen documented screw-ups, because some will be thrown out" (ibid., 99). Ballou approvingly cites the opposition of his interviewees to seniority-based school transfers when he claims, "As principals have noted, it takes only one or two of these teachers to poison the atmosphere in an entire school" (ibid., 95). Ballou relates the opposition of these principals to virtually every aspect of teachers' working conditions that receives some form of protection in the UFT contract. These conditions include seniority-based staffing (though he notes that only about 500 transfers occurred in 1999 for 1,100 schools and 68,000 teachers), the inability of principals to unilaterally or more easily implement SBOs, the disciplinary stages and requirements for evidence needed to terminate teachers, fixed class sizes (thirty-four students for high school, with exemptions for Special Education) and the rights of teachers to duty-free lunch breaks and self-directed prep time (ibid., 99–109). It is not uncommon to find administrators wishing to have more managerial authority in relation to the staff they supervise.[14] They find their champion in academics and policy advocates such as Ballou (and other contributors to *City Schools*), who see principals as the "protagonists," the front-line implementers of the (neoliberal) policies they envision will improve public education. What is interesting about this laundry list of complaints is the extent to which so many were subsequently addressed under Bloomberg in his general effort to empower school administrators. A large part of his success in doing so was owed to implementing labour policies that resulted in an increasingly precarious workforce subject to high turnover rates.

In this section, I contend that significant changes to the composition of NYC teachers and their employment status, namely, a shift to an increasingly young workforce with fewer median years of service (suggesting a higher turnover) and a much larger proportion without the job security provided by tenure, has had a fundamental impact on teachers' professional autonomy. An increasingly precarious, short-term workforce, spread over many small worksites and many with

Figure 3.1. Median Years of Teaching Experience of Classroom Teachers, 2000–2014

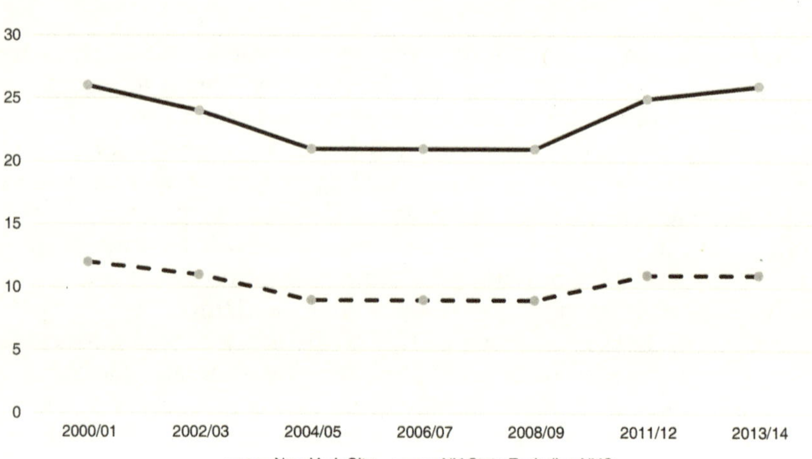

fewer than thirty staff members, has weakened school-level union chapters, as teachers lack the confidence or interest in placing themselves in a potentially adversarial position with their administrators. With weakened or non-existent school union chapters, administrators, as the front line managers tasked with implementing policies such as raising test and exam scores at all costs, have greater power to prescribe curriculum or pedagogy or increase time spent on test preparation, thus circumscribing teacher autonomy. Their effectiveness in doing so is directly judged by the DOE and the State Education Department.

Academic and grey literature has tended to de-emphasize teachers' experience in discussions of education policy, despite their role as the ultimate implementers. Much of the literature discussed above in this chapter is indicative of a general tendency to see school administrators and superintendents as the principal actors to whom policy advocates voice their appeals and teachers (and students) as the objects upon which they act. Teachers themselves are seldom asked for comment.[15] This section draws heavily on teacher accounts of changes in working conditions.

Figure 3.1 shows the disparity over the 2000s of median years of teachers' years of service in NYC and elsewhere in New York State. The biggest decline between 2002 and 2011 coincides with the peak of large high school closures and openings of small schools (graph by Paul Bocking, using New York State Education Department data, 2000–14).

Figure 3.2. New York City Teacher Age Distribution, 2013–14

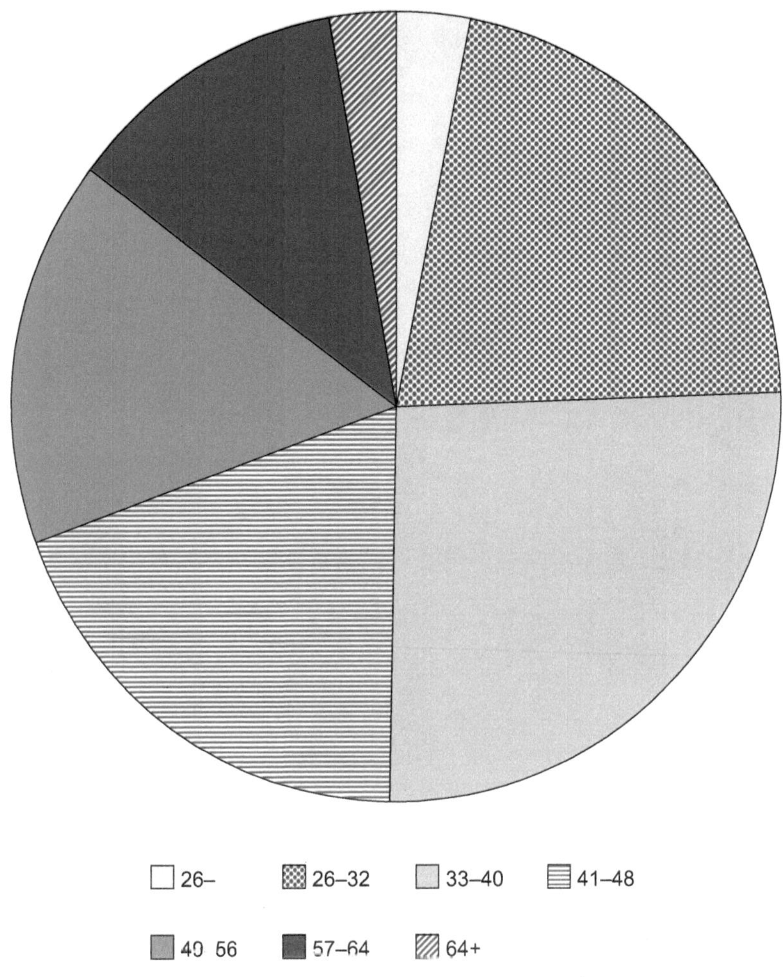

Figures 3.2 and 3.3 demonstrate how in the 2013–14 school year NYC teachers were disproportionately younger than their colleagues in neighbouring, predominantly affluent suburban Nassau and Suffolk counties on Long Island, with nearly double the proportion of teachers in their mid- to late 20s. Nassau and Suffolk counties have proportionally far more mid-career-aged teachers in their forties through mid-fifties. Interestingly, both areas have comparable proportions of senior teachers in their late fifties and early sixties, coinciding with the top

Figure 3.3. Nassau-Suffolk Teacher Age Distribution, 2013–14

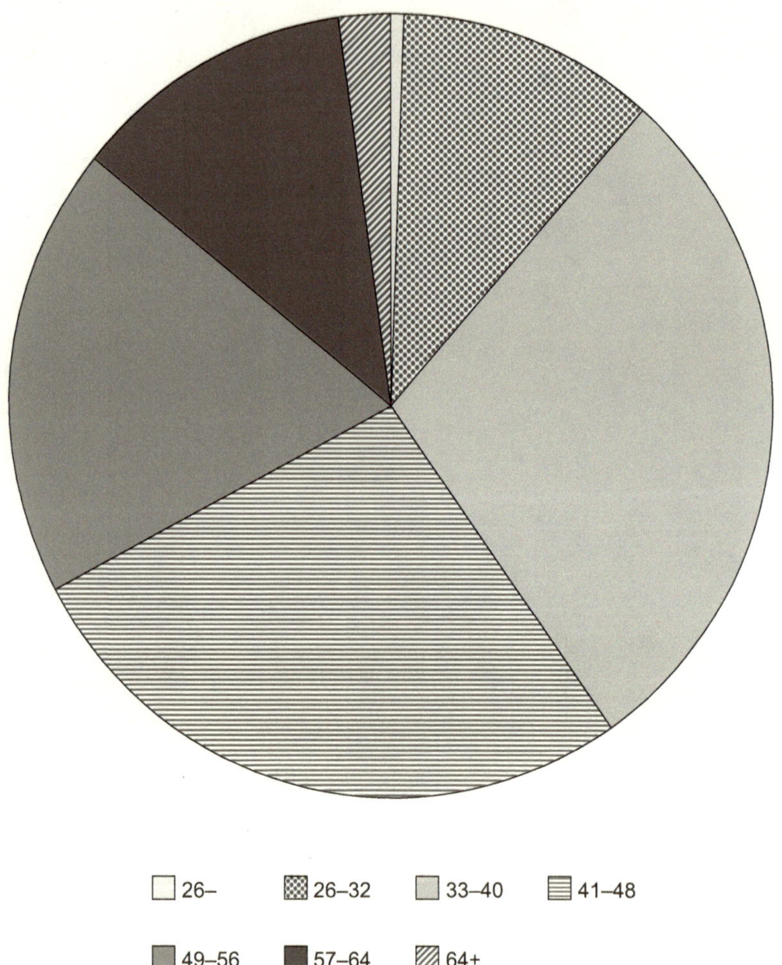

salary scales in these districts (charts by Paul Bocking, using New York State Education Department data, 2013–14).

Figure 3.4 demonstrates the widely divergent salary ranges of teachers across New York State. Teachers in Genesee-Finger Lakes, an upstate region including the city of Rochester and some mainly rural counties, are among the lowest earners. By contrast, since the onset of province-wide negotiations in 2004, teacher salaries are uniform across Ontario. Teacher salaries vary slightly across Mexico, according to three regions

Figure 3.4. Median Teacher Salary, 2013–14

defined by cost of living, the highest-earning areas being in Mexico City and the north and the lowest in the poor rural south (graph by Paul Bocking, using New York State Education Department data, 2013–14).

The 2005 contract between the UFT and the NYC DOE, the only one signed under Bloomberg,[16] marked a significant turning point in the composition of the teacher workforce. After years under Mayor Giuliani during which teacher salaries declined in real terms and the gap between their median compensation and those of more affluent Long Island districts grew substantially, UFT members won increases adding up to 35 per cent over inflation by the end of the contract in 2008 (Fullan and Boyle 2014, 42). Also included in the deal, however, was the elimination of seniority placement of teachers who had lost their position because of declining student enrolment or the closure of their school. Affected tenured teachers became Absent Teacher Reserves (ATRs), who like substitute teachers were deployed full time to cover regular teacher absences, but kept their original salaries and benefits. In the midst of dozens of school closures and conversions to small schools, perhaps 1,200 to 2,000 teachers lost their regular positions, according to a network of ATRs, who have attempted to gain recognition as a member subgroup by their union (New York Teacher 10, interview Apr. 2015). An ATR teacher explained how the intersection of teaching to the five Regents exams, small schools with generalist faculties, and a policy to encourage turnover at closed schools led to teachers' becoming ATRs:

> Within [large schools], it could be like a miniature university because you could have a foreign languages department with multiple language choices. Now it's largely the norm that there's only Spanish available. We used to have professional non-academic, commercial classes like typing, carpentry, metal work. So for the non-core academic subjects, things that are not English, Math, Science, Social Studies, there's no place for these teachers anymore. With the small schools, they've shredded these programs ... The other part of this is that when they close these schools, the new schools are supposed to take half of the staff and then shed the other half. The surviving staff are divided up among the three to four new schools that succeed the original school and then the other half are put in this pool. An interview determines who gets to stay and who has to go. The administration is often displaced too. (Ibid.)

For the first several years, this ATR teacher described the system as relatively satisfactory, though inferior to holding a permanent position, as he covered semester- or year-long absences. This situation was similar to that of a long-term occasional teacher in Toronto, who receives the standard teacher salary for level of experience and holds the full range of classroom responsibilities. In 2010–11, however, the system changed, so that ATRs were on four- to six-week rotations between schools, in which they acted as daily supply teachers or as assistants in the classrooms of other teachers. New evaluation structures were also created to assess their performance as substitutes. He contends that this change was made to push ATRs to resign (ibid.; Antush 2014).

Despite the removal of seniority provisions, ATRs are still able to regain their status as a regular school faculty member by successfully interviewing for a new position. However, a policy change by the NYC DOE in 2007 outside of the contract but with the consent of the UFT, discouraged this change from happening for teachers with higher levels of service:

> There was a giant turning point in 2007, where this idea of Fair Student Funding got implemented. It gave [principals] a limited budget for hiring staff. So it gives a *huge* incentive to the principal to choose someone that's of

> lower salary. The starting salary last time I checked is in the $40,000 range. Mine is over $70,000. If you're looking to fill three teachers, with a budget for $120,000, you can get more teachers for your money at this level. Now what happened in the past was principals were allocated teacher units. That would bring in whatever number of teachers you needed regardless of salary. (New York Teacher 10, interview Apr. 2015)

As a result, principals had a strong disincentive to hire experienced, tenured teachers who had been surplussed through the ATR process, or through a regular transfer. According to the UFT (2014), the 2014 contract signed with de Blasio included a provision exempting ATR salaries from the school's average salary calculations, removing this incentive for principals to save money by not hiring higher seniority ATRs. In Ontario, the number of teacher positions in a school is tied to student enrolment, since principals have no control over salary budgets, leaving no incentive for individual principals to hire lower-paid teachers. In New York, however, according to a teacher employed at a small school, this structure still largely defines school staffing:

> instead of all teachers being paid from the DOE, you're paid from a school budget, and so the budget each school gets is an average of all teacher salaries. And so it discourages small new schools from hiring experienced teachers because there's one teacher who taught for fifteen years, so she brings the average up. Now each teacher costs more. (New York Teacher 5, interview Dec. 2014)

She argues that placement programs like Teach for America (TFA), which don't assume its recruits will make a career commitment to teaching, work well within this context of lowering costs and have consequences for union capacities, especially at small schools:

> It seems to me that it's a really great way to keep costs low for paying teachers. When I came in it was like high forties … they kept it really low because the top scale is a hundred and change. So they hire enough teachers, but they only get first-, second-, third-year teachers, because that's how they're able to afford a whole staff. So my first year at that new school, there were seventy kids, because you build year by year; you're trying to get to about 250–80. There were like three of us who were brand-new Teaching Fellows or TFA people … There were a few more who were one or two years in, so a lot of inexperience. We had one woman who had fifteen years in the building, and another who had eight. Everyone else was under three years. That's how they built it. Part of it is budgetary,

> but part of it to me seemed to me this way to ... nobody's tenured, a lot of them are teachers that are cycling in and passing through, they're not really committed to any union or fairness practice among their colleagues. Especially with TFA, it's community service you do before you go to law school. (Ibid.)

The NYC DOE hired 5,500 new teachers at the start of the 2015–16 school year, of which about 1,000 came through the Teaching Fellows program, which, like TFA, provides an intensive, fast-track, several-week-long training program prior to entering the classroom, in place of holding a university degree in education (Darville and Decker 2015). Teaching Fellows complete a subsidized master's in education degree while working in the classroom. Unlike TFA, Teaching Fellows recruits individuals interested in education as a second career, resulting in a considerably lower turnover. Several New York teachers I interviewed entered the profession through the Teaching Fellows. Many felt under-prepared when they entered the classroom, emphasizing the value of conventional teacher training programs, but were happy with the program's ability to attract a diverse cohort with a serious interest in teaching. Several remarked that a divisive "new versus old teachers" dynamic and general anti-unionism, which they perceived as pervasive in TFA, were not present in the Teaching Fellows training they received.[17]

TFA members employed in NYC schools declined from a height of 536 in 2008 to 400 in 2014 and 230 in 2015, half of which were placed in charter schools (ibid.). TFA closed its NYC training site in 2014, owing to growing difficulties in recruiting candidates. Its NYC director cited, "a contentious national dialogue around education and teaching in general, and TFA in particular" (quoted in Darville 2014a), alluding to criticism of the limited training offered to its members, who generally do not stay in teaching. Others attributed the decline to an improving post-2008-recession US labour market for university graduates (ibid.). One special education teacher I interviewed came to education through TFA. Entering her seventh year of teaching in 2015–16, she was virtually unique among her cohort for still being in the profession. She was also among the most senior of the thirty-five teachers at her middle school in Washington Heights (New York Teacher 11, interview Apr. 2015).

However, a teacher shortage identified at the start of the 2015–16 school year for many cities in the United States (Rich 2015) did not materialize for NYC. Despite the large number of new hires, it was still well below California's total, with 21,000 openings (and only 15,000 new teacher graduates from the state's faculties of education) (Decker 2015). Unlike California and other states and urban areas, NYC is not making up for mass layoffs during the 2008–9 recession and subsequent years of austerity. AFT president Randi Weingarten and other union activists attribute declining numbers of students entering teacher preparation programs to high-profile attacks on the teaching profession by politicians such as Governor Cuomo and his ideological brethren in other states. In New York State, however, despite declining numbers of entrants, education graduates still overshot available new positions in 2015 by about two-thirds, according to the State Education Department (NYSED). While hiring at elite public schools is far more competitive than at struggling schools, overall NYC appears to maintain its attraction for new teachers, offering salaries well above most upstate districts (but below its suburban neighbours) and, perhaps just as important, because of its more qualitative allure as *New York City* (ibid.).

A significant NYC DOE policy change was enacted in 2010–11, which dramatically changed the way teacher tenure is granted. Despite being virtually unmentioned in analyses of the Bloomberg education era, it has had a profound impact on the system's large number of newer staff according to several interviewed teachers. In Ontario and Mexico, the attainment of permanent employee status for K–12 public school teachers means greater union protection under seniority-based provisions for layoffs and due process on disciplinary issues, among other rights. Using the word "tenure" to describe this status, as is done throughout the United States, is misleading, as the term is more commonly associated with the far broader rights of permanent full-time university professors. In any case, the job security that tenure provides, especially as it limits the power of administrators, has an impact beyond the working life of an individual teacher that affects the culture of the school as a whole. As one teacher said, "The last public school I taught at was great … Partly because it was overwhelmingly senior teachers. So they were tenured, they were not frightened of taking risks in the classroom, but also in terms of grieving things" (New York Teacher 2, interview Dec. 2014)

Obtaining tenure became much more difficult under Bloomberg. This difference has had a significant impact on institutional cultures, as the proportion of teachers working precariously for years under probation has risen. Previously, provided that teachers received Satisfactory annual ratings by their principals during their three probationary years, they were virtually guaranteed to receive tenure by their superintendents, as they had been effectively vetted by their principals. Teachers who entered the profession at this time reported obtaining tenure relatively painlessly. A teacher activist who obtained tenure under this system explained the shift:

> There's Race to the Top coming from Obama, and so [Bloomberg] wanted a more stringent evaluation system. And New York State bought into that. So the state adopted the new observation system … essentially you apply for tenure to the chancellor or to your superintendent, that are appointed under the chancellor. Under Mayor Bloomberg, he just changed the policy and said to his chancellor, who said to his superintendents, "Only allow 50 per cent of the people who apply tenure to get it." (New York Teacher 3, interview Dec. 2014)

A younger colleague joins us and adds:

> I'm in my fifth year and I'm untenured. So I'll be going up for tenure again this year. When you go through the process, it just becomes supremely evident, it's a completely subjective, arbitrary, and political process. If you look at data and statistics across the city, because tenure decisions are made by the superintendent not the principals, you'll see it's arbitrary. So Queens has one tenure-giving rate, and Manhattan has another one. The tenure rates are ticking up a little bit. A lot of that has to do with the orientation of the mayor [de Blasio] and the superintendent. But it used to be a guaranteed shot when you went up for tenure that you would get it. (New York Teacher 4: Interviewed Dec. 2014)

He explained the post-2011 application process:

> You have to submit a portfolio that has lesson plans, your observations from your principals and administrators, anything that can document contributions that you make to the school community, any leadership roles that you take. Student work, your data, your test scores for Regents exams. Your student pass rates in your classes … So this is a big fat binder, and then you've got hundreds of teachers for each borough applying for tenure, and they're supposed to go through these binders and then make a decision whether you should get tenure or not. So they never see you teach. (Ibid.)

This teacher had been denied tenure twice and each time had his probationary status extended for a year by his principal. He is frustrated by the lack of feedback from the superintendent concerning his unsuccessful submissions, adding to his sense that the process is highly arbitrary. He echoes New York Teacher 5, quoted above, and New York Teacher 7, who recalls her principal's refusing a suggested hire with ten years experience for being "too expensive," and argues that low rates of granting tenure are part of an effort to have a lower-paid, high-turnover workforce:

> It's a labour shift going on … senior, expensive veteran teachers, to that of a transient labour force. Where people like me who came in through Teaching Fellows typically only stay for five years. Before, after five years you were vested in the pension system … Then under Cuomo, our governor, they passed a law … it's ten years before they're vested in the pension system … new teachers more generally, they're leaving after five years. In addition to that, the big pay increases in the contract don't come until year eight. So there's a huge incentive to deny us tenure because they know that before you get to year eight, you're a cheap teacher essentially. (New York Teacher 4, interview Dec. 2014)

Like New York Teacher 5, he contends that the increasing proportion of untenured teachers has a powerful impact on staff relations in the school and on the relative strength of the union chapter. His tenured colleague, a UFT delegate for the school and member of MORE explains:

> The tradition in New York is, "If you don't have tenure, don't say anything!" You shouldn't be on any union committees. Just keep your head down. If you have a concern, you should talk to someone who has tenure … it's really hurt the teachers' union movement that it is like that. There're people who are like, "Don't sign anything, don't sign a petition, don't put your name on anything." (New York Teacher 3, interview Dec. 2014)

His untenured colleague has given up trying to maintain a reputation unsullied by labour activism, writing articles for MORE's blog and participating in conferences: "I've gone into the mode where, 'I don't give a fuck anymore.' Pretty much. Because it's not a fair process. You forced me to speak out, because your system is so corrupt!" (New York Teacher 4, interview Dec. 2014). The tenure policy change increases the power of principals over untenured teachers, according to informants, who say that, in addition to the absence of a publicly available rubric for superintendents to assess teacher portfolios, the endorsement of their school administrator is actually pivotal for the superintendent making this decision. Whereas tenure previously depended on successful classroom observations conducted by principals, including pre- and post-observation meetings where feedback is provided, the submission of the portfolio for tenure and its approval or denial constitute a more mysterious process.[18]

A common theme throughout this chapter on New York City has been the propensity of the neoliberal education policies discussed here to increase the extent to which the characteristics and personalities of individual administrators define the working conditions of teachers on their staff. This is acknowledged by both teachers who report good relations with their principals (New York Teachers 5 and 11) and those whose experience has been mostly negative (New York Teachers 1, 2, 7, 12, and 13). These are the circumstances that give rise to laboratory-like schools such as Jen and Karen's described at the start of this chapter, where top-down changes to pedagogical practices are made on a yearly basis, irrespective of teacher input, and in which their professional autonomy is substantially degraded.

3.4. Scaling-Up: Initiative in Neoliberal Policy Shifts from New York City to Albany

The election of progressive Democratic Mayor Bill de Blasio in November 2013 marked a major shift in the neoliberalization of public education in New York. Elected on a platform of combatting growing inequality in the city, one of his priority areas, like Bloomberg's, was education. However, in seeking to redistribute public resources from the city's charter schools back to the municipally run school system, while curbing the weight of standardized test scores on the evaluations of teachers and schools, he threatened the legacy of his predecessor. This section will discuss how, in a scalar shift during the tenure of de Blasio, the initiative in neoliberal education policy passed to the state governor's mansion in Albany, occupied by Andrew Cuomo since 2010. Utilizing the constitutional authority of the state government over the city, aided by powerful ideological allies, Cuomo defeated many of de Blasio's most substantive education proposals. Cuomo's success in subsequently advancing the neoliberalization of public education through standardized testing and tying it to teacher evaluations will be studied in the next section. We will first look at the initial progressive efforts under de Blasio and then consider how the shifting of power in education policymaking authority from the NYC to Albany created a problem of scalar strategy for the UFT. Because of changes increasingly being made to the working conditions of its membership by a state government with which the union holds no formal rights to collective bargaining, the UFT had to adopt a new geographical strategy in the sense articulated by Andrew Herod in his seminal *Labor Geographies* (2001), in order to regain its leverage.

De Blasio's election was heralded by many progressives as an opening for left-leaning urban policies in a context where Democrat-led administrations across the country, exemplified by those in Chicago and Washington, DC, were bastions of neoliberal orthodoxy. In an article for the *Huffington Post*, "The de Blasio Mandate for Education," written shortly after his victory, Ravitch underlines the impact of his win on the education policy zeitgeist as "a major national setback for the agenda shared not only by Mayor Bloomberg, but by George W. Bush, Michelle Rhee, Arne Duncan, Jeb Bush, Scott Walker, Bobby Jindal, ALEC (the American Legislative Exchange), the Koch brothers and many others." She adds optimistically, "Make no mistake: In New York City, the drive to privatize public education has ground to a halt with de Blasio's election" (Ravitch 2013b, n.p.). Repudiating Bloomberg's record, the education scholar urged de Blasio to reinstate default neighbourhood middle and high schools for students, dismantling the complex school choice mechanism. She also recommended a review of the system's principals, citing many who had been hired with minimal qualifications under Bloomberg, and she backed de Blasio's plan to prevent charter schools from further usurping space in public schools with which they are co-located and requiring them to pay rent and accept a broader range of students. Finally, she advocates a general rollback of his predecessor's testing and "flawed" school accountability mechanisms, "whose sole purpose seems to be to set up schools for closure and privatization" (ibid.).

De Blasio succeeded in making some significant early changes in areas that were firmly under the control of the DOE. In contrast to Bloomberg, De Blasio selected for chancellor Carmen Fariña, who had started in the classroom and risen through the DOE and was well regarded by the UFT and advocates outside the system for her reasonableness and integrity (Former UFT Official 1, interview Jan. 2015). Several of her early policies were especially relevant to teachers' professional autonomy. A minimum of seven years' teaching experience would now be required for applicants for principal, up from zero under Bloomberg, who had justified the lack on the basis of administrator shortages in the early 2000s and his neoliberal ideology that private sector managerial experience was more valuable than a teaching background (Darville 2014b). Extreme incidents of teacher mistreatment by administrators were more rapidly addressed, as in the case of a Bronx primary school principal pushed to early retirement after she threw her teachers' desks and cabinets to the curb in a statement against sitting while teaching

(Edelman 2015). According to MORE activists, Fariña enforced a contractual rule in the UFT agreement that principals are required to participate in monthly consultation committee meetings convened by school chapter leaders.[19] Under Fariña, rates of tenure granting slightly increased to 65 per cent by 2015, still far below the 90 per cent rate prior to policy changes in 2010 (Zimmerman 2016). Bloomberg's school letter grades based on test scores results, resembling the Board of Health's posters found near the entrances of the city's restaurants, were replaced with assessments based on broader criteria, downloadable from the DOE website.

In other crucial areas of education policy under his control, de Blasio kept the status quo. With support from a broad-based coalition of education groups, including some smaller charter school chains, he obtained an extension to mayoral control from the state legislature in 2015, arguing that the policies of his administration needed more time to reach fruition. They included the Renewal Schools program, in which ninety-four city schools otherwise subject to closing due to low state test scores received additional resources and support. In a move viewed by political commentators as another example of Cuomo's antagonism towards de Blasio and the influence of his other principal adversary, Eva Moskowitz, CEO of Success Academy (New York's largest charter school chain), the renewal was limited to one year rather than three years, the mayor's compromise proposal after initially requesting that the policy be made permanent (Shapiro 2015b).[20] Meanwhile, parent advocacy groups Class Size Matters and NYC Kids PAC criticized de Blasio for what they saw as little empowerment of the Community Education Councils and School Leadership Teams, which had lost much of their influence under Bloomberg to the chancellor and local principals, respectively. While praising de Blasio's success in stopping punitive school closures, they also charged him with not meeting his campaign goals to make the city's stratified school choice system more equitable. These parent groups also criticized his decision to maintain the centralization of power under mayoral control (Haimson and Tanikawa 2015; NYC Kids PAC 2015).

De Blasio suffered one of his largest education policy defeats by Governor Cuomo over his proposals to make student standardized test scores less punitive for teachers and schools. Two other plans overturned by Albany were a new wealth tax to fund the expansion of pre-kindergarten and the return of hundreds of millions of dollars earmarked for charter school construction to public school funding (Lois Weiner, interview Dec. 2014). Following a \$3.6 million advertising campaign against de Blasio's anti-charter school policies in spring 2014 by the Families for Excellent Schools lobby group, high-profile rallies of Success Academy pupils and staff led by Moskowitz and publicly endorsed by Cuomo, capped off by the state legislature's overruling of municipal measures to limit charters, de Blasio backed away from his efforts to curb their proliferation (Singer 2014; Hernandez and Craig 2014). Weiner (interview Dec. 2014) contends that the defeat of the key planks of his campaign policy on education were foreshadowed by Joe Williams, executive director of Democrats for Education Reform (DFER), an influential pro-testing and charter school think-tank and lobby group affiliated with the Democratic Party, whose principal donors are Wall Street hedge funds. "The much-maligned standardized tests aren't going anywhere," he commented in an article in January 2014 reporting on the new mayor's education mandate. "The Bloomberg haters are going to have to settle for a change in style rather than major changes in substance" (Willen 2014). DFER donated $72,000 to Cuomo in 2015 (Gonzalez 2015).

Neoliberal interventions in New York State's K–12 education system did not begin with Andrew Cuomo. Three-term Republican governor George Pataki (1995–2006) authorized the creation of up to 100 charter schools across the state in 1998, raising the cap to 250 in 2006. During the course of his tenure, he refused to increase state funding for public education and fought against a high-profile legal suit by Campaign for Fiscal Equity to raise funding for NYC schools. At Bloomberg's urging, he led the authorization of mayoral control for NYC (Traver 2006, 502). Nevertheless, under President Randi Weingarten, Pataki was endorsed by the UFT (Former UFT Official 1, interview Jan. 2015). Arguably Pataki's most significant intervention in K–12 education was maintaining an overall context of fiscal austerity while Bloomberg's administration proceeded with its agenda.

The election of a mayor with a left-leaning education agenda brought substantial financial backing from pro-testing and charter school lobby groups financed by Wall Street hedge funds and major US education policy philanthropists to Andrew Cuomo. They apparently considered Albany to be a strategic bulwark for maintaining the momentum of neoliberal education policy in New York. Students FirstNY Advocacy, the Coalition for Opportunity in Education, and Families for Excellent Schools spent over $8.3 million[21] lobbying state legislators to support charters in 2015. The latter alone spent $9.7 million in 2014 (Bragg 2014). Public education activists and investigative journalists reported over $4.8 million in political donations received up to 2015 by Governor Cuomo directly from hedge fund managers (Gonzalez 2015). De Blasio remarked, "The hedge-fund contributors loom very large in Albany, and they have way too much influence; that is a fact" (quoted in Goldman and Klopott 2015).

Cuomo rejected efforts by Fariña and the DOE to negotiate with the UFT reforms to the teacher evaluation process that would have made the process less onerous and tied to value-added metrics on standardized test scores. Over the course of 2015, he led an effort by the state legislature, assisted by the NYSED, to increase the weight of these test metrics in annual evaluations while making tenure more difficult to obtain. The new will of the state government under Cuomo to aggressively formulate and roll out education policy, the details of which will be fully outlined in the following section, creates a scalar problem for the UFT and other local teachers' unions across the state. Whereas these unions hold statutory collective bargaining rights with local school districts and, under mayoral control, the NYC municipal government, the state legislature wields increasing power over teachers' working conditions. This situation resembles Peck and Tickell's (2002, 401) influential scalar analysis of the tendency under contemporary neoliberalism of senior governments to upload policymaking authority in the public sector, resulting in weakening avenues for locally based dissent.

This scaling-up of teachers' labour relations to higher levels of government follows developments in Ontario and Mexico (Sweeney 2013; Bocking 2015a). However, in these two jurisdictions, education finance originates from the senior level of government, inspiring a credible argument to negotiate with the actual holder of the purse strings. School district funding in New York is provided in roughly even measures from local and state sources, with under 10 per cent contributed by the federal government. Even more significantly, unlike the centralized structures of teachers' unions in Mexico and Ontario, the New York State United Teachers (NYSUT), controlled by UFT through the large proportion of the delegates, dues, and officers that it contributes, primarily acts as an umbrella association for local unions to lobby the Albany legislature, lacking legally binding collective bargaining rights or significant power independent of its affiliates. Absent these structures for formally scaling up contract negotiations to the state level, NYSUT could apply its statewide presence in public campaigns, as it has around education funding. It has attempted to support the parent-led Opt Out movement, the state's most powerful grass-roots education mobilization, which seeks to undermine the state's standardized 3rd to 8th grade testing regime. However, while joining calls to parents to opt their children out from the tests, NYSUT has been limited by the official stance of the UFT, which in 2015 did not support the movement. While 20 per cent of children were opted out of the exams across the state in 2015, the rate was less than 2 per cent in NYC (Shapiro 2015a). In the absence of participating in and leading strong statewide opposition, the UFT found itself with a weakened capacity to resist Cuomo's 2015 reform of teacher evaluations, which, by increasing the power of standardized testing, has far-reaching consequences for teachers' professional autonomy.

3.5. Cuomo's Expansion of Standardized Testing into Teacher Evaluation: Undermining Professional Autonomy

The eclipse of teachers' professional autonomy in New York by punitive evaluation structures developed in the 2000s within the context of the first major federal interventions in US education policy since the Elementary and Secondary Education Act of 1965.[22] A key plank of President George W. Bush's NCLB legislation enacted in 2002, was mandating states to annually administer high-stakes tests to students from 3rd to 12th grades. The results were used to reward or penalize districts and individual schools and justify funding charter schools, part of an ethos of fomenting competition to mimic the economic consequences of globalization (Hursh 2007; Ravitch 2013a). However, NCLB required states to ensure that virtually all of its students passed all exams by 2014 and, faced with this unreality and the legislative inability to amend NCLB, the US DOE consistently granted waivers to states on this requirement, so long as they presented evidence of pursuing desirable policies (Hursh 2013, 578).[23] The NCLB provided another strong example of the tendency of neoliberal governance to scale up policymaking while limiting local autonomy and downloading accountability for execution (Peck and Tickell 2002; Hursh 2013).

The Regents exams served this purpose at the high school level in New York State. Believing its actions justified by fears of rising mediocrity, as were so many other education policies harkening back to the 1983 *A Nation at Risk* report, the state made its optional five high school Regents exams mandatory for graduation in 1996 (Hantzopoulos and Tyner-Mullings 2012, xli). Hursh (2007, 2013), Winerip (2012), and teachers interviewed here[24] have contended that, reinforced under NCLB, this mandate has resulted in a narrowing of both school timetables (i.e., the selection of available courses) and the actual content of individual courses in order to emphasize learning content directly related to the five mandatory Regents. A teacher at a small school describes the imperative of teaching the test:

> So my English class: I'm getting ready to give an assignment tomorrow on question 27 on the Regents exam, which is a very specific way of writing a short literary analysis. I wouldn't be giving that garbage if I could be

> giving exactly what I wanted to do. But I have to teach them the language of the test. The specific language of it is *controlling idea*. That's what they have to write, a controlling idea. That's not in the Common Core![25] They don't use the language of the *controlling idea* in the Common Core. Nobody uses the word *controlling idea* in their pedagogy, in their instruction. It's not a universal word like *thesis* or *argument* or *claim*; it's none of that. But this is what you ask, because you have to know what a controlling idea is when they take that test. (New York Teacher 4, interview Dec. 2014)

Despite the original progressive ideals of NYC's small schools movement as described above, the vast majority of small schools created under Bloomberg, facilitated by their narrow course offerings due to scale, tended to teach to the Regents exams, often encouraged by their principals. According to a 2008 Policy Studies Associates survey[26] of teachers and administrators at seventy-six small New Century High Schools from 2002 to 2006, "Teachers provided successively higher ratings of the alignment of instruction with Regents requirements over time" as well as "successively lower ratings of student discipline and their own influence on school policy and curriculum."[27] (Foley et al. 2008, 14). Teachers indicated that their influence was diminishing, in the face of consistently high rates of observation and control by principals over their classroom instructional practices (ibid., 23).[28] This study concurs with the view of Brian Barrett, at the State University of New York (SUNY), who concludes that the influence of NCLB policies such as high-stakes testing, has the "capacity to fundamentally alter teachers' professional practices and identities" (2009, 1018).

A history teacher explains how interventions from principals to teach to the test in order to raise school scores has degraded the professional craft of educating:

> To some degree, in the major subjects the tests [Regents exams] always dictate things ... At the same time, there can be a lot of freedom. You can take risks as a teacher in a school with a principal who doesn't micromanage ... But if you have a principal who's not sympathetic or who doesn't understand history, or how to teach it, or just looks at the review books and says,"follow this curriculum," as a teacher you have even less freedom. In some ways, the tests always dictate what you have to teach, but when you have a bad principal, they'll even dictate how you're going to teach it, at what pace, what you'll emphasize ... some of the tests are pretty good, and force the students to do some thoughtful intellectual work ... The problem is the punitive nature of it – if the students don't do well, the school loses its funding. (NY Teacher 2, interview Dec. 2014)

This teacher's reference to schools' losing funding due to low test scores refers to Bloomberg's school letter grade rating system, under which schools would be rewarded or punished, which was ended under de Blasio. A former elementary teacher and MORE co-founder relates:

> This was fourth grade, East Harlem ... we were in the middle of a week-long [science] investigation, in the middle of that day's time in the investigation. The kids had all these materials out, they were measuring, looking, making notes, and the assistant principal tells me to put all that away and start doing test prep right now. And I said, "Well yeah, sure, okay. As soon as we're done with this, we'll clean it up and we'll get started." She said, "No, right now." So in front of the kids I had to beg her to let us continue the experiment. I failed. And we literally had to take everything as it was, notes and everything, and just put it away. Turn to page 39. Answer question 28: a, b, or c. (New York Teacher 1, interview Dec. 2014)

The formal basis of power between teachers and the principals in terms of establishing time that is dedicated to test prep can vary dramatically:

> In some schools, test preparation is a course; it's like considered a separate block of time; time is taken out for just pure test prep. In some schools it starts from the very first day of school, with assessment tests, drills ... everyone's thinking about the tests. They have to, in order to survive. And so what some principals do to protect teachers and children from the pressures of the test and test-based ideas of education is try to encourage teachers to integrate things they know or suspect will be on the tests into their regular teaching. (Ibid.)

How do those varying conditions get negotiated? Is it solely at the discretion of the principals, in terms of the policies or their philosophical inclinations? His response suggests the school-by-school nuance of teacher and principal power relations and the limits of existing union protections for professional judgment in NYC:

> On paper, presumably the teacher has a lot of leeway to determine precisely how a given lesson will be taught. However, the reality is that if a principal gives a direct order, a teacher who doesn't carry out that order ... is subject to accusations of insubordination. So what the union often advises teachers to do is go along with it, but if you feel the contract has been violated, then you can grieve it. But in practice ... people essentially

> defer to what the principal says we're all going to do … Or if they attempt to subvert it, they do it on the down-low. They close their classroom door or try to do something different … In general, the first schools where you see teacher resistance to testing, where teachers have organized to refuse to administer the tests, to refuse to do test preparation … the principal has one way or another given a signal. (Ibid.)

This passage again illustrates the decisive influence, post-Bloomberg, of administrators in setting the tone of the school in relation to the ability of teachers to act with professional autonomy, especially in the context of high-stakes testing.

These accounts of frustrated teachers compelled to spend class time teaching a concept of limited use because of its adoption by the Regents exam, the history teacher whose professional capacity to plan lessons is curtailed, and the science teacher forced to shelve an interactive lab for test prep, all serve as snapshots of the outcome of NCLB's mandate for high-stakes testing.[29] Educators summarized that the most significant consequence of the Obama administration's RTTT was taking these high-stakes tests beyond defining what is taught in the classroom to directly determining teachers' job security. Unlike NCLB's legal mandate, which compelled states to implement standardized testing, RTTT implemented its agenda through a $5 billion fund, particularly attractive to state governments suffering from significant loss of tax revenue in the aftermath of the 2008–9 recession. Winning applicants (nineteen of forty-six states and DC that submitted) secured the agreement of local school boards and teachers' unions to raise limits on the number of charter schools, to institute processes to close schools with low test scores, and to determine at least 20 per cent of teachers' annual evaluations through value-added assessments, based on "growth" of student scores between tests taken at the beginning and at the end of the school year. For meeting these requirements, in 2010 New York State received $700 million spread over four years.[30] However, with half of these funds mandated for spending on student testing and observations tied to teacher evaluations, the actual additional amount districts would receive per student is just $33.50 per year (Ravitch 2013a, 99; Hursh 2013, 574–6). With such a modest contribution to education budgets in exchange for considerable administrative restructuring, the extent that pursuit of RTTT funding was ideologically motivated will be further suggested through the description below of Governor Andrew Cuomo's dogged efforts to ensure value-added assessments determined teachers' evaluations to the fullest extent possible.

Another teacher, currently at a critical small school where all but the English Regents exam is waived, described her past experience at a conventional high school prepping students for the math Regents:

> The tests can test anything out of twelve different chapters. Most teachers I know, if they get through all twelve chapters it's because they're a speed racer and there's not a lot of depth of learning ... my colleague and I went over fifteen years of exams and tallied the topics, all this statistical analysis to decide which six we're going to teach this year because that's all the time we have. And they scored great on all the past exams, and then that year for whatever reason, it's [the actual exam was] just totally different ... What the hell! We just spent nine months working our butts off, doing the best they can – Saturday school, after school, sitting in an office with tick marks for a test we don't even care about. And then they flunk. So now I'm a shitty teacher. Because based on this test score I didn't do my job, and I didn't prepare kids, and now there goes my MOSL score. (New York Teacher 5, interview Dec. 2014)

Measures of Student Learning (MOSL) is the New York State value-added assessment. At the high school level, Regents exams fulfil the role of the MOSL at the end of the school year. Since receipt of RTTT funds began in 2010, New York State's Annual Professional Performance Review (APPR) for teachers has consisted of two components: (1) a series of informal or formal observations of classroom teaching by the school's principal or an outside evaluator and (2) the MOSL. Official observations in New York State are based on the patented Danielson evaluation rubric, which specified twenty-two distinct areas of teacher competency. It was narrowed to eight areas in the 2014 UFT contract, covering lesson planning, professional responsibilities, the classroom environment, and instructional methods, the last two categories holding greater weight (UFT 2014). Initial requirements of two observations per year were raised in 2014 to at least one formal (mutually scheduled, period-long) and three informal (unannounced, fifteen-minute) observations, or to six informal observations. Teachers with Effective or Highly Effective ratings require one to two fewer observations. Some teachers interviewed report having received fewer observations, noting the practical logistical difficulties for administrators of potentially scheduling hundreds of observations a year for all of their staff members. Overall, they reported far more concern about the impact of the MOSL test scores on their evaluations[31] (Hursh 2013, 583; NYC DOE 2015).

In 2011, Cuomo's legislature doubled the MOSL component to count for 40 per cent of the APPR, and observations were reduced to 60 per cent. NYSUT and the UFT responded with legal challenges, but the new 40 per cent threshold stood, with the caveat that teachers at each school could choose to have part of the extra 20 per cent evaluated through an additional locally developed standardized test. However, faced with more paperwork, many schools opt to simply give the existing Regents exams the 40 per cent weighting (Hursh 2013, 584). Cuomo and others strongly advocated for increasing the weight of student testing in teacher evaluations, claiming that it is scientifically possible to isolate and quantifiably measure a teachers' contribution to student knowledge year over year.[32] Factors such as the socio-economic status of students and parental education levels were minimized in this formula by the argument that considering them is tantamount to lowered expectations for poor students (rather than a rationale for greater student supports). Accordingly, proponents argued that value-added assessments of the impact of teachers on their students' test scores offered the most *objective* measure of the quality of an educator. Teachers who did not "add value" could then be justifiably fired (Kuhn 2014, 45). As Texas School Board superintendent and anti-testing activist John Kuhn explains, "The real magic – and faith – comes in when the algorithm attempts to set a predicted amount of improvement that each student *ought to have made*; the teacher is rated based on how often he or she outperforms the individual improvement called for by the algorithm" (ibid.; emphasis original). Ravitch explains how this idea initially proposed by William Sanders, an industrial statistician from Tennessee, and subsequently promulgated by economists at the conservative Hoover Institute entered public discourse in 2010 through its adoption by travelling neoliberal education advocates Michelle Rhee and Joel Klein (Ravitch 2013a, 100–3). It was then appended as a key aspect of RTTT and diffused to states across the country. With strong support from Bloomberg and the new governor but with the UFT refusing to agree to its form of implementation, it was imposed in NYC by the state education department, while other school boards and unions across the state enjoyed greater room to negotiate more local autonomy (Tisch and Berlin 2014, 2–4).

The professional capacity of high school teachers is subordinated to the fear they will lose their jobs if the exam scores of their students do not sufficiently rise. Rather than interpretation of broad curricular requirements through student-centred and project-centred learning based on teaching deeper, more qualitative principles through "authentic tasks,"[33] the emphasis shifts to rote-learning of quantitative data. A major impetus behind NYC's critical small schools movement has been the substitution of the Regents exams for these alternative forms of evaluations (Hantzopoulos and Tyner-Mullings 2012, xxxiii). In 2016, these schools enrolled a few thousand high school students, a tiny portion of those governed by the NYC Department of Education.

After the full implementation of the APPR in the 2013–14 school year, Hursh (2013) anticipated that the evaluation system driven by student test scores would result in mass firings, as, he argued, NYSED's bell-curve rating system intended. However, in the 2013–14 teacher evaluation, less than 1 per cent of teachers in the state were rated Ineffective, and over 95 per cent were rated Highly Effective or Effective. When NYC's results were more closely tied to state test score MOSLs, 1.2 per cent of teachers were rated Ineffective, but only 9.2 per cent were rated Highly Effective, compared with 58.2 per cent across the rest of the state (Tisch and Berlin 2014, 3). In a highly publicized response, Cuomo decried the results as "baloney," claiming that more teachers must actually be Ineffective, to account for insufficient improvements in student test scores (Smith 2015). Retired (in 2015) Long Island principal and anti-standardized testing activist Carol Burris explained Chancellor Merryl Tisch and Cuomo's motivations:

> To Tisch's dismay, APPR, which she helped design, has not produced the results that she and Cuomo wanted … The plan, according to the state's Race to the Top application, was for 10 percent of all teachers to be found ineffective, with small numbers designated as highly effective. The curve of the sorting bell was not achieved. (Strauss 2015)

As part of the 2015–16 budget, in April 2015 Cuomo pushed through the state legislature new measures he believed would result in a higher number of teachers being labelled Ineffective and on the path to termination. School districts would be compelled to renegotiate their union contracts and implement the policies locally by the following November or lose increases in state education funding. First, the 60/40 balance of observations and MOSLs would be replaced by a more ambiguous matrix, with an even weight between both but with negative (Developing or Ineffective) results on the MOSL, thus lowering Effective or Highly Effective ratings on the observation component. After two consecutive Ineffective ratings, a teacher *may* be charged with "incompetence," leading to dismissal for untenured teachers and trials within ninety days for tenured teachers. After three consecutive such ratings the teacher *must* be charged, and a decision reached within thirty days. Next, the number of years' service before a teacher was eligible to apply for tenure was increased from three to four, and Effective or Highly Effective ratings would be required in at least three of the four years.

Finally, schools in the bottom 5 per cent of total state testing results for ten years may be restructured by a board- or state-appointed "receiver," who can fire any or all staff (Bakeman 2015; Brody 2015).

The response of NYSUT and the UFT to these attacks on the job security of their members mainly took the form of intense lobbying in Albany. Union negotiators claimed victory in limiting the increase in probation to four years (Cuomo wanted five years) and eliminating a proposed tax credit for donors to private schools that would have been an initial step to subsidizing private tuition and was fiercely fought for by charter school lobbyists. They were unsuccessful in forestalling the further influence of standardized testing results over teachers. Where they failed, New York state's Opt Out movement claimed some success. Coordinated by parent-led networks such as New York State Allies for Public Education, the cumulative effort of parent associations in districts across the state resulted in over 220,000 students in 3rd to 8th grades sitting out their math and/or science state tests in April 2015, over a fifth of all eligible students (Harris and Fessenden 2015). The Opt Out Movement was present throughout the state, but the highest concentration of test refusers was in the predominantly middle-class Long Island suburbs of Norfolk and Suffolk counties, where it received vocal support from superintendents, elected trustees, and local teachers' union leaders, contributing to an overwhelming majority opting out. Opt Out was a minor presence in poorer, rural districts and in NYC, where, despite tripling in numbers from the previous year, was still less than 2 per cent of all elementary test takers.[34] Of NYC's 7,900 students who were opted out, over 1,650 were in District 15, the affluent Park Slope neighbourhood in Brooklyn (Rodriguez 2015; Harris 2015).

The teachers' union president[35] of a small Long Island school board explained how parents in her district became galvanized in response to state measures to quash the budding dissent and ensure the exams were administered:

> These school districts were going to pass resolutions that they were going to "discuss" whether or not to even give the test in their district ... both districts were told, by the State of New York that if they did that ... the state would remove every member of the board of education and the superintendent and put in their own representatives to run the district. That doesn't happen in America. In America, we believe in local control. We believe that in fact, if we elect a board of education, that board of education is supposed to represent *us* locally. The state is not allowed to tell us what we can and cannot discuss! (New York Teacher 9, interview Apr. 2015)

The state government's intervention helped build opposition to the tests: "The parents went crazy! ... [the] school board never brought the resolution to the floor. Superintendent, the news media, everyone was there. The superintendent said, 'I've been advised by council not to talk about this.'" In response, activist parents began to organize: "I don't really know the politics in your country ... I don't know if you know mine. What I'm telling you is, this is revolution stuff in America. This is crazy shit." She later remarked during our interview:

> NYSUT's agenda has not been an anti-testing agenda. It is only now becoming, because the parent groups are standing up and they've decided they're going to protect public schools, and they're going to protect their children. So unfortunately, my state and national union have not been setting the pace. They have been reacting to the fact that *they* are going to be thrown out of office, just like the legislative members, and the senators and the governor. This will destroy Cuomo. It will, because he will never be able to run for president. (Ibid.)

Since Cuomo and his bipartisan allies were facing an electoral threat, the scaling-up of the initiative in neoliberal education policy in New York may have reached its point of vulnerability. The groundswell of public opposition in some politically influential swing vote regions of New York State to what are widely viewed as excessive testing of children and, for some, an attack on teachers has reverberated across the state. Teachers in NYC would benefit, despite the much weaker Opt Out Movement in their city, including at the secondary level and despite public organizing and protest focusing on 3rd to 8th grades, as these are statewide policies affecting both elementary and secondary.

Following a high-profile statement by Obama that testing should be reduced, NYSED and Cuomo announced in late 2015 that MOSLs and value-added assessments would be suspended entirely from annual teacher evaluations until at least 2019, accompanying an overhaul of the Common Core State Standards on which the standardized tests were based. NYSED also announced that school districts with high opt-out rates would not be punished by having their funding levels frozen, as state authorities had threatened earlier. The results of the 2014–15 state teacher evaluations revealed that 92 per cent of NYC teachers were rated Highly Effective or Effective (Zernike 2015; Taylor 2015; Clukey 2015). If their own unions lack the capacity to do so, will it be New York's organized parents who save their children's teachers?

3.6. State of Our Union, State of Our Schools

Throughout this chapter there have been references to the response of the UFT to the neoliberal policies that have transformed teachers' work in New York City by limiting their professional autonomy. We have seen many aspects of this transformation: the impact of mayoral control in concentrating power in the hands of the mayor and the chancellor, weakening official community forums; the proliferation of small schools and "school choice" that changed the spatial organization of the workplace; policies that increased the precariousness of teachers by making tenure more difficult to obtain and surplussed teachers easier to eliminate; and finally, the scaling-up of policymaking beyond the local plane on which collective bargaining is conducted, to make fundamental changes to the teacher evaluation process. Beneath all of these dynamics we have the political economy of austerity financing for public education, the rise of charter schools, and rising socio-economic inequity experienced by poor and working-class and racialized communities that represent the overwhelming majority of NYC's students.

Underlying policy shifts initiated chiefly by Bloomberg and later Cuomo have constituted a largely consistent tendency to remake the teaching profession towards one that is disempowered and precarious. In doing so, we have seen a hollowing out of the power of the union, at the level that matters most: the school site. Unlike most once powerful teachers' unions in the United States that have lost institutional capacity from the passing of "Right to Work"-style laws that hemorrhage dues revenue, as happened in Wisconsin after 2011, or lost thousands of members from the expansion of non-union charters, as happened in Detroit and Los Angeles, on paper the UFT remains as powerful as ever. Yet all of the policies I describe above add up to weakening the capacity of teachers to defend their ability to exercise their professional autonomy in their schools.

Some of these defeats are due to decisions by the leadership of the UFT, which have concentrated power and initiative at the top of the union, thereby neglecting the chapter level, and a political strategy that has striven unsuccessfully to contain these policies through high-level lobbying while eschewing more confrontational grass-roots alliances such as the Opt Out Movement. From these decisions, one can see an ideological orientation on the part of a leadership that is unwilling to support bottom-up insurgent mobilization. It does not acknowledge the contemporary attacks on public education as being consistent within a context governed by the neoliberal variant of capitalism, let alone a perspective that sees beyond the legislative programs and actors of

City Hall, Albany, or Washington, DC, to horizons of similar policies crossing borders elsewhere and the resistance that they encounter, whether in Ontario or in Mexico. Because of a lack of systemic analysis, a comprehensive alternative vision is not forthcoming and the battle continues to be fought in an isolated fashion. For these reasons, I devote a substantial focus here to the Movement of Rank and File Educators (MORE), which has put forward an alternative concept for the union in this context.

The final section of this chapter focuses then on how the UFT has attempted to change, and has been changed, during these circumstances, to help explain the unevenness of neoliberal reform across my three case studies. I begin with an overview of the current structure of the UFT's leadership and school chapters, attempting to understand some reasons behind the weakness of the union's presence in many schools. I will then trace the development of the MORE caucus, its use of policy mobility "from below" through its inspiration from Chicago's Caucus of Rank and File Educators (CORE), its struggles to both gain a critical mass of support from colleagues, and, following the CORE model, build meaningful alliances with parent groups. I draw heavily on interviews with union activists, many affiliated with MORE, and to a much lesser extent former UFT officials.[36] I also utilize notes from MORE caucus events, meetings, and rallies; UFT delegate assemblies; and MORE, UFT, and the incumbent Unity Caucus materials.

A former UFT official describes how the union leadership confronted the education challenges of the Bloomberg era. He notes a dichotomy between critics of the union executive, who equate unionism with comprehensive contractual rights but do not recognize structural crises facing the school system and a more farsighted leadership:

> There are people – particularly internal opposition in the union – who have this vision that unionism is industrial unionism, and they will see this as union betraying some fundamental interest. But the union has – the union leadership ... this sense that you need to change public education. You can't continue to have a system – this drop-out rate leaves so many poor kids and kids of colour behind ... in the United States, the way in which education reform in the corporate sense gains its power is by pointing to the kinds of failings of the school system with regards to race and class. Even though it's not like teachers or unions devised this system, or that they approve of it. Nonetheless, the charter schools in New York City were originally put into three of the poorest communities, huge concentrations of people of colour: Harlem, South Bronx, central Brooklyn ... The problem with charter schools is not the structural relationship. It's

> not because you don't have the government officially running the school ... that's the problem. The problem with the charter school movement [is] the people who have seized control of it and run its leadership. So the idea was how we could produce a different vision of what a charter school should be, including a different vision of collective bargaining where we would have a contract that wasn't this kind of long, detailed industrial style contract with regulations, but had in it teachers having voice and control over all the work decisions; sort of taking that bargaining we had made with the new small schools and elaborating it. (Former UFT Official 2, interview Apr. 2015)

He acknowledges that most charter school advocates aren't interested in this experiment by the union. Many are politically aligned with conservative coalitions that aim to weaken teachers' unions in order to remove their counterweight to corporate wealth in US elections (ibid.). A MORE activist had a harsher critique of the UFT leadership's effort to create a progressive model for charter schools, which he viewed as indicative of a conservative approach to working within the system:

> From the beginning their whole strategy is to retain a seat at the table. Stay in the conversation. On charter schools, they said, "we can't straight out oppose charter schools, because parents love them! Therefore, we're going to start our own charter school! And prove that a unionized charter school is the best way to go" ... we later discovered, when they had one of these privatization summits, where somebody secretly videotaped a presentation of a guy on how to trick the unions, that *that* was a strategy! They were like, "We're going to tell the unions to start their own charter schools. If they buy it, then they can't oppose charter schools because they're part of it." (New York Teacher 1, interview Dec. 2014)

With the rapid proliferation of charter schools in urban US school districts, the UFT, like other teachers' unions, has worked with the AFT's Alliance of Charter School Teachers and Staff (ACTS) to organize the non-union schools and have had some modest successes at smaller independent charters in NYC (Winslow 2013; Zionts 2015). Eight per cent of NYC's approximately 1.1 million students in publicly funded schools attend charters (McKenna 2015).

Alongside the structural transformations in the organization of the NYC DOE under Bloomberg discussed above, a disruption in how the union intervened on day-to-day workplace issues and school-level grievances occurred. A former official described the previous system:

> The power dynamics in a traditional school, there are various sorts of checks on principal's authority, but they're not so great that we're dealing with a mythical world in which there were no abusive principals … In those days… depending upon the relationship, if things got really bad, more often than not, the union would be able to go to the superintendent and they would be able to work out some changes, some accommodations. (Former UFT Official 2, interview Apr. 2015)

The collapsing of geographically defined community school districts into various forms of support networks resulted in the shifting of administrative authority. While principals gained increased power within their 1,800 schools through a broad range of policies, power over them came to be wielded to an increasingly direct extent from DOE headquarters via surveillance and intervention based on student test scores. The intermediary structure of superintendents weakened, which, according to this former UFT official, coincides with a push by Bloomberg's DOE to diminish the union's capacity to effectively resolve workplace problems through grievances and arbitration:

> They make a decision at the DOE to basically destroy the grievance system. Because the grievance system is based on a kind of funnel where you only want to take a small number of grievances to arbitration: the highest level. So you try to resolve these at lower levels … The DOE refuses to solve any grievances at lower levels. They create this massive bottleneck at the top of the system, because the way arbitration works for us is we have a limited number of days that we have arbitrators to hear arbitrations. So we can only schedule so many arbitrations … the union [is] constantly trying to increase the number of arbitration days. Because what's happening is too many things. We win all the arbitrations, because they're taking stuff that they can't win, but the object at the top is to block up the system. So that is one dynamic that makes it hard for us to use the grievance system. They do the same thing before a teacher gets tenure; they are at that point an at-will employee. There is supposed to be an appeal for your year-end ratings, which is really the only means of redress that a teacher that's not tenured would have. They basically decided that they're not ever going to overturn a principal's unsatisfactory year-end evaluation. (Ibid.)

Though obscure to those outside the union's leadership and unreported in standard accounts of contemporary education policy change in NYC, the results are significant in terms of reduced support from the larger union for school chapters locked in conflict with administrators. This change helps shift the balance of power to the latter's benefit:

> Those principals that are malevolent have a much freer reign to be malevolent, which is still not by any means a majority in the school system. And they make the superintendents into empty shirts ... You have a system in which it becomes very difficult for the union to do the kind of servicing stuff that it did before. It doesn't keep a union chapter from organizing; it simply makes the system that was in place for resolving conflicts impossible to work. (Ibid.)

A former senior UFT staff member describes the duties of the school-level union chapter chair:

> The eyes and ears and mouth of the union at the chapter level. The chapter leader is involved in grievance procedures and leads at grievance hearings. The chapter leader negotiates with the principal to withdraw charges, or finesses that those charges aren't filed in the first place ... it's a real job. People want to be chapter leaders for three reasons: one is they're militants, two is they're militants who also want to be in the leadership [Unity] caucus, three, they're militants who hate the leadership caucus. But for the most part, these are tough guys and women; it's mostly women who recognize that things ain't getting better, with the exception of the extraordinary principal. (Former UFT Official 1, interview Jan. 2015)

He provides an overview of the health of the union's school-based chapters in this context:

> Of the 1,400 institutions, there are not 1,400 active chapters [there are over 1,800 schools]. Depending on who you talk to, there are either 800 or less. Now of the 800, they tend to work fairly well. Sometimes, a chapter leader is a kiss ass, so they bury any problems and will finger troublemakers. Then you have chapter leaders who will put their necks out on the line every day and risk Unsatisfactory ratings – a couple of U ratings and you're out. The union goes out of its way to defend the chapter leaders, whether they're part of the Unity caucus or part of the opposition caucuses, because you lose one of them, and the camel's nose is under the tent! (Ibid.)

MORE activists concurred that roughly half of all schools have functional union chapters.[37] All teachers interviewed were asked to comment on the activity and health of the chapters in the schools where they have worked. Their responses indicated a wide diversity of experiences. One teacher explained why some chapter leaders were "kiss asses":

> There's a lot of terrible chapter leaders now because we've had years of turnover and there [are] these schools where everyone's a young teacher and no one knows their rights, and the principal will even encourage a teacher they like to become chapter leader so that they can then impose ... Yes, in some schools it is a company union. It's awful. (New York Teacher 2, interview Dec. 2014)

The role played here by the absence from many NYC schools of large numbers of veteran teachers, frequently replaced by untenured staff, reiterates the arguments made above of the impact of these trends on the capacity of teachers to assert their professional autonomy in the face of administrative pressure to teach to the test. The extent that untenured teachers are vulnerable to retaliation by administrators for participating in union activities led facilitators at a MORE workshop on building school chapters to advise against their taking any form of visible leadership role in the union.[38] Teacher 2 also described how he experienced this retaliation while untenured, thus placing his employment at risk:

> We had a union meeting once where the guy everyone knew was the principal's person, who's now an administrator ... [he] just came in and took some notes and left. And everyone knew he wasn't there because he was a union guy, and I was observed [evaluated] the next day. He was coming to take attendance on who goes to the union meetings! (Ibid.)

This teacher and many others also described working at schools with strong union chapters and leaders.[39] Nevertheless, it is surely a sign of institutional weakness that many administrators are able to create an intimidating environment surrounding participation in the union at their school (recall Jen and Karen, at the start of this chapter, explaining that their school's only veteran teacher, being the chapter leader, was isolated from other staff), how so many schools do not have a functional union presence, and how in some it has been co-opted to serve managerial prerogatives. A major critique by MORE activists is the lack of initiative in many school chapters for involving its members in a participatory fashion to address significant issues. A MORE member described meetings at his former school:

> It's during a lunch break or something; then there are cookies and chips. You can ask a few questions, and that's it. But it's never like *the chapter* makes decisions ... There are some things the chapter has to vote on, like if we're going to make changes to our schedule, there are some things within

> our rights. But it's never like "a charter school's going to colocate with us, what's our action plan for how we're going to fight that? How are we going to stop this, how are we going to rally the community to our side?" (New York Teacher 1, interview Dec. 2014)

MORE activists tended to blame the UFT leadership for not creating or supporting structures within the union that would encourage greater school site activity.[40] For them and others, this lack has served as a major impetus to join the MORE caucus as a means of making structural changes within the union.

A Washington Heights middle school teacher who became a MORE activist describes how, coming from overwhelmingly non-union North Carolina as a self-identified progressive, she was eager for the opportunity to be involved in her new union:

> I was very excited to join a union. I really liked the idea of it! My union rep at the time was like, "OK, well, here's a form you can fill out ... we don't really have issues with our administration ..." He did invite me later ... to a restaurant reception to welcome the new UFT president, who at the time was Michael Mulgrew. I remember going and being very unimpressed, because the primary thing that was discussed was parking spaces ... really, parking spaces? [Laughs] Parking around the school. Which is an issue in New York City, getting to work on time, parking can be really expensive. I sort of get it, but I was surprised that was such a big topic of conversation. I was generally very unimpressed with Michael Mulgrew's demeanour and choice of words, all of those things. The food was really good at that reception though. I think they also had mixed drinks ... So that was my first exposure to union stuff. (New York Teacher 11, interview Apr. 2015)

For her, the official activities of the union both at her school and in the larger institution and its narrow "business unionist" focus were unsatisfying. They did not appear to her to serve as vehicles to address the sprawling range of equity and social justice issues affecting both her students and her colleagues. At the end of her second year, she ran for the position of school chapter chair and was defeated. She attributes her loss to a rumour spread by the incumbent that she was hand-picked by the principal, with whom she had a good relationship. Other teachers viewed her suspiciously as a TFA alumna and for her limited teaching experience. She does not regret the loss in hindsight, reflecting on a friend who won the chapter chair at her school while untenured, became embroiled in conflict with the principal, and was soon fired. A year later, now holding tenure and with stronger relations with her colleagues, she was elected chapter delegate, a position similar to vice-chair. She became active in the broader union, leading to her awareness of MORE:

> I started going to Delegate Assembly meetings. Of course my chapter leader was like, you don't really have to go. It's not important, no one goes. I went to a couple and I was like, "Wow these aren't important, nothing happens!" [Laughs] It also kind of sucks. The speakers are really loud. It's like Mulgrew talking. My attendance that first year was not great. But towards the end of the year, there were a couple of times when people from MORE would speak up. Actually there was the resolution about specialized high schools and how they were unequal. That got my attention. I wanted to hang out with those people; they're saying smart things, they're bringing up good ideas. They're not just sitting here doing nothing. (Ibid.)

Adopting some ideas from her MORE colleagues, she was pleased with increased levels of activity she saw in her school chapter, leading to plans for further involvement on her part:

> People have become more interested in union stuff because this year for every meeting I've sent out detailed minutes ... When we did our evaluation petition [an initiative by MORE concerning teacher evaluations], I got our chapter to endorse it. People said yes. There have been a couple [of] other little actions we've done as a chapter. And to the UFT's credit, they've started to do a little more stuff that calls for people to be participatory. So whenever that happens, I jump on it and try to get my chapter to do it. Or whenever there's an event, I say, "I'm going, who wants to come?" So more people have taken an interest in union stuff. But we don't have regular meetings or anything like that ... I've been frustrated with my chapter leader in the ways he's not been doing his job, now that I have a clear picture of what that job is, and so I've been thinking about running for a while. (Ibid.)

Meanwhile, she increased her involvement in MORE. From 2013, she served multiple six-month terms on its steering committee, participating in discussions on the direction of the caucus. In her time, the group overcame various internal political tensions. According to her and other participants, generational differences among activists were sometimes evident. As a large generalization, across gender and race (though MORE, reflecting the composition of teachers in NYC, is predominantly white) older activists were more likely to focus on strategizing and organizing to win chapter elections and expand the presence of the caucus in the larger union, leading to the 2016 UFT elections. Younger teachers tended to be drawn to discussions and workshops focused on building alliances with parents and high school students, emphasizing an anti-racist framework. They were also more likely to identify politically with the radical left than their older colleagues, who were more social democratic. The caucus was concentrated in the city's high schools, despite several primary and middle-school teachers among its founders and steering committee. At a meeting looking ahead to the fall 2016 union elections, the caucus set goals to double its share of the vote for executive positions from 18 per cent to 35 per cent and increase its base of supporters among chapter chairs and delegates in the union's monthly Delegate Assembly from roughly 80 to 200. The caucus was notably lacking in hubris over the prospects of actually winning seats on the union's executive.

In addition to joining the Opt Out coalition against standardized testing as discussed below, MORE has collaborated with "Right to Play," a group of teachers, students, and parents campaigning for athletics funding for the city's small schools. According to the group, 17,000 students of colour attend city high schools with no sports activites, owing to the DOE's funding structure, which favours larger schools. Their struggle is an intersection of how small secondary schools have facilitated a narrowing of focus on test preparation and perpetuated inequity amid racial and class segregation. Led by students, Right to Play has rallied outside DOE offices and met with city councillors. Three activist teachers have been fired, accused of supporting students engaged in civil disobedience at a rally in Albany; to the charges was added a critique of MORE for the official UFT's protection of its members. Right to Play members claim to have received little official support from the UFT, but they attend MORE's organizing meetings, where the caucus agrees to support their campaign.[41]

I arrived at Carroll Public School, set in the heart of a neighbourhood of well-groomed brownstone townhouses in Brooklyn for a MORE conference in October 2015. Two high-end toy stores and two private tutoring companies operated within a block. Suggesting the political power of the neighbourhood, they were joined by the cheerful storefront office of the district's state assemblywoman. The primary school was immaculately clean, the hallways and auditorium covered with beautiful student artwork. The classrooms where we held our sessions were like a photo from a government press conference on education policy. An American flag hung from the wall next to the blackboard, waving over neatly labelled baskets of picture books and art supplies. It was difficult to imagine here that any sort of crisis existed in US education.

About 120 people, including a contingent of parent activists involved in the Opt Out movement, assembled in the auditorium. A plenary panel included one of these parents, who explained why she joined the movement after seeing a narrowing of her child's 3rd grade curriculum to test prep. "My teacher knows my daughter better than any test score," she said, to cheers from the audience. Outspoken anti-testing activist, elementary teacher, and union chapter chair at the Earth School in Manhattan, Jia Lee was introduced as MORE's candidate for union president, to challenge Michael Mulgrew, candidate for the governing Unity caucus.[42] Through Lee's efforts in April 2015, parents at her small K–4 school opted 104 students out of the state reading and math exams, a majority of those enrolled (Rodriguez 2015). She hailed a successful recent strike by Seattle teachers for having won the elimination of value-added assessments in teacher evaluations, guaranteed thirty-minute recesses in primary schools, limits to Special Education and ESL workloads, and investigations on the racialization of student discipline – all of which were greatly needed in NYC, she argued. Lee explained, as would others throughout the conference, that the defining issue on which the Caucus of Rank and File Educators (CORE), MORE's greatest source of inspiration, built community alliances and ran successfully for leadership of the Chicago Teachers Union was opposing waves of school closures in predominantly black and Latinx neighbourhoods. The issue on which MORE would seek to define itself would be offering a clear voice against high-stakes testing and as an enthusiastic ally of the emerging parent-led movement.

Alongside a determination to build alliances with parents, evident in the discourse and the content of the conference, was a self-conscious effort to engage in a form of policy mobility, sharing the strategies of other US teacher caucuses and unions. Participants in a workshop on racial justice sat among several tables, each with an "artefact" representing the activism of teachers' caucuses and unions in NYC, Seattle, Chicago, and Los Angeles. Lessons learned about policies promoting restorative justice, lower class sizes, prioritizing recruitment of teachers of colour, and delinking teacher testing from evaluations were discussed and proposed for MORE's upcoming election platform. Present on the closing plenary were members of the Social Equality Caucus, MORE's equivalent within the Seattle Education Association, and Philadelphia's version, the Caucus of Working Educators. All are affiliated with the United Caucus of Rank and File Educators (UCORE) described in chapter 2.

I encountered Jen in the hallway. It was six months since I had interviewed her and her colleague Karen at their school on the Upper West

Side. At the end of last June, Karen was fired by her principal after receiving an Ineffective rating in her annual evaluation and being burdened by low student test scores on the Regents. Jen had been elected chapter delegate. "Overwhelmingly," she said proudly. Jen was still unsure of her future employment prospects. "I've already filed two grievances. No superintendent in NYC is going to give me tenure," she said. Now in her sixth year, she would go up for tenure again in spring 2016. Her principal was still pushing the Learning Cultures curriculum on the staff. According to Jen, most of her young colleagues still keep their heads down and work towards gaining tenure. Despite her precariousness, she presses ahead with her activism, wanting to do more but limited by the time constraints of the job.

In the 2016 UFT election, MORE and their allies won all seven seats reserved for high school teachers on the union's executive board. President Mulgrew and his colleagues were handily re-elected, but MORE presidential candidate Jia Lee received over 10,000 votes, doubling the caucus's presidential vote in the previous election in 2013. Overall UFT member turnout in the 2016 election rose from 18 per cent to 24 per cent (MORE 2016). After a year serving as a chapter leader, having not received tenure, Jen left teaching and entered law school. Following the 2016 US presidential election, NYC teacher activists organized inside and outside of the UFT to oppose the entry of immigration agents into the city's schools to deport undocumented students. President Trump's education secretary, billionaire Betsy DeVos, had no experience within public education and was a major proponent of private school vouchers in Michigan. In the aftermath of the high-profile 2018 Supreme Court Janus decision allowing public sector employees in unionized workplaces to opt out of paying dues, DeVos subsidized campaigns urging teachers in New York and elsewhere to do so. While she is a powerful national figurehead of the neoliberal agenda for education, so far, she has fortunately lacked the legislative power of her predecessors under George W. Bush and Barack Obama.

Of the three case studies in this book, it is in New York City that the work of teachers has been the most transformed by neoliberal policy. This is not to say that the context here for public education or, for that matter, teacher unionism is the most acute or dire. (For that view I guide my reader to the next chapter.) However, in terms of the subordination of professional autonomy, what it means to be a teacher has to the greatest extent been neoliberalized here. Like other major US cities with predominantly black and Latinx working-class students, in the North under the Democratic Party's electoral hegemony, old ward patronage politics converged and acquiesced to new technocratic forms of neoliberal governance such as mayoral control. Just as important as understanding the extent of this project, is its unevenness across local and state jurisdictions. NYC as a site of experimentation in transforming teachers' work can be contrasted with its immediate suburbs, where far more continuity exists, ironically the base of the strongest contemporary movement against the neoliberalization of education in New York State. Even among other old racialized and gentrifying urban centres, important differences can be found. Charter schools have not expanded at nearly as rapid a rate in NYC as they have in Philadelphia, Detroit, Chicago, Los Angeles, and DC, despite the unparalleled concentration of corporate power in downtown Manhattan and its far-reaching political alliances (McKenna 2015).

However, the workforce has been profoundly remade through the intersection of small schools, managerial principals, school choice, and changes to tenure from the tying of annual evaluations to student test scores. Nevertheless, in response to the strength of the Opt Out movement, the Cuomo administration abruptly reversed its misguided plan to fire teachers by increasing the linkage of evaluations to test scores. This experience suggests how, even in this context, neoliberal policy is politically vulnerable to organized resistance. Meanwhile, the scaling-up to Albany resembles similar dynamics in Illinois, Pennsylvania, Florida, and Michigan, where conservative state capitols move to establish rule over spatially removed contentious urban centres. As the local UFT is faced with a new spatial vulnerability, could the network building of grass-roots caucuses offer a possible future model of social movement teacher unionism? MORE has made a start, but so far, faced with a far vaster terrain on which to organize and a much more entrenched incumbent leadership to challenge, it has not yet made the same breakthroughs as its allies in Chicago and Los Angeles have.

4 Mexico City

Preface: Día del Maestro

I arrived at Isabel's secondary school in the borough of Iztapalapa in the early afternoon, during recess.[1] Around 1,000 students were enrolled from 7:30 am to 1:40 p.m., with 800 more from 2 pm to 8:10 p.m. Most primary and secondary schools in Mexico City operate on this two-shift structure, owing to a shortage of buildings in crowded poor and working class neighbourhoods.[2] It was the day before 15 May, Día del Maestro (Teachers' Day), a national holiday when schools are closed. School loudspeakers blared the 1960s ballad "To Sir, With Love" while students mingled in the crowded central courtyard. A special lunch was served for teachers in the staffroom, of chicken mole and rice, followed by cake. In front of the assembled staff, the principal read a prepared speech on the importance of educators. Some teachers were presented with large, home-made thank-you cards signed by their students. The festivities soon ended, and teachers dispersed to meet their classes.

I chatted for a few minutes with Mauricio, who was not scheduled to teach in the next period and was marking a stack of math tests. It was his first year here, having previously worked in a private school. The public system offered higher salaries and more labour rights, but working conditions in the private school were better, with classes of around twenty students and more parental support. Asked about the limit on the number of students in a secondary school class, he thought for a moment and replied, "Well, fifty is the maximum number of students and desks that can physically fit into a room." Under these conditions, he observed, "You can't turn your back to work individually with a student because the rest of the class will be out of control." While I was talking with Mauricio, another teacher walked in and sat at a nearby table with his lunch, making a face in my direction. "Don't worry, he's not with the INEE" (the national education evaluation agency), Mauricio laughed, pointing at me. "You're not though, right?" he quickly asked. My answer was sufficiently reassuring that his colleague joined our table and shared his cookies. Later, Mauricio showed me a couple of his classrooms. The walls were bare and grey, with a large whiteboard at the front. There was no art, student work, books, or any other distinctive features. Nearly all of the room was taken up by desks and chairs. All of the classrooms I saw in the school were the same. Each period, teachers rotated between rooms that housed several classes and a couple of hundred students over the two shifts.

I returned on another day and joined Isabel's civics and ethics class. It is now near the end of the school year and students were preparing for their exams. A civics teacher for eight years, in addition to an education degree she had a degree in psychology. Like most teachers with less than twenty years' service, she was employed part time, assigned twenty hours spread over afternoons. To augment her income, she practised psychology from her home in the morning. Some colleagues ran convenience stores out of their homes with their families or drove taxis. Her class offered an exciting respite for the students. After the students stacked their desks and chairs along the wall, she placed a portable speaker connected to her MP3 player on a desk in the middle of the now cleared room. Their task was to practise their flash mob routine, which they would perform in front of the school the next week. Several mothers were there to participate. Isabel presses "play," and everyone began dancing, adjusting their moves to the changes in tempo and rhythm prescribed in the instructional song. After a couple of rounds, Isabel told the students to reorganize their desks and sit down. She reiterated the purpose of the activity: to de-stress and to promote non-violence and cooperation. The students and parents moved into the groups they had been in since the start of the semester, in order to plan their performances. Each student had been assigned a role within their group, overseen by Isabel. I said goodbye and left the classroom, walking across the now quiet courtyard, through the gate, and onto a busy street where I caught a bus back to the Metro.

This chapter describes how the neoliberalization of education affected the professional autonomy of Mexico City's teachers from the mid-1990s through 2017. In contrast to the previous chapter, which focused on initiatives led by municipal and state authorities with the federal government in the background, far greater attention is placed here on the impact of national policies on education governance. This is due to the highly centralized nature of the Mexican state, a tendency that, despite some reversals during the decline of the Institutional Revolutionary

Party (PRI) in the 1990s, has only increased in the early twenty-first century. Another major difference is the interweaving throughout this chapter of the opposing roles of the official "institutional" National Union of Education Workers (Sindicato Nacional de los Trabajadores de la Educación; SNTE), and its internal dissident movement, the National Coordination of Education Workers (Coordinadora Nacional de los Trabajadores de la Educación; CNTE). Historically, the SNTE has been controlled by the state, while the CNTE has struggled since its founding in 1979 to democratize the union while aggressively challenging policies of the Mexican government, which it considers harmful to its members and public education more broadly. Both have a higher relative prominence than the New York UFT or MORE, discussed in chapter 3, for proposing or contesting policy affecting the teachers at the centre of this case study.

I begin by contextualizing attempts by the Mexican government to decentralize the burgeoning education authority in the 1990s, centred on the Mexico City megapolis, through efforts to curb the power of the SNTE over the system under the tightening control of Elba Esther Gordillo (section 4.1). I then describe how the Quality Schools Program (PEC) of President Vicente Fox, while purporting to increase "school autonomy," in fact amounted to centralizing authority at the expense of teachers' professional autonomy, particularly by introducing the ENLACE standardized exam. The extent to which this national policy affected Mexico City schools is assessed (section 4.2).

Next, we consider the 2008 Alliance for Quality Education (Alianza por la Calidad Educativa; ACE) (section 4.3). A product of Gordillo's increasingly neoliberalized power over education policy, the ACE claimed to rationalize teacher hiring and make continued employment contingent on standardized exams taken by the teachers and, after 2011, the ENLACE. However, because the ACE was significantly undermined by the opposition of the CNTE, President Enrique Peña Nieto strove again to implement its key policies after his election in 2012 (section 4.4). He enacted an effective scalar strategy that undermined the regionally concentrated basis of the CNTE, including its relative weakness in Mexico City. To do so, he strengthened transnational policy alliances both with the OECD and with domestic business lobbyists and opposition parties, while marginalizing the SNTE.

The resulting Ley de Servicio Profesional Docente has had a strong impact on teachers' professional autonomy by undermining teacher training colleges (section 4.5) and through the use of an examination that does not recognize classroom teaching (section 4.6). All of these measures interact within a context of increasingly precarious employment conditions for Mexico City's secondary teachers and changing teacher-school director power relations, both affecting their ability to exercise professional autonomy (section 4.7). This chapter concludes by considering factors behind the uneven response of teachers in Mexico City to national education policies in relation to that of more militant teachers in southeastern states (section 4.8).

4.1. Transitions in State Power, Decentralization, and the Emergence of Elba Esther Gordillo's SNTE as a Key Neoliberal Actor

From the 1990s, Mexico's federalization process occurred within the context of decentralization as the dominant policy idea within education governance in Latin America. As discussed in chapter 2, this model of governance within the region was circulated through forums hosted by UNESCO and particularly the World Bank, which exercises editorial discretion in cultivating its roster of recommended policies (Peck and Theodore 2015) and offered loans for their implementation (Messina 2008). Graciela Messina makes a distinction between decentralization programs initiated from the top down as opposed to in response to popular demands. The latter are motivated by desires for increasing local participation while maintaining central responsibility for funding. The former are more common in both developed and developing countries, and are associated with processes of neoliberalization in which central state funding is typically substituted for private financing. Messina also identifies parallel or subsequent processes of "recentralization," in which the central government re-establishes power through national standardized tests and other top-down policies that have adverse impacts on teachers' professionalism. This is indeed the direction taken by Mexico's education policymakers from the 2000s onwards; strong examples are found throughout this chapter, including the Quality Schools Program (PEC), the ENLACE exam, the ACE, and the Professional Teaching Service Law (Ley de Servicio Profesional Docente). Policies like these have evoked strong opposition from teachers' unions across Latin America for their impact on working conditions, salary, and overall funding except in Mexico, Messina notes, owing to the corporatist nature of the SNTE (2008, 42–3). Resistance here has instead been led primarily by the dissident CNTE.

Secretary of Education Manuel Bartlett significantly furthered decentralization in 1992 by introducing the Acuerdo Nacional para la Modernización de la Educación Basica (National Accord for the Modernization of Basic Education; ANMEB) (Marquez Ayala 2008,

156). Responsibility for negotiations over teacher salaries and a wider range of economic issues shifted from the federal government to the states, along with oversight of day-to-day system administration, the ability to add some locally developed course content, and licensing of the growing number of private schools (Brambila 2008, 218–19). The SEP's national offices retained final oversight of programs of study and course curriculum, the free national textbooks, the school calendar, and the teacher education curriculum, among other areas (Marquez Ayala 2008, 158; Hecock 2014, 66–7). One of the ANMEB's most direct impacts on teacher professionalism was through a different trajectory of decentralization. The capacity of zone inspectors to evaluate teachers' work was increased by formalizing their oversight over annual exams and hence the way teachers interpreted the expansive curriculum, in forms that will be described below in relation to the PEC (Martin 1994, 88–90).

However, with the exception of the latter policy, these waves of reforms left Mexico City's school system relatively unaffected. As the Federal District lacked the constitutional powers of Mexico's thirty-one states, the governance of its basic education system from preschool through secondary school, as well as the normales, remained directly under the control of the national SEP (Arnaut 2008). To administer the second-largest system after Mexico State, with the largest overall budget, a sub-secretary for the DF was created in 1993. In 2005 it was renamed the Administración Federal de Servicios Educativos en el DF (Federal Administration of Education Services in the Federal District; AFSEDF), with new departments for secondary technical schools and a unified department for Iztapalapa, by far the city's largest borough in terms of students, schools, and staff (ibid., 147).

According to Alberto Arnaut, the DF's education system was not decentralized to the city government partially because of a mutual interest of the SEP and national SNTE leaders not to potentially destabilize the three largest SNTE sections in the country by undermining their subordination to the national union. The position of local dissidents, especially in Section 9 (primary teachers), could have been strengthened if they had been able to negotiate directly with a less monolithic city government, governed since 1997 by the centre-left Party of the Democratic Revolution (PRD). Until it won constitutional status equal to a state in 2016, the DF government also lacked many of the states' budgetary powers. According to one AFSEDF official, the DF government didn't want the complications of administering over 5,000 schools and tens of thousands of teachers (AFSEDF Official 1, interview Feb. 2015). However, writing in a publication of the Mexico City government, Messina (2008) and Marquez Ayala (2008) maintain that this has been a goal of the DF, complicated by political differences between its PRD administration and the PRI or PAN-led federal government. The Mexico City government created the Secretaria de la Educación del DF (SEDF) in 2007 to administer its increasing involvement in the provisioning of upper-level high school and post-secondary education. According to Arnaut (2008, 152), this change created a possibility for eventually taking over responsibility for the city's basic education as well.

The divergent experience of federalization between Mexico City and the rest of the country would contribute to the uneven rollout of national education policies impacting teachers' professional autonomy in the renewed centralism of the 2000s. The influence of the CNTE in Mexico City was confined by not being able to negotiate directly with the DF's centre-left administration, against which it could apply more pressure than it could against the national government. However, in various ways described below, from the quantifiable (Mexico City's relatively favourable education funding levels) to the more nebulous (the politically strategic position of its teachers), the DF was somewhat insulated from the more contentious policies that followed from the governments of Fox, Calderon, and SNTE leader Elba Esther Gordillo herself. Subsequently, it would also help explain the lower degree of militancy in Mexico City's Sections 9 and 10, compared with the bastions of the CNTE in the southeast of the country.

Gordillo flexed her muscles for the first time on the national stage with the negotiation of the Carrera Magisterial in 1993. At this time, early in her tenure as general secretary, Gordillo's control still rested to a great degree on the consent of the restive membership, earned through winning material gains, rather than on its later basis that was primarily in elite power relations and wealth. Following Hecock's (2014) description, she deployed her institutional influence among state and national political figures from the PRI and the PAN as well as the SEP, to ameliorate the impact of a typically anti-union, neoliberal policy of merit pay for some members, in both its establishment and its operation. In the process, Carrera Magisterial helped consolidate her influence and power over the union's membership and in relation to the government.

The PRI governments of Salinas and Zedillo developed and implemented Carrera Magisterial, presented to the public as a policy that would improve the "quality" of education, under a neoliberal rationale that teachers would work harder if they were rewarded for alleged improvements in their capacities. This improvement was measured "objectively" through standardized tests of their own competencies and those of their students. It was an "instrumental rationality, against a work ethic based on commitment and loyalty to education as an end" (Leyva Piña and Rodriguez Lagunas 2012, 560; author's translation). According to Leyva Piña and Rodriguez Lagunas, it also had a hidden agenda of slowly transforming labour relations and teachers' culture by contributing to a gradual undermining of the collective nature of the union (ibid., 553). This view was supported by a CNTE leader in Mexico City during the 1990s, who saw in it a strategy by the government to widely differentiate teacher salaries in order to prevent the kind of groundswell caused by a common low salary, which precipitated the 1989 national strike (CNTE Section 10 Activist, interview Feb. 2015). On the basis of its removal of salaries from a common ground of negotiation, it was strongly opposed by the CNTE (Leyva Piña and Rodriguez Lagunas 2012, 559). Carrera Magisterial was a system of economic incentives achieved by meeting a list of criteria. Seniority and degrees having been obtained, the traditional basis on which teachers (and many other workers) moved up salary scales totalled 25 per cent. However, under the new system the following gains would be possible: completion of professional development 17 per cent; results of tests measuring professional expertise 28 per cent; evaluation of a supervisor 10 per cent; and student test score results 20 per cent (Hecock 2014, 69).

Through Gordillo's successful negotiations, unlike conventional merit pay structures where teachers can see their salaries go up or down annually based on test scores, thus creating considerable insecurity (Ravitch 2013b; Kuhn 2014), salary increases gained through the system would be permanent. In contrast to schemes in the United States and elsewhere, participation was voluntary, but non-participants would receive smaller negotiated salary increases. The size of the increases offered through Carrera Magisterial would also be negotiated annually with the national SNTE. Teachers who obtained the first level, where 60 per cent of participants remained, earned a 24.5 per cent increase over their base salary. A further 25 per cent ascended to level two, but less than one teacher or school director in 2,000 ascended to the fifth and final level, which offered triple the base salary (Hecock 2014, 69). Estimates of the total number of teachers who elected to participate varied widely. Hecock reported about two-thirds during the 2000s (ibid.), while the CNTE activist cited above estimated that 40 per cent of his colleagues in Mexico City were enrolled, though he said the SEP claimed twice this number (CNTE Section 10 Activist, interview Feb. 2015). Responsibility for the program's data collection (e.g., performance on teacher tests, student test scores, completion of courses, seniority) was assigned to both state and national SEP offices, the latter tallying results and then sending recommendations for promotion to state governments. At the national level and in participating states, where administrative capacities and enthusiasm for the program varied widely, the SNTE was able to effectively apply leverage through various underhanded means, according to Hecock's informants in state SEP offices, to influence the passage of teachers into the program and turn the Carrera into "a potential patronage tool to strengthen the position of union leaders" (2014, 69). Although the Carrera's original neoliberal objective of removing teacher compensation from labour negotiations and making it contingent on external variables controlled by the state was to a considerable extent subverted – a shift that surely benefited many teachers – it left them subordinated to another authority. US academic Bradley Levinson found that among teachers in Michoacan in the mid- to late 1990s, it was entered into by some, but "maligned by most, who found it corrupt and divisive" (2001, 239). Aboites (2012) observed that the SEP was unable to provide significant evidence to the public that the Carrera Magisterial actually increased student achievement, claiming that mainly it provided useful information to the national SEP. Brambila (2008) reached similar conclusions. In this case, Aboites argued, teachers should simply receive regular salary increases (2012, 829–30).

Another initiative bundled with the Carrera Magisterial was a standardized exam on subject knowledge and teaching practices for entry into the teaching profession. It was opposed by the CNTE for undermining the ability of normale schools and faculties of education to determine successful graduates based on a command of pedagogy, on a comprehensive basis not possible on a written test. If implemented transparently, it would also undermine clientelistic practices employed by local SNTE sections and SEP officials of distributing jobs. Each state could decide whether to participate, but only thirteen of thirty-two were doing so by 2003, and only five assigned all new positions through the exam (Senate of Mexico 2016, 3). Its impact was limited. Believers in entrance exams as an effective accessor of teacher quality would push again for its implementation on a national scale through the ACE in 2008.

Meanwhile, Gordillo tightened her control over the union. She ensured that the calling of general conventions by which state executives were elected, and the confirmation of the legitimacy of their outcome, continued to rest solely with the national executive, which she controlled. CNTE-led states continued to exert considerable pressure on the SNTE via the federal government every three years for these conventions to be convened fairly.[3] Gordillo's power was demonstrated in 2004, through the creation of the new top position of president, to which she was summarily promoted from general secretary. In 2007, the national SNTE convention suspended rules prevalent in nearly all arenas of Mexican politics prohibiting re-election or setting strict term limits, allowing her to potentially become "president for life" (Leyva Piña and Rodriguez Lagunas 2012, 550–1). Her further entrenchment and sometimes ham-fisted efforts to impose her hand-picked leaders in state locals created dissent among a range of otherwise loyal, anti-CNTE officials who saw their own ambitions blocked or who opposed her rupture with the PRI.[4] However, in 2012 she was appointed to another newly created top position, that of president of the General Union Council for the Strengthening of Public Education by unanimous vote of 3,230 convention delegates (Bensusan and Middlebrook 2013, 78; Hernandez Navarro 2012, 394–5).

From this vantage point, Gordillo's "golden age" of power peaked under the PAN governments of Fox and Calderon, intervening in national politics and using her position to endorse the neoliberal reforms of the education sector of her allies or author them herself. She was widely viewed as the most powerful woman in Mexico. Leyva Piña and Rodriguez Lagunas (2012) argue that under Gordillo, the SNTE distinguished itself from other corporatist unions by ascending in influence rather than declining after the end of the rule of the PRI in 2000 under which it had been nurtured. Gordillo faced limits on her power under PRI presidents Salinas and Zedillo. By carrying her influence[5] over to the PAN she won the gratitude of Fox and Calderon, particularly in the case of the latter's tiny margin of victory, widely viewed to have been fraudulent (Bensusan and Middlebrook 2013, 79–80; Hernandez Navarro 2012, 410). She was appointed director of the National Lottery and of the Social Security Institute (ISSSTE), which administers healthcare and pensions for the nation's public employees. In addition to these patronage posts, she was given real power within the SEP: a veto over the appointment of sub-secretaries for basic education and senior administrators of Mexico City's school authority, the AFSEDF (highly strategic in her efforts to gain control over Sections 9 and 10). She had a voice in the presidential appointment of secretaries of education. One, Josefina Vazquez Mota (PAN presidential candidate in 2012), was substituted by Calderon halfway through her term, owing to conflicts with Gordillo, with a mutually agreeable replacement. To help rehabilitate the negative public image of herself and the SNTE, Calderon's administration subsidized an educational TV program on Televisa,[6] *All the World Believes in You*, oriented to parents and children, in which she and the SNTE were portrayed favourably (Leyva Piña and

Rodriguez Lagunas 2012, 539–42; Bensusan and Middlebrook 2013, 82). The SNTE under Gordillo held far more institutional power within the state (though generally not for the benefit of its members, students, or the broader public) than education unions in Toronto, Ontario, or New York City or State. In this context, where nearly full support from the SNTE was under Gordillo's control, the PAN administrations pursued policies that saw a re-centralization of education governance, though changes were less dramatic in federalized Mexico City. However, these policies posed serious challenges for the professional autonomy of all Mexican teachers.

4.2. Re-centralized Governance through School-Based Competition

The Quality Schools Program (Programa de Escuelas de Calidad; PEC) was the signature eduction initiative of the Vicente Fox PAN government of 2001 to 2006. It was expanded through the terms of Calderon and Peña Nieto, though in a diluted form. While the program was limited to urban primary schools, it had a significant impact on the basic education system as a whole. The PEC introduced both a large-scale national competitive structure for education funding, an organization external to the SEP to oversee competition in 2002, the National Institute for the Evaluation of Education (INEE); and also the premise for a national standardized exam for both upper primary and secondary students, the ENLACE, established in 2006. These developments led to a similar trajectory for Mexican teachers, as increased emphasis on the Regents exams and primary school testing in New York under Governor Cuomo made for his state's teachers: a subordination of classroom instruction to the imperative of test preparation and more space for managers (in Mexico's case, zone supervisors more than school directors) to intervene in pedagogy under the premise of raising scores. The school-based management mechanism within PEC also advanced privatization, where it succeeded in substituting private financing for federal funding. Each of these initiatives was supported by Elba Esther Gordillo's SNTE and strongly opposed by the CNTE, to the extent of succeeding in partially or fully exempting states from these programs where the movement was strongest (Leyva Piña and Rodriguez Lagunas 2012, 555). At the conclusion of this section, I will attempt to assess the specific impact of these national programs on Mexico City.

The PEC consisted of a national competition whereby urban primary schools would compete on the basis of a complex rubric of qualitative and quantitative measures for additional funding to be used according to a proposal authored by the school's director, teachers, and interested parents. It promised to improve student achievement as measured in graduation rates and with ENLACE through standardized test scores. In 2001, its first year, 300,000 peso grants were awarded to 1,500 urban primary schools. In 2004, the grants were halved to 150,000 pesos but extended to 20,000 schools, approximately 1 in 10 of Mexico's 194,775 public kindergartens, primaries, and secondary schools, of which 90,000 were considered to be in "deplorable conditions" regarding repair, according to the SEP (Aboites 2012, 839). The total number of participating primary schools had reached 40,000 by 2009 (ibid., 853). PEC grants declined to 20,000 pesos by 2015 (AFSEDF Official 1, interviewed Feb. 2015). The analysis below will focus on the first eight years of the program during its greatest influence.

Funding for the PEC was provided by grants and loans from the World Bank (Hernandez Navarro 2013). According to Teresa Bracho, an academic affiliated with the OECD and author of the definitive study commissioned by the SEP and the INEE on the effectiveness of the PEC from 2001 to 2007, the PEC emerged from ideas developed by education policymakers in the United States and the United Kingdom, subsequently endorsed and circulated in literature by the World Bank and OECD, around "school quality and effectiveness" and "social participation."[7] The latter was described as a hallmark of School-Based Management (SBM), increasing parental involvement to identify school needs, and the procurement of private sector support to finance them. Bracho locates the PEC within a continuum of decentralization policies within 1980s–2000s Mexico:

> [Decentralization] implicates combining various levels of government that in a vertical sense are implicated in the operations of programs (national, state, municipal and school-level), with the opening of spaces in a horizontal sense, for the participation of new actors from private and social sectors, through the reactivation of venues of citizen's participation ... as with the receipt of economic support on the part of parents and private organizations in a schema of co-financing. (2009, 37; author's translation)

She further distinguishes variations within SBM based on the concentration of decision-making to principals (as in NYC), teachers, or parent committees. Integral is the concept of school staff (administrators and teachers) being reflexive about how to improve teaching and whole school practices and collegiality. Power relations between administrators and teachers within these structures are not explicitly defined, though emphasis is placed on the importance of both the *quality* of administrative leadership (as in much of the mainstream US education policy literature) and buy-in from teachers (ibid., 17–39).

A key question is the line between teachers exercising their professional judgment through initiatives such as SBM to locally identify and respond to the specific needs of their students and becoming accomplices to neoliberalization by "taking ownership," often alongside parents, of the systemic under-resourcing of schools by the state. Perhaps this distinction can be made at the point where teachers (and parents) accept the use of standardized tests to measure the success of their schools through SBM initiatives, as is typically the case. By legitimizing this form of evaluation, the importance of systemic socio-economic context and the need for greater across-the-board funding increases is obscured. Instead, a debate on the effectiveness of individual teachers is brought to the foreground, in a zero-sum competition for essential resources amid systemic austerity. Parental involvement is manipulated to further the privatization of education when the identification of unmet needs is only to commit to fundraising or to pursue private sector sponsorships to meet them, as Bracho acknowledges, is in fact encouraged under SBM to augment a modest increase in resources from the state (2009, 37). In response to these dynamics, the CNTE-led union section of Michocan argued that the PEC removed the responsibility of the state to provide all schools with essential maintenance funding. In the context of a sympathetic PRD state government in the 2000s, its proposal for across-the-board funding increases was enacted in place of the PEC (Leyva Piña and Rodriguez Lagunas 2012, 556)

Bracho acknowledges that while the funds awarded through PEC were intended to support increased professional development and training for teachers to directly improve classroom instruction and thereby student achievement, in practice, most funding went towards more basic school needs. This fact was unsurprising, in light of the proportion of schools mentioned earlier in desperate need of such resources by the SEP's own reckoning. How these needs affected both the capacity of teachers to do their work and the students' experience of their school, were clearly visible in my visits to secondary schools in Mexico City from 2015 to 2017. The lack of space in overcrowded schools in working-class Iztapalapa, meant that desks and chairs occupied nearly all the space in each classroom, making it difficult to teach through instructional strategies such as group work, differentiated learning circles, or any form not based on rows. Teachers were not allowed to use the one photocopier, located in the school's office, and few classroom digital projectors functioned (installed several years ago as part of a technology initiative, but without funding for ongoing maintenance). Both shortcomings tended towards a reliance on teaching through the abundant, free textbooks and use of the whiteboard at the front of every room. However, many teachers demonstrated an ingenuity in classroom activities which required few costly material resources.[8] The most sophisticated technology in each school was a biometric scanner to verify teacher attendance. While peeling paint and dirty windows are common in New York's and Toronto's schools, in Mexico City most plumbing fixtures appeared not to work and free drinking water was non-existent (the case everywhere in Mexico). Most secondary schools had wireless internet, funded by the Mexico City government. As will be discussed below, with an above average rate of federal funding supplemented by greater municipal funding, the physical condition of Mexico City schools is among the best in the nation (Arnaut 2008).[9] According to the Citizen's Observatory of Education, two years into the PEC half of the funds at the school level were used for maintenance and construction. Most of the rest was dedicated to furniture, books, and equipment, and only 1 per cent was used for the professional development of teachers (Aboites 2012, 837).[10]

The competition for additional school resources through PEC had significant implications for teachers' professional autonomy. Participation in the PEC involved a substantial increase in workload for teachers, in an evaluative process that was in practice far more prescribed than was initially portrayed. The school's application for the PEC and its subsequent evaluation by the SEP required constant staff meetings to write reports on its ten Specific Objectives:

> The teacher ends up subsidizing – with a free increase in their productivity – the resources that arrive at the school from PEC, because the program converts into the extraordinary what should be ordinary: that each school should receive the resources to meet its basic necessities and create the necessary conditions to work. (Ibid., 837; author's translation)

The PEC utilized a progressive discourse of encouraging the participation of teachers, students, and parents through horizontal power relations centred on the school site. However, Aboites (2012) argues that, confronted by the established tendency in the Carrera Magisterial towards standardized evaluation, in practice it was highly bureaucratic. As happened in the NYC small schools movement, an initially progressive discourse that claimed to empower teachers' professional autonomy and combine it with greater community participation was, in practice, like school choice and its use of test scores to rate schools, subordinated to structures of neoliberal governance. Schools competed with others in their zone for increases in funding mainly for critical maintenance. Increased centralized control and surveillance through the use of standardized testing determined school applications for entry to PEC. Fox, his secretary of education, and the developers of PEC articulated a philosophy of education in which the intrinsic value of learning (for students) and service (for teachers) was an insufficient motivator for improvement. They needed to be pushed by competition for greater resources and the potential for their loss (ibid., 829, 833–4).

Aboites relates these dynamics to a "business strategy" of incentivizing worker productivity combined with deskilling, harkening back to Frederick Taylor, the father of scientific management theory in the United States. Aboites argues that school proposals were obliged to hew closely to criteria set by program evaluators at the national SEP offices or risk not getting approved, in contrast to the program's purported objective of empowering local schools, which best know local conditions. He cites an example given by the PEC director of the initial rejection of a proposal from a school in Hidalgo prior to his intervention. Its staff and parents had chosen to focus on improving "values," owing to significant social problems including drug abuse and absenteeism among students, rather than on the recommended emphasis on raising math and Spanish test scores (ibid., 835, 837). Contrary to horizontal collaboration, Aboites found that competition between schools in a local zone for PEC funding discouraged winning schools from sharing their strategies. The competitive structure of applications meant that the neediest schools frequently did not get grants. The process tended to favour the most organized schools with strong parental participation and the highest test scores.

The increased importance of exam results, particularly after the creation of the ENLACE in 2006 in PEC applications, increased the importance of zone inspectors and regional supervisors (superintendents) of schools in relation to their staff, whom they pushed to standardize their projects (ibid., 843) As in NYC, they now had a rationale for regularly intervening in the classroom. Beneath regional supervisors and immediately above school directors, zone inspectors were responsible for overseeing teaching practices and student evaluation and graduation policies in around a dozen schools, in one of which they had their office. From his anthropological observations of secondary schools in Guadalajara, Christopher Martin describes the role of the inspector:

> The basis of the inspector's authority is her forceful pursuit of technical controls on teaching ... [she] carries with it a particular discourse, a form of intercommunication in the zone with its talk of qualifications, paperwork,

> tests, competitions ... In addition the sheer weight and frequency of work load demands create a momentum from which the teachers find it difficult to escape. Finally, the inspector emanates a strong personal presence, the force of which make[s] the teachers work hard which, due to its all-embracing character, its relative constancy and its depth of penetration can only be described as panoptic. (1994, 91)

Though Martin's observations were made before the 2000s' wave of centralization reforms, contemporary comments from Mexico City teachers suggest that it remains accurate for inspectors owing their position to senior SEP officials. Many zone inspectors and regional supervisors held their positions more because of approval from the SNTE hierarchy under Gordillo's control than from their actual employer, making the zeal with which they pursued education reforms highly variable.

The process of the PEC evaluation included the following steps. Teachers and school directors had to assess the success of their school in meeting PEC objectives, which were officially claimed to be locally developed but in practice emerged out of a centrally defined rubric. The twenty-four primarily qualitative standards included usage of differentiated instruction, degree of teacher planning, extent that teachers support and encourage students to improve, the director "exercises academic leadership," "teachers and directors engage in continual training," "teachers encourage the protection of the environment, appreciation for art and good health," "[they] teach universal values like solidarity, tolerance, honesty and responsibility in the formation of citizenship," and participation of parents in decision-making (Aboites 2012, 848; author's translation). SEP central staff then evaluated the extent to which schools met the criteria. This was very difficult and time consuming in practice. The SEP reported that these parts of evaluation were completed for less than a quarter of participating schools in the first eight years of the PEC (ibid., 846). The Fox administration attempted to rectify this problem by creating the National Institute for the Evaluation of Education (INEE) in 2002, which as a body autonomous from the SEP would gather, analyse, and disseminate data on its functioning and later through the national ENLACE exam run directly by the SEP. In practice, test scores from the ENLACE, which were easy to compare and quantify, became the primary metric of comparison. The expanding influence of the ENLACE exam through the PEC will be discussed below.

To what extent did the PEC have a significant impact on teachers and schools in Mexico City? Since the late 1990s, the city government has increasingly covered school construction and maintenance, bursaries and uniforms for students, and other operating costs unrelated to staff salaries, as the national SEP pulled back its funding (Arnaut 2008, 151).[11] As a result, parents do not have to make up these costs as they do in other states. The AFSEDF posts notices beside the main entrance of every primary and secondary school in Mexico City stating that the institution is completely free and offering a complaints hotline for parents to call if they are told otherwise. Yet according to Aboites (2012), "voluntary" donations collected by the parent association rather than school staff still make a significant contribution to the maintenance budget. The sometimes ambiguous line between voluntary and obligatory fees is politically sensitive for education authorities, owing to the constitutional stipulation that basic education shall be free.[12] When explaining that all primaries and secondaries in Mexico City receive a flat amount of 90,000 pesos per year (approximately $8,500CAD in 2016) for their non-payroll costs, regardless of the number of students, a senior AFSEDF official acknowledged that this was not a generous sum (AFSEDF Official 1, interview Feb. 2015).

Prior to the re-uploading of direct responsibility for the administration of employee salaries to the national SEP in 2014, the funding provided from the federal government to state authorities for basic education varied drastically. While the average per pupil funding in 2005 was 8,767 pesos, the AFSEDF received 13,530 pesos, the fourth highest among thirty-two states, and the adjacent jurisdiction of Mexico State, large portions of which are also highly urbanized, received the lowest rate at 5,467 pesos (Marquez 2008, 179).[13] The DF's share of federal funding for basic education declined from 10 per cent in 1998 to 8.3 per cent in 2006, both a relative and a real decline (ibid., 180), yet Mexico City schools were still better funded than most.

In his anthropological study of a secondary school in Michoacan in the 1990s, Levinson describes an overall ethos of equity and an emphasis on human development: "There is a greater concern with educating the whole person in the secundaria. Students learn more about the art of getting along and appreciating the world. In the United States, subject matter reigns supreme" (2001, xv). Academic competition through test scores was de-emphasized. Secundarias are not streamed on the basis of academic ability, meaning that, as in their primary schools, students move with a cohort through most of their classes over three years. However, general secondaries offer the most direct route to continuing to upper high school and eventually applying to university, while technical secondaries offer more workshop classes and are more oriented to being the terminal institution (ibid., 27). The latter are more likely to be found in rural areas, or in poorer and working-class urban neighbourhoods, representing a degree of geographic streaming. In 2015, Mexico City had 539 public general secondary schools, employing 73 per cent of secondary teachers; 200 technical secondaries, which employed 23 per cent; and 47 *telesecundarias* (small schools predominantly located in rural areas, which, lacking a teaching staff large enough to cover all subject areas, delivered some classes by television), employing 1 per cent (SEP 2015).

In this context, the INEE was established with the purported objective of being a "transparent" gatherer of information about the national education system "autonomous" from the SEP (and therefore the SNTE). It would interlocute with the OECD and the World Bank in the analysis and reporting of statistics. Its testing function was initially promoted by Fox's government as a less intensive version of the controversial university entry exam, Ceneval. It would provide indicators of the status of education in Mexico. The chair of the board of the INEE was appointed by the Mexican president. Most directors represented education authorities, and others came from the Citizen's Observatory of Education (OCE) an NGO, parent groups, business lobbyists, and religious groups (Aboites 2012, 859). A complaint from Elba Esther Gordillo promptly won the SNTE a seat at the table (Leyva Piña and Rodriguez Lagunas 2012, 556).

Following unsuccessful attempts through the INEE to implement a national exam that would be used to assess PEC schools and be incorporated into the Carrera Magisterial as one of the criteria for salary increases (a form of merit pay), the ENLACE exam was created directly by the SEP in 2006. The INEE would not return to prominence until it was effectively relaunched by Enrique Peña Nieto's government as its primary testing vehicle. ENLACE annually tested approximately 16 million students from year three of primary through the three years of secondary. Like similar exams in Canada and the United States, it tested language comprehension (Spanish) and math, alternating a third subject such as history or science. It consisted of 150 multiple-choice questions. In its first iteration, results were used by the INEE to create tables of the "top 500" primary and secondary schools in Mexico and to rank the education achievement of each state. That students in rural Indigenous and poorer communities had consistently lower scores was acknowledged by the SEP. With arguments similar to those of Ravitch (2013a) and Kuhn (2014) in the US context, Aboites observed that this fact demonstrated the inherent flaw of standardized exams across incredible national diversity, that comparing impoverished rural schools with schools in Mexico City's elite Polanco neighbourhood was unfair and would yield predictable results. State government representatives objected to the ranking of their schools as dismal without additional federal resources. Academics cited the experience of the Chilean education system (a school choice structure similar to that of NYC), in which schools with high marks are inundated with applications and can choose their students, thus perpetuating high scores (Aboites 2012, 863). Implementation of the ENLACE faced significant resistance and sporadic obstruction from teachers where the CNTE was dominant, or where Gordillo was weak within the local SNTE (ibid., 846).

ENLACE's focus on testing Spanish and mathematics placed a mounting weight within the curriculum for increases in student grades in these subjects, just like the situation in New York, to the detriment of teaching in non-tested areas. To increase class time dedicated to Spanish and math in secondary schools, history and civics courses were reduced and physics, biology, and chemistry courses were combined. There was a greater intervention by administrators in monitoring the pedagogy of teachers in accordance with published guidelines for optimal forms of test preparation. The SNTE objected to potential job losses from closing courses and using disciplinary power against teachers who stubbornly tried to maintain their classroom autonomy, but the union didn't challenge the context behind this undermining of teachers' pedagogy and professional autonomy (Leyva Piña and Rodriguez Lagunas 2012, 557).

Under Fox, Gordillo held a veto over education policy. She never appeared to harbour strong disagreements based on principle or ideology, but raised objections when her institutional power could possibly be undermined, as happened with the initial establishment of the INEE. The PEC and the ENLACE exam were given her blessings, despite their ability to undermine the professional autonomy of her members and equity in education more broadly. Under the Calderon administration, in the context of mounting criticisms of the national education system from the left and the right, she took her combination of a pragmatic willingness to accommodate to the neoliberal drift and her apparently primary desire to further consolidate her own power to become, according to Hernandez Navarro (2013), the "central protagonist" of education policy.

4.3. From Clientelism to a Neoliberalized Teaching Profession

Elba Esther Gordillo's transition from a populist clientelism in the 1990s (exemplified by her negotiation of the Carrera Magisterial) to a consistently neoliberal politics sustained by elite alliances culminated in her central role in the development and implementation of the ACE in 2008.

The means by which this program was an innovation in the neoliberalization of the teaching profession, disrupting practices representing alternately the legacies of corporatist clientelism and Mexico's welfare state, are described in this section. Along the way we see the full realization of standardized student evaluation through the ENLACE on a national scale beyond the aspirations of No Child Left Behind (NCLB) and Race to the Top (RTTT) in the United States, but in a manner that was ultimately fatal. CNTE and non-CNTE teachers alike responded with widespread resistance, which undermined the ACE but set the stage for the more successful strategy of the next president, Enrique Peña Nieto.

An important antecedent preceded Gordillo's thoroughly neoliberal shift. As the ultimate authority over the public sector Social Security Institute (ISSSTE), responsible for the healthcare and pensions of the nation's active and retired government employees, in 2007 she presided with new PAN president Felipe Calderon in its conversion from a defined benefit pension plan to individualized defined contribution savings accounts. Her centrality in the change was emphasized by both the SNTE and the CNTE, the latter naming it the "Gordillo Law." It provoked strong opposition among teachers as the largest group of affected public employees, re-galvanizing the CNTE in both its bases and with new supporters in northern states. Despite massive demonstrations, Supreme Court and International Labour Organization legal challenges, strikes and occupations of SEP and ISSSTE buildings by the CNTE, and the insertion of grandfathering clauses, the shift was ultimately successful (CNTE Section 10 Activist, interview Feb. 2015; Hernandez Navarro 2012, 345–51; Leyva Piña and Rodriguez Lagunas 2012, 560).

The emergence of an increasingly vocal business lobby on education policy with considerable influence in Calderon's right-wing administration created the context for Gordillo's neoliberal turn. Mexicanos Primero (Mexicans First) was quietly founded in 2005 by a small group of socially conservative cabinet members in the PAN government and business leaders, led by Claudio X. González, son of the billionaire magnate of Kimberly-Clark de México, and Alejandro Ramírez Magaña, son of the owner of Cinépolis, Mexico's largest cinema chain. Its policies and tactics closely resembled those of its contemporaries in the United States. Hernandez Navarro described Mexicanos Primero as the "front group of the business rightwing on education issues" (2012, 422; author's translation). It made its first major public intervention in 2007 with the release of *Brechas: estado de la educación en México 2010*, a report that, citing test score results from the first years of ENLACE, described the education system as "mediocre" and accused the SNTE of coddling weak teachers. Its publication garnered significant government and media attention. Mexicanos Primero also presented awards to individual teachers for furthering a "more humanist" vision of education, despite their union, while issuing public statements denouncing the majority of teachers as "lazy, selfish" (ibid., 419; author's translation). Its influence in Mexican education policy would grow considerably in setting the terms for mainstream debate. Meanwhile, school physical plants deteriorated amid the expansion of secondary schools, owing to rising enrolment and retention, often poorly constructed and maintained, which undermined conditions for working and learning. However, these issues garnered little attention from either business leaders or the SEP and Gordillo in their diagnosis of problems facing the nation's education system (Leyva Piña and Rodriguez Lagunas 2012, 560).

On 15 May (the Mexican Teacher's Day) in 2008, flanked by Calderon, twenty-six state governors, and an assortment of business leaders and bishops, Gordillo introduced the ACE initiative (Hernandez Navarro 2012, 353). Leyva Piña and Rodriguez Lagunas (2012) argue that the ACE was in part about demonstrating the "harmonious relationship" between the SNTE and the federal government, while excluding the CNTE as a legitimate national actor. They contend that the ACE was arguably more a product of the SNTE than the SEP, a view shared by Hernandez Navarro (2013). The ACE covered three principal areas. Curriculum changes emphasized "citizenship, productivity and competitiveness," with an emphasis on the latter two, which, Leyva Piña and Rodriguez Lagunas claim, corresponded with a de-emphasizing of cooperation, humanism, and cultural diversity. Also present were measures resembling the PEC's promotion of public-private partnerships through school-based management, ostensibly to improve school infrastructure and student health. These measures consisted of technology procurement and outsourced food contracts (replacing school-run snack shops) along with parent committees that were encouraged to obtain private support to match public funds. Long hostile to the public normale schools, which had served as incubators for the teachers' movement, Gordillo described them as "unemployment factories" and recommended they be privatized and turned into tourism and hospitality training colleges (Hernandez Navarro 2012, 382–6). Hernandez Navarro observed: "The ACE opened for private interests and non-profits, an enormous space to participate in the running of schools through school councils, and from there to create political clients. For this, the employer councils were enthusiastic for it" (ibid., 428; author's translation).

The clause that provoked the greatest contention was titled "Evaluate to Improve." It proposed standardized exams for new teaching positions, for temporary and low-seniority teachers to obtain permanent status, and for promotions (Leyva Piña and Rodriguez Lagunas 2012, 558). In the process, it not only removed the right of successful graduates of the nation's publicly run normale schools to a teaching position, it removed graduation from a normale school or a university faculty of education as a mandatory prerequisite for obtaining a teaching position (Hernandez Navarro 2012, 356–7). A bachelor's degree in a relevant subject area and passing the teaching application exam would now be sufficient (Bocking 2015a, 81).

This clause would have a profound impact on teachers' employment in several ways. It increased the precariousness of teachers whose continued employment would now be conditional on passing an exam. Leyva Piña and Rodriguez Lagunas (2012) contend that this change undermined the importance of experience and performance in the classroom, a more accurate measure of professionalism, for newer and temporary teachers in their trajectory towards permanent employment. The teaching position exam purported to eliminate long-standing and much criticized practices in many regions of the country, where retiring teachers could pass on their positions to their sons or daughters or potentially, for a price, could recommend someone else for the position. Alternatively, teaching positions were awarded by school directors, other administrators, or union officials as a form of patronage. The argument that open competitions for jobs and promotions via exams would increase the system's professionalism was an easy sell in the context of popular awareness of corruption and the declining social acceptability of nepotism (ibid., 562).

The removal of normales and other faculties of education as mandatory prerequisites was based on the notion that knowledge of pedagogy, instruction, child and adolescent development, and classroom management were basic skills that initially could be evaluated on a standardized exam and further developed on the job. They would not require years of professional study and training beforehand. From this point of view, the professional characteristics of teachers, beyond the subject area knowledge an accountant would bring to the teaching of math or an engineer to science, were thin indeed. Leyva Piña and Rodriguez Lagunas describe how these changes led to the deprofessionalization and precarization of teachers:

> Flexibility in teachers' labour had the potential to corrode the character of the teachers ... developing individualist attitudes. From solitary unshared work it increases the anxiety, fear and grades of stress, with consequent

> physical and psychological consequences ... it removes the obligation of the state to train and professionally prepare teachers, because now they will have to pay for their own training; it reduces vacation time in the summer from time teachers spend in courses and diplomas as part of their certifications; it intensifies and increases the hours in the teachers' workday. In other terms, the reform implicates the spending and investment of money and time in the search of professionalization, masking a complete process of deprofessionalization of teachers. (Ibid., 562–3; author's translation)

Several key impacts, then, gave a significant section of teachers personal reasons to be strongly opposed to the provisions of the ACE, a policy whose originators could be easily identified: Elba Esther Gordillo and Felipe Calderon. The CNTE emphasized the deprofessionalizing aspects in its opposition to the ACE, particularly the diminishment of normale schools and the dubiousness of a standardized written exam for assessing teacher quality. The movement charged that administration of the exam lacked transparency and could be manipulated by the SNTE and the SEP in favour of their preferred candidates (ibid., 562). Fierce resistance emerged from both CNTE-led sections as well as traditionally pro-institutional sections of the SNTE, which broke ranks, including Morelos, Baja California Sur, Coahuila, Morelos, Zacatecas, Durango, Puebla, and Quintana Roo. Over 400,000 teachers in fourteen states participated in strikes at various times over 2008–9 in opposition to the ACE. In the most successful instances, teachers allied with parent groups concerned about school fees and commercialization, and *campesinos* engaged in struggles for land rights in states like Morelos and Chiapas with deep roots of rural collective struggle. In states with the most organized opposition, teachers refused to carry out aspects of the ACE. They blocked the administration of the ENLACE or the OECD's new PISA exam, which served for many dissident teachers as a manifestation of the international dimension of the neoliberal education agenda. The high levels of resistance created a crisis for Gordillo, who dealt with it by tightening control over the SNTE. National congresses now met in secret locations, and conventions to elect executives of state sections were postponed (Hernandez Navarro 2012, 388). While the host site for countless national mobilizations, which drew the participation of their active members, the CNTE was not sufficiently organized in Mexico City's Sections 9 or 10 to lead citywide strikes, though Section 9's strong presence in many primary schools did lead to parents joining marches and protests.[14]

Amid the mass movement united in its opposition to the ACE, a formal division opened among the dissidents of the teachers' union. In July 2008, just two months after the inauguration of the ACE, teacher activists from across Mexico gathered in the capital to launch the Democratic National Executive (CEND) of the SNTE. While sharing many principles and sympathizers, the CNTE did not recognize the new organization (ibid., 432–5; Leyva Piña and Rodriguez Lagunas 2012, 547). For years before, the CNTE's difficulties in organizing effective mass protests at the national level had been further hindered by the frequent inability of the leadership of its largest state sections to agree on shared strategies or dates for mobilization. The CEND emerged out of schisms between the leaderships of CNTE sections that had successfully gained some power in Michoacan and Guerrero (the former alienated the latter in pushing ahead with the CEND) from those of Oaxaca, Chiapas, and the DF.[15] The dissident leaders of Michoacan aligned themselves with non-CNTE activists in the state sections of Puebla, Morelos, Tlaxcala, Mexico State, and San Luis Potosi, among others, who were disgruntled with the ACE and the pension reforms overseen by Gordillo in the previous year (Hernandez Navarro 2012, 439–45; Cervantes Pérez 2012). The CNTE of Section 9 issued a statement refusing in its terms "to negotiate with charro leaders and betray the alliance policies of the CNTE" (Cervantes Pérez 2012). The CEND was launched with great fanfare amid over 1,600 delegates led by Michoacan, representing factions from most of the SNTE's sections (with the notable exceptions of Oaxaca, Chiapas, and the DF). Its supporters campaigned intensely within the CNTE, to which it still claimed affiliation. However, it suffered from division between non-CNTE leaders, whose goal was the creation of a national education union parallel to the SNTE, and the majority of dissidents from within the CNTE, who insisted on struggling to democratize the existing union.[16] Following the election of new leaders within the SNTE of Michoacan in 2011, who strongly backed the CNTE, the CEND shrank to largely coalesce among the non-CNTE, anti-Gordillo leadership of the Puebla, Morelos, and San Luis Potosi sections (ibid.). Dissidents grouped in both the official CNTE and the CEND maintained a steadfast opposition to the ACE, both groups claiming that fighting Gordillo and the neoliberal agenda for education was their primary objective, decrying sectarianism. Speculatively, however, it is difficult to see how these internal divisions did not undermine opposition to their powerful opponents, particularly their capacity to construct a cohesive resistance at the national level capable of fatally undermining the federal scope of the ACE.

Gordillo intensified the impact of the ACE on teacher evaluations, proposing in 2011 a modification of the Carrera Magisterial that would raise the portion of teacher pay increases based on the results of their students' test scores on the ENLACE from 20 per cent to 50 per cent (Leyva Piña and Rodriguez Lagunas 2012, 560; Hecock 2014, 69). This proposal elicited further opposition from her own members, whose incomes became dependent on a standardized multiple-choice test to which they had to orient their classroom instruction. The SNTE leader seemed to be taking one more step away from her earlier populist base to embrace the avant garde of neoliberal policy. The primary purpose of the ENLACE, rather than simply a national survey of student achievement as its advocates initially claimed, was to act as a form of value-added measurement, in the manner described in the previous chapter relating to New York, which would further discipline teachers. According to Aboites, the pressures created by the salary incentive had harmful consequences for meaningful student learning, since it

> pressured teachers to create a climate of bureaucratic demands within their classrooms, totally counterproductive to a true education process. It increased the use of fraudulent practices – such as the "loan" of children from one classroom to another when the evaluations arrived – and increased non-pedagogic strategies to train the children to answer on the exams. (2012, 831; author's translation)

Dissident teachers claimed victory in the spring of 2012, when tens of thousands refused to sit the ACE's teacher exams and did not face reprisals. Mexico City's elementary teachers in the CNTE Section 9 conducted hundreds of classes and activities the city's downtown Zocalo to demonstrate an alternative pedagogy, an estimated 20,000 parents and students participating. These teachers actively redefined their role, demonstrating the value and importance of their professional autonomy to the public (Hernandez Navarro 2013, 199–202). Meanwhile, it soon became evident to both critical education researchers such as Aboites and administrators within the SEP that the efforts by individual or small groups of teachers to try to "game" the ENLACE were so extensive that the validity of the exam was fatally compromised on a national level (AFSEDF Official 1, interview Feb. 2015; Hugo Aboites, interview Feb. 2015). As SEP officials saw no way to effectively bring its administration under their control, the national ENLACE exam for millions of students in years 3 to 6 of primary school and 7 to 9 of secondary school was scrapped in 2013. While the CNTE steadily protested the ENLACE and blocked its administration in Oaxaca, Michoacan, and elsewhere, it appears that countless unorganized individual acts of sabotage were the most effective. The test was partially revived by the INEE and renamed "Planea" in 2015 on a much reduced scale for the 6th and 9th grades, the final years of primary and secondary school, respectively. It was used in 2015 to identify for intervention schools with positive or negative results outside the mean of their area (AFSEDF Official 1, interview Feb. 2015).

Insurgencies from the grass roots and middle ranks threatened not only Gordillo's control of the union but her ability to effectively enact policy in cooperation with the SEP. In the arena of elite politics she continued to consolidate her position, swinging her PANAL party behind winning candidates in midterm elections. But as Calderon's PAN fell in the polls leading to the 2012 presidential election,[17] she sought a rapprochement with the projected restorer of PRI rule, Enrique Peña Nieto (Hernandez Navarro 2012, 415–18). While making education reform a priority of his administration, Peña Nieto was uninterested in her partnership. His policies would not be a significant departure from the ACE. However, he rapidly demonstrated an understanding of some of the scalar reasons behind its defeat, owing to the concentrated strength of dissident teachers, and he acted accordingly to further centralize the administration of education policy in Mexico. The results would provide the CNTE with their greatest challenge to date.

4.4. Enrique Peña Nieto and Fast Policy

The rapid series of events in the year following the election of President Enrique Peña Nieto in 2012 provide a textbook case of "fast policy" (Peck and Theodore 2015), revealing a fascinating convergence of actors in the production of neoliberal education policy.[18] Advancing beyond the failures of the Fox and Calderon administrations in education policy, Peña Nieto reversed the federalization of the system to firmly entrench the policies introduced in the ACE. He sought to do so in such a way that they could not be defied on a regional basis by the CNTE, which had had the effect of undermining the credibility of education governance on a national level. In doing so, he ruptured old political alliances in education governance and formed new ones. This section will provide a brief narrative of the events surrounding the launch of Peña Nieto's education reform to introduce the key actors and their convergence and will then discuss their relative influence.

Shortly after his victory in July 2012, Enrique Peña Nieto appointed a transition team on education policy led by Mexicanos Primero chair Claudio X. Guajardo, the nation's most prominent business advocate on education policy. President-Elect Peña Nieto visited the OECD headquarters in Paris, to meet over several days with its chair and former PRI politician José Ángel Gurría. In September, the OECD released a policy document, *Getting It Right: Strategic Reforms for Mexico*, with basic education part of its primary focus. Its recommendations overlapped with those of Mexicanos Primeros and centred on increasing the evaluation of teachers, aimed at undermining their permanent employment status, measures largely found in the ACE (Bocking 2015a, 78–9) – all to the detriment of the professional autonomy of teachers.

Recommendations from both organizations were reflected in Peña Nieto's proposals for education presented on 2 December, a day after he was sworn into office. Beforehand, the leadership of the "Pact for Mexico," a grand coalition of the three largest parties – the PRI, the PRD, and the PAN – had agreed behind closed doors to pass substantive legislation during the first few months of Peña Nieto's term on basic education, labour law, the tax code, and privatization of the energy sector (Hernandez Navarro 2013, 27–31). Cooperation from Gordillo's PANAL was not essential. On 10 December 2012 amendments to Articles 3 and 73 of the Constitution were moved in Congress, stipulating that teachers' employment would be contingent on evaluation, thus exempting public primary and secondary teachers from the labour law that covered all other employees. The amendments passed on 21 December 2012 with support from the Pact and entered law on 6 February 2013 (Bocking 2015a, 78–9; Arriaga 2013, 13–14; Bensusan and Middlebrook 2013, 84; Aboites 2015, 4–5).

Peña Nieto's new alliance with the business leaders of Mexicanos Primero, the OECD led by Ángel Gurría, and the Pact for Mexico had won its first victory. Recognizing that she had been sidelined, Gordillo denounced the education reforms for their adverse impact on teachers' employment, threatening to mobilize the membership of the SNTE in opposition. Her performance was unconvincing. Earlier in 2012 during an interview with *Milenio* newspaper, Gordillo had endorsed Peña Nieto's campaign promises to make the permanent status of teachers conditional upon passing regular tests, stating, "Permanence perverts proper evaluation, it goes against evaluation" (quoted in Hernandez Navarro 2013, 144; author's translation). According to Hernandez Navarro (2013), being such a consistent neoliberal advocate through the governments of Zedillo, Fox, and Calderon, she was unable to change gears when she realized the fix was in. Gordillo was imprisoned less than a month after the passage of the constitutional amendments, charged with embezzling hundreds of millions of pesos from union funds.[19] An opinion poll reported that 80 per cent of the public and 84 per cent of teachers approved of her arrest (Bensusan and Middlebrook 2013, 86; Hernandez Navarro 2013, 263; Bocking 2015a, 82). Gordillo's status as one of Mexico's last great *charro* union power brokers, a holdover from the corporatist era of the PRI, whose deft manoeuvring had gained her an extension on life through the administrations of Fox and Calderon, was over.

Under Peña Nieto, a significant realignment occurred in the composition of the political alliances behind education governance in Mexico. On the Mexican left and within the CNTE, considerable attention has been given to the involvement of the OECD. This is consistent with a foundational nationalist narrative within the left that frames opponents of neoliberalism as patriots and its advocates aligned with the OECD or the World Bank as foreign controlled and complicit in imperialism, usually American in origin.[20] Mexico entered the OECD in 1994, shortly after the inauguration of the North American Free Trade Agreement (NAFTA), as the first developing nation to join the "organization of rich countries." Through the tenures of Fox and Calderon, it enrolled in the OECD's increasing focus on education policy by participating in its international standardized test, the PISA since 2000 and in policy-sharing forums. However, it was under Peña Nieto's administration that this collaboration drew much closer for both the elaboration of policy and in winning popular legitimation. Peña Nieto's and Ángel Gurría's close political affinities were likely influential. A member of the technocrat wing of the PRI that came to power in the late 1980s with Carlos Salinas, Ángel Gurría was his chief negotiator for NAFTA. He was subsequently the secretary of foreign affairs and then of finance in the Zedillo administration. After being appointed to the OECD in 2006 with Fox's endorsement, he had only a nominal relationship with Calderon's PAN government. His collaboration with Peña Nieto became known within months of his election, the president-elect declaring, "I propose that the OECD become a strategic ally for the design of the policies that Mexico needs, and what greater contribution than to have a friend at the head of this organization" (Jiménez 2012, n.p.). Ángel Gurría replied, in the Foreword to *Getting It Right*, that "the new Mexican government should consider the OECD an extension of its own capacities" (OECD 2013, 4). Still, the OECD's role consisted largely of acting as a prestigious third-party legitimator for policies already in circulation, in a fashion described in chapter 2. Ángel Gurría and his staff gave Peña Nieto recommendations similar to those he received from Mexicanos Primero, some of which found their way into the constitutional amendments and later legislation. However, this acceptance occurred with the free volition of the Mexican government. Peña Nieto was not "under the orders of the OECD," as many of his critics claimed. As Brenner, Peck, and Theodore argue,

> it is problematic to assume that neoliberalization processes normally or necessarily move "downwards" along a global-to-national vector ... this

> superordinate gaze fails to take account of the strategic role of national, regional and local state apparatuses as active progenitors of neoliberalizing institutional reforms and policy prototypes, and as arenas in which market oriented regulatory experiments are initiated, consolidated and even extended. (2010, 195–6)

The CNTE became the primary voice for the growing ranks of teachers anxious about how the reforms would affect their employment. The Professional Teaching Service Law (Ley de Servicio Profesional Docente) was passed in September 2013, putting the constitutional reforms into practice. The 2013–14 school year began with a massive wave of teacher strikes and protests in twenty-seven of the thirty-two states, led by the CNTE but also drawing out unaligned teachers from new regions. They culminated in weeks-long strikes in the CNTE's southern strongholds and strikes for days at a time in the Yucatan, Veracruz, and the northern states, where teachers rapidly mobilized despite a limited history of organization. The highway blockades, mega marches, and occupations of airports, international borders, government buildings, and Mexico City's Zocalo rivalled the national strike wave of 1989 for its geographic breadth (Arriaga 2015). By early November, the movement had won vague agreements from state governments where the struggle had been strongest to work around the federal dictate for a standardized testing regime for teachers, often combined with firmer commitments to hire more teachers or meet community demands to cancel proposed school fees.[21] However, concurrent negotiations at the national level between the CNTE and the Interior Ministry for the abrogation of the reforms yielded no gains. By early 2014, in contrast to the defeat of the ACE two years earlier, state governments that had made side agreements with the CNTE came under strong pressure from federal authorities, which filed successful claims with the Supreme Court that they were in abeyance of the national constitution. These states soon reneged on their agreements (Aboites 2015, 2–5; *Aristegui Noticias* 2014; Bocking 2015a, 93–5. Dissident teachers retreated from the national scale to try to win exemptions in their strongest bases (Maria de la Luz Arriaga, interview June 2015). Peña Nieto's scalar strategy of re-centralizing control over education policy to the national level by embedding reforms in the Mexican constitution were proving successful. The new evaluation program began its rollout in most states during the following school year, and the standardized testing of existing teachers began in the 2015–16 school year. What did these new evaluation structures look like and how did they affect the teaching careers and professional autonomy of those under its examination?

4.5. What Makes a Teacher? Marginalizing the Normales and Teacher Education

On the evening of 26 September 2014,[22] dozens of students from the Ayotzinapa Teachers' College in the state of Guerrero commandeered five buses to travel to Mexico City and participate in marches against what they contended was discrimination in teacher hiring by the SEP against the graduates of public rural normale schools and the favouring of alumni of private urban university programs. Their struggle was within the context of Enrique Peña Nieto's reforms and its predecessors, which cumulatively diminished the role of the normale schools in the formation of the nation's teachers. In the town of Iguala and on its outskirts, two hours southwest of the nation's capital, the buses came under fire by local police, killing six students. Forty-three students were captured by the police. Passed off to a local drug cartel, they disappeared and were presumed murdered. The abduction of these activist student-teachers placed an international spotlight on the political persecution of the normale schools. It launched mass protests for months across Mexico, which drew tens of thousands, and strikes by CNTE teachers in Guerrero and students in Mexico City, who closed their university campuses in solidarity (Arriaga 2015; Bocking 2015b).

Explanations for the motivations behind the violent attack on the students vary. Many extend beyond the official version that it was the product of a corrupt local mayor and police force enmeshed, like many others in Guerrero, in a cartel, who hated the students, were upset that they had taken the buses, which unbeknown to the students may have been used for drug smuggling. According to the investigation of the Interdisciplinary Group of Independent Experts commissioned by the Inter-American Commission on Human Rights of the Organization of American States, local human rights groups, and *Proceso* magazine, military authorities responsible for communications between state, federal, and municipal police that were situated at a base less than a kilometre away, were aware of the movements of students that night and attacks upon them. Radio communications during key periods in the attacks were withheld by the military from the Interdisciplinary Group's investigators (Turati 2014). The likely complicity of upper levels of government in the disappearance of these students presents a chilling picture of potential state involvement in the murderous suppression of politically inconvenient student-teachers.

The rural college has produced eighty-eight generations of teachers since its founding in 1936 during the government of leftist president

Lazaro Cardenas. Since the beginning, its students, most from local peasant families, have led struggles for land reform while studying agricultural methods to, in turn, train the area's children in primary and secondary schools. In marked contrast to the national education system's official priorities of English, Spanish, and mathematics, the *normalistas* of Ayotzinapa also take courses in community organizing, Indigenous languages, and political economy. According to alumni and primary teacher Joel Amateco Venancio,[23] a leader in the campaign for justice for the abducted and presumed murdered students, "The goal of the school is to form teachers who are socially and politically aware and on the side of the vulnerable. Graduates of this school have a more profound understanding of the essence of what it means to be a teacher" (Bocking 2015b).

The Mexican government staggered the full rollout of programs associated with the Ley de Servicio Profesional Docente, beginning with measures that primarily affected new teachers. The SEP initiated the system of exams in July 2014 for new teaching jobs in the coming school year; 149,000 applicants competed for 16,505 positions, according to the government. The exam consisted of two segments, with eighty multiple-choice questions on teaching practice in the first, and ninety-five multiple-choice questions to assess general intelligence and ethics on the second; twenty questions on each segment were not evaluated. Throughout the country 344 application centres were established, and most of this process proceeded without incident. The CNTE blockaded exam sites in Michoacan, Guerrero, Chiapas, and Oaxaca, resulting in their postponement and relocation to nearby states (Poy Solano 2014; Poy Solano et al. 2014). Perhaps because this component of the Ley de Servicio Profesional Docente did not affect the employment of existing teachers, it did not provoke mass protests across the country, resulting in its more or less successful implementation.

The CNTE argued that the written exam was both a poor method of assessing whether an applicant would be a competent teacher, and that it undermined both the credibility of public faculties of education, particularly the normales, which were dedicated to training teachers, and thereby the overall professional autonomy of teachers. It also represented a further shift from conditions prior to 1992 when successful graduation guaranteed a teaching position (Enrique Enriquez Ibarra, CNTE Section 9 General Secretary, interview June 2015). Their opposition was also rooted in a historic understanding of teachers in Mexico, existing since the founding of the SEP shortly after the Revolution in 1921, that teaching held a distinct status from the "liberal professions" of law and medicine. Whereas duly certified lawyers and doctors were autonomous in the sense that they could set up a private practice or become employees of an institution, teachers were civil servants with a commitment to state institutions (Hugo Aboites, interview Feb. 2015). This section focuses on a significant change to teaching as a profession introduced by the Ley de Servicio Profesional Docente. Coinciding with the implementation of application exams, graduation from normales or faculties of education would no longer be a mandatory prerequisite for becoming a teacher. The federal government claimed that the principal rationale for the measure was to alleviate a teacher shortage by making it much easier for professionals in other fields to apply (AFSEDF Official 1, interview Feb. 2015). Prospective teachers would require a bachelor's degree (licenciatura) in their subject area (or equivalent years of trade employment for workshop teachers). Their grasp of pedagogy, professional ethics, and capacities for working with children and adolescents would be assessed through the multiple-choice exam. In effect, it reiterated the ACE's claim that there are limited professional skills intrinsic to the teaching profession beyond subject-area knowledge. As a result, this aspect of the Ley both had a profound impact on the collective identity of the Mexican teaching profession and threatened to considerably undermine its professional capacities.

It is the contention of education researcher César Navarro that the Ley de Servicio Profesional Docente's undermining of the normales is about fundamentally transforming the professional culture of teachers: "Teachers' identity has been formed to a great extent from the 'cradle' of the normales and for that reason, a central project of the reform culminates with its extinction and the sweeping out of the public school, teachers who graduated from these education institutions" (2016; author's translation). Mexico has 484 rural and urban normale schools, of which 274 are public institutions, accounting for 77 per cent of Mexico's 121,000 student-teachers. However, public normales were at 73 per cent enrolment and private normales at 52 per cent in 2013–14, the first year in which a degree in education became optional (Poy Solano 2016b). Funding from the SEP for these institutions has been in long-term decline, dropping precipitously in recent years.[24] The former president of the Escuela Nacional de Maestros described the state of normal schools as "paralysis, financial asphyxiation and academic abandonment" (ibid.; author's translation). According to Poy Solano, one factor has been the increasing withdrawal of support from the official SNTE, which provides some resources through funding it holds in trust from the SEP.

The general secretary of CNTE Section 9 of Mexico City's primary teachers, Enrique Enriquez Ibarra, explains why training in subject knowledge alone is insufficient to being an effective teacher:

> When these colleagues come in to give a class, they don't have all the elements necessary for classroom management, teaching strategies and pedagogy. It's different to do it in a study or a lecture hall, then to have 20, 25, 40 kids in a group. We see this a lot in the secondary [schools] … We have doctors, accountants, chemists, mathematicians from the universities. We're not saying they're not good, but when they enter the secondary, and they're in front of adolescents that are changing, they don't have control of the group … because these teachers don't have the profile of a graduate of the normales. And this will become more prevalent in the primaries and preschools. (Interview Feb. 2015; author's translation)

A secondary teacher adds that the Ley in fact exacerbated a long-term issue within secondaries, as the SEP lacked pedagogical programs for less common subjects like art or music, the system has tended to hire professionals in areas outside of core academic subjects rather than normale graduates (Mexico City Teacher 9, interview June 2015). According to a senior official of Mexico City's basic education system, AFSEDF acknowledges that graduates from normales are better trained in classroom practice than graduates from private and public non-education universities and those without education degrees. Its first hiring round is open only to graduates of the normales; then it opens a second round for remaining positions to all other applicants (AFSEDF Official 1, interview Feb. 2015).

The contention of the SEP and Enrique Peña Nieto that a degree in education is not necessary for effective teachers is tantamount to arguing that there is only a limited base of abilities and skills, apart from subject-area knowledge, which is intrinsic to teaching (Hugo Aboites, interview Feb. 2015). According to these proponents, it is something that can be picked up on the job or, as the leaders of Teach for America (TFA) claim, through a three-week crash course. This is a profound devaluation of the concept of teachers' professionalism. While TFA has received considerable public pushback in the United States, as discussed in chapter 3, this form of deskilling of teachers has not yet sparked popular concern in Mexico. Nevertheless, it is already transforming the profession in a far more profound way, with implications for the nature of being a teacher and the education that students receive.

4.6. Testing Teachers

The resistance provoked by the implementation of standardized exams for existing teachers through the fall of 2015, though geographically concentrated much like the protests against the entry exam, proved to be more disruptive and the resentment it represented far more widespread. What was the source of this strong opposition? According to a report issued in May 2016 by the Mexican Senate's policy think-tank as protests began anew:

> The teacher evaluation system instituted by the reform of 2013 is one of the *highest impact* in the world because it determines each step in the employment trajectory of teachers that work in basic education, approximately 1.3 million in the publicly operated system. It is unique in its objective of evaluating in a manner completely external, without the participation of school authorities, each teacher in the immense Mexican education system. (Senate of Mexico 2016, 3; author's translation; emphasis original)

This passage clearly presents the ambition of Peña Nieto's government through the Ley de Servicio Profesional Docente and its dependence on the federal government. The legislation ultimately determined the employment conditions of teachers across Mexico, negating collective bargaining over the most important aspects of the profession. In the absence of firm control over many state education systems and even less at the school level, considering the questionable loyalty of school directors to the Reform, themselves being subject to the exam, the national SEP and the INEE were obligated to directly administer the exam. This remarkable degree of centralization contrasts with New York State, where school districts and principals were relied upon to supervise at the smallest scale equivalent forms of teacher evaluation.

The standardized exam was structured to function within a fully centralized system. Lacking participation by local school officials, direct observation of teaching, as is common in US and Canadian teacher evaluations, was ruled out. The SEP and INEE established a schedule reaching to 2020, whereby Mexico's 1.3 million primary and secondary teachers and school directors would participate in their first round of evaluations at the rate of 300,000 a year, divided over two periods in the spring and fall. Selected teachers reported to a local examination hall consisting of a computer lab, where over the course of up to four hours they completed a multiple-choice exam on teaching practice, wrote and uploaded a fully annotated lesson plan, and uploaded examples of student work, representing both high and low achievement. Teachers who passed with at least a Sufficient grade, were required to take the exam again in four years, while those deemed Insufficient must take remedial courses at their own expense and try again the following year. Failure for a third time would result in automatic dismissal for teachers hired before the implementation of the Ley in 2013. Those hired before this date would be transferred to a lower-paid secretarial position (Senate of Mexico 2016, 1).

The first round, in fall 2015, was "sensibly reduced" to only 106,000 participants. The second round, in spring 2016, was postponed to the following school year, pushing back the initial schedule (ibid.). At this rate it would take over twelve years to evaluate every teacher through the three steps, significantly weakening the practical effect of the Ley De Servicio Profesional Docente.[25] These administrative setbacks were caused by a combination of technical glitches in the national computer-based exam system[26] and large-scale resistance by teachers in states where the CNTE predominated. In these states, tactics varied from mass blockades of exam sites, which prevented their operation, to alleged widespread cases of sabotage of computer equipment within the halls by the test takers, on a sufficient scale to fully disrupt exams, as all attendees claimed that the technology was dysfunctional and that they would leave (Cano 2015; Briseño 2015). According to the Senate Report, 90 per cent of teachers and directors called for evaluation in the first round participated. Of the 16,000 who did not, 75 per cent were located in Chiapas, Guerrero, Michoacán, and Oaxaca and would be assigned a new exam date in the following year. The 3,360 teachers located elsewhere were fired (Senate of Mexico 2016, 17).

Of the 103,313 teacher participants,[27] 15 per cent were considered Insufficient, 38 per cent Sufficient, 40 per cent Good, and 8 per cent Outstanding.[28] If the teachers are subtracted who failed, because they submitted only one piece of the three components rather than received low marks, the Insufficient rate is cut in half (ibid., 14). With its breakdown into four possible ratings, this evaluation system bears some similarities to New York State's contemporary APPR (see chapter 3.7). While the Mexican criteria are based on an exam taken by teachers (since the demise of the ENLACE) rather than on the results of those taken by their students, as is the case in New York, in both cases politicians claimed that the exams would act as a sorting mechanism that would pinpoint the system's bad teachers.[29] Yet New York State's Cuomo claimed that less than 1 per cent of teachers being found unsatisfactory was "baloney" and vowed to create a new exam, whereas the SEP welcomed the test results, stating that they revealed "only the best prepared are giving classes" (ibid., 14). However, the Senate's report on the Ley acknowledges the challenge of prominent academics, who argued that the results undermined the fundamental claim behind Peña Nieto's education reforms, that the shortcomings of the nation's school system were primarily due to bad teachers. They also questioned the validity of a multiple-choice exam to evaluate teachers' capacities in the first place. The report strikes a critical note in observing that, while the INEE recognized the existence of various technical glitches and said it would "perfect" its instruments, not only did the SEP not question the results of the initial evaluation, it declared them "satisfactory and sound," claiming that they "reflect the teaching competencies and the knowledge of those who were evaluated" (ibid., 17)

The CNTE pledged to resist the Ley until its abrogation, continuing protest actions through 2015 against the exams despite mounting government repression, particularly against the Oaxaca section. These actions included the freezing of the union's bank account, police attacks on marches, and the sporadic imprisonment of leaders, including the general secretary (Casco Peebles and Ocampo Merlo 2019). Though carried out in the absence of resistance in most of Mexico, a sizeable number of teachers across the nation continued to hold the exams in contempt. Nearly all Mexico City teachers I interviewed prior to the implementation of this exam, treated it with suspicion. Returning to my two case study schools in the delegation of Iztapalapa in February 2016, where several teachers from each had been selected, their earlier views were confirmed. One teacher who had taken the exam explained that she had done so because there was no alternative, but she did not believe that it was an effective evaluation of her teaching. Given the test's nationwide application, the questions were designed to assess as many realities as possible within the diverse country. However, she argued, this meant that many were not relevant to the context in which she taught: "In twenty years in Mexico City, I have never taught a student for whom Spanish was a second language. How would I know those teaching strategies?" Or the questions were inane: "A spider enters the classroom. Do you: A) Kill it. B) Ask a student to kill it. C) Capture it. If I answer A, does that mean I'm against scientific inquiry or am I maintaining safety?" Only a school union representative affiliated with the official SNTE Section 10 leadership seemed to think that this form of testing was the way of the future.

Opposition to the Ley from both the CNTE and many non-affiliated teachers can be grouped into at least three principal categories. First is the objection that standardized tests cannot effectively evaluate the capacities of a teacher, substantiated both by self-identified "critical" education researchers such as Aboites and even by the president of the INEE, Sylvia Schmelkes. In an extraordinary interview in July 2016 with the Mexico City newspaper *La Jornada* in the midst of ongoing protests by the CNTE, she stated that the Ley in its current form, "may not be what the country and teachers need," recognizing that it was strongly opposed by many teachers and musing that changes could be made. She admits that the Ley in its current form was an inferior version of what would have been a more meaningful measure of teacher competencies:

> But then we calculated numbers and overall the logistics required to train evaluators who would be capable of evaluating teachers in the classroom, and not once but at various times, and not one trainer, but at least two. When we confirmed this, we saw that it wasn't possible; for this reason we designed qualitative instruments. (Poy Solano 2016a; author's translation)

While the Senate report purports to primarily serve as an objective analysis of the Ley de Servicio Profesional Docente without drawing its own substantive conclusions, its sympathy with this view is suggested, not least by its prominent citations of American education policy critic Diane Ravitch in describing similar teacher evaluation programs in the United States (2013; part of a brief section on international comparisons). As will be discussed below, the fact that Peña Nieto's education reforms drew broad criticism from within the senate and even from the head of the agency that designed its testing instruments was precipitous for dissident teachers.

A second objection, voiced especially from the CNTE, is that the purportedly "objective" system is not so. Given that the SEP and leaders like Peña Nieto apparently concur with Mexicano Primero that the primary cause of the deficiencies of the education system are "bad teachers," and that they can be identified with a multiple-choice test on professional knowledge, there is a widespread belief among CNTE activists that the exam can and will be structured to yield a desired pass/fail rate (Mexico City Teacher 9, interview June 2015; CNTE Section 10 Activist, interview Feb. 2015). Based on this fundamental mistrust of the intentions of the SEP, the INEE, and the politicians who govern them, CNTE activists fear the exam would be used to purge experienced teachers and activists. They point to similar reasons for opposing an additional rule of the Ley de Servicio Profesional Docente, which sets out a series of reasons for which teachers will be automatically fired. A particularly contentious one consists of having three consecutive unexcused absences. In a national context, where legal strikes are virtually unknown,[30] activists fear that the law will quash militancy by creating a strong penalty for participation in work stoppages of more than brief duration (Casco Peebles and Ocampo Merlo 2019, 484). As will be discussed in the final section of this chapter, this rule did not prevent the eruption of open-ended strikes in the CNTE's core states in the spring of 2016, despite thousands of firings. Whether the dismissals limited the spread of the action is difficult to ascertain, although a senior official of the AFESDF believed that strikes certainly were limited as of 2015 in Mexico City, due to the law's judicious application here (AFESDF Official 1, interview Feb. 2015). Suggesting awareness that the rule could have an effect on participation, the general secretary of Section 7 in Chiapas stated at the outset of a strike in May 2016, "the first thing that we have to do is break the fear, because if we are thinking of the three days, well then we're screwed, truly. I've said at various times that there are no alternatives" (Alerta Chiapas 2016; author's translation).

Thirdly, CNTE members and critical academics explain that the terms within the Ley that determine teacher employment were not implemented through negotiation with the CNTE (or with the official SNTE leadership). They were unilaterally imposed. As an extension, the clauses of the Ley that stipulate when teachers may be fired (for not taking the exam, failing the exam, unexcused absences, among other reasons) may not be appealed. With the elimination of these rights to due process, public school teachers are exempt from federal labour law, which covers all other workers. The capacity of the union to intervene in defence of its members is also significantly limited. Continuing in this general spirit of intransigence, the federal government subsequently refused to modify any aspect of these central aspects of the Ley (Hugo Aboites, interview Feb. 2015; CNTE Section 10 Activist, interview Feb. 2015).

> It's an attempt to subordinate teachers who have been revolting for many years, decades, and who have become a very strong opponent to public neoliberal policies ... We're talking about a half million teachers who were active in 26 states in 32 that form this nation. So it's an attempt to control a political force. On another level it's a way of getting rid of some nuclei of resistance that are more important, as in Oaxaca, Guerrero, Chiapas, Michaocan, especially. On another level it's a way of fighting that teacher who's a troublemaker or this one who's a leader. (Hugo Aboites, interview Feb. 2015)

For Aboites and CNTE activists, the Ley has profound implications for the capacity of teachers to engage in contentious politics. The following section will explore how these measures interact with and increase the precarious employment conditions of secondary teachers in Mexico City and the considerable impact on their professional autonomy.

4.7. Precarious Employment and Professional Autonomy

This section explores how workplace relations and power dynamics between teachers and school directors in Mexico City have been affected by the waves of neoliberal reforms described above in this chapter. As will be explained, school directors are not nearly as integral to the front-line implementation of neoliberal reforms affecting teachers' professional autonomy as are their colleagues in New York City. This difference is reflected in the extreme top-down nature of the education reforms embodied in the Ley, as discussed in the previous section. The structure of non-director participation is perhaps one of largest factors undermining the success of neoliberal reforms, since it limits the ability to influence school-level dynamics among staff. As a result, teacher-director relations vary depending more on individual rather than on structural factors. In many of Mexico City's secondary schools, the real source of weakness in autonomous teacher culture in the face of top-down edicts is the virtual absence, according to many teachers, of the official SNTE to represent their interests in workplace-level disputes. The second part of this section will explain how one of the fundamental sources of teacher precariousness predates the Ley but has worsened in recent years. Mexican teachers overwhelmingly are employed on a part-time basis and required to apply for more hours. The nature of this employment is perhaps so taken for granted that it is hardly ever mentioned in analyses published by Mexican teacher activists or their allies. Yet it is a foundational cause for the insecurity of teachers' work lives and has a strong impact on their professional autonomy.

It was highly significant in the context of many conflicts over education policy that school directors in Mexico remained part of the teachers' union. They were removed in 2017 and reclassified as management by government decree. Whereas in Canada and the United States, school administrators' membership in teachers' federations was mostly a hold-over from when these organizations acted as professional associations rather than labour unions,[31] in Mexico it was largely a product of the union's corporatist origins. The SNTE was formed to group all education workers into one organization for the purposes of state-driven political mobilization. It was also an integral part of the union's clientelistic structure. Because promotion in many states was controlled by the union and used to reward loyalty, a 1992 reform stipulating that directors be appointed by the SEP on the basis of a written exam was observed in the breach (Hugo Aboites, interview Feb. 2015). However, in school delegations (districts) where teachers were able to democratize the structures of the SEP and the SNTE, usually in states where the CNTE was consolidated, new practices emerged whereby school directors were elected by their peers (Cook 1996, 194–5). As a result, school directors in these areas are frequently movement leaders. Enrique Enriquez Ibarra, general secretary of Mexico City's CNTE Section 9, directs a primary school on the morning shift. Changing the role of school directors to become front-line managers capable of implementing top-down administrative policies is a key priority for neoliberal reform advocates. The Ley de Servicio Profesional Docente established a centralized written exam for aspirants to school leadership, wresting control of appointments from both the corrupt official SNTE, weakened since the departure of Gordillo, and the democratic practices of its dissidents. After the implementation of standardized teacher exams, the highest demand of Mexicanos Primero was the removal of school directors from membership in the SNTE (Bocking 2015a, 92). Peña Nieto waited until near the end of his term and, interestingly, after the defeat of his signature education agenda, to do so. The non-response from SNTE leader Juan Diaz de la Torre, even considering his reputation for acquiescence, was noteworthy, considering how removing tens of thousands of members holding strategic positions of responsibility in the workplace significantly undermined the institutional strength of the union (Bocking 2019, 15). The OECD's *Getting It Right: Strategic Agenda for Reforms in Mexico* published at the start of his term, recommended giving school directors the power to hire and fire teachers in order to increase "school autonomy." This term borrows from the school-based management discourse previously used to advocate for the Quality Schools Program (PEC) and defend parent fundraising (OECD 2013, 129–30). School directors do not have the power to hire or fire teachers. Most disciplinary authority continues to be held by zone supervisors and inspectors. Under another late-term policy intended to increase the disciplinary capacities of the SEP, additional zone supervisors were hired, enabling each to be responsible for six, instead of ten schools (González, Rivera, and Guerra 2017).

The capacities of school directors to intervene in teachers' classroom practice has increased over the past few years. However, a senior AFESDF official describes how much still depends on their individual characteristics and those of the teachers at their school:

> Technical secondary schools have a very hierarchical structure ... They're militarized ... In the case of the general secondaries, it depends on each

> one, there's some with a very successful leadership and others where it's a disaster. In the primary [schools], much depends on the director … But I'll say that the reform indicates that leadership needs to be participatory and inclusive … I've observed that there's some where they've really achieved a level of co-action, and they are very respected; they've earned their place in the hierarchy as a director. There are others who haven't, and they're questioned [by their teachers], and others who utilize the power relationship. (AFESDF Official 1, interview Feb. 2015; author's translation)

This official describes a policy intended to increase the ability of school directors to observe classroom teaching, while creating a more formal school-level leadership team:

> As a part of the strategy to implement the reform in the DF, we're striving to strengthen the director with a new structure. Because normally in primaries, it's easier to see it, to know the teachers and the director, in front of the classroom. Now schools that have ten or more groups per grade, which in the DF are 75 per cent … have an administrative subdirector to download administrative work from the director, an academic subdirector, a promoter of reading, and a promoter of new technologies. (Ibid.)

At face value, such a structure could well offer benefits for improving the professional practices of teachers. This is assuming that resources, such as time from the classroom to pursue professional development, which historically has been scarce, are actually available for teachers and provided that, while showing ways for teachers to improve, their capacities for professional judgment are also respected. One participant complained that the "promoters" were dictating how they should teach and added that school directors now have the ability to reject or approve teachers' transfers to their school (Mexico City Teacher 6, interview Feb. 2015).

A secondary teacher active in the CNTE considered that school directors still don't generally intervene in teachers' work, but if there is a conflict, then there is wider scope for them or inspectors to observe their classroom teaching. According to him, such interventions were typically of a disciplinary rather than a collegial nature. Much depends on the power dynamics in a given school: "Lately, the idea has been increasing that the director is the law. That's to say, he will determine everything, when a few years ago, we could still, especially in the meetings of the technical committee [monthly staff meetings], debate what we should do in the school" (CNTE Section 10 Activist, interview Feb. 2015; author's translation). He believed that the SEP was pushing this culture shift, and that eventually they would want to give directors the power to hire and fire.[32] It is interesting in this context that Mexico City teachers are not only older on average than NYC teachers (forty-two years compared with forty) but also substantially more experienced, with an average of seventeen years of service,[33] compared with less than eleven in NYC[34] (INEE 2015, 35). A much lower rate of turnover in Mexico City's schools may be significant in shaping workplace cultures where teachers are more likely to be confident enough to assert their own ideas on both classroom teaching and how the school should be run.

Several interview participants, especially subdirectors, directors, and a tutor for new teachers, emphasized a distinction between their criticism of contemporary policies, which they saw primarily as impacting teachers' employment conditions, and a belief that many teachers lacked innovation in their pedagogical practices and needed an external push to change. A subdirector voiced his belief that

> many teachers defend their method, their form of work and they don't want to leave their comfort zone. But some dynamic teachers are versatile, adapting to the necessities and socio-economic conditions of the country and they are the ones promoting these changes. So we have a contradiction between those who do it and those who don't and the government says, "Some teachers in these contexts in primary and secondary [schools] are having success, why not you?" And we're in this dilemma, to make a Reform approved by law is not what we want, [so] we have to adapt ourselves to this new change. Teachers should reflect daily on their practice. They should also keep themselves updated, so that education can improve in this country. (Mexico City Teacher 4, interview Feb. 2015; author's translation)

A secondary science teacher with twenty-three years' experience contends that the ideas of classroom teachers are seldom taken into account in policymaking, resulting in a disjuncture with classroom experience and creating cynicism among teachers:

> What I would like is that they take into consideration our perspectives as teachers in elaborating their plans, programs, strategies ... they never call us. They say they do but it's not true, who knows who they call, but it's not people in the classroom. Those of us in the classroom, we have different challenges with the children ... Whoever it is that elaborates the programs and whatnot, they're not in the classroom, they're people in an office, working at a desk, and they don't see the problems that there are in every school and each classroom. (Mexico City Teacher 2, interview Feb. 2015; author's translation)

Scepticism about top-down policies, formed without their participation and felt to be divorced from their working experience, is common among Mexico City teachers, even if it is seldom expressed in the highly visible manner by their colleagues in more militant states.

The precarious employment of Mexican teachers is structurally determined in the assignment of positions, with a profound impact on their capacity to exercise their professional judgment. The issue exists on two levels. First, the vast majority of teachers are underemployed, assigned less than full-time status. Second, teachers receive little to no time during their regular workday for professional duties outside of classroom teaching. The time to do so must be found beyond extensive hours in the classroom for those teaching full time or the second jobs of underemployed teachers. In this sense, the employment structure for Mexican primary and secondary teachers is strikingly different from that of their colleagues in Canada or the United States, where the job is structured in the overwhelming majority of circumstances as a full-time occupation.

The standard teaching load for a primary teacher working in a school with morning and afternoon shifts consists of 18.4 hours of classroom time a week, amounting to daily responsibility for one grade-level class during one of these shifts. This work schedule does not recognize or compensate any time for non-classroom professional duties (Hernández, Llamas, and Garro 2012, 329). The work schedules of secondary teachers are more complex. While teachers in Canada and the United States are usually assigned a full-time course load at the start of their employment, new secondary teachers in Mexico are typically assigned two or three daily fifty-minute classes, amounting to twelve to fifteen hours of work a week. They may apply to teach additional courses as they become available, to eventually reach a maximum of forty-two hours a week, typically attained only in the last few years of a career. According to the INEE, teachers assigned full-time hours (thirty-six to forty-two hours a week) have remained static at around 10 per cent from 1999 to 2015. The number of those at three-quarters of full time was also static at around 12 per cent. However, teachers employed half time (twenty hours) declined from 32 to 22 per cent from 1999 to 2014, and teachers with hourly employment less than part time increased from 43 to 55 per cent, with the biggest growth since 2008 (INEE 2015, 56–7). Less than full-time work is increasingly the trend; in secondary schools opened between 2010 and 2014, 70 per cent of teachers are on an hourly basis, whereas only half are in schools created between 1999 and 2004 (ibid.). As a result, most secondary teachers approaching full-time hours work in two or even three schools, frequently commuting from one to the other in the afternoon (INEE 2015). In this way, the employment conditions of secondary teachers in Mexico bear a resemblance to itinerant sessional university lecturers in the United States or Canada.

Historically, the objective held by most teachers of increasing their hours towards full-time status, obtaining assignments at schools closer to home, or consolidating their hours in one school has created rich opportunities for patronage and clientelism for both SNTE and SEP officials (Hecock 2014; Hernandez Navarro 2012, 432; Martin 1994, 94–9; Mexico City Teacher 7, interview May 2015). While the application exams of the Ley de Servicio Profesional Docente were supposed to remove this opportunity for graft, informants suggested that opportunities were still abundant for authorities to confer favours in employment assignments. Meanwhile, regarding another dimension of employment security, the proportion of secondary teachers with permanent status, formally gained after successfully completing six months in a permanent position, has declined from 94 per cent in 2002 to 76 per cent in 2015 (Hernández, Llamas, and Garro 2012, 330; INEE 2015, 61). This statistic may suggest a growing number of teachers working in back-to-back interim positions, covering teachers on long-term absences, which suggests that the SEP is increasingly assigning work through these interim positions rather than through new permanent positions.

Two problems exist with the assignment of work in units of several hours for secondary teachers. On one end, teachers lack enough working hours and therefore have to do other work to support themselves, often outside of teaching. A subdirector observes of his colleagues:

> Here the average is twenty-one hours [a week], but there are those that only have nine, twelve, fifteen. There are some that have more hours because they work at more schools … but you can't live with twenty-one hours of work in this country; you need to do your forty-two hours to live marginally decently. (Mexico City Teacher 4, interview February 2015; author's translation)

A secondary visual arts teacher in his first year got by with twelve hours of work a week, teaching six groups for two hours each (Mexico City Teacher 9, interview June 2015). Senior teachers who have obtained a "double shift" in primary schools, teaching in both the morning and the afternoon, and secondary teachers who have accumulated thirty-six to forty-two hours have an adequate salary but no time to prepare for their classes. A secondary teacher of civics and "orientation" (counselling) for nineteen years, who has gained full-time status, works for twenty-two hours a week from 9 a.m. to 1:30 p.m. at one school, and for an additional

Table 4.1 Secondary School Classroom Teaching as a Proportion of Recognized Work

	Mexico	United States	Canada	OECD average
Percentage of recognized work time in classroom	90	71	60	—
Total yearly hours of classroom teaching	1,047	981	743	694

Source: (OECD 2016, 428)

twenty hours from 4:30 p.m. to 8:10 p.m. at another school (Mexico City Teacher 1, interview Feb. 2015). His colleague, a science teacher for twenty-three years, works for nineteen hours from 7:30 a.m. to 11 a.m. in one school and then teaches at another for nineteen hours from 2 p.m. to 7:20 p.m. (Mexico City Teacher 2, interview Feb. 2015).

The OECD statistics shown in table 4.1 demonstrate that Mexican secondary teachers spend a far higher proportion of their recognized working time actively engaged in classroom teaching than their colleagues elsewhere in North America do. By "recognized" working time, I refer to the period of time that teachers are contractually or statutorily mandated to perform teaching-related duties. For example, education legislation in Ontario stipulates that teachers must be present fifteen minutes before the start of classes and for ten minutes past the end of the school day, though in certain (unusual) circumstances teachers can also be asked to perform duties until 5 p.m. Professional preparation periods during which teachers are not responsible for students are included within this recognized workday in both Ontario and New York State. Not so for Mexican teachers. Unofficially, "recognized" work of teachers occurs in their evenings and on weekends, usually outside the school. Table 4.1 explains the significance of these statistics.

> The proportion of statutory working time spent teaching provides information on the amount of time available for non-teaching activities such as lesson preparation, correction, in-service training, and staff meetings. A large proportion of statutory working time spent teaching may indicate that less time is devoted to tasks such as assessing students and preparing lessons. It also could indicate that teachers have to perform these tasks on their own time and to work more hours than required by statutory working time. (OECD 2016, 428)

Mexico City's school authorities at the AFESDF acknowledged that their teachers must use their own time to perform many of the tasks described above that are essential to classroom teaching (AFESDF Official 1, interview Feb. 2015). According to a school director, when secondary teachers were hired, the AFESDF assigned them a proportional number of weekly "co-curricular" hours for which they are paid to do non-classroom professional activities. The ratio was close to three hours for thirty hours in the classroom, but part-time teachers often received none (Mexico City Teacher 8, interview May 2015). The subdirector who earlier voiced his frustration over a perceived lack of innovation among many teachers acknowledges the difficulties of being creative with a full-time teaching load:

> A teacher with forty-two hours in my country is not going to have time to train or update themselves because you're up at 6 a.m. and you're working until 7 or 7:30 at night. When do you have a shower, eat or sleep? When do you see your family? Here a class of fifty minutes per group, if I have thirty-nine hours and I teach science, that means I give six hours a week to each group ... it doesn't leave me time before or afterwards. So I have to bring my marking home, but that's on my time. But if I had forty-two hours full time, I would have to mark and teach at the same time in the classroom; I wouldn't be able to take away extra work. As a result, the only moment that I have to work and meet with my colleagues is during recess or during the technical committee [staff] meetings. There we have time to share. Every month directors and teachers spend a full day evaluating the situation of the school to be able to make adjustments and changes. (Mexico City Teacher 4, interview Feb. 2015; author's translation)

It is noteworthy that neither the OECD nor the SEP nor senior elected officials within the Mexican government have recommended or campaigned in recent decades to improve the quality of teaching by giving teachers paid preparation time. A major World Bank report, *Great Teachers: How to Raise Student Learning in Latin America and the Caribbean* (Bruns and Luque 2014) found that Mexico City teachers routinely spent a significant amount of time marking or doing administrative work while in the classroom.[35] They argue, based on correlations with test scores, that such practices, which take teachers away from directly engaging with students, have an adverse impact on learning. Consistent with neoliberal ideology, they blame the quality of the teachers for these practices, raising few questions about the fact that more resources may be required on the part of the state. It is difficult for teachers to fully use their professional capacities to do the time-consuming tasks of preparing and delivering pedagogy oriented to the specific needs of their students when most are compelled to commute between schools, teach long hours, or work at a second job in order to earn a decent living. Recognized daily preparation time is critical to enabling teachers to exercise their professional autonomy.

4.8. Acquiescence, Resistance, and the Challenges of Scaling-Up: The CNTE in the City and the Countryside

We have explored in this chapter the evolution of national-level neoliberal education policies, the integral role of the official SNTE under Elba Esther Gordillo in their implementation, and the resistance of the CNTE; this final section explores labour relations for Mexico City teachers since 2013. It seeks to explain why secondary teachers in Mexico's capital have responded differently to similar education policies, especially from their more militant colleagues in the southeast of the country. Explanations include differences in the nature of work for primary and secondary teachers, the historical position of the teacher in rural and urban contexts, the presence of political allies, and the relative disciplinary capacities of education authorities. This discussion will help us understand the CNTE's upsurge against the education reforms over the summer of 2016 and assess its outcome.

The day after Gordillo's arrest for embezzlement in February 2013 (without public protest), the union's national executive appointed General Secretary Juan Diaz de la Torre to take her place at the annual convention (Hernandez Navarro 2013).[36] The departure of Gordillo did not lead to a collapse of the hold of the "institutional" forces over the national SNTE and most of its state sections, despite de la Torre's far weaker political power (Enrique de la Garza Toledo, interview Feb. 2015). After being virtually invisible during the initial CNTE-led upsurge against the reforms in the fall of 2013, de la Torre received public recognition from Peña Nieto, and began the international charm offensive described in chapter 2. Despite the strength of the upsurge, the CNTE and other dissidents were unable to contest control of the national union to the extent achieved by the movement in 1989. A Mexico City CNTE activist emphasized that the national executive's hold is reinforced by entrenched *caciques* (local political bosses) at the state level, who needed to be challenged there (CNTE Section 10 Activist, interview Feb. 2015). However, despite the emergence of strong movements in new states, including Veracruz and Jalisco, these dissidents were unable to win control over the official structures of their union sections, which could be ceded only by conventions called by the national executive (Maria de la Luz Arriaga, interview June 2015).[37] Advances for the movement have been considerably impeded as a result of these mutually reinforcing state and national structures of control, even with a weaker leader at the top.

De la Torre's eagerness to appease Peña Nieto at the national level filtered down to affect Mexico City's secondary teachers in the absence of a strong dissident movement in Section 10. According to one secondary teacher, "With the new reform, the union disappeared. Now we don't have a union. The union exists but not for teachers; that is to say, we're not protected by the union" (Mexico City Teacher 5, interview Feb. 2015; author's translation). A school official attributes labour stability in Mexico City in part to de la Torre's closer alignment with the government:

> If we compare the DF with other states, obviously there [are] a great deal of stability and very good relationships ... [owing] to very fluid communications, to giving technical-pedagogical elements that strengthen the [local] union in a technical-pedagogical position, but also to the national context, where the SNTE is since the departure of Gordillo and the identification of corruption, in a position of greater alliance, we say, with the secretary of public education. Not the Coordinadora [CNTE], but the SNTE. (AFESDF Official 1, interview Feb. 2015; author's translation)

A secondary teacher for twenty-three years bitterly described the situation of a dominant institutionally aligned Section 10 leadership and a weak CNTE dissidence for rank-and-file members:

> The union has never truly helped us. One nearly always has to go out independently to solve problems ... It's no more than a symbol and the truth is that it's divided between the democraticos [CNTE] and the charros [institutionals]. It's always a constant struggle between them and this doesn't benefit us. (Mexico City Teacher 2, interview Feb. 2015; author's translation)

The comments of this teacher are a reminder that while many in Mexico City dispute the validity of the education reforms (most were opposed in the two secondary schools where I conducted interviews), relatively few align themselves politically with the CNTE or the official SNTE. Two teachers active within the CNTE of Section 10 attributed the sentiments of their colleagues to a reluctant resignation to the reforms and a disbelief in their ability to challenge them. They held little optimism about the likelihood of a mass upsurge among the city's secondary teachers in the manner of their colleagues in the southeast (CNTE Section 10 Activist, interview Feb. 2015; Mexico City Teacher 9, interview June 2015).

However, interview participants active in the movement also identified significant differences between the experiences of secondary and primary teaching to explain why the dissident movement in the latter was far stronger in Mexico City. Various respondents described the nature of secondary teaching as more individualistic, where teachers came together only in severe circumstances (Mexico City Teacher 5, interview Feb. 2015). A Section 10 Activist adds that the tendency of many school directors to not encourage professional collaboration is augmented by the secondary level's division into subject areas, whereas primary teachers teaching the same grade level more frequently shared resources (interview Feb. 2015). Some also argue that secondary teachers are not as collegial as primary teachers because, while the former had long been a heterogeneous combination of graduates from public normale schools and university faculties of education, under the Ley of 2013, they were now joined by professionals lacking any degree in education. By contrast, a majority of primary teachers were still graduates from the public normales. As four-year boarding colleges, they were long the incubators of a distinct teacher identity, and many graduated together from Mexico City's large Escuela Nacional de Maestros. Another explanation is the differing structures of employment. Whereas primary teachers arrive and leave together for the morning and afternoon shifts, under their hourly employment contracts, secondary teachers have unique schedules. A secondary teacher whose employment is geographically fragmented with nine hours of classes each in two schools is also less likely to develop a strong identification with either community (Enrique Enriquez Ibarra, interview June 2015; CNTE Section 10 Activist, interview Feb. 2015; Mexico City Teacher 9, interview June 2015).

The CNTE has a longer and deeper history of organizing among Mexico City's primary teachers, first winning the local executive in 1989 through an open election convened by the national union in the aftermath of that year's upsurge. CNTE supporters were re-elected in subsequent elections. The CNTE Section 9 has also faced significant obstacles. In 2007, Gordillo staged a *charrazo* (takeover of the union). At the last minute, she ordered that the electoral convention be changed to a location unknown to the vast majority of the delegates, 80 per cent of whom had pledged support to the CNTE slate. Gordillo's candidates won by a landslide. Although CNTE supporters secured judicial recognition that the election was unjust, they have been unable to compel the SNTE to respect this finding.[38] According to CNTE Section 9's general secretary, he and other members of the parallel executive can continue representing members (on their personal time and without renumeration) because the AFESDF is aware that they have the support of most teachers (Enrique Enriquez Ibarra, interview June 2015; CNTE Section 10 Activist, interview Feb. 2015; Hernandez Navarro 2012, 386–8, 446–8; Leyva Piña and Rodriguez Lagunas 2012, 548).

One of the biggest reasons given for the greater strength of primary teacher dissidents is their greater ease in building alliances with parents (Hugo Aboites, interview Feb. 2015). A young secondary teacher explains its importance for building a movement:

> In the primary schools it's easier because the parents are more active. In secondary it gets more difficult, but you have to do this work. At the end of the day, if you do a good job, they see that you're there in the classroom, they see how education is being destroyed not by the teacher, but by external conditions ... constant work gives you legitimacy. (Mexico City Teacher 9, interview June 2015; author's translation)

Primary and secondary teachers share the same SNTE locals in all other states in Mexico, making this effort at alliance building easier outside the capital. When asked to explain why their colleagues protested less than teachers in the south, Mexico City secondary teachers suggested that in addition to having fewer opportunities for coalition building with parents than primary teachers have overall, the school and their staff play a more central role in community life in the south. A teacher blamed school directors who ushered staff out of the building once their shifts were done and lacked interest in starting extracurricular activities that could directly link the school with its surrounding neighbourhood.[39] A custodian who worked in the school she had attended as a child, and a long-time prefect (responsible for student discipline), emphasized how teachers who lived in the school's neighbourhood tended to have an easier time connecting with both the students and their parents. They estimated that 30 per cent of the teachers at their school lived nearby in the culturally vibrant but economically struggling neighbourhood in Iztapalapa (Mexico City Support Staff 1 and 2, interview June 2015). The custodian recalled arriving at the school to find that parents had blockaded the entrance, protesting the shortage of certified teachers in all subject areas. She explained that while parents can support the struggles of education workers, reciprocation is risky:

> If I support a parent who's blocking the door to the school, I'll be the one who's disciplined ... For this reason, when the teachers demonstrate, they

> do it away from the school, not here. They don't close the schools, they simply stop work, go to demonstrate in the Zocalo, [Monument to the] Revolución, etc., but not here at the school, because then we could lose our jobs. (Mexico City Support Staff 2, interview June 2015; author's translation)

Yet moving demonstrations from the school to the distant city centre arguably makes parental participation more difficult (Mexico City Teacher, interview Feb. 2015).

Strong differences in the political cultures of Mexico City and the southeast states are also important for explaining the unevenness of teachers' agency. Reports from Chiapas during the waves of teacher strikes and protests from May to July of 2016 against Peña Nieto's education reforms provide abundant examples of highly organized parents and community allies providing support that would make the discipline feared by Mexico City teachers less likely. On 23 May, "Before the march arrived in the central park [of state capital Tuxtla Gutiérrez] the group 'Organized Chiapan Businesspeople' delivered to the teachers a ton and a half of supplies, among them bottles of water, biscuits, soap, canned tuna, beans and rice" (Henríquez 2016a). The following weekend, *La Jornada* reported that thousands of parents and other supporters marched in 80 of the state's 122 municipalities in solidarity with the teachers' strike (Henríquez 2016b). On 13 July, *La Jornada* related:

> The blockade installed by residents of this city at the access to Tuxtla Gutiérrez, to support the ... CNTE in their struggle, has taken on a life of its own. It has constituted itself as a permanent popular assembly, broadening the demands of the teachers, and at 15 days it is a reflection of the popular reach that the teachers' movement now has in Chiapas. Hundreds of people, up to 3,500 in recent days, remain here, day and night ... everything started on June 27, when faced with the threat of repression against the blockade here ... people mobilized to create a "security corridor" around the teachers. In a few days it transformed into a centre of ... movements that defended the land, opposed the privatization of energy, demanded street paving, drinkable water, and defence of the region's nature reserves. (Bellinghausen 2016; author's translation)

As mentioned in chapter 2, the CNTE emerged in the late 1970s and early 1980s in the southeast states out of strong alliances with established *campesino* and other community movements. They are largely without equivalents in Mexico City's context, but distinctions also exist among its boroughs. Several CNTE members described Iztapalapa as the most politically active delegation (Mexico City Teachers 7 and 9, interviews May and June 2015; CNTE Section 10 Activist, interview Feb. 2015).

Government strategies for responding to teacher and popular protests vary dramatically between Mexico City and the southeast states. Sociologist Enrique de la Garza Toledo suggests that the administrations of the Party of the Democratic Revolution (PRD) since 1997 in Mexico City contributed to de-radicalizing and co-opting dissident movements, whose members may have been reluctant to alienate the government with protests when possibilities for dialogue existed (interview Feb. 2015). This tendency has declined with the election of Mayor Miguel Mancera in 2013, who moved closer to Peña Nieto. Little parallel of "progressive" governments and social dialogue has existed in Chiapas or Oaxaca, states, where the PRI has long wielded control and maintained a reputation for violent repression of protest.[40] Authorities in Chiapas, Veracruz, and Guerrero alienated parents at the outset of the education reforms in 2013 by interpreting increases in "school autonomy" to allow the government to download the cost of various school operations onto the parents themselves. By contrast, as mentioned earlier in this chapter, the AFESDF has emphasized that no parent would ever be obligated to pay a fee and, with support from the Mexico City government, it provides free school uniforms and other supplies, as well as some bursaries. The AFESDF also has retained stronger administrative capacities for enforcing discipline among its staff. It is easier for regional and zone inspectors to regularly visit schools when they are within a contiguous urban area rather than spread across hundreds of kilometres of rural territory. Arnaut argues that the traditional administrative hierarchy of directors, sector chiefs, supervisors, and school directors is relatively stronger in Mexico City, which has remained continuously under direct federal control, than in many states that have experimented with various forms of decentralization since 1992 (2008, 148). A senior official of the AFESDF contrasts the ability of teachers in the southeast to engage in illegal strikes, with their firmer grip in Mexico City:

> Sections 9 and 10 … the relationship is very good. The leaders of these sections are of the SNTE, and up until now we haven't had [strikes] in Mexico City … Because the law stipulates that if you are absent, you are not paid. If you miss three consecutive days, without justification, then you lose your employment. There are states such as Oaxaca, Guerrero, etc. that haven't paid attention to this and they haven't made deductions. On the contrary, as the newspapers say, they [CNTE] have been able to negotiate lost wages for everyone who came to protest. In the case of the DF, no. It's very punctual. The teacher who's absent is reported and [the pay] is deducted. The teacher who's absent three times … we proceed with the firing if there's no justification … this has meant, in addition to

good communication, that we have a very stable and organic relationship with the leaders of the Section. (AFESDF Official 1, interview Feb. 2015; author's translation)

The upbeat national website of the SNTE provided no indication that another massive wave of strikes and protests by teachers across Mexico was unfolding against education reforms through May to July 2016. Press releases on successful meetings of its leadership with state officials and international dignitaries were interrupted only by a statement of concern on the killing of eleven protestors by police in rural Oaxaca on 19 June while they were clearing a highway blockade organized by the CNTE. Some were relatives of teachers and one was a local journalist (McDonnell 2016; Hernandez Navarro 2016). While urging authorities to exercise due diligence in its investigation, the SNTE expressed its "profound concern" that "under the banner of education reform, some actors had entered the debate with a belligerent position that precipitates violence" (2016a), appearing to blame the CNTE for the deaths. That the SNTE felt compelled to issue a public statement on the conflict, which otherwise it strenuously ignored, indicated the significance of this incident. The attack made international news. Some commentators drew comparisons with the disappearance of the forty-three Ayotzinapa student teachers in 2014. Teachers' unions held solidarity rallies at Mexican Consulates in Canada and the United States. Many organizations, including Education International, denounced the killings. The negative publicity for Peña Nieto was compounded, as the incident coincided with a meeting of the North American heads of state in Toronto.

Section 9 of the CNTE then convoked a strike over the last two weeks of school in July (except for a final day to deliver grades and meet with parents), with the estimated participation of 400 of over 1,300 primary schools across Mexico City. While a minority, it was a mobilization not seen for years by Mexico City teachers. Militants also rallied outside the Mexico City SEP headquarters and district offices in Iztapalapa (Mexico City Teacher 7, interview Oct. 2016). The work stoppages were joined by another unprecedented dynamic. Morena, the left-leaning party that had split from the PRD following the 2012 elections and since 2015 had comprised the largest political force in the capital, mobilized its extensive network of neighbourhood committees in support of the teachers. It hosted a 100,000-strong march to the Zocalo.[41] Amid the road blockades, occupations, and strikes in the CNTE's strongholds and sporadically elsewhere, the Interior Ministry agreed to formal negotiations on the structures of teacher evaluation, the fate of 8,000 teachers who had been fired during the strikes, and several imprisoned leaders. The

CNTE refused to meet with the adversarial education secretary, who convened a parallel series of closed-door meetings with the SNTE that produced proposals around incentive pay, but nothing related to the contentious evaluation system (Poy Solano 2016c). Meeting with CNTE leaders, Morena, the PRD, smaller leftist parties, and a handful of PAN deputies in the congress and senate voiced their interest in revising Peña Nieto's education legislation.

The SEP announced, as the 2016–17 school year began, that the standardized teacher exam would be voluntary, except for those who had failed it in the previous year – a major victory for the movement. This reversal suggested the importance of both Mexico City teachers and the movement's intervention in national politics to tip the balance in a conflict that previously was largely regional. Despite the sentiments of demoralization and resignation about the national education policy expressed by secondary teachers in 2015 and in 2016 prior to the upsurge in Mexico City, the conflict is a reminder of how the political culture of Mexican teachers remains in flux. The government did not fire thousands of teachers who were absent for the exams in 2015 and 2016, but it fired 586 with more than three unexcused absences in a month, principally those who had participated in the strikes at the end of that school year.[42] Twenty-one of these teachers are from Mexico City, including all eleven classroom teachers of the small Leonardo Bravo primary school in Mexico City, where CNTE leader Francisco Bravo is the school director. He has been threatened with termination. I met with several of these teachers and the director at their school in October 2016. They were continuing their regular classroom duties, despite not having been paid since the end of September. The school's parents had physically blocked the entry into the building of replacement teachers sent by the SEP, which refused to meet with delegations of parents requesting the reinstatement of the teachers. The CNTE of Section 9 held fundraisers to support them.

I met again with Isabel at her school in October 2016, a few months after the showdown that helped force significant compromises on Peña Nieto's education policies. When we last met, she was frustrated with the movement and disillusioned over its internal tensions. Despite always being encouraged to do the difficult job of organizing their colleagues at school, few women entered the leadership of the movement in Mexico City or at the national level. Other activists were trying to challenge from within the official SNTE Section 10, which was pouring resources into social activities. She started attending CNTE secondary teacher meetings again in June 2016 as protests across the country picked up steam, and Mexico City CNTE primary teachers planned to join in. She and other teachers at her school first attempted a one-day strike in early June. They established a picket line at the entrance, but when the school director arrived, the official SNTE union representative at the school opened the door to allow him in: "When the director enters then that's it, you have to enter," she said. The picketers were demoralized, and the protest collapsed.

There were successful short strikes in a few dozen Iztapalapa secondary schools later that month, which avoided the three days' absence leading to firing rule. Teachers at her school were hesitant, but were spurred on by hundreds of primary schools already on strike. The national delegate assembly of the CNTE also voted that in order to have a seat at the negotiations table with the Mexican government alongside striking states, Mexico City's secondary teachers would have to join the work stoppage. The decisive factor was the arrival of a group of politically active parents from a friend's school also in Iztapalapa, who organized the parents, who then encouraged teachers to participate in one-day strikes on the afternoon shift. The school director's subsequent efforts to intimidate the parents, according to Isabel, backfired and bolstered their resolve. A few parents attended CNTE assemblies, where they emphasized the need for the movement to communicate that Peña Nieto's policies did not improve education and would lead to good teachers being fired, and that the government should focus on repairing crumbling schools.

Mexicanos Primero and some leaders from the PAN maintained counter-pressure. The Business Coordinating Council (CCE), Mexico's most important corporate lobby group, urged the government to not concede to "acts of extortion" (Carlos Miranda 2016). Constant direct actions by teachers, including blockades of highways, malls, and airports, have fed their portrayal by conservative media as violent and disruptive. Weeks of school closures in some regions have alienated some parents, despite the efforts of striking teachers to engage with them (Ahmed and Semple 2016). The imperative for teachers' unions of constantly renewing relationships with parents and incorporating their demands (Brogan 2014), has been evident throughout the movement's experience, weighing heavily on the conditions for victory or marginalization.

Teachers have proven their capacity to render inoperable widely contentious policies, as they did with the ACE or the ENLACE exam that determined teacher pay. It is yet to be seen if the three-step teacher evaluations of the Ley de Servicio Profesional Docente will be implemented over the long term. Visible at the peaks of national mobilization in the fall of 2013 and summer of 2016, the CNTE has expanded and reinforced its networks in the north and centre of the country, beyond its bases, in the context of an official SNTE with a diminishing impact on the work lives of its members. Yet the control of Juan Diaz de la Torre and his supporters over the union's institutional apparatus did not weaken.[43] The movement did not appear to have significantly grown among Mexico City's secondary teachers, whether as a result of the greater governance powers of the education system or because of its division from the better organized primary teachers and their stronger parental support.

Scalar strategies, though geographically uneven, will no doubt remain central to the struggles of both rural and urban teachers. Outside of states like Chiapas and Oaxaca, the CNTE has lacked powerful allies beyond the regional level, contributing to the fragmentation of attempts to scale its struggle upwards. The CNTE's tactical alliance with the Morena party in Mexico City in the summer of 2016 introduced new political dynamics. Despite Morena's dominance since 2016 in the Mexico City legislature, the party had little influence over education policy, owing to the centralization of education governance. However, the party's many active members strengthened the CNTE's organized support in Mexico City. Reinforced in the capital, the CNTE was better placed to confront education policies on the national level. Alliances with Morena create the potential for conflict within the CNTE, which historically has mitigated internal division by eschewing relationships with political parties. Many in the CNTE, having long fought the PRI's domination of the SNTE and, more recently, soured relationships with state-level PRD governments, are concerned about the potential for co-option. Yet in the waning months of Peña Nieto's presidency, CNTE activists shifted their focus to campaigning with Morena in advance of the national election, despite some internal criticism that the implementation of neoliberal reforms has advanced in the meantime (Poy Solano 2018; Antonio González 2018).

By the end of his term, many of Peña Nieto's signature policies had been discredited. The historic unpopularity of Peña Nieto's presidency and his party was evident in the PRI's crushing defeat in the 2018 presidential and legislative elections. Following the presidential victory of Morena's Andres Manuel Lopez Obrador in 2018, his education secretary declared that his government would fundamentally revise the evaluation of teachers to be more collaborative and less punitive, earning cheers from CNTE activists. When this discourse did not appear to be matched by a significant change in policy, the CNTE conducted multi-day strikes in several states and blockaded the national legislature on various occasions over the spring of 2019. Lopez Obrador personally intervened, chairing negotiations with CNTE leaders. The process yielded legislative amendments that specified that the standardized evaluation system not be used for disciplinary purposes and that the 586 teachers fired for striking in 2016 be rehired (La Jornada 2019; Antonio Roman 2019). A new period appears to have begun for education in Mexico.

5 Toronto

Preface: School Workroom Cultures

As is true in any workplace, teacher subcultures vary widely from school to school and department to department. From my teaching experiences and the observations of colleagues, I found particularly deterministic the degree to which a student population was considered challenging to work with or whether it was an "academic" school. In my socially conscious, progressive classes at the Faculty of Education, we were warned about the toxicity of department workrooms. This was the propensity for stressed-out teachers, safe from the prying ears of minors or the principal, to let off steam at lunch or in between classes with angry tirades about clueless students, "helicopter parents," and our nettlesome superiors. At the first school in Toronto from which I drew my interviews with teachers and observations for this chapter, which was considered a difficult place to teach, my colleagues during the year I worked with them generally restrained themselves from excessive venting. Despite the cliques, there was a sense of solidarity, of trying to make the day easier for each other. As a relatively new teacher I was a particular beneficiary. Beyond the frequent willingness to offer advice, my older colleagues lent me resources and in the case of a particularly hyperactive grade 9 class, invited me to refer particularly challenging students to work for a period in their mature grade 12 class. Although generally not politically active in their personal lives, they were interested in bringing social justice and a critical appraisal of the larger world into their classrooms. During the Occupy Wall Street movement in 2011, which inspired a protest camp in Toronto, all but one of the teachers in this English department devised lessons drawing on the issues raised of economic inequality and activism. They were pro-union, but rarely attended Ontario Secondary School Teachers Federation (OSSTF) events.

In 2014, I completed a semester-long position in the high school that provided the second source of interviews and observations for this chapter. It was located in an affluent neighbourhood and university admission was taken for granted by all in the school. Collaboration between teachers with similar courses was organized and efficient, and many teachers spent their lunch periods supervising student clubs or sitting on committees. Non-work conversation was segmented between the thirty-somethings, who discussed their young children, and the over-fifties, who reported on their home renovations. A month could pass without an overt political discussion, and there was scarcely a mention of the union. I withdrew into my own lesson planning and marking. I was excited one day when a union meeting at lunch was called for the whole staff. It featured two local OSSTF leaders, who were released full time from teaching to work in the union office. We filed into the staffroom (generally used only by substitute teachers), and smiles were elicited by the supplied warm pizza, though one teacher mumbled, "Why are we thanking them? It's our dues money." After an introduction by the teacher who was the school's elected union rep, the two full-time officers launched into a presentation for twenty minutes on the upcoming provincial election, stressing the anti-labour agenda of the Progressive Conservative (PC) party. The staff were then asked for their feedback on OSSTF's electoral strategy. After a few seconds of silence, a teacher raised her hand to ask about the benefits plan. The meeting concluded soon after, as teachers gathered their keys and binders and rushed to their classrooms.

At the end of the day, I was in the English Department office, with a dozen teachers present. "Sisters and brothers," began the department head sarcastically, "What a load of crap!" Several others murmured in agreement. I listened uncomfortably as the officers were described as "arrogant" and that the union meetings were always top-down.

"Why didn't anyone respond when they asked for feedback?" I asked. They answered that more specific questions should have been asked, that it was all so general and vague, and that member involvement was superficial. "You know I'm on the executive of the supply teachers' union," I ventured. "We still like you." another teacher retorted. Some began to gather their coats, others thumbed through piles of marking. I didn't know what else to say. I took it for granted that the union was an essential, positive force, without which we would be at the mercy of the authority of school principals and whatever policies were devised by the government, irrespective of how they affected our work lives. I feared that the generalized scepticism, often justified, that many teachers exhibited towards the policies of the education ministry and the school board, had extended to the union itself – that the union was just another incomprehensible authority, as "union avoidance" attorneys would frame it. At the very least, "the union" for these teachers signified its full-time leadership, not themselves. I turned to my desk. To obtain a reference for my next job, I had requested a classroom observation and formal evaluation by the principal during the following week. I had to prepare.

School-level cultures are significant for understanding the capacity of teachers to exercise their professional autonomy in the classroom. In Toronto, Ontario, as elsewhere, the macro-level context is often shaped by forces considerably distanced in terms of formal structures of authority, if not spatially as well. Education policy in Ontario over the early twenty-first century has broadly followed the dominant trends of other Canadian provinces. Despite the absence of an intervening federal government, as in the United States, let alone a centralizing national government as in Mexico, there has been policy mobility between provincial education ministries and academics (Wallner 2014). Yet perhaps because of the absence of a neoliberalizing strong central government, distinctive waves of neoliberal policies have not passed through the provinces with the same rapidity as they have transformed US education. As Jennifer Wallner explains, "the regimes at work within each province mediate the introduction of new ideas and influence the likelihood that they will be adopted" (ibid., 221). Though all provinces have their own standardized student exams from which data are gleaned to purportedly judge the system's overall effectiveness, they differ in their consequences for students. None is paired with disciplinary mechanisms comparable to the original No Child Left Behind (NCLB) Act of the United States, which would close and "reconstitute" schools with low scores.

Understanding the legacy of the PC government of Premier Mike Harris (1995–2003) for education politics in Ontario is essential for contextualizing the succeeding Liberal governments led by Dalton McGuinty and Kathleen Wynne (2003–18). Yet there is a paucity of published academic research analysing the post-Harris era of education policy and governance (Pinto 2015). Following the ideas of Ontario Institute of Studies in Education (OISE) academic Michael Fullan and his colleagues, who became top advisors to McGuinty and Wynne on education policy, is one approach I will be taking here. In keeping with the central premise of the book, this chapter relies on the perspectives of secondary teachers in Toronto, reflecting on how the policies rolled out under the McGuinty and Wynne provincial governments have affected their professional autonomy as educators.

I demonstrate here how the education policies of the Liberal governments of Ontario drew upon a profound centralization of power under the previous PC government and its implementation of standardized testing as key metrics for defining education "success" to shape many of their own policies. It begins, as did previous case studies, by explaining the importance of scalar centralization, in this instance from the Toronto District School Board (TDSB) to the Ontario Ministry of Education, for establishing the context for contemporary neoliberal education reform in section 5.1. Next, in section 5.2 I analyse the rapid rollout of provincial policy under the Liberals as it was understood from the centre. The perspective shifts in section 5.3 to consider its impact from the perspective of teachers in an "inner city" secondary school, where the imperative of raising graduation rates is felt through the increasingly managerial role of principals and vice-principals as they encroach on the ability of teachers to exercise their own professional judgment in the classroom. Section 5.4 demonstrates how teachers' professional autonomy faces different challenges in a secondary school serving an affluent area. In this context, parental intervention with administrators over the children's grades is prevalent. For schools in working-class and affluent areas a common stress, but affecting each differently, is the existence of "school choice" policies, which, it is argued, are contributing to a racial and class sorting of secondary students in Toronto. In section 5.5 I consider the impact of the scaling-up of teachers' collective bargaining for professional autonomy and the strategies of the OSSTF.

5.1. Centralizing Governance: Increasing Ontario Ministry of Education Control of the Toronto District School Board

The centralization of governance and policy proceeded from the shift of control over funding from school districts to provincial governments, beginning in the late 1990s and becoming the dominant trend across Canada by the early 2000s, reversing decentralization in the 1960s through the 1980s (Wallner 2014, 76–7). Chief among political motivations was a perceived greater capacity of provincial governments to control the large proportion of education expenditures determined by teachers' collective bargaining. In Ontario, the PCs uploaded education finance from locally levied property taxes to centralized funding from the provincial government under Bill 160 in 1997 (ibid., 219). This move resulted in the ratcheting-down of funding to a lower common denominator that squeezed Toronto, as the city had previously financed its schools at an above-average rate. Overall education funding was cut by $5.4 billion in 1997. Some smaller rural boards, which previously had drawn from a limited property tax base, did receive funding increases (Fullan and Boyle 2014, 62).[1] Among its many impacts, another means by which Bill 160 promoted centralization was through the amalgamation of 129 school districts into 72 (including all public, Catholic, French, and French Catholic systems). The TDSB was formed from the school boards, each of which was larger than many rural boards, of the six former cities of metropolitan Toronto, which at this time were also forcibly merged into Metropolitan Toronto (ibid., 60). Whereas New York City lost its elected school board trustees with the implementation of mayoral control, the school trustees remained in Ontario, but their annual stipend was capped by provincial legislation at $5,000. Trustees who were not wealthy or retired were hampered in representing their constituents on a full-time basis, as was formerly the case in Toronto (ibid., 62). The provincial government reasserted its drive to fiscal austerity and centralizing control in 2002 by declaring it illegal for school boards to approve a budget deficit. Districts in Toronto and Ottawa passed them anyway and were taken over by provincial supervisors. They were also unable to create balanced budgets without drastic cuts to programs and staff. With an election on the horizon, the increasingly unpopular PCs restored modest portions of funding (ibid., 63).

While avoiding altering the formal structure of local collective bargaining, the government used its power over education finance to legislate provincial control over key aspects of teachers' professional autonomy previously negotiated between boards and federations. These actions included removing the following issues from the purview of collective bargaining while imposing changes generally intended to reduce funding: class sizes (increased), staffing allocations (reduced), professional development (reduced), preparation time (cut in half), and teachers' administrative duties (increased, in addition to mandatory "voluntary" activities). The outcome of these policies imposed by the provincial government was the reduction of approximately 10,000 teaching positions through retirements and layoffs (ibid.). As Goli Rezai-Rashti explains:

> All of these policy reforms served to centralize educational decision-making and increase the ministry's control over matters of finance and curriculum that had previously been under the jurisdiction of local boards of education. In just five years (1996–2001) the Ministry of Education and Training became the main source of funding and principal regulator of education, drastically reducing the power of school boards. (2009, 309)

The final straw was perhaps an unpopular law in 2001 providing tax credits to parents for sending their children to private schools. This amounted to a step in the direction of school vouchers and was a profound form of privatization by which public funding would be redistributed to subsidize private schools (Fullan and Boyle 2014, 65). Soon after the implementation of this law, academics at OISE, many of whom would later play important roles within succeeding Liberal governments, released *The Schools We Need: Recent Education Policy in Ontario & Recommendations for Moving Forward*. It was a strong critique of PC education policies for being too many and often harmful (Leithwood, Fullan, and Watson 2003). It was heavily cited in the Liberal Party's campaign in the 2003 election, won by McGuinty with a majority government. The tax credit was promptly repealed. The PC defeat in the 2007 election was widely attributed to their proposal for a revised tax credit for students attending private religious schools, resulting in another majority government for the Liberals (Fullan and Boyle 2014, 66).

This structure of governance largely remained intact under the Liberals, establishing the context in which, under McGuinty and Wynne, the provincial government had a significant influence on teachers' work and professional autonomy. During his first term, from 2003 to 2007, Dalton McGuinty carried out a key campaign promise as the self-described "education premier" and restored $2.6 billion in education funding (of the $5.4 billion cut by Harris) to hire specialist and classroom teachers to lower elementary class sizes and fund a "Student Success" teacher in every high school as part of a priority discussed in the next section to raise graduation rates (ibid., 67). However, Elizabeth Shilton observes, "More fundamentally, the McGuinty Liberals have shown no interest in repealing the keystone of the Harris-era centralizing reforms: central control of education funding, reflected in the provincial education funding formula" (2012, 235). Taxing power would not be returned to local districts. Despite increases in the per pupil student grants through which most provincial funding was directed, considerable pressure remained for districts to close small schools, as fixed costs were covered by declining enrolment, as will be discussed below in section 5.5. It was also the primary mechanism facilitating the competition for enrolment in Toronto and other large cities through school choice.

The leadership of the TDSB enjoyed a much better relationship with the Liberals than with their predecessors, who had drastically reduced their autonomy and funding while temporarily taking over their administration (Fullan and Boyle 2014, 86). Trustee compensation was raised to $25,000 (leaving it still mostly a part-time job). From the 2003 provincial election through the 2014 election, nearly all of Toronto's twenty-two provincial electoral districts elected Liberals, making the city along with the surrounding "905" suburbs the core of the party's support in the legislature.[2] Not insignificantly, Kathleen Wynne's political trajectory began as a TDSB trustee in 2000, where she opposed the mass school closures threatened by the Harris government's budget cuts. Elected to the provincial legislature with McGuinty's victory in 2003, she served as education minister from 2006 to 2010. Meanwhile, the TDSB was restructured into twenty "families of schools" led by superintendents, which, unlike New York City's more amorphous school networks, were still generally aligned geographically with the city's trustee wards, each with a total of twenty-five to thirty elementary and secondary schools. Fullan and Boyle explain how these "families," larger than many districts in northern Ontario, functioned in relation to the ambitious rollout of reforms from the provincial Ministry of Education:

> The families of schools enjoy high levels of professional autonomy led by the superintendents with the close involvement of trustees. This independence, coupled with less direct connection from the centre to the schools in a larger organization, meant that the Ontario reforms were slower to gain traction in the TDSB compared with most other school boards across the province. (Ibid., 87)

Fullan and Boyle also observe, "the district had a tradition of operating with a degree of conflict and turmoil at the top (among the trustees, with the government)" (ibid., 86). Tension with the Liberal government was limited to frustration over the disparity between its mandate to run new provincial programs such as full-day kindergarten and insufficient funding provided to do so. However, internal conflict made headlines in 2013 and 2014, challenging the legitimacy of its elected board as an institution. A charismatic TDSB director[3] known for "culture-building" events such as a motivational rally of thousands of teachers and board staff at the start of one school year resigned in 2013 after being found to have plagiarized a newspaper column and his PhD dissertation. Together with the district's struggle to balance its budget with received funding, one conservative columnist called it a "crisis of governance" and looked south for an alternative model, "In big cities like New York or Chicago, the head of schools is a high-profile position filled by high-calibre individuals. The TDSB needs a chief executive with experience in the business world or the broader public sector at complex administration" (Gee 2013). In late 2014, scandal ensued again when it was revealed that the new director had awarded herself a substantial raise while teachers and other employees were subjected to a wage freeze by the provincial government. Among other sources of near violent boardroom conflict, she refused to share her employment contract with trustees, despite their duty to provide its oversight.[4] Pundits and politicians called for a takeover by the provincial government or, inspired by US models, mayoral control (Lorinc 2014; Canadian Press 2014). The Liberal government commissioned an "outside expert" to conduct a public review of the TDSB's top administration. In addition to a "culture of fear" among senior managers and dubious "pet projects," she reported that a particular problem was trustees who "retained a 'full time' mind-set," despite their "symbolic" compensation (Wilson 2015, 5). They would intervene regularly in the work of principals in their ward, demand their participation in political events, and even influence their appointment (Wilson 2015).

The discrediting of the district leadership created a context for the Ministry of Education to intervene in an unpopular and seemingly unrelated agenda of closing schools with declining enrolment to sell off its valuable real estate. In the final few pages of a report focused on interpersonal dynamics and management culture, the reviewer pivoted to underutilized schools, arguing the need to sell them off to bring much needed revenue to the system and criticizing trustees for obstructing this process due to the interests of their constituents (ibid.). Within days of the release of the review in early 2015, the education minister issued an ultimatum for the board to address these findings (Sandals 2015). The budget for trustees, access to assistants, and office space were considerably reduced. New plans were made to close secondary schools with low enrolment due to demographic changes and, as will be discussed in section 5.6, a lack of success in the context of school choice. Embarrassing dysfunctional conflict and alleged corruption at the TDSB ultimately facilitated the further centralization of power in the provincial government. In this context, the governments of McGuinty and Wynne held considerable sway over the rollout of policy from the centre to Toronto's classrooms.

5.2. Quantifying Student Achievement: Policy from the Centre

This section details the development of education policy primarily from the vantage point of the provincial Ministry of Education. I describe it as "policy from the centre" to emphasize its top-down origins whereby most initiatives began with the ministry, which actively participated in global policy networks. They were then pushed out to school districts, which had varying but generally limited leeway for adaptation to local circumstances. As before, to provide context I begin with a brief overview of the significant intervention of the Harris PC government on teachers' professional autonomy. Then I will consider how the education policy imperatives of the Liberal McGuinty and Wynne governments, particularly their emphasis on EQAO test scores and high school graduation rates as key metrics to define their success, emerged from the Harris era to underpin ever increasing "layers" of top-down policy (Pinto 2015), which have increasingly defined the work of educators.

This section particularly draws on and critiques a detailed account by Fullan and Boyle (2014) of this era in which Michael Fullan served as a prominent advisor to the provincial government. For his prolific and high-profile interventions into provincial education policy over more than two decades, Fullan is among the few policy consultants whose name would be familiar to many Ontario teachers. His influence radiates far beyond the provincial scope he might otherwise have as a professor emeritus and former dean of OISE. He is arguably one of the world's most well-known and influential education policy consultants. Toronto-based People for Education executive director, Annie Kidder, describes Fullan and the UK-based policy advisor Michael Barber as "rock stars that zoom around the world" (interview Nov. 2015). In March 2018, the home page of Fullan's consultancy website, where he is described as a "worldwide authority in educational reform," touted his ongoing work with authorities in California, the Peel District School Board of Mississauga and Brampton, Ontario, and a workshop tour in Australia (see michaelfullan.ca).

Near the apex of his influence, in 2010 Fullan co-chaired with Barber a large-scale international conference on policy, Building Blocks for Education: Whole System Reform, sponsored by the Ontario government and hosted by Premier McGuinty. Ministry of Education and senior school board officials spoke on "international benchmarks," comparing recent changes in the systems of Australia, Finland, Singapore, Ontario, and the United States (Fullan and Barber 2010, 2). Keynote speaker Andreas Schleicher, director of the OECD's Program for International Student Assessment (PISA), argued for the importance of generating data through standardized testing, earning strong agreement from Fullan and Barber. They explained that it would constitute "collective autonomy," arguing, "We should not interpret the call for autonomy as a return to the autonomy of the individual teacher. 'Behind the classroom door' is decidedly not for fans of whole system reform" (ibid., 13). US Secretary of Education Arne Duncan extolled merit pay for teachers and his Race to the Top (RTTT) program (described in chapter 3). Fullan disagreed in his final report, citing insufficient evidence of merit pay's efficacy and argued that it would be a "huge distractor," which the Ontario government was not interested in (ibid., 13).

Fullan's success comes in considerable part from codifying policy lessons[5] from his experience as a senior advisor under Dalton McGuinty into a "brand of education reform" (Sue Winton, interview Dec. 2015). I take a critical approach to some of the McGuinty-era policies that he stands behind, particularly the reliance on Education Quality Accountability Office (EQAO) standardized test score results to evaluate the Ontario education system and the drive to raise graduation rates without considering its effects on the integrity of classroom teaching. Overall, I am critical of his embrace of top-down policy in the Ontario context, insofar as it does not take seriously the capacity of teachers to effectively exercise their professional judgment. As a result, this chapter contends that their classroom autonomy has been undermined. However, as Annie Kidder observed (see chapter 2), in the context of the dominant policy discourses in the United States, Mexico, and many other countries, including the United Kingdom, "his brand is not to attack teachers." In his later writings, Fullan (2016) clarified his criticism of NCLB's punitive approach of firing teachers and closing struggling schools. He also recognized that teachers draw significant satisfaction from exercising their professionalism well, so merit pay is a "wrong driver" for reform. Fullan has even critiqued top-down reform more generally (but not in reference to Ontario), recognizing that more often than not these policies fail to connect with the realities of teachers' work lives. However, his chief remedy is to scale down from working through civil servants, administrators, and politicians at the national or the state/provincial level to the district level. The voice of classroom teachers remains marginalized because he does not acknowledge or take seriously the contradictory power relationships of schools and school districts as hierarchical workplaces. Administrators and superintendents do not necessarily understand or sympathize with the realities of teachers' work or share the same interests, as teachers and principals themselves will argue in the following sections. While Fullan is a focus of critique, he is symptomatic of the post-Harris PC experience in Ontario, of a softer neoliberalization of education, in contrast to the pro-privatization, anti-labour approach of Governor Cuomo in New York State or President Enrique Peña Nieto in Mexico.

Drawing on recommendations of the Royal Commission on Learning from the preceding New Democratic (NDP) government, soon after their election in 1996 the PCs established the EQAO as an independent agency responsible for administering standardized testing within the public education system.[6] The EQAO introduced tests of reading, writing, and math in grades 3 and 6, math in grade 9, and reading and writing in grade 10 (Fullan and Boyle 2014, 61–2). The tests were strongly opposed by teachers and their federations, among other reasons because they would narrow instruction. Under pressure to obtain high scores for a school's record, teachers would divert time otherwise spent on regular course content to drilling students on the specific knowledge most likely to be found on the tests. "Teaching to the test" would constitute a significant threat to professional autonomy, as teachers in the United States and Mexico could corroborate. Except for the grade 10 literacy test,[6] the EQAO tests would not be considered "high stakes" for teachers or students in the way that such tests are in New York State, where they decide teacher employment and student graduation (in the case of the high school Regents exams) or in Mexico where the ENLACE determined teacher employment and salary increases. Elsewhere in Canada, provincial exams comprise 40 per cent of a student's final marks in grades 10 through 12 in British Columbia and 50 per cent of final grade 12 marks in Alberta (Wallner 2014, 79). The primary significance of the EQAO test scores was indicative, to provide an analysis of the system as a whole as well as of individual schools. While lacking the direct punitiveness of standardized tests under NCLB, through which consistently low-scoring schools could be closed and their staff fired, the results similarly received a wide public release and, as will be argued below, were linked to more subtle forms of pressuring and shaping of teachers' work. As Spencer (2012) contends, the highly centralized record-keeping practices to which the school-level administration of the EQAO contributes, is a form of "governance at a distance" through the audit of local authorities.[7]

The Conservative government created the regulatory Ontario College of Teachers (OCT) in 1997. It produced the *Standards of Practice for the Teaching Profession*, which defined teacher professionalism in broad terms that were largely taken for granted. More controversially, in 2001 the OCT was tasked by the government with administering the Ontario Teacher Qualifying Test (OTQT),[8] an exam for all new applicants for teaching positions, and a requalifying test every five years. Both resembled the standardized evaluations of the Ley de Servicio Profesional Docente discussed in the previous chapter that have been bitterly resisted by the Mexican teachers' movement. The system for evaluating teachers through principals' observations was standardized with the introduction of the Teacher Performance Appraisal (TPA) process, consisting primarily of two formal classroom observations every two years and the New Teacher Induction Program (NTIP) of two observations of teachers in each of their first two years (Rezai-Rashti 2009, 309–10; Fullan and Boyle 2014, 62; Shilton 2012, 234). Interviews by Pinto et al. (2012) with forty-one Ontario elementary and secondary school administrators about what makes a good teacher found that they drew largely on two popular archetypes: the "charismatic teacher," who possessed intrinsic intangible qualities (caring, firm, good communicator, etc.); and the teacher whose "competency" was more reflective of the official discourse of the ministry of knowledge of curriculum and policy. Pinto et al. conclude, "NTIP reflects a knowledge transmission model of induction, whereby the focus is on conformity and the transference of so-called 'expert' knowledge" (ibid., 79). They argue that neither the criteria used in NTIP nor those of individual administrators encouraged independence on the part of teachers. While arguably superior to Mexico's standardized teacher exams in assessing how teachers work in the classroom, Ontario's NTIP and TPA rely heavily on the subjective perceptions of principals, which mostly align with dominant discourse from the ministry and do not tend to encourage alternative or critical approaches to pedagogy and instruction by teachers.

Rezai-Rashti (2009) summarizes the impact of the Harris era on teachers' work as intensification (new curriculum squeezing new content into fewer courses, budget cuts leading to larger class sizes and less prep time) and reorganization. The latter consisted of replacing high school department heads who had subject-area expertise with a system of around four teachers as Curriculum Leaders, each responsible for several subject areas. As Curriculum Leaders would usually not be personally experienced in all of the several subject areas for which they were responsible, their duties veered away from actually being curricular leaders. Rezai-Rashti describes this situation as a shift from veteran teachers to "teacher-managers," "whose main responsibility is to administer government-mandated policies in local schools" (2009, 316). Meanwhile the new provincial curriculum was more prescribed, and detailed lists of "overall expectations" and "specific expectations" meant less teacher discretion in interpreting courses. Some teachers interviewed by Rezai-Rashti suggested that this change could provide students with a clearer idea of where marks came from. Overall, he argues that these changes had a profoundly adverse impact on teachers' professional autonomy, and that the "impact of restructuring was felt most strongly in Toronto, where more progressive ideas and support mechanisms had been in place" (ibid., 312).

Rezai-Rashti found that at least some veteran teachers were able to continue to exercise a fair amount of autonomy in the face of these top-down reforms, supporting Larry Cuban's research on the persistence of classroom autonomy despite major top-down policies (2009, 2013). One experienced teacher explained:

> I have been teaching long enough to see a number of different things come and go through the years, and generally what you do, if you're in a

> position where you already have a permanent contract, and it is unlikely you would be called up on the carpet, and you have seniority … is take what you like from these changes that come about, and the things you think are best suited to the particular subject area that you're teaching … if I were a beginning teacher or even mid-career looking at another ten or fifteen years, then I would definitely address these things in a much more serious way. (Rezai-Rashti 2009, 313)

Accordingly, Rezai-Rashti argues that the strongest impact of the Harris era reforms on teachers' professional work was on new teachers with less experience, ability, or confidence to push existing professional autonomy to the hilt in response to reforms. He concludes pessimistically:

> there have been no substantial structural changes in the everyday practices of schooling. The reorganization of the education system institutionalized by the former Conservative government is now so entrenched that the potential for any substantial changes to the system are limited. (Ibid., 318)

Sears and Cairns (2019) and Laura Pinto concur that, from the PCs to the Liberals, "Ontario's core education policy has remained largely unchanged while the neoliberal rhetoric has persisted" (Pinto 2015, 143). I will now attempt to assess the extent to which this belief is the case.

Dalton McGuinty's government intervened quickly after taking office to change some significant aspects of teacher evaluation instituted under Harris. The OTQT qualifying standardized test and recertification requirements were eliminated, while the performance appraisal was shifted from every two years to every five years, and the NTIP was retained (Rezai-Rashti 2009, 309; Shilton 2012, 234; Pinto et al. 2012). The broader trend under Harris of rolling out layer upon layer of top-down policy from the centre continued and arguably intensified. Pinto et al. did not see substantial changes towards more democratically engaging educators and communities in curriculum development during McGuinty's first term (2012, 206–7). Under McGuinty, the ministry substantially expanded its capacity as it centralized control from local school districts over education policy. Through this process, policymaking became more politicized, according to OSSTF president Paul Elliot:

> It really came to fruition, the whole shift in power, after Harris left, but he was the one who started the ball rolling. When he shifted the funding to the provincial government, it really became more political than it ever

> was before. Locally, it was just locally political, some people couldn't even tell you who the trustees were ... McGuinty, as much as he may have been known as the education premier – it really all had to do with the directives and policies that came out ... the exponential growth of the Ministry of Education, of policy advisors specifically ... Because now, if they were funding it, they really took control over the direction of education. That's when we began to see the drive to increase graduation rates. (Interview Sept. 2016)

Elliot continues, explaining how in his opinion the steady expansion of the Ministry of Education under McGuinty and Wynne created its own rationality for ever expanding policy:

> Every time I go over there, you're always meeting new policy people. And they come and go so quickly. Case in point, when I went to the last central table in bargaining, we talked about ministry initiatives. We got them to agree to a one year hiatus on ministry initiatives. They were just aghast. They said to us, "you have no idea what you're asking us to do." Because it was almost impossible for them to do that because they are driven by new initiatives. Without initiatives, they don't exist for any reason. You had whole floors of people who would continue working on new initiatives because that's what they do. (Ibid.)

Certainly, this explanation of institutional self-perpetuation is far from Fullan and Boyle's account below of "morally driven" policy reform.

The most significant part of the McGuinty government's education policies centred around measures intended to raise the scores in the annual EQAO tests instituted under Harris, as they were assumed to be the most accurate form of measuring the system's overall effectiveness, and raising high school graduation rates while requiring youth to remain in school until age eighteen. Fullan and Boyle attribute the Liberal government's emphasis on improving "literacy and numeracy" to a trip by McGuinty to England in the late 1990s, where the future premier observed Fullan's work as an assistant to Prime Minister Tony Blair. They credit McGuinty with leaving behind Blair's more punitive policies, in which schools performing badly on tests were subject to "assertive name-and-shame accountability" (2014, 67). The Ontario government established a Literacy and Numeracy Secretariat in 2004 to coordinate school strategies aimed at improving scores. Raising graduation rates would be the subject of projects grouped under the Student Success Initiative (ibid., 67–70). In contrast to Pinto's views, Fullan and Boyle claim that the McGuinty government did increase the involvement of teachers in developing the Student Success, Literacy, and Numeracy programs, especially relative to the policies of the preceding Harris government:

> The unwritten message was that schools and teachers needed to be key participants in improvement and that their ideas and knowledge mattered. This was a smart move early in the strategy, as it demonstrated trust in the profession, an essential ingredient for an effective partnership and buy-in from teachers. (Ibid., 68)

Fullan and Boyle tout their model of a balance of "pressure and support," which they contend was followed by the McGuinty government during this period, with the subsequent successes that ensued in terms of higher EQAO scores and graduation rates. Rather than the punitive consequences for low scores seen in the contemporary United Kingdom or the United States under NCLB, in 2006 the Ontario Focused Intervention Partnership (OFIP) was created through which elementary schools with low or stable scores received additional support. Initially, $25 million was spread over 1,100 schools ($27,000 each), including 150 TDSB schools, reduced to 10 by 2013, as their scores rose (ibid., 72, 89). Fullan and Boyle describe the basis behind the program's success, claiming that it motivated teachers to be proactive where they previously were not:

> Before intervention, more teachers blamed external factors such as poverty roughly 2:1. After OFIP, the opinions shifted 1:2, with more teachers admitting they could do something about it. Across the province the OFIP program was a big success. Combining high expectations, nonjudgemental (positive) stances towards the schools, and targeted and ongoing support for capacity building. (Ibid., 91)

The number of low-achieving schools was reduced, owing to the "involvement of superintendents, a shift from professional development to professional learning, more sophisticated use of data, and a deliberate focus on improving teaching" (ibid.). EQAO scores and high school graduation rates rose during McGuinty's first term from 2003 to 2007, Fullan and Boyle say, because of "a combination of focus, new resources, and mutual commitment between the government and schools" (ibid., 73).

To make it easier for more students to graduate, the Specialist High School Majors (SHSM) program was launched in 2006, through which schools developed "specialist programs" with connections to local businesses and industry. Students could earn additional credits through work placement programs and free community college courses. Within a few years, 38,000 students had enrolled in 1,500 programs at 647 high schools, representing 12 per cent of all secondary students (ibid., 70). Fullan and Boyle give credit to this program for substantially boosting graduation rates. The program had much lower enrolment in the TDSB, with only 1,700 participating students as opposed to 4,800, if involvement was in proportion to the rest of the province. They blame TDSB trustees for obstructing the program for reasons that are unstated (ibid., 91). Fullan and Boyle also herald a shift from formal professional development sessions to improve teaching to "ongoing learning in schools" collectively facilitated by teachers, especially in high schools. "Through moderated marking and co-teaching, this form of professional learning has also moved schools on. Some refer to it as the deprivatization of the classroom." It was "not being mandated or part of a deliberate strategy" (ibid., 95), suggesting it was bottom-up, though they later explain that these programs were launched by superintendents.

Fullan and Boyle describe the ministry's activity from 2008 to 2012, in which Fullan was embedded: "The reforms picked up momentum in the second phase, and the sheer volume of work is enormous" (ibid., 74). The *Energizing Ontario Education* (2008) policy document retained the prioritization of increasing the proportion of students scoring above 70 per cent on math and literacy tests and set a target of 85 per cent of high school students graduating within five years by 2011, up from 68 per cent in 2003.[9] Initiatives were also launched to raise EQAO scores among marginalized groups, including Indigenous students, recent immigrants, and students from low-income families (Ontario Ministry of Education 2008, 5–9). By 2010, 72 per cent of students graduated high school within the standard four years, and by 2012, 84 per cent did so within five years. Meanwhile, the proportion of students achieving 70 per cent and up on the grade 9 math score increased from 59 per cent in 2007 to 73 per cent in 2012. The numbers on the grade 10 literacy test declined slightly over these years from 79 per cent to 77 per cent (Fullan and Boyle 2014, 80, 81). In the TDSB, EQAO test scores for grades 3 and 6 closely tracked Ontario averages from 2003 to 2012. They consistently remained a couple of percentage points below on the grade 9 math and grade 10 literacy tests, as well as on the graduation rate. Consistent with their focus on the agency of their policy and dismissal of structural causes, they blame this drop on the lower TDSB uptake of the SHSM program (ibid., 98–100). Fullan and Boyle attribute the success of McGuinty's "Ontario Strategy," of which Fullan was a part, as having a "small number of ambitious goals" and a "focus on data as an instrument of continuous improvement" (ibid., 85). They note approvingly that the "TDSB is one of the leading boards in the province in using data to measure outcomes and inform decisions and instructional practices" (ibid., 88). As in New York, an Office of Accountability and Student Achievement reports to the director.

People for Education's executive director, Annie Kidder, head of Ontario's most prominent education advocacy group, contends that the government's encompassing focus on increasing test scores has created distorted priorities of helping a specific range of students reach a specific metric, in this case, obtaining at least 70 per cent (level three of four). While lauding the province's less punitive approach towards teachers and schools in comparison with that of the United States, she comments:

> So it's definitely we're going to work together [teachers, schools, and the government], but it's still having very very strong overall goals. Despite it being not commonly copped to at a provincial level, it certainly has been, if our political goal is getting X per cent of kids up to level 3, then certainly, high schools were told, work on the kids who are at 2.7 … To us that's a bastardization of what we should be doing in our classroom. (Interview Nov. 2015)

Ann Vibert observes in the context of education reform under Harris and McGuinty in Ontario, "So highly do proponents of accountability value the demonstration of improvement that the *appearance* of improvement becomes the primary consideration. As in the market, perception is reality" (2009, 296; emphasis original). A high school teacher and education activist adds even more sceptically:

> The McGuinty government and subsequently the Wynne government is very data driven. It's all about graduation rates, and test scores too, but in particular credits earned, graduation rates … and so they came up with all these initiatives like credit recovery, credit rescue … to basically grant credits … So we've seen massive mark inflation … but of course they have the data. So graduation rates have gone up under the Liberals – not a surprise. When you take the Enron approach to education, if the numbers don't add up, just figure out a different way to add up the numbers. I'm speaking as somebody who doesn't even care about marks. I would be happier teaching a system that didn't give marks. (Toronto Teacher 10, interview July 2015)

This teacher's language, implying a deliberate effort on the part of the provincial government to skew grades upwards to support their political agenda, may sound like an exaggeration or assigning too much intent and agency. Consider, however, this account by a teacher, hired by EQAO to score grade 6 reading and writing tests, of an incident during the grading process:

> After two days of scoring, we were informed that whatever we'd been scoring as a code 20 was now a code 30. (Laughs) We were organized in pods. Pods are two groups of approximately thirty teachers in each group, so there [were] sixty teachers in each room, and there are supervisors at the front ... and there was an audible outcry. People were like, "What do you mean? What do you mean all of a sudden what you told us was this is now this?" That was the curve, right? They weren't getting the results that they wanted from that particular question ... there were some people who said, "I don't think I can do this." They wanted to leave. They just felt that the integrity of the process, if there was any to begin with, was completely undermined ... my guess is that the results that were coming in on the language score were lower than they wanted. ... the difference between a code 20 and a code 30 could be the difference between some students passing and some students failing. (Toronto Teacher 2, interview Aug. 2014)

This teacher's experience of shifting grading criteria used by EQAO was corroborated in a separate interview with Toronto Teacher 4, who had also graded these exams.

Fullan and Boyle claim that the "Ontario Strategy" was "Not top down or bottom up," citing the involvement of some school district directors in policies ultimately determined by the provincial Ministry of Education as "policy leadership from the middle" (2014, 88). After publication of *Big City School Reforms*, Fullan developed the concept of "Leadership from the Middle." Critiquing policy reforms from national or state/provincial governments as being too top-down, he also dismisses bottom-up (i.e., teacher-led) reform as "too piecemeal" (Fullan 2016, 203). His "middle" is the directors of school districts, whom he urges to work together horizontally for finer-grain policies than can be meaningfully elaborated and implemented from the top. The top remains important for developing the right "drivers," such as standardized test scores, to measure schools (ibid., 203–4).

Fullan and Boyle articulate their technocratic orientation underpinning many of the assumptions behind McGuinty and Wynne's "Ontario Strategy" in explaining why test scores and graduation rates improved in the TDSB:

> The alignment of data was important, coupled with the growth of skills and ability to compare and manipulate the data ... The intense focus on

> higher expectations with accountability led to more precise conversations between district and school leaders about which students needed most support and how it was going to be provided. Then it was the resources, human and financial, that came with the Ontario Strategy that made the difference. Today the district and the schools feel that they are part of a larger plan. (2014, 90)

It is a version, albeit friendlier towards classroom teachers, of the same assumptions guiding the centralization of education governance in New York and Mexico in which only when subjected to sufficient external pressure will educators improve their schools and that ultimately it is up to experts and top officials to generate the means by which this improvement will occur. Accordingly, they are willing to share credit: "Donna Quan, Director of Education at TDSB, has evidence showing that District Reviews of schools have made the biggest impact on student achievement in recent years" (ibid., 92). The District Reviews consist of high schools first completing a "School Effectiveness Framework" to self-assess room for improvement, then review teams visiting schools to speak with staff and students and observe them in classrooms, and scrutinizing student work. "Communication is open, honest, and transparent throughout the process. The District Review Team adopts a supportive and nonjudgemental approach" (ibid., 93). Fullan and Boyle note that the process was developed with union consultation. This likely helped create a process that was less punitive or adversarial than New York Mayor Bloomberg's initial letter grades for schools. They note optimistically, "Current conversations focus on the differences between a good and a great school" (ibid.). In addition to all high schools completing these reviews within three years, principals in consultation with teacher Curriculum Leaders complete annual "School Improvement Plans," which are appended to the "Board Improvement Plan for Student Achievement" submitted to the ministry. Individual schools and the TDSB as a whole must explain how they will make improvements in "literacy, numeracy, learning pathways, community, culture, and caring" (ibid.). At least the first two are defined by EQAO scores. Anecdotally, according to teachers cited in the following section and administrators interviewed by Pinto (2015), it is these more quantitative criteria that are politically more significant, making such policy plans reminiscent of the "Quality Schools Program" (PEC) instituted in Mexico during this period.

Fullan and Boyle take pains to distinguish their endorsed strategy in Ontario from the punitive contemporary ones of New York and England, yet retain the use of standardized test scores as a primary metric to judge the system's progress. Moreover, there is a very clear imperative woven throughout of the necessity of year-over-year, sustained, rapid improvement on all fronts. How feasible is it to maintain this plan indefinitely? How does it affect the system? Is there a dumbing-down of credit integrity or of the standardized exams themselves? Teachers interviewed in the following section do believe that constantly rising progress has been achieved at least partly through weakened standards. Their voices are not found in Fullan and Boyle's accounts, though they criticize contemporary trends in "negative accountability, isolated school autonomy, the continued deterioration of the teaching profession" (2014, 145).

The policy imperative of constantly rising graduation rates is thornier. Students without a high school diploma hold limited options for a life without poverty. Raising the percentage of youth in high school also requires increasing resources, as OSSTF president Paul Elliot explains: "It's at about 85 now? If they want to get to 90, it's a huge step in support to get to 90 because the next 5 per cent are going to take such an increased level of support, attention, different kinds of programs" (interview Sept. 2016). Additional Special Education classes with very low teacher to student ratios, more educational assistants, youth workers, and counsellors are required to effectively accommodate students who often suffer from a range of emotional and mental health issues. If they had a choice, by the age of sixteen or seventeen, many would drop out of school, as was the case in previous decades. The gritty realities of this situation are not captured in Fullan and Boyle's bird's-eye system analysis. What we see instead is a parade of good intentions from the McGuinty government and their colleagues at the top of the TDSB. Providing the necessary resources to keep a growing proportion of youth in school precipitates a collision with austerity politics, which, with regard to education, became pronounced in Ontario from 2012 onwards, threatening the incremental improvements in funding of the Liberal government's first two terms. These developments will be further discussed in the final two sections of this chapter.

Criticism of the top-down education policy of the Liberal premiers and traditional scepticism of academics and civil servants were opportunistically employed in the 2014 education platform of the hard-right PC leader Tim Hudak. His education white paper claimed to champion "a teacher and principal driven system" and dismissed the work of Fullan and other policy advocates contracted by the Liberals:

> Only the classroom teacher really knows the particular needs of your child. When it comes to education, a key principle for the Ontario PC Caucus is that decisions made by individuals closest to students and parents work better than those made by big bureaucracies. We believe that

> the community school ought to be the key unit in the system, and that the teachers and their principal are the most important players. Right now, education bureaucrats at Queen's Park, the school boards and teachers' unions are the key players. The teacher is the most un-empowered person in this top-down system ... We believe teachers should be respected enough to make decisions in their own classrooms. (PC Party 2013, 10)

The PCs' strategy here of lauding teachers as a profession in their appeal to parents should be considered in the context of the backlash towards Conservative premier Mike Harris, who in television and radio ads attacked teachers for protesting the policies of his government. It also suggests that while populist resentment or scepticism about top-down policy is widespread, the PCs believed a juxtaposition of "out of touch" technocracy against classroom teachers would help garner support from voters. On the following page of the policy document under the heading "A Realistic Definition of a Teachers' Job," it is clear that, despite the PCs' claimed view of top-down policy, teachers would continue to be disempowered. Principals would have increased power to assign them additional non-classroom duties and change the composition and size of their classes, as the government would remove these issues from collective bargaining (ibid., 11–12).[10]

For Fullan and Boyle, success in school districts can be attributed chiefly to the agency of directors, superintendents, and provincial ministry officials. In this hierarchical view, the role of the classroom teacher is more implicit, reduced to being accountable for carrying out policies dictated from above. In reading their account, one gets a strong impression that little consultation was done with school staff (teachers and administrators), and a great deal was done with policy leaders at TDSB headquarters and the ministry offices. According to OSSTF Toronto vice-president Leslie Wolfe:

> The levels to which the provincial governments under McGuinty and Wynne have infiltrated extended themselves into the development of curriculum, the implementation of curriculum, the funding, the standardization of curriculum, and the standardization of expectations of performance by teachers and students; all of that has come together to, whether in actuality or in perception, make teachers feel like they have very little professional control over what's happening in the classroom. (Interview Sept. 2016)

Wolfe subsequently qualifies her comments in relation to the later Wynne government since 2013: "To be fair, I think she's been more sensitized to our complaint that too much, too fast, too many changes, not enough time or professional development to implement any of them properly" (ibid.).

The official record of the success of the McGuinty and Wynne governments' test-score and graduation-rate driven interventions into education policy, as presented by Fullan and Boyle, is open to challenge. Some argue it has distorted a significant part of the focus of education policy by fixating on improving the abstract metrics given so much political weight. It will be argued in the following section that such policies have had a significant impact on teachers' work and an adverse effect on their professional autonomy.

5.3. Quantifying Student Achievement: The Impact on the Classroom and Professional Autonomy

It's always better to give a higher mark than a lower one. Always. Cause of those three, you know, the parents, the admin, and the colleague? That'll make it easier for you in all of those circumstances. And the kid. It makes your life easier, so just hand out the high marks and pretend ... swallow your integrity and give the high marks because it makes everything easier. Everyone's happy then. (Toronto Teacher 8, interview July 2015)

It feels less and less like a respected profession, and more like being a hired babysitter, in terms of my feelings of how I feel like I'm treated by the board and the admin ... I don't feel as valued or respected. It's harder and harder to do my job effectively in the classroom cause I don't feel that there are as many supports. (Toronto Teacher 6, interview Mar. 2015)

The previous section gave an overview of how the Liberals drew on the centralization of governance to implement layers of policy downwards onto the TDSB in a context where education remained politically sensitive. I now draw on teachers' perspectives on how this pattern has affected their work. The following two subsections will emphasize how these provincial policies affect schools differently. An important variable is the socio-economic context of their students, which creates varying pressures depending on graduation rates, EQAO test scores, and the school's desirability under school choice. I begin by exploring how the downward flow of policies from the ministry to the TDSB and the principals to implement in their schools has affected the latter's relationship with teachers. I find that changes in the responsibilities of administrators have contributed to modifying their power dynamics with teachers, as the work of principals becomes increasingly centred around ensuring compliance with ministry and district policies. The professional autonomy of teachers, enabling them to assess how to best meet the specific needs of their students, is continually challenged by the pressure to meet provincially set targets for test scores and graduation rates and by the imperative of implementing "layers" of centrally devised policies towards these ends (Pinto 2015). As in New York City, the imperative of showing continual, quantifiable improvement creates the pretext at the school and classroom level for administrators to intervene in teachers' work.

As noted earlier, a watershed moment in the working experience of Ontario teachers occurred when the Mike Harris PCs legislated the removal of principals and vice-principals from any form of union organization under the provincial Labour Relations Act (Shilton 2012, 223). OSSTF Toronto vice-president Leslie Wolfe explains it as "a punitive measure after they supported teachers in our political protest in 1997" (interview Sept. 2016). For teachers employed during this period, a shift in power dynamics and roles was perceptible:

> Definitely, since when I first started teaching to now, the role of the admin has become very adversarial; whereas when I first started teaching, it was much more collegial ... As soon as they were taken out of the union they were made to choose if they wanted to continue on being administrators. Or if they wanted to stay in the union, then they went back to teaching in the classroom. As soon as that happened, you could feel a definite shift to a them versus us feeling. The role of the principal seems to be a lot more punitive towards teachers. It feels like they're middle-managers. They don't feel like teachers. (Toronto Teacher 6, interview Mar. 2015)

Another veteran teacher at a different school used similar terms to describe the shift from collegiality to a hierarchical "manager versus employee system" (Toronto Teacher 3, interview Aug. 2014). Wolfe argues that, even without returning school administrators to the federations, greater collaboration could have been fostered:

> There could have been a focus on creating a model of education where principals were seen as lead teachers ... What's happened instead [is] that principals have become truly, I call them on-site managers. They're not lead teachers. They have nothing to do with curriculum development and implementation. (Interview, Sept. 2016)

Instead of striving to understand the particularities of their school's community and to build consensus for improvements derived from that context, as Wolfe contends was more commonly the case when she began teaching in the mid-1980s, now they are mainly responsible for implementing and managing top-down policies and reporting on local results. Consultation with teachers is not as important:

> They are now small business/public relations managers whose job it is to implement at the school level what's trickling down from the government and through the board to the schools. I would say that that approach to change and the separation of the principal from being the lead teacher into being the "manager" of these people, who must implement the changes they're being told to implement, has also created that sense of loss of autonomy and increased stress … it started under Harris, but really under McGuinty all this top-down kind of new curriculum, new expectations, new approaches to teaching is really the culprit. Principals have been probably as much a victim of it, although they probably don't recognize that necessarily as a group, they might as individuals, as teachers have been. (Ibid.)

Pinto argues that "policy layers" around literacy, numeracy, and graduation rates from the Liberals, following on from the actions of the PCs, have been overwhelming for principals and teachers; she notes a "neoliberal move to mandate staggering volumes of new policy," and in the context of Ontario, she describes "policy texts as regulatory mechanisms that increase state control over educators" (2015, 140–1). According to Pinto, a key form in which neoliberal education policy has affected the professional autonomy of principals and teachers has been the use of standardized tests, arduous reporting, and "highly prescriptive policy," which has placed their work under greater surveillance as a form of "audit culture." She explains:

> Audit practices intensify educators' labour processes by encroaching on technical control through management systems with reductive and prescriptive mandates. Within this accountability vacuum, schools find themselves privileging certain practices, while detracting from educators' autonomy to make choices that they believe would better serve the needs of students. (Ibid., 142)

A similar conclusion is drawn by Vibert on the impact of top-down policy on teachers' work in Ontario, describing a process of deskilling and disempowering, where educators lose their capacity to exercise professional judgment:

> The consequence for teachers and especially for principals is that their time is increasingly taken up with documenting their work, filling forms, and

> sending information back to the system. In the process, of course, the work of teachers and principals is redefined in technocratic terms: no longer agents in the ongoing debate about purposes and practices that historically was central to education, they become technicians who "implement" a given curriculum and "administer" prescribed tests. (2009, 301)

Reporting to the provincial government on the culture of the TDSB's senior administration, Margaret Wilson cited a principal's account, "Every Executive Superintendent generates work for the principal in terms of reports as do the constant flow of new initiatives. Life becomes a paper chase leaving little time for the real job, curriculum leadership" (2015, 13).

Ontario high school principals and vice-principals interviewed by Pinto most frequently cited the government's Student Success Initiative – lauded in the section above by Fullan and Boyle as being responsible for higher graduation rates – as particularly onerous and frustrating. Key concerns were that the policies were frequently disconnected from school realities and that they had to implement them, regardless, or face disciplinary consequences (2015, 146). Pinto found that the

> intensity of accountability measures within policy results in the inability for educators to step back from their immediate demands and consider broader educational issues or look at these practices in a more holistic sense. This amounts to intensification: profound changes through more of the same work, or signification of different work tasks being assigned, such as record-keeping and administration. Characteristics in school settings include: a perceived lack of time; chronic work overload; replacing time spent caring for students with meeting administrative demands; enforced diversification of expertise; and pre-packaged curricula and pedagogy. (Ibid., 142)

Many of these issues are similar to those raised by teachers noted in previous chapters as well as below in this section. School administrators frequently viewed the policy as the product of an "ivory tower" outlook, removed from school realities, or of political imperatives to get quantitative results on test scores and graduation rates. They also complained that policies were sometimes contradictory and were generally top-down in conception and implementation, involving little consultation with school staff. Their standardized character meant they did not meet the specific needs of individual schools and their communities. Time was lost for addressing local issues not identified by central policy (ibid., 146–8). One principal interviewed by Pinto explained:

> The way for me to get promoted in this system is to be very initiative-driven. And I can let the whole school fall apart, but if my [policy]

> initiatives have very good scores, I'm going to have a circle of people thinking I'm doing a good job. Not the kids, not the teachers, but at the board level, because my spreadsheets look good. (Ibid., 150)

Sue Winton and Katina Pollock concur:

> Under neo-liberalism, strong and poor performance are attributed to schools and individuals rather than socio-political, economic, or cultural factors. School leaders are individuals who are increasingly held responsible for students' academic achievement (defined as high test scores). Thus, a successful school leader under neo-liberalism is one whose students demonstrate high achievement on standardised tests. (2016, 21–2)

Researchers differ to some extent on the degree of agency held by school administrators in pushing back against top-down policies that they do not find to be in their school's interests. Vibert (2009) reports that the Toronto principals she interviewed consciously tried to minimize time spent on ministry and board initiatives that they believe have little direct benefit to their students. However, they also know that career security and advancement depend on at least their nominal participation, what Pinto (2015) refers to as "fear driven compliance." While Ontario principals and vice-principals interviewed by Pinto complained that their professional autonomy was undermined, she found that participants did not actively or even passively resist provincial policy, however much they disliked it. Some would engage in self-conscious "performativity" to elicit desired responses from the ministry (ibid., 150). Despite their lower rank, teachers may have more agency in this regard, owing to union protection through the option to grieve infringements on professional autonomy and due process rights if accused of insubordination. Moreover, in a typical secondary school, the ratio of teachers to principals is higher than principals to superintendents within the TDSB's "families of schools," making surveillance of principals easier. The study by Winton and Pollock (2016) of Ontario elementary school principals suggests that administrators do in fact exercise some agency in prioritizing school activities towards goals identified by the local community, such as school climate, student well-being, as well as student academics, rather than the ministry's singular neoliberal focus on boosting EQAO and international test scores. This is particularly the case when they are supported by an active group of parents (Sue Winton, interview Dec. 2015). However, as in New York and in Mexico under the ENLACE exam, EQAO test scores (especially at the elementary level) and high school graduation rates have become a key basis for supervising principals. The ensuing pressure flows downwards (Sears and Cairns 2019).

A Toronto OSSTF leader and several high school teachers interviewed suggested that provincial and thereby school board pressure on educators and schools to raise EQAO test scores is much more significant at the elementary level. A Curriculum Leader at one of the case study schools explains:

> I don't hear the English Department complain about it much. Heck, most of these teachers started teaching around the same time the literacy test came into being in the first place. It's so second nature. It's always been there, so I don't think they question it. How much time goes into prep … most English teachers argue that they do everything that is on the literacy test. I remember more talk about that before. (Toronto Teacher 5, interview Mar. 2015)

The implication here is that the EQAO has little direct impact on teachers' instructional time outside of time spent directly writing the test, since they feel that most skills tested by the exam are addressed through the existing curriculum and they do not receive any direction otherwise. This position was borne out in my prior experience teaching grade 10 English to students who were strong academically. I applied my professional judgment, supported by the department, that only two classes of practice drills directly related to the test were necessary. Another teacher of grade 10 English commented:

> I used to be super resentful of it, I thought we could be spending our time in much more constructive ways. And I also really used to feel that if a kid passes English, that should be enough to show literacy. It definitely does encroach on our professionalism, and it does feel like it undermines our judgment. I guess I'm just so used to it now that I don't get as annoyed. But it does feel like the month of March is kind of a waste. In some schools they spend all of grade 9 and all of grade 10 leading up to it, preparing for the test, which I think is such a shame because – there're things on that test – I don't know who decided that that's what literacy is, but it's hilarious. (Toronto Teacher 4, interview Nov. 2014)

In 2011–12, the proportion of the TDSB's grade 10 students enrolled in academic courses who passed the literacy test the first time was 87.8 per cent, dropping to 37.4 per cent for students in the applied stream (Parekh 2013, 5). A teacher of an applied-level[11] English class recounted the considerable class time she must focus on preparing students for the literacy test, leading her to also question the pedagogical value of some of its segments:

> With the grade 10 applied class, my real goal is to get them to pass the literacy test ... While I wouldn't say I teach directly to the test, I'm definitely very aware now in my planning for that grade 10 course of what sorts of skills I need to build in ... Now granted, they're important communication skills regardless, so I don't have a problem with that aspect of teaching to the test, in terms of working more on reading comprehension, that's a very important skill ... There are, however, and especially in the last two years, additional kinds of questions ... I am sometimes not even sure what they're asking in some of those questions. So, I do find that I end up, again, teaching somewhat to the test. I spend a lot of the year just formulating questions, formulating units in ways that prepare the students for the test. (Toronto Teacher 2, interview Aug. 2014)

The Curriculum Leader above who suggested that the literacy test (OSSLT) had little impact on the work of English teachers in his department added that the test did seem to carry significant weight with the district. He did not share Fullan's respect for the ministry's mandated School Improvement Plans:

> The metrics seem to matter, it's my impression that they matter more than they did before. That there's less discussion about individual cases and more on, "well, we see your numbers are like this, we'd like to get them like this." And of course, the charade we go through every year of looking at the School Improvement Plan, saying, well, our plan is to get the OSSLT scores up by 3 per cent next year. And we realize that whatever we do never has an impact ... it never does. Nothing I have ever seen or heard of at any school – has anyone ever actually made a 3 per cent impact because they said to make a 3 per cent impact? It's made up. (Toronto Teacher 5, interview Mar. 2015)

According to an OSSTF Toronto leader, whenever the union convenes a discussion on forms of job action short of a full strike, the boycott of EQAO-related tasks is always recommended, teachers describing it as a waste of time and money and an unnecessary stress on their students. When an attempt by EQAO to move the literacy test online resulted in a computer system crash, shutting down the exam for dozens of schools in Toronto in the fall of 2016, dozens of OSSTF members were quick to express their contempt for the test in a union Facebook discussion group. OSSTF took the opportunity in a press statement to question the value of the EQAO.

Among Toronto secondary teachers, a stronger consensus is found on the overall impact of the provincial imperative of constantly rising graduation rates on their professional autonomy. Teachers described how their professional judgment to determine grades is frequently challenged:

> A lot of admin – it feels like they're disconnected from what goes on in the classroom … they're stuck between a rock and a hard place because they're getting policies coming down from the board that they have to implement whether or not they actually make sense from an educational perspective … Like the "pass the students at all costs." It's more important to look good on the books and our pass rates than to actually do what's right for the kids. I'm teaching kids in grade 12 who have never actually passed a single grade in their life. If you look at their transcript for high school, [in] almost every class they've been gifted the 50, and they were transferred all the way through elementary school from grade to grade. So I feel absolute pressure to pass kids who are illiterate in English. It doesn't sit well with me. (Toronto Teacher 6, interview Mar. 2015)

This teacher, echoing a similar story described by a colleague, explains how the pressure is realized through the direct intervention of their principal, who rounded up from nine the grades of every senior student:

> I think the big issue is that she didn't consult or tell us ahead of time … There're small things that feel like they undermine our professional judgment. We've gone to school for X number of years to learn our craft. We've done tons of volunteer work before we've even started our teaching careers. Many of us have been teaching for decades … it makes us feel like we're not professionals. If we can't make that judgment call on final marks, what power or authority do we have in our job? (Ibid.)

OSSTF president Paul Elliot concurred that principals can employ various means to intervene in teacher grading to make it easier for students to pass courses and thereby increase graduation rates (interview Sept. 2016). A common unofficial policy enforced at the school level is that students could not receive a final mark between 43 and 49 per cent; typically, their grade would be rounded upwards. Likewise, school and district policies dictate that students may have until the end of a semester to hand in an assignment. OSSTF Toronto vice-president Leslie Wolfe explained:

> The principal, under pressure for their school to be a top performer, in turn pressures teachers, whose students' marks might not be reflecting what the principal wants the school to look like … teachers feel under pressure to basically falsely inflate student marks in order to meet these

needs. Or the other thing we hear is: if the students aren't succeeding to the expectations of the principal, there must be something wrong with the teacher. It's not that the teacher has tried everything and the student can't do it, it's that the teacher isn't good enough. (Interview Sept. 2016)

For schools with below-average rates of graduation and credit accumulation,[12] which tend to place high on the TDSB's Learning Opportunity Index,[13] various interventions by administrators and/or ministry staff occur in the classroom as part of the Student Success Initiative. In the case study school that fits this description, a teacher explained how, at the behest of a vice-principal, English teachers were required to use the same readings and assignments:

> It takes all the joy out of my work. I feel like a robot, just handing out handouts I didn't make and talking about things I don't care about. The vice-principal pushed ... who also wanted Shakespeare removed from the texts. They wanted to do comic books instead ... but I think they [the students] can handle Macbeth, so I planned to do it. I went rogue and taught the elevensies Macbeth! Imagine getting in trouble for doing that. (Toronto Teacher 8, interview July 2015)

Her use of professional judgment as an experienced English teacher to determine the most pedagogically appropriate materials for the specific needs of her students was dismissed. This teacher then explained how, assisted by ministry and TDSB staff, administrators led staff in all departments through exercises where targets for increases in student grades are set based on diagnostic activities at the start of the year. Teachers are then required to adopt in their classrooms one of several specific Evidenced Based Instructional Strategies (EBIS) endorsed by ministry and TDSB staff, after creating a model lesson plan to demonstrate the teacher's comprehension of the strategy. This teacher, with fifteen years of experience, noted her frustration that, while being able to choose among several strategies, there was no space in which to question their pedagogical value. She also commented that by the apparent ages of the TDSB facilitators that they could not have had more than four or five years of experience as classroom teachers, despite being "totally motivated, totally on it." She explained from her perspective how the targeting of student grades worked in her school:

> I'm willing to learn new strategies, but the measuring and predicting ... okay, now it's higher because I don't want to look like I haven't done my job, and they say, well, the system obviously works, look how much

> higher it is! Because they took what the kids did at the beginning, the first time they evaluated it, they didn't do so well. Then I did the instructional-based strategies, and so then I evaluated them on a completely different assignment, and their marks ended up being higher … or they'd say, well where do you think they'll be … and some of them ended up doing well on a very different assignment, so therefore there had been progress. It was the least scientific thing I've ever seen. (Ibid.)

This teacher described how the school staff was made "accountable" by administrators for their progress in relation to the targets:

> Then they had, at the end of the year, all of these graphs put up on the board in the staff meeting, and they said, "look, look, look at the change! This is the beginning of the year, this is the end of the year." … math especially got hammered … with English, okay, you didn't understand the reading comprehension, but you wrote something interesting later on … we can give you marks for your thoughts. In math, you know how to do the process or you don't, so it was harder for them to … (Ibid.)

The teacher noted the absence of a "control group" of comparable classes in the school. In her opinion, this lack undermined claims that adoption of the new teaching strategies is responsible for changes in student performance. She also expressed frustration about how little attention was given to the context of her students, some of whom had seldom attended school for a few years and who received little parental support. This comment should be considered in light of Fullan and Boyle's description above of the Focused Intervention Program in schools with low graduation rates. Here an effort is indeed made to de-emphasize the importance of a student's socio-economic and familial context in the minds of teachers, while increasing the weight assigned to an individual teacher's performance in determining the success (or failure) of a student. In sharing this experience (as this teacher also stressed), it is not my intention to look cynically at or dismiss all efforts by administrators, school districts, or higher-education officials to introduce better pedagogical techniques into classroom teaching. Virtually all the teachers I spoke with (and with whom I have personally worked) would agree that self-improvement is an integral part of their professional responsibility. The problem I wish to identify here is education strategies elaborated from the top (whether by the ministry, the TDSB, or school principals) and then imposed on teachers with minimal consideration for their expertise. This is how teachers' professional autonomy is undermined.

Meanwhile, the role of Curriculum or Assistant Curriculum Leader has shifted some teachers towards the role of the "teacher-manager" described by Rezai-Rashti (2009), Vibert (2009), and Robertson (2000). Over the past several years, the two schools in this case study and many others in Toronto moved independently from the initial model under Harris of four or five teacher Curriculum Leaders responsible for all academic subjects as well as ministry initiatives such as preparation for the EQAO tests and Student Success to twice as many Assistant Curriculum Leaders, each responsible for a smaller subject area (Toronto Teachers 1 and 3, interviews Aug. 2014; Toronto Teacher 5, interview Mar. 2015). This structure came closer to the restoration of the old department head structure and brought more teachers onto the "leadership team," assisting in making decisions affecting the school as a whole (Toronto Teacher 1, interview Aug. 2014). However, their role of participating in school-based management and "School Autonomy" type tasks of micro-budgeting has increased. Assistant Curriculum and Curriculum Leaders at both schools noted that final decisions always rested with the administrators, but that to varying degrees their opinions were considered. While these respondents were clear that this position did not give them any form of managerial authority over other teachers (in large part due to the intervention of OSSTF), in other ways they have been implicated in an adversarial conflict with their peers over resources. Toronto Teacher 3 (an Assistant Curriculum Leader) described how meetings have sometimes been dominated by debates between Assistant Curriculum Leaders over the allocation of money between departments:

> There are these discussions where you watch the power of the school being allocated by dollars … And certainly, seeing shifts in that balance of power … I've watched teachers attacking other teachers around the needs of their department, saying, "are these truly needs?" Because I feel like we're all competing for limited resources, there's a little bit more conflict there than one might think … Because before it just came from a magical box and people would just dip into that box as much as possible. There's an effort to be more transparent. I wouldn't say completely transparent, but more transparent. So we can help inform the decision-making around that …On the other hand, it provided another source of conflict, or competition over limited resources. (Interview Aug. 2014)

Since school budgets increasingly are placed in defined, small funds rather than in just a "general fund," amid a context of overall budget reductions, this form of School-Based Management extends the work of some teachers not only into a time-consuming managerial role of administering budgets, but into a competitive one at that. Rather than uniting in solidarity across departments and subject areas to press for more funding from the school board or the ministry, an externally imposed context of scarcity is taken for granted and teachers are pushed into a zero-sum competition with their colleagues. Another Assistant Curriculum Leader described these competitions as, "the way you get co-opted away from the real conflict … that education is not being funded enough" (Toronto Teacher 1, interview Aug. 2014). Vibert (2009) describes this situation as another form of "accountability" from the fiscal perspective of central authorities, as teachers and administrators discipline each other while engaging in increased bureaucratic reporting procedures.

The continual rollout of new policy "layers," especially under McGuinty, built on the Harris era removal of school administrators from the teachers' federations to make principals and vice-principals increasingly subservient to the imperatives of the provincial government and, to a lesser extent, the TDSB. This redefined role with increased "accountability" to meeting provincially defined graduation targets, and to a lesser extent EQAO scores, flowed downwards from administrators to place more pressure on Toronto's secondary school teachers, undermining their professional autonomy in the classroom. These accountability measures undermined autonomy in distinct and uneven ways, depending on the diverse constituencies of Toronto's schools. Most of the accounts by teachers included in this section were from a case study school with predominantly working-class students, approximately half of them of colour and many from families newly immigrated to Canada. Pressure here on administrators and teachers was primarily derived from a need to raise course credit accumulation and thereby graduation rates.

5.4. Quantifying Student Achievement: Intersection of Race, Class, and School Choice on Teachers' Work

> If I had to choose one thing that was particularly challenging and has an impact on so many different aspects, it would really be related to evaluations and what we can and cannot do with respect to evaluations. (Toronto Teacher 2, interview Aug. 2014)

The following section will draw more on the experiences of teachers at a predominantly middle-class (overwhelmingly white) school, where greater pressure on professional autonomy comes from parents and the Toronto form of "school choice." While this school receives less attention and concern from the ministry and the district, owing to its high graduation rates and EQAO scores, teachers here report that administrators are more likely to intervene in their work at the behest of parents looking to raise their children's grades, particularly with respect to university applications. Teachers here also argue that, in addition to the policies and programs described in the previous two sections, ministry documents regarding the assessment and evaluation practices of teachers, particularly *Fresh AER* and its successor, *Growing Success*, have had a particularly large impact on their professional autonomy. The predominantly affluent and well-educated parents who tend to intervene to increase the marks of their children are also active participants in Toronto's school choice practices. Similar to that of New York in some respects, this competition between schools to enrol predominantly white and affluent students has increased racial and class segregation within the school system, with deleterious effects on the classroom.

Although not raised by Fullan and Boyle in their review of policy-making under the McGuinty government, a significant example of the ministry's intervention into teachers' professionalism were policy documents that determined how teachers should conduct student evaluations, especially *Fresh AER* (Assessment, Evaluation and Reporting; TDSB 2006), and its successor, *Growing Success* (Ontario Ministry of Education 2010). Some educators considered *Fresh AER*'s emphases on transparency to students as to how evaluations are conducted and greater lenience on accepting student assignments, to be pedagogically progressive and in the interests of equity for marginalized students. Ultimately, these policies were in line with the Student Success Initiative's objective of increasing student pass and graduation rates. However, for many teachers, since marks of zero were all but banned, being required to accept assignments up to the end of the course and prohibiting late marks (to name a few issues), *Fresh AER* epitomized the top-down policy's effect on diluting curriculum standards and undermining professional autonomy. OSSTF president Paul Elliot described how *Fresh AER* resulted from a drive by the government to standardize instructional practices across Ontario:

> That was all provincially driven until people started pushing back, saying there needs to be some changes here, there needs to be some autonomy in terms of what I do in the classroom. Because they tried to make sure that an urban school in Toronto is the same as a school in the suburbs, is the same as the schools in Ottawa, [is the] same as the schools in Kenora, which just isn't the case. (Interview Sept. 2016)

Four years later, *Growing Success* was released by the government with revised policies on assessment, evaluation, and reporting procedures. It included an explicit acknowledgment and a detailed definition of professional judgment, in response to teacher and union intervention (Ontario Ministry of Education 2010). Compared with *Fresh AER*, this document left more of the more specific details of policy to the interpretation of teachers. As a teacher at an affluent school argued, however, the perception remained among parents that marks and grades assigned by teachers could be negotiated:

> We were given back the power of the zero, but I think that the mentality is still, do whatever it takes to not give a kid a zero. Again, that tension in the relationship and sort of this nudge-nudge wink-wink expectation between the students and you and the parents and you and the admin. and you, that you can make a zero disappear … By even suggesting that a teacher should not give a child a zero, it suggests that there's no professional judgment. (Toronto Teacher 2, interview Aug. 2014)

Related to these pressures, OSSTF Toronto vice-president Leslie Wolfe described how over the Harris PC and McGuinty/Wynne Liberal eras, teacher complaints about (course) "credit integrity" issues had changed:

> Credit integrity before meant, did the student complete the work, did the student get the information, did the number of hours get completed. Now teachers talk about it in terms of "did the student actually earn the mark they've been given." Or, "has our focus on success only being measured by standardized tests and marks outcomes meant that we're forcing teachers to inflate the marks, and really the credit is lost," because the mark is about creating a perception of the school. (Interview Sept. 2016)

Under *Growing Success*, teachers cannot be told to change a student's grade (Ontario Ministry of Education 2010). However, under the Education Act, the primary provincial legislation governing K–12 education in Ontario, principals are the ultimate assignees of grades, enabling them to subsequently change grades, which they frequently do according to Wolfe. She also says that this practice is most prevalent in Toronto's affluent schools:

> They change marks because parents demand it, and they change marks because they think a teacher has been unfair. I've had teachers called in and disciplined because the principal thinks they're not marking fairly because the student class average is lower than … the principal wants to see it at.

> There's a whole equity piece in this because I would say that in the largest part, the greatest incidents of this kind of interference by the principal in the integrity in the teachers' professionalism in terms of assessing and evaluating a student, happens in the neighbourhoods where there is the highest socio-economic factor. Where there is the greatest parental pressure and involvement, and there are much higher expectations from the community on the kids ... in the schools that we consider high needs, we don't hear about this at all, or very rarely.[14] (Interview Sept. 2016)

Following in the context of an affluent school with policy-aware parents, the perception exists that marks can be leveraged with the proper application of influence:

> There seems to be this idea, not among all the parents, but I think in the community that I've been teaching in, that teachers should make bad marks disappear. There is the flip side of a marks-driven culture ... So there's a lot of pressure on us ... to do whatever it takes to get a student a particular mark for some school [university] that they have their eye on. But essentially those marks become meaningless ... because of all these limitations and all of these pressures that are exerted on professionals. And it does create conflict between teachers if two teachers are teaching the same student, and one decides to exercise their professional judgment in a way that isn't in accordance with what another teacher might do, or what the admin might do. The admin will say it's your call, but what they really mean is "don't cause more shit for us." (Toronto Teacher 2, interview Aug. 2014)

Many activist teachers and academics, including those interviewed here, call on their colleagues and unions to build alliances with parents as one of the most important strategies for combatting the deleterious effects of degrading professional autonomy of teachers. This call is made particularly in reference to working-class and racialized parents who are socially (and often geographically) distant from middle-class and predominantly white teachers (in Canada and the United States) (Hagopian 2014a; Weiner 2012). In Toronto as in New York, absent a strong outreach effort, parental involvement at school is generally weak to virtually non-existent at the secondary level.[15] Unfortunately, where parents tend to be considerably more active, in middle-class or affluent neighbourhoods, teachers suggest that in the context of strong societal pressures and competition for entry to post-secondary education programs,[16] parents intervene with the objective of securing an advantage for their child. How teachers should respond requires more investigation by education activists and intellectuals. At the case study affluent school, parental intervention over grades can go as far as litigation:

> I think there's a real fear that administrators are driven by fear of parents. In fact, some of them talk that way, "we have to please the parents." And the corollary to that is it feels like teachers aren't as supported ... There's a thing in all of the documents that talks about teacher's discretion. It's put in there, but I feel that is being taken less and less seriously, due to this fear of accountability, this fear of: can you actually back it up? And I think sometimes it's done from the best of reasons. Principals and vice-principals are trying to protect people from negative consequences through parents, who are increasingly litigious. Certainly, there have been more lawsuits in the last couple of years at my school than I've seen in my career. (Toronto Teacher 3, interview Aug. 2014)

Policy openings by the provincial government to question the professional authority of teachers in the evaluation of students are predominantly utilized by parents who, through their socio-economic status, already exercise substantial agency within the education system. Self-interest, especially among the most class- and racially privileged parents, has had an adverse impact on Toronto's public secondary schools through the institution of school choice.

In 2006, the TDSB counted approximately 17,000 teachers and 272,000 regular elementary and secondary students (Fullan and Boyle 2014, 87). In the context of a demographic decline of families with teenage children in Toronto due to rising housing costs but also aggressive recruitment by the publicly funded Catholic school board and the opting of some wealthy parents for private schools, by the 2015–16 school year these numbers had declined to 15,615 and 243,000, respectively[17] (TDSB 2016). The TDSB has responded by initiating specialty programs for students outside of the regular course stream and eliminating neighbourhood boundaries for all but the most in-demand secondary schools. These few are located in the most affluent communities in the city and, in the face of great demand, limit overcrowding by enforcing neighbourhood residence as a prerequisite for enrolment. Meanwhile, other schools have increasingly opted to create their own specialty programs to attract choosy parents and avoid demographic losses to other schools. In this sense, the institution of school choice by the TDSB can be seen as more of a reaction to a specific context than a primarily ideologically driven decision based on the supposed efficacy of competition for driving school improvement as it was in New York under Bloomberg (see chapter 3). Nonetheless, this competition has had an adverse impact on equity.

Rather than empowering all families, evidence has emerged that school choice, as in New York and elsewhere, has increased racial and class segregation in Toronto (Kurek 2016; Francis 2016; Kunin 2016).

As was explained in chapter 3 in relation to New York, school choice is a form of neoliberal education policy specific to urban areas sufficiently large and dense enough to include a significant number of local schools that children could plausibly commute to, with more or less assistance from their parents, in order to generate market competition between the schools for enrolment. Claude Lessard and André Brassard observe that it has existed informally for as long as affluent parents and those familiar with the system have known how to work it. In Canada, Alberta set the precedent in 1996 (following a few US states, which had done so earlier) to remove school boundaries (2009, 267). The TDSB followed in 1999 with the "optional attendance policy," which gave parents the opportunity to apply, space permitting and at the discretion of the receiving school, to schools outside their neighbourhood. Unlike the situation in New York City, all students in Toronto retain a right to attend their neighbourhood elementary or secondary school by default (TDSB 2004). As stated above, schools at maximum capacity may have a "closed" status, restricting enrolment to the neighbourhood catchment area. An annual "Report Card" on Ontario schools published by the pro-privatization Fraser Institute think-tank, which in part uses EQAO test scores to rank schools, is widely cited in the media. It is considered highly influential in establishing perceptions of "good" and "bad" schools and is even attributed with affecting real estate values as parents strive to move into the neighbourhood catchment areas of in-demand elementary schools with closed enrolment (Lessard and Brassard 2009, 267). Regardless of the stated intentions of the Ministry of Education that the EQAO tests are purely indicative and, unlike their equivalents in the United States or Mexico, do not carry punitive consequences, in the context of the credibility assigned by the public and the media to the Fraser Institute's report, this is not the case in practice. The viability of schools subject to Toronto's competition for enrolment depends at least in part on these metrics. Another large part depends on the racial and class-based determinations by many mobile parents of a local school's desirability.

A TDSB teacher from a secondary school experiencing significant declining enrolment explained how school choice tends to segregate schools on the basis of race and class:

> North Toronto, Northern, MacKenzie, Lawrence Park … these are schools whose populations are swelling. And it's coming at the expense of other schools. So schools that are … more mixed racially, economically … those schools are seeing a lot of their diversity disappear because of this white

> middle-class … I'm generalizing, but this kind of consolidation at these schools … The more racialized the school becomes, the less desirable it becomes in the eyes of people who are shopping for good schools. And that includes racialized parents, who evaluate a school based on whether white kids go there. (Toronto Teacher 10, interview July 2015)

Likely as a result of these dynamics, Vaughan Road Academy, a school with a significant black population, had its enrolment decline from 770 in 2006–7 to 220 in 2016–17, as more local elementary students went on to Forest Hill Collegiate in a neighbouring affluent and predominantly white area. Parents whose children remained at Vaughan Road Academy believed the school was the victim of racial and class segregation. The TDSB closed Vaughan at the end of the 2016–17 school year (Kurek 2016; Francis 2016).

In the context of declining demographics, many "closed enrolment" secondary schools reach this status by operating specialty programs, chief of which is French Immersion, in which students outside the neighbourhood may enrol (TDSB 2004). According to the demographic statistics maintained by the TDSB on program enrolment, the students in its most prestigious specialty programs, French Immersion and Gifted, tend to be among the most privileged.[18] Their families are much more likely to be in the top income decile (23.9 per cent and 22.4 per cent, respectively, with conversely 3.1 per cent and 1.8 per cent in the lowest decile) and are much more likely to be university educated and white (55.4 per cent and 41.6 per cent); by comparison, 28.3 per cent of all TDSB secondary students are white (Parekh 2013). The TDSB teacher above explained how his school participated in this context:

> Schools no longer have a community; it's now a service provider. Parents can shop around and it's about catering to the customer. But of course the parents and families who most often opt for optional attendance are those who have some mobility … who can drive their kids across the city, or kids for whom even taking the bus twice a day is not a major expense. So it tends to appeal to a certain demographic of family … So in order to keep us alive, we were drawing in kids from outside the catchment area. Middle class … Predominantly white. And these families were interested in the program only insofar as the demographics of the program pretty much kept to that. (Toronto Teacher 10, interview July 2015)

As this teacher implies, specialty programs affect school cultures and by extension teachers' work by in effect segregating students with particular characteristics into specialty programs. In practice, this typically means that the most academically inclined students, with much lower suspension rates (as a quantifiable means of measuring student behaviour), are skimmed from the top, leaving their peers behind. At a macro scale, it reproduces the spatial segregation seen in New York City's exclusive magnet schools with difficult entrance requirements but operating within the same school building.

Vaughan Road Academy attempted to sustain enrolment by offering an International Baccalaureate (IB), which was successful in terms of growing to over 100 students, but it did not stop the regular program's decline in enrolment, which in the school's final year was only slightly larger than the IB program. According to a long-time teacher at the school, in response to parent preferences the IB program was fully segregated from the rest of the school, with dedicated teachers and a separate set of non-academic elective courses. Working in the IB program can be an intellectually rewarding experience for teachers, as its students universally tend to be highly committed. Some aspects are more prescribed for teachers than the regular curriculum, as final assignments are determined by the IB program, which oversees this level of evaluation (ibid.). Another consequence for teachers' professional autonomy would appear to be that, as in many of New York's small schools, low enrolment makes it unfeasible to offer a broader range of courses beyond those essential for a high school diploma. However, the largest impact on teaching is the unbalanced nature of classrooms caused by further stratifying the existing system of academic streaming[19] with an additional elite level, whether French Immersion, IB, Gifted, or Advanced Placement courses, which tend to be primarily accessed by parents with the highest social capital (Parekh 2013).

Across the city in southwest Scarborough, Birchmount Park Collegiate, a school with a reputation for discipline issues, located in a racially and socio-economically mixed area, added a Gifted program consisting of self-contained classes in most academic subjects in the 2016–17 school year. It aimed to draw in students who would otherwise attend neighbouring Malvern Collegiate in the predominantly white and affluent Beach community. However, recruitment of only fourteen students, some of whom would likely have attended the school in any case and taken academic courses, placed the viability of the program in doubt.[20] School choice is a particular concern for the People for Education research and advocacy group. Executive Director Annie Kidder expressed her concern that cumulatively it would undermine public education by creating enclaves of privilege within the system:

> There's a real love of alternative schools, French immersion … various ways to stream my perfect, precious child – and I speak as one of them – into a

> place where they'll be with children like them. That's an inexorable, less visible shift, where you start to make public education ... work for those with social capital ... But they're just wonderful little bubbles of upper-middle-class white people where they teach social justice math. (Interview Nov. 2015)

The publicity and social weight associated with EQAO test scores is the most easily comparable quantitative variable used to facilitate school choice at the elementary level in Toronto. These scores can also be easily located online by the parents of prospective students for secondary schools. According to accounts cited earlier, however, it is likely that pressure to raise EQAO scores has a greater impact on the work of elementary teachers than their secondary peers.[21] The pressure described in the previous subsection by secondary teachers to inflate marks in order to increase the pass rate for courses and thereby the overall school graduation rate finds its expression in the context of school choice in the more qualitative realm of school reputation. Schools with students from predominantly white and affluent families are considered as de facto being the most academically rigorous. In practice, however, at the schools that appear to "win" under school choice, teachers report that academic integrity and their ability to exercise professional judgment is continually under challenge from these mobile and status-oriented parents. School choice cannot be considered solely liable for the rise of a culture in which education is treated as a transactional consumer good, but it and the class and racial segregation which it facilitates appear to bear some responsibility. Meanwhile, elite programs that pull in the highest academically achieving students, who are also usually the easiest to teach, having fewer special needs and facing the lowest systemic barriers, leave behind everyone else. The nature of teaching changes in these contexts, but, more profoundly, the overall equity of the system is undermined to the detriment of the most vulnerable students.

5.5. Scaling-Up: The Centralization of Bargaining and the Negotiation of Professional Autonomy

The centralization of labour negotiations for Ontario teachers under the Liberal governments of McGuinty and Wynne followed the uploading of financing to the Ministry of Education under the PC government of Mike Harris described at the start of this chapter, thus completing the succession of the provincial over the municipal as the most important scale in education governance. This development had important implications for teachers' professional autonomy when an initial collaborative period between the McGuinty government and the federations ended with a drive for public sector austerity. Under the Wynne government, the new provincial scale of negotiations coincided with the increasingly active Ontario Public School Boards Association (OPSBA), which advocated to increase the managerial power of principals to define teachers' work as a cost-saving mechanism for insufficiently funded districts. Along with the Ministry of Education's now well-established policy interventions, provincial bargaining became an opportunity to press for Ontario-wide concessions in professional autonomy.

Centralized collective bargaining is the dominant trend in Canada for teachers, with Ontario and Alberta the latest provinces to join British Columbia, Saskatchewan, Nova Scotia, and Quebec[22] with two-tier[23] district/provincial negotiation structures. The smaller maritime provinces of Newfoundland, New Brunswick, and Prince Edward Island have completely centralized negotiations for teachers (Sweeney, McWilliams, and Hickey 2012, 251). Two-tier negotiation structures typically delegate issues that are most directly determined by funding levels, such as salaries, pensions, benefits, and usually class sizes, to negotiation between the provincial government and the provincial unions. Other less directly economic issues relating to working conditions are left to negotiations between school districts and union locals. The centralization of funding created a strong rationale for Ontario's teachers' unions to scale up negotiations to deal directly with provincial policymakers, while striving to keep other issues, such as the managerial prerogatives of principals to assign non-classroom tasks to teachers, at the local level if strong contract language already existed there. For employers, a major incentive was a perception that school districts could not hold their own against local unions that also counted on the support of their provincial federations. Many of OSSTF's historical gains, such as the large salary increases of 1974–5, were done by "whipsawing" school boards: winning a precedent-setting salary in one district and pressing to have it met or surpassed elsewhere. British Columbia, considered an important influence on the Ontario and Alberta governments' subsequent shifts towards centralization, was motivated to do so to counter the highly effective coordinated local bargaining of the British Columbia Teachers' Federation (BCTF) (Schucher and Slinn 2012, 20; Rose 2012, 216; Shilton 2012).

This section sets the context with a brief overview of the Harris government's disruption of the existing structures of local collective bargaining. I then look at how during its first two terms, from 2003 to 2011, the McGuinty government's political strategy of pursuing labour peace with teachers led to the increasing formalization of two-tier collective bargaining with OSSTF and the other federations. Next, I will show how this scaling-up of negotiations was transformed in the highly adversarial context of McGuinty's and Wynne's push for fiscal austerity from 2012 onwards. There was little diminishment of this underlying conflict in the 2015–16 round of collective bargaining, despite the legal formalization of the two-tier structure in 2014. At this juncture, the government, in concert with the OPSBA, tabled significant concessions on teachers' professional autonomy as well as compensation increases below the rate of inflation. Ultimately, the former was defeated by the federations, at the cost of the latter. The political approach taken by the provincial government has been the decisive factor throughout the experience of centralizing negotiations in Ontario. These contentious rounds of negotiations have also precipitated debate among OSSTF members over the balancing of union demands relating to compensation versus professional practice. This discussion is significant insofar as it also signifies an opportunity, as it did for activist teachers allying with parents over onerous standardized testing in New York State, to reinforce a broader interest of teacher unionism in matters of the public interest.

In 1997, the PC government repealed Bill 100, the legislation governing teacher labour relations since teachers won the right to strike in 1974, replacing it with provisions under Bill 160, which, as referenced above, had a multifaceted adverse effect on the federations. Teachers were placed within the Ontario Labour Relations Act, which was significantly revised to eliminate anti-scab legislation and card-check certification for union recognition, the latter not relevant to public school teachers who remained statutory members of the federations. Bill 160 removed class size and instructional time from collective bargaining, promptly increasing both (Rose 2012, 208). Reasonable class sizes and sufficient preparation time are critical to the ability of teachers to meaningfully exercise professional judgment. The five federations representing 126,000 teachers launched a two-week illegal strike in November 1997, as mentioned in chapter 2. They did not defeat this legislation but did build public awareness of Harris's austerity agenda for education (Gidney 1999). The fight over Bill 160 was emblematic of the frequent strikes and occasional lockouts of teachers under Harris, chiefly over the loss of prep time, with a strike rate of 23.8 per cent, versus 2.2 per cent under Bill 100 from 1974 to 1996 (Rose 2012, 210). The federations were often ordered to end strikes by the Ontario Labour Relations Board, but teachers responded by refusing to do extracurriculars. The government partially capitulated in 2001 by redefining instructional activity to begin to restore lost prep time (Rose 2012).

The uploading of education finance combined with the imposition of a rigid funding formula "gave the government an effective veto over meaningful local bargaining on crucial monetary and non-monetary issues and took other major issues off the bargaining table altogether" (Shilton 2012, 222). In the context of an aggressively neoliberal, pro-austerity Ontario government, the "real quarrel was not about the new collective bargaining framework per se. It was about a shift in power within the school system from the local to the provincial level" (ibid., 221). Shilton explains further:

> the government used its legislative and regulatory authority to circumvent the collective bargaining process, deliberately constraining the flexibility of local parties to negotiate local solutions to the challenges created by the new funding formula. It was an approach calculated to alienate all parties to local bargaining, since it clearly reflected the government's view that school boards were captive to the teachers' unions, incapable of asserting the strong management control needed to keep both teachers and tax levels in line. (Ibid., 232–3)

While undermining local negotiations both by imposing policies that were loathed by teachers and by a highly restrictive finance structure that offered no room to manoeuvre for school boards, the Harris government did not attempt to implement any form of formalized central negotiations. This response did not prevent the federations from waging political campaigns targeting the government, as it had when Ontario set a ceiling on school district expenditures to combat inflation in the 1970s.

During their campaign and upon taking office, the Liberals stated a desire for a shift from "intense and confrontational government-teacher relations to an approach based on consensus and cooperation" (Rose 2012, 212). Union contracts were reached with informal provincial coordination for 2005–8, which, in addition to gains mentioned earlier including the hiring of more specialist teachers, restored prep time lost under the Harris PCs, made voluntary activities voluntary again, and reintroduced negotiated class size limits, gaining overall federation support for Dalton McGuinty's education policies (Leslie Wolfe, interview Sept. 2016; Fullan and Boyle 2014, 71; Rose 2012, 213). The 2008–9 negotiations for the 2008–12 contracts involved a "more open and formal approach" (Rose 2012, 213), including a consultation to determine central issues and the participation of ministry representatives in local negotiations. A 12 per cent salary increase over four years provided a strong incentive for OSSTF to settle, especially in the context of the approaching economic recession. Through these two rounds, the

Provincial Discussion Tables (PDTs) functioned, despite the government's not having an official legal mandate to conduct bargaining. The PDTs guaranteed central funding for salary and workload, enabling a decline in class sizes. Local negotiations subsequently occurred within this context, subject to a deadline by the ministry in order to receive agreed central funding for salary increases, creating a de facto two-tier bargaining system (Leslie Wolfe, interview Sept. 2016; Rose 2012, 212; Shilton 2012, 235). This shift was facilitated by the legal assigning of local bargaining rights to provincial teachers' federations.[24] According to Joseph Rose, the key factors for success in these two rounds were the "Liberals' close ties with teacher unions" (2012, 215), tangible improvements on working conditions from the Harris years, and real salary gains in the second round at a time of recession and austerity. Teacher salaries rose faster than those of private sector workers and other public sector workers from 2004 to 2009 (ibid.).[25]

The emergence of two-tier bargaining created new dynamics within OSSTF and the other federations. A critical, recurring issue was the lack of clarity around the defining of central and local issues. Shilton observed that the government could use financial pressure through proposed salary increases to force central negotiations on issues that unions prefer to be local (2012, 238). Unions can also disagree internally about the central/local split, depending on whether local leaders hoped below-average contract terms could be brought up to a higher provincial average or feared that it would fall to this level. Within OSSTF, the Toronto local lobbied for on-call supervision and workload language to remain at the local bargaining table, as it believed it had the best contractual language in the province (Leslie Wolfe, interview Sept. 2016). Sweeney, McWilliams and Hickey reported from interviews with union leaders a tendency for local officers to have more reservations about central bargaining than staff at the provincial level (2012, 255, 259). Through two-tier bargaining, provincial union negotiators became increasingly important within the federations in relation to local, elected union executives.

Significantly, the OPSBA was not an influential organization during the 2005 and 2008–9 negotiations. This fact favoured easier resolutions, as despite sharing federation demands for greater school funding, OPSBA was sharply at odds on issues governing teacher working conditions and professional autonomy insofar as they curtailed the management prerogatives of principals. Rose wrote presciently, "Two-tier bargaining has benefited from favourable economic conditions and funding assurances. How sustainable it will be in leaner economic times is uncertain" (2012, 217).

The Liberals shifted from a "partnership" to an increasingly adversarial approach to the OSSTF and other education sector unions. The 2008–12 union contracts bridged a global recession, during which the Ontario government engaged in some mild stimulus spending to ameliorate the effects of the downturn. The provincial deficit rose significantly as tax revenue also declined.[26] McGuinty and the leadership of the Liberal Party emerged with a new approach, in which provisioning the education sector was not a priority. OSSTF lagged behind this political realignment. While issuing strong public statements denouncing the political direction of the Liberals, engaging in protests, and assisting the New Democratic Party (NDP) in some strategic wins, other actions suggested that provincial and perhaps the Toronto leadership held out hope for a high-level compromise and were less than fully committed to confronting the government. Through this process, the centralization of negotiations to the provincial level continued, while McGuinty's government flexed its power over education policy in a manner reminiscent of the Harris PCs. In the aftermath, a formal two-tier bargaining structure was created. It was immediately demonstrated that beyond newly defined legal parameters, the decisive factors determining the character of the negotiations were the intentions of the employers, the provincial government, and the school boards, which continued to press for austerity and concessions. The following account and analysis draws heavily on the author's experience as a local leader within OSSTF Toronto during this period.

McGuinty's Liberals won re-election in 2011, one seat short of their earlier majority. In the context of shifts in US politics associated with the so-called Tea Party movement and the election in Toronto of charismatic mayor Rob Ford, the opposition PCs moved further to the right on economic issues in the midst of the recession, using populist conceptions of government waste to accuse public sector workers, including teachers, of being overpaid. The Liberals responded shortly after their victory by commissioning a high-profile bank economist to analyse the province's fiscal situation and provide recommendations on eliminating the deficit by 2017–18 through reductions in public expenditures. Measures to increase revenue, such as raising taxes, were explicitly rejected (Ontario Government 2012a). The report recommended cutting \$2.8 billion by 2018 from K–12 education, the largest ministry after health, by limiting increases in funding to a rate below inflation. The salaries and wages of 294,000 K–12 teachers and education workers, accounting for 76 per cent of the provincial education budget, would be the target (ibid., 363).

The widely publicized release of the Drummond Report in February 2012 coincided with the start of negotiations by OSSTF and other education unions through the PDTs. The report suggested that threatened job cuts of thousands of support staff and larger class sizes could be traded for salary concessions (ibid., 223).[27] The government subsequently demanded salary freezes, furlough days, reductions in paid sick days and elimination of a gratuity by which retiring teachers received a cash bonus for unused sick days[28] (Ontario Government 2012b, 1; Fullan and Boyle 2014, 85). The 2012 Ontario budget released soon after included a $500 million cut to education funding by these means. Toronto OSSTF member Caitlin Hewitt-White described the focus that left "intact relatively decent features of the school system, like class size caps, a clever strategy that made use of the public's perception of teachers as well-off and spoiled" (2015, 173). The provincial government avoided proposals directly related to classroom practices and professional autonomy. It appeared to be a ploy to convince the public that the conflict was purely monetary in a political context where fiscal austerity had popular support. Negotiations came to an impasse, despite a full-page newspaper advertisement by the provincial leadership of OSSTF stating that the union was willing to accept a two-year wage freeze. Intended to win public support by emphasizing the union's moderation, the concessionary stance alienated many activist members. It failed to elicit any change in the government's approach (personal notes). The government reached a concessionary deal with the English Catholic Teachers' Association (OECTA) in July that closely resembled its opening position (MacNeil 2014, 134–6).

As the OSSTF and the ETFO decried this substandard deal and planned job action as the 2012–13 school year began, the Liberal government set a precedent for a legislated attack on trade union rights by proposing that the Catholic contract be imposed on the hold-out unions. Bill 115, the Putting Students First Act, passed in September with PC support. It required OSSTF and ETFO to reach agreements that were "substantively similar" to the OECTA deal, and set a deadline of 31 December, after which contracts would be imposed. The Ontario Labour Relations Act prohibits strikes during the life of a contract. Teachers' protests would thereby be effectively curtailed, regardless of their consent or dissent over the outcome of this imposed structure. Provincial OSSTF negotiators initially tried to work within this constrained framework in an effort to limit losses, but five of seven local union tentative agreements were voted down by members. OSSTF abandoned any further deals under the circumstances. While ETFO conducted a series of rolling one-day district strikes over the fall, OSSTF boycotted non-teaching administrative and extracurricular activities, the latter drawing significant, often negative, public attention to the conflict. Weekly pickets were held outside Liberal provincial parliament offices across Ontario. Toronto OSSTF members at the school level organized leaflet distribution at subway stations. Despite this activity by many members, Hewitt-White critiqued a lack of alliance building with parent groups or other unions, noting that these protests seldom attracted outside supporters. Other unionists criticized the apparent lack of coordination between the ETFO and OSSTF in the organization of protests. Thousands of Ontario high school students did organize one-day walkouts, including several high schools in Toronto, culminating in a rally at the provincial legislature. Ostensibly over the lack of extracurriculars, most had an overall pro-teacher approach, demanding that the government negotiate fairly (Hewitt-White 2015, 180–3; Sweetman 2012).

Dalton McGuinty resigned amid rising conflict[29] in October 2012, after nearly nine years as premier. New contracts were imposed on most OSSTF and all ETFO locals in January 2013, at which point Bill 115 was rescinded, having served its purpose. Kathleen Wynne was elected interim premier by the Liberal Party, touted as being to the left of McGuinty and her contenders. As a former education minister, she was considered well placed to resolve the conflicts with teachers. While organizing rallies against the Liberals, the OSSTF Toronto executive donated a total of $30,000 to candidates for their party's leadership including Wynne, causing considerable controversy when this fact was published by Elections Ontario. Many active members expressed their frustration that the payment was done without their knowledge or consent, and they thought the "realpolitik" it represented smacked of cynicism.[30] The incident generated a caustic editorial in the pro-Liberal daily *Toronto Star*, which accused OSSTF Toronto of "playing an old-fashioned political game" by donating to politicians against whom they were simultaneously protesting (*Toronto Star* 2013). Retiring as OSSTF president in the aftermath of the Bill 115 conflict, Ken Coran shocked many members by running that summer for the Liberals in a provincial by-election. He was defeated by the NDP (Hewitt-White 2015, 182–5; MacNeil 2014, 138–9).

Wynne publicly acknowledged that Bill 115 was a mistake for having generated considerable conflict and mistrust, but she did not act to ameliorate the financial losses it inflicted on teachers,[31] holding the austerity line of lowering education expenditures. Her government consulted the education unions for the creation of the School Boards Collective Bargaining Act (2014), which formalized a two-tier negotiations structure of central (provincial) tables and local tables (Leslie Wolfe, interview Sept. 2016). Its first round from 2015 to 2016 yielded major conflict. In the context of the government's intention to further limit funding, the Ministry of Education tacitly or explicitly encouraged the OPSBA to propose significant concessions on professional autonomy that could give districts and school administrators more flexibility in the use of provincial funding. The OPSBA was not conceived in the two-tier Collective Bargaining Act as a full party, representing directors, superintendents, and principals who had aligned their interests against the professional autonomy of teachers. To the frustration of the federations, it appeared to be delegated this role by the provincial government.

Negotiating over which issues would be dealt with at central and local tables consumed most of a year before collective bargaining could formally begin (Jones 2016). According to OSSTF president Paul Elliot, this delay was in large part due to the intervention of OPSBA. Elliot explained how this structure made for a very slow start:

> two of the parties may agree, but one of the parties may hold up the rest of this or have a veto power over the deal ... Really in fact, what we're bargaining is some local issues, and also over the provincial issues ... We went to an arbitrator; for us it became obvious that this was going to take so long that we actually said, "if you agree that this will be a central item, then we'll agree on these two items that you said will be central items." Our goal was to minimize the central items, just big ticket items, that's it. But they wanted things like class size, supervision, all kinds of things that vary all over the province. That took far too much time, as opposed to having a defined number of issues that are in regulation or legislation. (Interview Sept. 2016)

Elliot explained some of the differences in emphasis between the ministry and the school boards, blaming the latter for scuttling deals reached with the government:

> The government is about policy and initiatives ... But for school [boards], it's really local management issues. Class size, supervision, number of on-calls ... in our estimation, at the central table, if you want to have the school boards there, they should be in an advisory capacity ... The central table, just the government and ourselves, we talk about money. Then we have local bargaining where we really talk about local issues. (Ibid.)

Education minister Liz Sandals, previously a long-time school trustee and past president of the OPSBA, championed the association's issues according to Elliot. She would push for the elimination of class size caps, arguing that with declining enrolment they were leading to program cuts at small schools. Elliot argued that this policy conveniently overlooked the provincial government's power to determine per pupil funding (ibid.). Again suggesting the asymmetrical relationship between the Ministry of Education and school boards, Elliot believed that the former did not trust districts to disburse their funds to signature provincial programs, rather than to other areas with budget shortfalls. However, a priority for increasing the managerial power of principals in relation to teachers seems to have prevented school boards from otherwise making common cause with the teachers' federations in demanding more funding for education.

From the opening of provincial negotiations in February 2015, OPSBA and the provincial government demanded an aggressive series of concessions from OSSTF and other education unions. Moving beyond Bill 115's imposed salary freezes and back to the Harris era, employer demands included removing class size limits, eliminating all preparation time for several categories of teachers and significantly reducing it for all others by increasing the authority of principals to assign on-calls and other forms of unscheduled supervision. Striking at the heart of professional autonomy, "[School] Boards would determine the type, frequency and timing of diagnostic assessment tools used by teachers. Boards would establish the mechanism to be used by all teachers to record the results and these would be used to inform teacher practices." (OSSTF 2015b). OSSTF locals in four school districts struck near the end of the school year, and more were planning to walk out before the Ontario Labour Relations Board ruled that the strikes were illegal, as they were not "local" strikes but were in fact in response to provincial bargaining issues. The confusing and labour unfriendly nature of two-tier bargaining was again demonstrated. By the start of the 2015–16 school year, as OSSTF was now threatening a full provincial strike, the ministry and OPSBA dropped their extensive demands relating to professional autonomy. The union won a year's hiatus on new ministry initiatives and contract language recognizing teachers' professional judgment. Also won were modest salary increases below the rate of inflation.[32]

According to OSSTF Toronto vice-president Leslie Wolfe, beyond its economic consequences for teachers, an impact of Bill 115 was to "exacerbate what was already a sense of a lack of control over their own professional worlds" in the context of previous policy layering under McGuinty (interview Sept. 2016). She recognized that many members also felt mistrustful of the union, adding to the overall frustration of teachers. One OSSTF Toronto member, who described herself as pro-union and had participated in the protests, looked back on the Bill 115 conflict:

> It was so crazy last time with the contracts being imposed. It felt like this shocking breach of democracy, and we, at our school anyway … were ready to do illegal strikes, we were ready to really take strong action, and our union was not on that page at all. And we felt pretty let down last time around … So that was really strange to see, when we were all fired up and ready to do whatever we needed to do, and stand up not just for our own contract and salary and what not, but just basic democratic rights. (Toronto Teacher 4, interview Nov. 2014)

An activist member within OSSTF Toronto explained the dynamics of the Bill 115 struggle by the top-down nature of the union, which came to rely heavily on connections with politicians during the McGuinty era while neglecting grass-roots forms of exercising political power:

> Ken Coran, who had spent many years building solid relationships with the Liberals was, I think, genuinely dumbfounded when the terms [of the imposed contract] were presented to him in 2012 …he had built relationships with these people and he trusted … it was like he was trying to explain to them, "don't you understand, we're the good guys." People were completely unprepared. I think this is something that happens in labour leadership, with our managerial class of union managers. Many of them are in their positions for a long time, they build relationships with these people they think they can come to count on. Then everybody looks for the electoral fix. To be honest, right now, in terms of negotiations, I don't really see a lot more that our union can be doing that they're not doing. But the big problem is what they haven't been doing for many years, which is really about building community links and community supports. (Toronto Teacher 10, interview July 2015)

As a co-chair and an active member of OSSTF Toronto's Political Action Committee, it is my experience that non-electoral strategies to build political power that require the involvement of large numbers of members, such as systematic outreach to parents or potential community allies, did not figure in the union's core strategies during the McGuinty-Wynne era. The official "labour-community" organization for this purpose, the Campaign for Public Education, acted as a coordinating body for union leaders and progressive trustees to issue public statements and advertisements. At the same time, through member-led committees, OSSTF Toronto supports a range of causes beyond the pecuniary interests of its membership, through donations, advocacy at the TDSB, and direct participation.[33] However, these efforts are seldom conceived as part of a deliberate strategy of the union for building political power in the context of defending public education. In this way, OSSTF Toronto and the provincial union as a whole, like many unions, engage in "social unionism" if not "social movement" or "social justice" unionism (Ross 2012; Camfield 2011, 50–2; Fletcher and Gapasin 2008).

Preventing the provincial government from framing labour struggles with teachers as being primarily over compensation issues is critical for OSSTF and the federations if they are to gain popular support in a context of stagnant wages for most working people and financially squeezed public services. During the fight over Bill 115, the unions framed it as an attack on democratic rights. This approach gained some public support, especially from those already disillusioned by other instances in which the government's interpretation of law was questionable during McGuinty's long reign. Some teachers interviewed (Toronto Teachers 3 and 4) expressed a desire that OSSTF be more proactive on curriculum, pedagogy, and other areas more integral to professional practice. The 2015 central agreement was ratified by 78 per cent of members (OSSTF 2015c). In Toronto member attention was more attracted to the below-inflation salary increases, coming after two years of salary freezes under Bill 115,[34] than to the victory on professional autonomy, which was taken for granted.

Considering the context of education governance after the Harris PCs and thirteen years under Liberal premiers McGuinty and Wynne, Wolfe observed:

> Secondary teachers today in Toronto experience their jobs with a great deal more sense of stress and pressure than when I began teaching in the late 1980s, Pre-Harris. I would put that down to the amount of change, the speed with which change is implemented, the lack of inclusion of the front-line worker, in this case the teacher, in developing the change. So there's no opportunity for a teacher to … have a sense of control over, or a sense that their professionalism is being recognized or honoured in any way. (Interview Sept. 2016)

A clear continuity existed, despite major changes in discourse and the early restoration of funding, from the Harris government to the Liberals, through the inheritance of disciplinary institutions such as the College of Teachers and the EQAO. The initial centralization of authority to the provincial level under Harris, through the transformation of education finance, facilitated far more sophisticated forms of governance under the Liberals, which steadily increased the capacity of the Ministry of Education to regulate the professional lives of teachers. For secondary teachers, this change occurred chiefly through pressure for steadily increasing graduation rates at all costs. Simultaneously, as in New York City, albeit in a less extreme form, the neoliberalization of education manifested itself in the specific context of the big city. School choice introduced a competitive market for enrolment to the public system. The result was structured along already existing racial and class inequities in Toronto, grounding segregation more strongly in schools, with a resulting adverse affect on students and teachers.

Finally, shifting economic circumstances during the 2008–9 downturn saw McGuinty change his alliances, to the detriment of OSSTF, whose leadership appeared slow to comprehend that their organization was no longer considered an essential partner. At both the provincial and the local levels in Toronto, leaders struggled to adapt to the new context, to the frustration of members, some of whom saw the union as another unresponsive bureaucratic intrusion in their work lives, like the school district and the ministry (Toronto Teacher 1, interview Aug. 2014). Formal two-tier negotiations under the School Boards Collective Bargaining Act did nothing to improve the 2015–16 round. Rather, it demonstrated that the key ingredient, in the context of unions on the defensive, was employers willing to compromise on the rollout of top-down policy affecting teachers' professionalism and willing to ensure that their real compensation was not eroded. In the context of neoliberalized governance and fiscal austerity, this was not the case. Amid a return to conflict and the ongoing neoliberalization of education among many other sectors in Ontario, an OSSTF Toronto teacher argued that ultimately a deeper rethink of union strategy is needed:

> We've got members who say, we should just all walk out, we need to take a hard stance … I actually don't agree with that. We'd be legislated back to work, eventually. We'd blow through our budgets, we would be fined massively, like in BC, for every day that we were out illegally. We couldn't sustain a full walk-out … unless you know you've got … a massive social movement behind you. We don't, and we wouldn't, because we haven't done that work to lay the foundation for that. I think it means that we're really bargaining right now from a position of weakness. There's a lot of work on the ground that needs to happen, and I don't think anyone in our leadership know how to do that. I don't think too many people in the labour movement these days know how to do that, because it's all been about … negotiating contracts and enforcing contracts, and that's it. But that ends up keeping us in these silos. That for me is why we're weak. It's

> not just us, it's right across the labour movement. Unless we can figure out a way to build social movements, I don't know how we're going to exist. (Toronto Teacher 10, interview July 2015)

One way to build trust with parents and a sceptical broader public that teacher job actions are not just about salaries and benefits and also to create a deeper role for the union in the work lives of many members could be to more prominently and articulately champion their professional autonomy. Doing so means making the case again that classroom teachers are best placed to understand the needs of the students they serve. The election of a PC government led by Premier Doug Ford in 2018 and a return to the level of conflict in public education seen during the Harris era have made it imperative.

6 Conclusion

Preface: Confronting the Neoliberalization of Education

In November 2018, months after the election that defeated Wynne's Liberals and brought Ford's PCs to power, I participated in a "Lobby Day" organized by OSSTF, in which dozens of teachers and education workers from across Ontario descended on the provincial legislature at Queen's Park to meet as many members of Parliament as possible. Individual meetings were held with nearly all members of the opposition New Democratic (NDP), Liberal, and Green parties and about half of the governing Progressive Conservatives (PCs). Our objectives were to explain our jobs, especially for the dozens of first-term politicians, and how students would be affected by the loss of the services we provided. The task was especially important for the educational assistants, school secretaries, custodians, and youth counsellors, who lacked both the stronger contractual protections and the broader public recognition enjoyed by teachers. We were also to raise awareness of the dangers for public education of school vouchers and charter schools, suggested in a report prepared by multinational consulting firm Ernst and Young on restructuring the public sector and commissioned by the new PC government.

With another teacher, I met with Christina Mitas, a PC representative for a district in Scarborough. Mitas had taught for a few years in Scarborough high schools. When she was hand-picked as a candidate in June 2018 by future premier Doug Ford, she was pursuing her master's degree at the Ontario Institute for Studies in Education (OISE). Before our meeting, I studied her online profile to understand how she was politically situated. She was president of the graduate student association at the academic institution with arguably the most left-wing reputation in Canada, previously drawing the scorn of her party, and had received the endorsement of an ideologically committed PC leader.

Mitas recognized the shortcomings due to a lack of funding experienced by schools in Scarborough, taking notes as my colleague provided specific examples from within her own district. Mitas then asked, "What do you think about school choice?" We hesitated. She continued, saying that providing more options for parents was always a good thing, and she explained that she strongly supported school vouchers. "I'm against them, they would hurt public education." I replied. "Are *you* against them, or is your *union* against them?" she pressed."Both."

If parents were given some form of tax credit or voucher to send their children to private schools (as was proposed in 2001 by the PCs during their previous government and again during the 2007 election), a likely outcome would be the exit of wealthier families from the public system, I said. I outlined the effects of school choice in New York, detailed in chapter 3. She acknowledged some of the ensuing problems of teaching to the test and of inequity between students, but she politely insisted that vouchers would be positive.

As we left the meeting soon after, I was frustrated that, despite having written this book, I hadn't thought of more to say. Could I have been more persuasive? What is the point of an intellectual analysis of the neoliberalization of education if you can't win debates in real life? Of course, I was probably naive if I thought there was anything I could say that could change what was apparently a core ideological belief: the market mechanism of choice is good, even at the expense of the public system.

This book has argued that the neoliberalization of education and challenges to teachers' professional autonomy have advanced through governments that have applied a softer touch, combined with some relative improvements to education that have won the support of many teachers and parents, at least for a time, as did the McGuinty and Wynne Liberal governments in Ontario. Neoliberalization has also been pushed forward by more abrasive leaders such as Bloomberg and Cuomo in New York and Peña Nieto in Mexico, though provoking a strong backlash, which in the latter contributed to the election of Andrés Manuel López Obrador.

Under the administration of Doug Ford, Ontario has again become a flashpoint for conflict. His opening salvos attacked the math and health curriculums and launched a short-lived "snitch line" to report teachers who defy the provincial government's edicts. Continuing his electoral campaign claims that the Education Quality Accountability Office (EQAO) math test scores signified the education system was in a crisis for which he blamed teachers' lack of knowledge of math, his government instituted a mandatory Math Proficency Test for all new certified teachers (OTF 2019). Ironically, EQAO, the agency tasked with administering the test, subsequently published a report concluding that there was a limited correlation between teacher testing and the academic performance of students (EQAO 2019). In the most aggressive attack on public education since the Harris government, Ford's 2019 provincial budget included a rise in high school class sizes by an average of six students and grades 4 through 8 by one student, over four years. High school students would also be required to take at least one course online per year. Taken together, these measures are projected to eliminate over 10,000 teaching positions, nearly 1,000 in elementary schools and over 9,000 in secondary schools (FAO 2019, 2). The latter number represents approximately one in four teachers in Ontario's public secondary schools. In this context of increasingly crowded classrooms with fewer teachers, private schools are advertising their low student-to-teacher ratios. As I write, Ontario's teachers' federations are engaging in a battle in defence of public education, with historic consequences.

This book has explained the differences of history and politics between Canada and the United States, and even more between both of them and Mexico, to help understand why teachers and their organizations have responded in diverse ways to neoliberal reforms. I hope I have also convincingly explained the commonalities of experience in the transformations of the work lives of the teachers of New York City, Mexico City, and Toronto. My principal method of research, interviews with educators on how their work has been affected by various policies, comes from my belief in the importance of individual and collective worker experiences in shaping their social worlds. Teachers in various contexts and circumstances have demonstrated considerable agency in challenging the rollout of top-down policies that they consider to be harmful to their craft. While they have experienced many setbacks, teachers have shown that the political space for the implementation of education policy remains far from empty, and that policymakers dismiss the power of education workers at their own peril.

This chapter begins by summing up the evidence throughout the case studies of the fundamental role of assault on the professional autonomy of teachers in the neoliberalization of education. It then argues for the importance of teachers' unions' taking seriously the defence of professional autonomy, both to protect the integrity of their members' work and in the broader public interest. Finally, I offer some thoughts on a strategic multi-scalar geography for teachers.

6.1. The Centrality of Teachers' Professional Autonomy in the Struggle against the Neoliberalization of Education

The ability of teachers to exercise their professional autonomy in determining how best to meet the unique needs of their students is a crucial issue determining the future of public education in the contemporary context of its neoliberalization. I have analysed five dimensions of comparison across the three case studies in order to understand how the neoliberalization of education in North America is undermining professional autonomy.

The first dimension is a common trend towards the centralization of education governance, away from local school districts and towards the state/provincial or national level. Centralization facilitated the rollout of subsequent policies, as institutions and structures that may have provided resistance, such as elected school boards, parent organizations, and local teachers' unions, found themselves out-scaled in the mismatch of locally based power and centrally made executive decisions. In New York City, this disparity occurred at three levels. The first was through the implementation of mayoral control, which removed meaningful authority from locally elected trustees, empowering the agenda of billionaire "education mayor" Michael Bloomberg. This application occurred in conjunction with a significant increase in federal intervention into education under the provisions of the No Child Left Behind Act (NCLB) of President G.W. Bush in 2002 and the Race to the Top (RTTT) program in 2009 under President Barack Obama. These federal measures mandated the "test-based accountability," which Bloomberg subsequently implemented. The importance of the national level diminished with the Every School Succeeds Act in 2015, returning the primary scale of neoliberal intervention to the state level. When Bill de Blasio succeeded Bloomberg with an education vision that conflicted with the dominant neoliberal agenda, his capacity to implement it via mayoral control was considerably undermined by Governor Andrew Cuomo's superseding authority from the state capitol. In Mexico, the key scalar shift in the centralization of education governance was from the state to the national level under the "structural reforms" of President Enrique Peña Nieto in 2013. This move followed earlier initiatives under the preceding administrations of Vicente Fox and Felipe Calderon, which returned the initiative in education policy, typically of a neoliberal character, to the national level after decentralization in the 1980s and 1990s. However, by mandating standardized teaching evaluation in the Mexican constitution and by simultaneously uploading responsibility for payroll to the national level, Peña Nieto's government made it far more difficult for the teachers' movement to win state-level exemptions from national policy, as it had done previously in Mexico City and elsewhere. Through this period, the centre-left administrations in Mexico City, which assumed the authority of both municipal and state governments (especially after 2016), though perhaps sympathetic, could not significantly intervene because of the centralized nature of education governance, particularly here, as a result of the subordinate status of the old Federal District up to 2016. In Ontario, the scaling-up of education governance began with the provincial government's uploading responsibility for financing local school boards from municipalities in the late 1990s. Under the succeeding Liberal provincial governments, a steady stream of ministry policies, especially under "education premier" Dalton McGuinty, coincided with the primary level of collective bargaining "following the money" to the provincial level.

The second dimension is an intense rollout of top-down education policy that has transformed the roles of school administrators, who are responsible for supervising its front-line implementation, in varying degrees in all three case studies. Such responsibilities can include school autonomy or school-based management initiatives where principals are given managerial control over elements of school funding and an interest in cutting costs. This was the case in Mexico City through the Quality Schools Program, in which schools led by their directors competed for additional funding via test scores. It was even more the case in New York City, where principals were given control over the school budget under Bloomberg, including a fixed amount for staff payroll that encouraged the hiring of low-seniority, and thereby low-cost, teachers. The relationship between principals and teachers has shifted from its earlier basis in collegiality to become increasingly hierarchical, as the former are now tasked with ensuring their staff are in compliance with the policy of the day. Their success in doing so is now a primary measure of their own effectiveness as managers. This shift has been particularly evident in Toronto since the removal of principals and vice-principals from the teachers' unions in 1997 and the subsequent increase in the "layers" of Ministry of Education policies (Pinto 2015) that they are required to oversee in their schools. In the process, the capacity of principals to intervene in the classroom work of teachers as well as to redefine the scope of their professional duties has increased. This has particularly been the case in all three cities over the preparation for and administration of student standardized testing. The integration of school directors within this system was slower in Mexico because of their membership in the union until 2017 and their allegiances to either its institutional leadership or the dissident movement. However, it is unfolding here too, particularly in Mexico City, where the disciplinary capacities of the system are stronger.

The precariousness of teachers' employment varied significantly between the cases, affecting workplace power relations and the capacity of teachers to exercise professional autonomy. New York City saw the most drastic decline, from the vast majority of new teachers' obtaining permanent status after three years to a slight majority continuing to work on year-to-year contracts even after the initial, now four-year, probationary period. This change had a major impact on workplace cultures, since probationary teachers dependent on principals' evaluations were far less likely to be assertive. Mexico City saw new teachers remain under probationary status for longer periods, modestly increasing the overall proportion of teachers without permanent status, which coincided with the more consistent application of employment exams. The more significant factor here is likely the decades-long process undergone by teachers from the start of their careers to when they obtain full-time status. A further major change in Mexico with the stated intent of broadening the labour market, which will also have a serious effect on teaching and workplace culture, is the elimination of a degree in education as a mandatory prerequisite for teaching. Employment conditions for permanent teachers in Toronto changed very little, maintaining a high degree of union-backed security.

The third dimension deals with the various policy measures that move through this relationship; quantitative performance metrics with politically determined thresholds have the greatest impact on professional autonomy. In all three cities, this aspect took the form of the publicized results of standardized student exams. In Toronto, it was supplemented by course credit accumulation towards rising graduation rates. Teachers in all three case studies reported that their freedom to exercise their judgment on how best to interpret curriculum and pedagogy is subordinated to the imperative of showing progress in these metrics, requiring them to varying extents to "teach to the test." The degree and form of pressure is uneven, depending on school contexts, and teachers of academically struggling students generally are the most affected. In New York City, student test score results were at one point decisive in determining the success or failure of a teacher's annual evaluation. In Mexico City, quantitative metrics suffered a major reversal after the cancellation of the national ENLACE student exam in 2013 following widespread individual and collective acts of resistance by teachers. In that year in Mexico, a new standardized exam to assess teachers' performance was introduced. The exam provoked waves of strikes and protests led by the CNTE, as many educators strongly believed that the exam was a poor means of judging their teaching, and they suspected that it would be politically manipulated to justify the firing of dissidents. In late 2016, Peña Nieto's government conceded, making the exam voluntary for teachers who had not previously failed the test.

In the fourth dimension, the power of these quantitative metrics over teachers' work is particularly insidious when combined with the creation of a competitive "market" for student enrolment through school choice, a significant form in which the neoliberalization of education has specifically unfolded in urban districts in Canada and the United States. It was much less evident in Mexico City, likely owing to the more entrenched pre-existing structures of class segregation by neighbourhood and enrolment in private schools and the elimination of the ENLACE exam. In New York City and Toronto, staff compete to avoid the closure of their schools due to low enrolment because of a negative reputation from standardized test score results and/or class and racial stereotypes. They do so through the marketing of specialty programs, to varying results on teacher professional autonomy. One consequence has been the rise of the self-conception, particularly in more affluent communities, of the student/parent as customer, having the power to challenge teachers' professional judgment. Where large schools have been replaced with many smaller schools, as in New York City, a consequence of the smaller faculty has been the narrowing of course offerings to classes subject to standardized exams. Rather than compel all schools to do better, as free-market advocates theorize, in practice these local systems become increasingly segregated, and the most mobile students, who tend to be the most privileged on the basis of race and class, are concentrated in a handful of "good" schools. This inequity has a strong effect on teachers' work, but especially on the life opportunities of students left behind by their more privileged peers. At its worst, as in New York City during the era of Mayor Bloomberg and NCLB, rather than receive additional support, struggling schools are stigmatized and reconstituted, their teachers losing permanent status at the discretion of administrators. The consequences were less punitive in Toronto under the Liberal governments, epitomized by Fullan's (2016) doctrine of "pressure and support." Secondary schools with low test scores and graduation rates have instead received some additional provincial funding (along with additional oversight over teachers' work) in recognition of the greater socio-economic challenges experienced by their students. Teachers at schools with declining enrolment are reassigned according to seniority rules overseen by the union. As a result, while neoliberal school choice is significant in both New York City and Toronto, it is more harmful in the former.

Finally, a fifth important dimension in the effect of neoliberal policy on professional autonomy has been the responses of teachers' unions. In all three case studies unions whose primary scale for contention with the state had been at the local district level were confronted by an increasing scaling-up to state/provincial and/or national levels of governance. This change has placed teachers' unions at varying degrees of disadvantage. New York City's United Federation of Teachers has been perhaps the most vulnerable. It has depended on the political lobbying of state and federal officials, as formal collective bargaining rights remained at the municipal level, higher-level state and national-level union structures were relatively weak, and the union leadership was reluctant to fully engage in broader community coalitions that were more confrontational. In Mexico, the context is wholly different. The national leadership and many state executives of the official teachers' union (SNTE) gives its full support to the federal government's education policy, regardless of its impact on its members. While drawing the sympathies of hundreds of thousands of teachers nationally, the capacity of the dissident teachers' movement (CNTE) for sustained collective action remains geographically confined to the southeast. The participation of Mexico City teachers in this movement has given them more strength than they would ever have resisting national policies on their own. The dissident movement is held back from consolidating in Mexico City to the same extent as it has in Oaxaca or Chiapas chiefly by the stronger administrative structures of the city's education authorities, which appear to exercise more powerful administrative and disciplinary capacities than exist in many other states. Despite considerable effort by the Secretary of Public Education (SEP), the reliability was in doubt of many school directors throughout the country to carry out neoliberal reforms affecting teachers' work, such as the standardized evaluations. As a result, one of the greatest difficulties faced by neoliberal education reform in Mexico City has been the lack of reliable agents for enforcement at the school level. The CNTE was greatly undermined by the scalar shift to the national level under Peña Nieto. What appears to be its success in fundamentally undermining his "structural reforms" after a difficult war of attrition from 2013 to 2016, filled with numerous strikes, reprisals, protests, and repression, is also related to a transformed national political context. The "Pact for Mexico" parties (PRI, PAN, and PRD), which drove the reforms in 2013 were progressively sidelined, leading to the electoral triumph of Morena in 2018.

Collective bargaining for Toronto teachers officially accommodated the uploading of governance to the provincial level with the institution of two-tier negotiations. However, they also face a much higher degree of unity from districts and administrator associations in the advancement of policies against teacher autonomy. Unlike New York, Ontario teachers are weakened by being divided into four federations that have lacked unity at critical junctures. They also face an adversarial Principal's Council and Public School Boards Association. In New York State, these authorities have split on issues of education finance, standardized testing, and teachers' evaluations to align with teachers (Hagopian 2014b). In Ontario, the priorities of these bodies have conflicted with teachers' professional autonomy, and they aligned themselves with the provincial government. The election of Doug Ford's PCs in 2018 has lead to significant new challenges. Yet overall, teachers' unions in Ontario find themselves at the end of this period with greater institutional resources than their colleagues in New York or Mexico experience. Despite many layers of provincial policy, teachers in Toronto, Ontario, continue to enjoy substantial professional autonomy. Public opinion is strongly divided on the utility of the EQAO tests, the ruling PCs emphasizing their value and the opposition NDP advocating for their elimination. Although, as in New York City and Mexico City, control over teachers' work is often subject to the micro-dynamics of power at the school level, especially as defined by the balance of relations between teachers and administrators.

However, even in New York State, a continental epicentre for neoliberal education policy, the peak of standardized-testing mania and its use to discipline and regiment teachers and their work appears to have been in the fall of 2015. Given the shift in political winds, in great part due to the parent-led Opt Out movement, Governor Cuomo moved on to other issues. In 2016, the UFT negotiated a de-emphasizing of standardized student test scores in teacher evaluations (Zimmerman and Disare 2016). New York State lawmakers in 2019 removed stipulations that standardized tests be used for teacher evaluations, considerably undoing much of Cuomo's earlier agenda (Amin 2019). The formal rescinding of NCLB in 2015 by the US Congress appeared to mark the end of an era of ambitious bipartisan neoliberal federal intervention into K–12 education under G.W. Bush and Obama. It has not been revived under Trump. The experience in Mexico City shows the repeated failure for myriad reasons, of top-down federal education policies such as the ACE, the ENLACE exam, and the Ley de Servicio Profesional Docente, which dismiss the concerns of teachers. The Morena government promises a more constructive relationship with teachers.

Key policy advocates such as Michael Fullan (2016) suggest that the dominant scale of education governance reform will return to the subnational state or district level. On the other hand, the political influence of global "standards" or "competencies" for education appears to be growing. This trend is especially represented by the OECD's PISA exam, which grew from twenty-eight participating countries in 2000 to seventy-two in 2015 (Addey and Sellar 2017). Within participating countries, media interest has risen accordingly. Unfavourable national scores have led to a new opportunity to argue that the problem is not a lack of funding, but a lack of private sector involvement and an overabundance of teacher autonomy (Steiner-Khamsi, Appleton, and Vellani 2018). The struggles by teachers in North America to defend their autonomy have many parallels around the world. Because of the continued political dominance of neoliberalism globally, the potential lucrativeness of privatized schools, and the general weakness of the labour movement and of alternative political visions, we can expect to see a continued push for the neoliberalization of education in the foreseeable future.

6.2. Teachers' Unions as Champions of Professional Autonomy

In all circumstances, teachers' unions grapple with perennial issues of balancing workplace issues relating to autonomy and workload, which offer more immediate bases for building alliances with parents and community groups, with compensation, especially amid widespread fiscal austerity. In contexts where the professionalism of teachers is consistently undermined, unions are challenged to avoid being seen as another overbearing and unintelligible institution and instead to fight for greater democracy in the workplace. Part of this struggle emerges from the changed composition of many education unions, particularly in Canada and the United States. From their roots representing teachers, UFT and OSSTF have grown to embrace the breadth of education workers from paraprofessionals to clerical staff. In the interests of building power in relation to their employers, this is a positive step. McAlevey (2016) and others have argued for sector-wide unions that unite workers across job classes and with the most and the least bargaining clout. However, professional autonomy in the classroom is no longer a unifying issue relevant to the entire membership. While maintaining its sectoral scope, perhaps OSSTF could learn from the Alberta Teachers' Association. It has developed a relatively higher provincial prominence on issues related to pedagogy and teacher practice, in part by being an important centre for producing and diffusing education research (Annie Kidder, interview Nov. 2015). The retention of administrators in Alberta's union likely helped sustain this activity as a shared priority. Teachers' unions must become the primary, popularly recognized authority on what constitutes good teaching, and they should gain this status by devoting considerable effort to obtaining a deep participation of its membership. The alternative is for advocates of neoliberal education policy or external disciplinary agencies such as the Ontario College of Teachers to successfully make this claim. Teachers' unions should make professional autonomy, including the ability of teachers to interpret curriculum, devise appropriate pedagogy for their students, and limit standardized evaluation and testing – integral issues in collective bargaining – potentially subject to strike action.

Renewing the role of unions in developing teacher professionalism is not without significant pitfalls. Prior to the upsurge of militancy in the 1960s and 1970s, teachers' federations in Canada and the National Education Association in the United States defined themselves as professional organizations, which in their contexts resulted in a lack of capacity or of willingness to assume the role of a labour union and confront their employers. While leading in the devising of curriculum and pedagogy, they shunned "unprofessional" activities such as strikes or political advocacy in order to challenge school districts and governments. Teachers' salaries and working conditions languished. It is easy to imagine that, transported to the contemporary context, such organizations would have struggled to mount a resistance to privatization and the undermining of autonomy. Since the 1990s, many US and Mexican union leaders have responded to a popularly perceived crisis in education and calls for standardized testing, "school choice," and more prescribed curriculum by adopting these proposals in the belief that doing so would renew the professional authority of their organizations and blunt anti-union attacks. Given the broader neoliberal context in which these policies were being developed, their approach was unsuccessful in protecting the integrity of the profession, and instead contributed to the undermining of working conditions and the capacity of the union to engage in contentious politics.

Nevertheless, it is a political dead end to dismiss the importance of unions becoming authorities on teacher professionalism as a distraction from militancy on conventional collective bargaining issues. This means losing a powerful basis for engaging many members through their devotion and concern for the craft of teaching. It is also the most effective way to build a position counter-hegemonic to that of government authorities and neoliberal "experts," which will have credibility with parents and the broader public. In the contemporary context, state authorities have demonstrated an increased willingness to intervene against teachers' strikes through legislation in Canada and the United States and repression in Mexico. In all three countries, teachers have most successfully defended themselves when they have won the battle of public opinion, creating a heavy political penalty for governments. As members of a caring profession, K–12 teachers must be able to demonstrate how their expertise serves their students better than the prescriptions of neoliberal policy advocates.

If teachers' unions develop comprehensive and politically significant positions on professional practice, a thorny question emerges about how they should respond when members fail to meet these standards. The conduct of doctors and lawyers is governed by their professional associations, but teachers do not have a similar degree of freedom to determine their conditions of employment. They are salaried, skilled workers subject to the authority of their supervisors. Teachers also have a more complex relationship with the public. Demands by parents and broader communities for a voice in teacher practice emerges from both their fundamental role in child development and the broader political significance of schools as sites for the reproduction of ideology. These claims pose limits to teachers' professional autonomy.

If teachers' work is deskilled, debased, and disempowered and professional autonomy is lost, we will see the potential extent of the neoliberalization of education. If the growing number of cut-rate, for-profit, charter school chains in the United States are an example, for the publicly funded schools of the working class it will consist of the replacement of professional educators with non-union technicians responsible for administering an entirely prescribed curriculum of daily lesson plans with no time or space for pedagogical experimentation. Aside from marching students through preparation for standardized exams and online work modules, their other major task will be maintaining discipline.

6.3. A Multi-Scalar Geography of Teachers' Professional Autonomy

The past two decades have seen a significant growth in international connections at both the top and the grass-roots levels between teachers' unions and movements across North America. Much of this expansion can be attributed to an increasing awareness of the similarities of struggles faced by teachers across jurisdictions and borders. Unlike other groups of workers in the context of globalization, teachers do not share the same employers (this situation could change if we see the rise of multinational private school chains) and we do not see forms of geographical competition for employment and investment that are the same as in other sectors such as manufacturing. However, among union leaders and activists, local exceptionalism and parochialism is giving way to an understanding that there are dominant forms of neoliberal education governance that share strong similarities from place to place. As a result, the impetus for solidarity has grown from a moral imperative to support workers in struggle to recognizing the usefulness of sharing strategies for confronting similar policies whether concerning high-stakes, standardized exams or school choice. As teachers struggle for professional autonomy, a geographically informed multi-scalar strategy that is not reduced to "scaling-up" or "localizing" actions needs to be developed . To have a greater impact on the work lives of teachers, the understandings involved ultimately must be rooted in the classroom experience.

Since the successful strike of the revitalized Chicago Teachers' Union in 2012, its leaders and organizers have been hosted by Toronto's teachers' unions and groups at least five times to share the lessons behind their victories. Toronto has not experienced the expansion of charter schools and standardized testing as Chicago has over the past decade, pushed by neoliberal governments more extreme than have been seen in Ontario. Yet hundreds of Toronto teachers have been enthusiastic to learn about the transformations that occurred within the Chicago union to enable it to score victories and build strong political alliances with parent and community groups, recognizing the applicability to their own context. Without neglecting the significance of geographical context in determining distinct strategies, teachers in Toronto and elsewhere have benefited from this policy mobility from below. The biennial Labour Notes and Trinational Coalition in Defence of Public Education conferences have increased in importance since the 2000s as physical gathering points, building long-term relationships based on familiarity with others' struggles and a shared analysis of common issues. Internet communication between conferences has opened up between grass-roots groups of teachers across great distances as never before. Practical forms of solidarity remain the familiar forms of demonstrations at embassies and consulates, letters, morale-building visits of guests to rallies, and donations. The new element of transnational teacher unionism is how, in the spirit of education, it precipitates radical learning communities,[1] through the strategic sharing of experiences regarding similar issues about confronting neoliberal reform. Such radical learning communities could gather ideal conceptions of teachers' professional autonomy by unions and movement activists, the governing discourse from education authorities, and qualitative assessments of the actual status of professional autonomy across jurisdictions. This research could then be used both to inform collective bargaining by individual unions with their employers and as a means of intervening in public debate on education policy.

Struggles against multilateral neoliberal education institutions such as the OECD's PISA exam, subject to a call for protest by the Trinational Coalition in Defence of Education, are unlikely to galvanize more than symbolic activities by teachers' unions in the intermediate term. The local, provincial, and national levels still have primacy in the education sector, leaving labour struggles highly bound by place.[2] The key strategic political question for teachers is still how to deal with the state. Historically, North American teachers' unions have been among the most active participants within organized labour in electoral politics. In the context of relatively open electoral systems, as exists in Canada, union political strategies could involve forming long-term, meaningful alliances with local parent and community groups that could then evolve organically into electoral coalitions to support progressive politicians who subscribe to the movement's democratically determined priorities. The "short cut" of union leaders simply donating large sums of money to influence election campaigns has generated cynicism in the absence of member involvement. Cash donations have limited effectiveness in light of intensifying counter-pressures to neoliberalize education, without grass-roots union participation and substantive efforts to shape the policies of political parties and candidates.

Despite the prominence of multilateral institutions such as the OECD and the World Bank in advocating publicly and privately for neoliberal education policies, particularly in Mexico, in the North American context it is still government officials and politicians who make the decisions. Shifting the direction of education governance is not simply a matter of replacing the people who are feeding ideas to policymakers and searching for new "good ideas." It is the structures of governance and the interests policymakers serve that must be changed if we are to have a more democratic and socially just public education system that is protected from privatization. This is a profoundly political struggle rooted in every place-bound jurisdiction in North America.

The contradiction of the scaling-up of negotiations is that it could become more distant and abstract from the experience of members, removed by further layers of representation from active participation in the absence of job actions and strikes. Likewise, in part due to sustained top-down policy from state authorities, the day-to-day work of leaders and staff members of teachers' unions revolves to a considerable extent around interlocution with these senior officials or interpreting their edicts. While necessary, this work considerably reduces the opportunity for union officers to work directly with groups of members. In this environment, the markings of a union leader are fluency in a technocratic form of policy and quasi-judicial knowledge. A technocratic union becomes autocratic when these specific forms of expertise become unchallengeable by rank-and-file members, leading to their apathy and demobilization.

The institutional health of a local teachers' union remains the aggregate of its presence at school sites, and the degree to which a union culture prevails among its members. The retention and sustained development of worksite stewards recognized as leaders by their peers are critical. Job expertise is strongly associated with workplace leaders recognized by their peers, with or without formal titles. School-site union leaders are most likely to hold the respect of their colleagues, enabling them to make calls for solidarity if they are considered to be good teachers. Good teachers are defined by their peers as well as their institutions, in large part by their effectiveness in exercising the full breadth of their professional autonomy through their pedagogy, instruction, and social support for students. A greater emphasis by teachers' unions on analysing and advocating the elements of good teaching could bring the spatial centre of gravity within the union back to the school site and the classroom. The technical skills of lawyers, negotiators, and grievance officers are essential so long as employment within K–12 education remains complexly regulated, but the time and energy this demands of leaders and staff come with the corollary effect that teachers' unions lack skilled member organizers. Professional autonomy and practice offer a substantive basis to engage members that are much more meaningful to their working lives than charity fundraisers. Were a union to research and debate professional practice with an approach that drew on the workplace knowledge of a significant number of its own members, rather than merely hiring outside experts to draft a position, unions could be more substantively participatory and thereby more democratic.

On a professional development day during which schools are closed at the Toronto District School Board, OSSTF offers over two dozen workshops, most developed by teachers for their peers. These sessions are among the most popular, in large part because their colleagues are considered best able to cater to the realities of schools and classrooms. They are one of the principal means by which the CNTE in Mexico organizes teachers outside of protests. Unions survey their membership on their priorities for salary and working conditions before entering negotiations. More could be done to train school-site union leaders to canvass the perspectives of their peers on contemporary curricular and pedagogical issues. Doing so could shift power dynamics within schools. With a collective position, teachers would be better able to curb the tendency towards the concentration of managerial power in principals and school directors, and challenge policies that don't work well in their classrooms. At a higher scale, unions with positions on teacher practice developed through a bottom-up process will have a stronger mandate to negotiate, knowing that their members have been deeply engaged in their development. Such approaches could form part of a multi-scalar strategy for defending and supporting teachers' professional autonomy.

Appendix: List of Interviews

New York

New York Teacher 1	December 2014
New York Teacher 2	December 2014
New York Teacher 3	December 2014
New York Teacher 4	December 2014
New York Teacher 5	December 2014
New York Teacher 6	December 2014
Lois Weiner, Professor of Education	December 2014
New York Teacher 7	January 2015
Former United Federation of Teachers Official 1	January 2015
New York Teacher 8	April 2015
New York Teacher 9	April 2015
New York Teacher 10	April 2015
New York Teacher 11	April 2015
New York Teacher 12	April 2015
New York Teacher 13	April 2015
Former United Federation of Teachers Official 2	April 2015

Mexico City

Mexico City Teacher 1	February 2015
Mexico City Teacher 2	February 2015
Mexico City Teacher 3	February 2015
Mexico City Teacher 4	February 2015
Mexico City Teacher 5	February 2015
Mexico City Teacher 6	February 2015
CNTE Section 10 Activist	February 2015
Enrique de la Garza Toledo, Professor of Sociology	February 2015
Graciela Bensusan, Professor of Politics	February 2015

Hugo Aboites, Professor of Education	February 2015
Mexico City SEP Education Official (AFSEDF) 1	February 2015
Mexico City Teacher 7	May 2015
Mexico City Teacher 8	May 2015
Mexico City SEP Education Official (AFSEDF) 2	May 2015
Mexico City Teacher 9	June 2015
Mexico City Support Staff 1	June 2015
Mexico City Support Staff 2	June 2015
Enrique Enriquez Ibarra, CNTE Section 9 General Secretary	June 2015
Maria de la Luz Arriaga, Professor of Economics	June 2015
Secretary of Public Education Official (SEP) 1	June 2015
Secretary of Public Education Official (SEP) 2	June 2015
Secretary of Public Education Official (SEP) 3	June 2015

Toronto

Toronto Teacher 1	August 2014
Toronto Teacher 2	August 2014
Toronto Teacher 3	August 2014
Toronto Teacher 4	November 2014
Toronto Teacher 5	March 2015
Toronto Teacher 6	March 2015
Toronto Teacher 7	April 2015
Toronto Teacher 8	July 2015
Toronto Teacher 9	July 2015
Toronto Teacher 10	July 2015
Annie Kidder, Executive Director of People for Education	November 2015
Sue Winton, Professor of Education	December 2015
Leslie Wolfe, OSSTF Toronto Vice-President	September 2016
Paul Elliot, OSSTF President	September 2016

Notes

Preface

1 Local "school districts" are referred to here interchangeably with the Canadian term, "school boards."
2 The Ontario term for the teacher who oversaw a broad department of multiple subject areas.

1 Introduction

1 Publicly employed K–12 teachers are automatically members of their unions in all three case studies because of contractual labour rights and, in Ontario, statutory membership in a teachers' federation.
2 An additional 6,000 unionized teachers are employed by the publicly funded Toronto Catholic school board. They are excluded from this study because they work under a separate local employer.
3 An analysis gained from Panitch and Gindin (2012) and, in the context of education policy, from Verger (2009).
4 However, it was accompanied by the further downloading of school operations and maintenance costs to the states, which can then pass them on to municipalities, which can decide to shift this burden again directly onto the parents of students themselves through annual fees. Mexico City has taken on many of these costs (though in the case of school maintenance, arguably not yet sufficiently), ensuring that no fees are charged to parents, whereas in other states, parents contribute to the upkeep of the school.
5 Numerous other issues exist, particularly the tradition of awarding school directorships as a form of patronage to teachers loyal to the official SNTE leadership and to local bosses of the ruling political party.
6 The 1971 strike by the Newark Teachers Union to eliminate "unprofessional duties," including hall and lunchroom supervision, while driven by a desire to ensure its members had guaranteed breaks, developed a similarly

racially divisive dynamic. Without the groundwork to build community alliances and incorporate the demands of predominantly African-American parents who were already struggling with the inadequacies and inequities of the school system, the narrowly conceived contract fight was perceived and portrayed as a strike by relatively privileged, majority white teachers against struggling black families (Golin 2002; Weiner 2012).

7 Identified in the preceding subsection.

8 Referred to in Ontario as Curriculum Leaders and Assistant Curriculum Leaders.

9 Instituto de Estudios Educativos y Sindicales de América (IEESA), which, while a branch of the SNTE, regularly issues far more critical reports and commentaries on the government's education policy. See, for example, IEESA (2013), *Algunas Consideraciones del Pasado Reciente del Sindicalismo Docente Latinoamericano* (Some Considerations on the Recent Past of Latin American Teacher Unionism); downloadable at www.ieesa.org.mx.

10 Ranging from a very strong influence by the Mexican Secretary of Public Education, the employer of all public primary and secondary teachers in Mexico and determiner of the education policies of Mexico City, to the New York City Department of Education, which sets its terms for negotiating with the UFT, though influenced by state and federal policies. The TDSB lies in between, as the signatory to the union contracts of Toronto teachers, though its role has diminished with the assumption of negotiations over monetary issues since 2009 by the Ontario Ministry of Education and the provincial unions.

11 Private institutions in Mexico accounted for 20.5 per cent of enrolment in upper-level high schools (medio-superior), and a high of 38 per cent of vocational schools in 2003. However, only 8 per cent of primary students and 7 per cent of secondary students attended private schools (Brambila 2008, 221).

12 In New York State, students must pass Regents exams for five core subject areas – history, math, science, English, and geography – to obtain a full high school diploma.

13 "Teacher's college" is also interchangeably referred to here as a faculty of education or a normal school (normale in Spanish).

2 Geographies of Professional Autonomy and Neoliberalism in North America

1 "Isabel" is a pseudonym.

2 The adjective "socialist" was added by the left-leaning nationalist president, Lazaro Cardenas, in 1934 and removed by his successor Manuel Avila Camacho in 1946 (Brambila 2008, 213).

3 Vasconcelos advocated paying rural teachers at twice the rate of urban teachers to encourage graduates to leave cities, "there is no better training for a young teacher than to discover in the countryside the needs of the school, and to have to improvise their solution" (quoted in Curiel Méndez 1982, 442). His vision never came to pass. Urban teachers and their schools historically have had considerably better working conditions and more resources.

4 Rural normale schools became the spiritual home of the dissident teachers' movement that coalesced into the CNTE. In the 1980s, a third of all teachers in Oaxaca and Chiapas were Indigenous bilingual instructors at the time when the movement emerged and established its stronghold in these states (Poy Solano 2016). They were considered centres of leftist organizing by the Mexican government, according to declassified Mexican intelligence agency reports, leading to efforts since the 1960s to restructure or close the schools. Elba Esther Gordillo, SNTE president from 1989 to 2013, described them with hostility in 2010 as "guerrilla seedbeds" (Padilla 2013, 24).

5 The Women Teachers' Association of Toronto formed in 1888. It was the first group in Ontario to pursue the distinct occupational interests of teachers as opposed to earlier associations controlled by school board trustees and administrators. As late as the 1950s, confronted by the opposition of male elementary teachers to their struggle for pay equity and to base pay scales on seniority rather than the grade level taught, women teachers opted for a separate gender-based organization until attacks by the Harris government pushed the organizations to merge as the Elementary Teachers' Federation of Ontario in 1998 (Spagnuolo and Glassford 2008, 56–8).

6 They affiliated to the Ontario Federation of Labour and the Canadian Labour Congress in the mid-1990s, in the context of significant attacks by the governing PCs on public sector unions.

7 SEP officials emphasize the Mexican government's close relationship with UNESCO by explaining how most other governments appoint their foreign ministry as the principal contact point, rather than the actual education authorities (SEP Officials 1, 2, 3, interview June 2015).

8 Rapid gains above the rising rate of inflation contributed to the federal government's instigating wage and price controls. The November 1974 to January 1975 strike by OSSTF Toronto ended with an imposed contract well below these gains (Head and Hutton 2005, 20–4, 31).

9 Subject to intervention based on perceived harm to students from extended strikes or lockouts (Hennessy 1975, 53). The body established to adjudicate on this basis, the Education Relations Commission, forty years later prohibited a series of local strikes conducted in 2015 by the OSSTF in the context of provincial negotiations.

10 University graduates' taking blue-collar jobs to organize in strategic industrial sectors was practised by Marxist groups across North America in this period (Glaberman 2002; Owen 2005).

11 Shanker denounced calls for a general strike, describing it as "a political weapon associated with the communist unions of Europe" (Freeman 2000, 267). Instead, he and the union leader representing municipal employees, including school custodians, teachers' aides, and secretaries, acceded to a corporatist plan to use the municipal workers' pension to buy $2.5 billion in city bonds to get out of the crisis, shifting the risk of default from the banks onto their own members (Freeman 2000).

12 These are not necessarily the most extreme neoliberal education test cases, which would include New Orleans since Hurricane Katrina, Arizona's de facto voucher system and private charters, and Michigan's patchwork of completely privatized small school districts. However, they have not had as much influence in setting the debate nationally (or beyond) as the larger centres and their key advocate leaders have.

13 Initially due to the prevalence of much higher sectoral minimum wages covering most urban workers and later due to the complicity of state-controlled unions, Mexico's minimum wage has historically been relatively far lower than the legal minimum in Canada or the United States. Statisticians calculate salaries on the basis of how many multiples of the minimum wage a worker earns; the bare minimum is earned in the most exploited sectors (Bensusan and Middlebrook 2013, 49–51).

14 Author's notes from People for Education conference, University of Toronto, 7 November 2015.

15 The CNTE benefited in the early years of the Salinas government from Education Secretary Manuel Bartlett's decentralization of administration to state governments, curbing the power of the national SNTE controlled by Gordillo. Salinas replaced him in 1993 with future president Ernesto Zedillo who made a rapprochement with Gordillo (Brambila 2009, 218–19). At a conference he organized in Mexico City in 2016 for opponents of the Trans-Pacific Partnership trade agreement, Bartlett described the SNTE to me as "very, very corrupt."

16 An important reason for the differences in durability of the dissident movements in Sections 9 and 10 may be attributed to the former's deeper roots in school-level and zone committees in the years prior to the 1989 upsurge (Enrique Enriquez Ibarra, CNTE Section 9 General Secretary, interview June 2015).

17 Ravitch observes, "when we contrast the rhetoric of *A Nation at Risk* with the reality of the No Child Left Behind legislation of 2002, *A Nation at Risk* looks positively idealistic, liberal, and prescient" (2010, 29).

18 The pivotal role of the Salinas regime, following the profound austerity administered by his predecessor (and the IMF), for neoliberalizing the

Mexican state, can be summed up in the halving of the public sector's share of GDP from 41.8 per cent to 23.2 per cent. Salinas privatized hundreds of state-owned enterprises, which, combined with corporate and income tax cuts, perpetuated chronic budget austerity (Marquez Ayala 2008, 154).

19 Hess and Meeks cite a survey of US school board officials in which 40 per cent oppose hiring non-traditionally trained teachers (e.g., through TFA), half oppose charter schools vouchers and eliminating neighbourhood schools, and 80 per cent oppose new charter schools. They admonish them for favouring "genteel measures" such as more professional development for teachers and principals, "while steering clear of more disruptive proposals" (2013, 109). For Hess and Meeks, it's the thousands of school board officials who are wrong. As is true of teachers, working within education makes them biased, rather than informed parties.

20 The largest academic association for studying education in the United States.

21 The federal government has intervened in provincial education through decisions of Supreme Courts on labour conflicts. Recognizing the precedent it would set for other provinces, the Ontario, Manitoba, Saskatchewan, and Quebec governments intervened in support of the British Columbia government in an appeal by the BCTF that BC had illegally removed clauses on class sizes and specialist teachers from the union contract. The BC government was required to hire hundreds of teachers to restore class sizes to pre-2002 levels. The BCTF's victory took fourteen years (O'Neil and Sherlock 2016).

22 Also see Wallner 2014, 230–1.

23 Founded in 1928, the CEA became the Latin American affiliate of the World Federation of Teachers' Unions, a branch of the Communist-aligned World Federation of Trade Unions. Most provincial teachers' unions conducted international activities through the Canadian Teachers' Federation. Throughout the Cold War it avoided engaging with Latin American teachers' unions, as they were seen as too "politicized" or, in other words, too left wing. The strength of the CEA was a symbol of this. Leaders of the BCTF representing the Canadian Teachers Federation in the late 1960s at the World Confederation of Organizations of the Teaching Profession disclosed that 85 per cent of the latter's funding came from the CIA. The World Confederation was dominated by the NEA, which routinely paid the dues of member unions in developing countries. It tried unsuccessfully to undermine the CEA. The International Federation of Free Teacher Unions led by AFT president Albert Shanker was even more ideologically committed to the US side of the Cold War (Kuehn 2006, 20–2, 26, 59–60).

24 An international conference convened by the SNTE in 2015 in Monterrey, featured directors of the INEE responsible for administering standardized testing and the Confederation of Mexican Employers (COPARMEX) (*El Universal* 2015).

25 I became involved in the Trinational Coalition after attending its 2010 conference in Montreal as a representative of OSSTF. I have since participated in many events organized by the Trinational in Mexico, including as a spokesperson for OSSTF at an "International Solidarity Conference" in November 2013 near the height of the first wave of strikes and protests against the Ley de Servicio Profesional Docente of Peña Nieto.

26 The latter has provided the most consistent financial and infrastructure support for the Trinational. Larry Kuehn, a BCTF researcher, Dan Leahy, an academic who organized the initial meeting in Olympia, and Maria de la Luz Arriaga, an economics professor at the National Autonomous University of Mexico (UNAM) have provided crucial continuity (Kuehn 2006). As participation within the Trinational for OSSTF is not an official duty to the extent of its membership in the Ontario Federation of Labour or the Canadian Labour Congress, its ongoing participation owes much to the role of Domenic Bellissimo, director of communications and political action.

27 I attended biennial Labor Notes conferences in Detroit and then Chicago, participating in workshops and caucus meetings for teachers. These meetings grew year over year to reach approximately 300 participants of the conference's over 3,000 attendees by 2018.

28 Personal observations from attending the CORE conference in Chicago, July 2011.

3 New York City

1 The experiences of "Jen" and "Karen" (both pseudonyms) are drawn from interviews and a school visit by the author with New York Teachers 13 and 14 in April 2015.

2 The Initiative was begun under his predecessor Mayor Giuliani but expanded at a massive and rapid scale under Bloomberg.

3 Unlike Bloomberg's administration – under most of which Joel Klein served as chancellor, enjoying strong support from the mayor – several chancellors led the Board of Education under Giuliani. Despite their varying ideologies and organizational priorities, all ultimately clashed with him (Rivera-McCutchon 2012, 26).

4 However, aside from the years 1989 to 1994, Chicago mayors have appointed the school board and its superintendent and intervened in education policy. This power and, in some periods, control over the education budget were an important source of political patronage, notably for Richard M. Daley and his father, for which Chicago's politics are (in)famous. In 1988, community activists won the creation of strong elected school councils with the power to hire and fire the principal, set priorities, and approve a discretionary budget. Elected district structures

and nominating committees for the central board were abolished with the return to mayoral control in 1995, but the empowered local school councils remain, though contested. The charter schools that have replaced dozens of public schools over the past two decades lack this structure, giving principals considerable power. Mayoral control was the dominant form of urban school administration in the United States at the turn of the twentieth century, prior to decentralization reforms in favour of greater parental and community voice. It was never abolished in Philadelphia, Baltimore, New Haven, or Jackson, Mississippi, among other cities (Shipps 2009, 118–20; Henig 2009, 23). None is prominently cited as a model for mayoral control, likely both because of the greater prominence of New York and Chicago and because the historic institution of mayoral control in these cities is not an integral component for policy advocates of a larger package of contemporary neoliberal reforms, which this chapter seeks to establish is the case for New York.

5 During the reign from 2007 to 2010 of charismatic policy advocate and schools chancellor Michelle Rhee.

6 In Toronto, becoming a trustee has traditionally been the first step for would-be politicians to become elected to higher (and better remunerated) office as a city councillor, or a member of the provincial or federal parliament, drawing many ambitious candidates into the race.

7 This is a common argument among neoliberal advocates for mayoral control (see Hess and Meeks 2013). Frederick Hess is the director of education policy studies at the American Enterprise Institute. Dorothy Shipps repudiates this claim of teachers' unions highjacking local school boards in her essay on Chicago's experience for *When Mayors Take Charge* (2009, 137).

8 Henig cites ineffective textbook distribution to explain DC school chancellor Michelle Rhee's initial desire for more power over personnel in 2007 under mayoral control. He acknowledges the concerns of parents and teachers in DC, particularly of African Americans, who felt excluded from exercising a political voice and saw mayoral control as a white power structure asserting control over educators and the black grass roots (2009, 28). In 2010, Rhee's patron, Mayor Adrian Fenty, lost his re-election bid (and with it, her job) in large part owing to her divisive attacks on teachers' collective bargaining rights and school closures in black communities (Ravitch 2013a, 286).

9 Education professor Michael Kirst cites the Chicago experience of mayoral control to argue that business lobbyists were principally interested in exercising fiscal discipline over schools. They were less successful in Boston, where career civil servants played a stronger role (Kirst 2009). In contrast, Wong praises the practices in Chicago (and subsequently in New

York) of mayoral control, resulting in the importation of management staff from outside the public education sector, who shared a mindset with business leaders (2009, 83).

10 Ravitch (2013a) points out that this can sometimes be a misleading statistic, however, as the graduation rate in five years is considerably higher. Five years was the standard in Ontario until 2003, under which I graduated in its final cohort.

11 Hantzopoulos and Tyner-Mullings attribute the ability of critical small schools to expand in the 1980s and early 1990s to "both the centralization (and the attendant inability to supervise all parts of the system) and decentralization (creating spaces that allowed new ideas to develop) of the New York City Board of Education" (2012, xxvi).

12 Michelle Fine, another early New York leader in creating critical small schools wrote, "It soon became clear that the small schools movement was being co-opted and commodified; Xeroxed and distributed across the city, with most of the key radical commitments of participation, equity, inquiry and dignity 'left behind' … in New York, a strategy that produced competing, overcrowded and under resourced small schools fighting with each other within the same building … small became the chrysalis for hatching charters, the sac for drip fed privatization into the public school system" 2012, x).

13 However, Hantzopoulos and Tyner-Mullings (2012) analyse several institutions that opened during this period, such as the James Baldwin School, which, despite challenges – notably pressure to focus on Regents exam prep – maintained a social justice vision. Many are among the twenty-seven schools affiliated with the New York Performance Consortium, a network of schools with waivers on requiring students to complete most Regents exams. In these schools, teachers report a high degree of respect for their professionalism in structures of collaborative decision-making. In large part this has been sustained by retaining veteran teachers, resulting in these schools' having higher rates of seniority and more capacity for challenging principals who go against the school's egalitarian distribution of power (Rivera-McCutchen 2012, 30–1; Shiller 2012; Feldman and O'Dwyer 2012).

14 Ballou does admit it was difficult to find eleven principals willing to speak critically about the contractual rights of NYC teachers, even when their confidentiality was assured.

15 Exceptions include works such as Kretchmar (2014), Aggarwal, Mayorga, and Nevel (2012), Shiller (2007, 2009, 2010, 2011), and Hantzopoulos and Tyner-Mullings' (2012) book on critical small schools in NYC. All employ a social justice lens. Nuñez, Michie, and Konkol (2015) is written in accessible style by teachers who became professors of education. It exhorts teachers to activism on education policy, drawing examples from the 2012 Chicago teachers' strike.

16 As relations with Bloomberg worsened, the UFT leadership determined to wait out his term, though doing so resulted in working under an expired contract for over four years. The union signed a deal with de Blasio within months of his taking office on 1 January 2014.
17 New York Teachers 1, 2, 4, 5, 7, 12, interviews Dec. 2014 – Apr. 2015.
18 A teacher activist in Nassau County explains the contrast between high teacher turnover in NYC and stability in the Long Island suburbs as a choice of school boards on whether to prioritize retaining teachers through adequate mentoring and good working conditions: "What you see in the city with a lot of the churning and churning out of teachers, that causes a lot of chaos. Because you're constantly having new teachers in the building. You don't have anyone who's seasoned. That really makes a huge difference. That doesn't occur in most Long Island schools. Because what happens is, if you get a job on Long Island, it's like, Mecca. When people come in, like in my district, very very rarely do you hear [of] people not being granted tenure. They really work with teachers … I'm a mentor. In my district we have a really good mentoring program, we work really closely with our new teachers and really nurture them and work hard with them if they're struggling. I don't think they do that in the city. So people are more likely to get tenure out here on Long Island because they're invested" (New York Teacher 8, interview Apr. 2015)
19 Personal observations at MORE Conference, 24 October 2015, New York City.
20 A subsequent extension negotiated in 2017 was limited to two years, the expansion of charter schools again being a primary issue of contention.
21 Donors to these lobbyists are not evident under New York State non-profit reporting laws, though some have been traced to conservative "free-market" groups (Bragg 2014).
22 Which topped up local and state funds in school districts with low-income children (Ravitch 2013a, 280).
23 This issue was finally addressed with a bipartisan revision of NCLB into the Every Student Succeeds Act by the US Congress in December 2015, devolving significant powers of the US DOE back to state governments (Strauss 2015).
24 New York Teachers 1, 2, 3, 4, 5, 7, 12, interviews Dec. 2014 – April 2015.
25 The Common Core State Standards is a significant issue impacting the professional autonomy of US teachers that is not addressed in this chapter. Common Core is an attempt at creating a standardized national set of curriculum expectations by grade and subject. It has been lauded as an effort to ensure all students are taught according to the same high expectations, overcoming vast race and class inequities. Its outcome for secondary education is debated by education activists. Its provisions for expanding standardized testing for kindergarten to 2nd grade has attracted significant opposition (Lois Weiner, interview Dec. 2014). NYC

teachers reported that it has had a minimal direct impact on their work. Among the various criticisms it has received, perhaps the most relevant here are that Common Core's curricular expectations are impossibly high for many struggling schools in impoverished areas and that, when it is tied to RTTT, a pretext is created for blaming and firing teachers for the low test scores of their students.

26 Funded by the Bill & Melinda Gates Foundation, among other institutions, to evaluate the effectiveness of the many new small schools that they had financially supported.

27 Aligning instruction with the Regents is identified as "Selecting curricular materials, developing curriculum, designing classroom assessments, developing a school improvement plan, designing or selecting professional development opportunities" (Foley et al. 2008, 15). Influence on school policy and curriculum is defined as "Establishing school discipline policies, Establishing and shaping the school curriculum, Selecting instructional materials that support the curriculum, Determining student retention and promotion policy, Making staffing and/or hiring decisions" (ibid., 23).

28 Teachers strongly agreed with statements, for instance: "My principal monitors the curriculum I use in my classroom to see that it reflects my school's educational focus" and "My principal monitors my classroom instructional practices to see that they reflect the school's educational focus" (Foley et al. 2008, 21).

29 Not only do educators argue that high-stakes exams like the Regents frequently have poorly constructed questions, but Hursh (2013, 580) cites research by Winerip, to argue that the difficulty of the state Regents is manipulated year to year in order to meet political objectives of demonstrating either rising scores or renewed toughness. He also cites acknowledgments of grade inflation in the English Regents exam by former NYSED chancellor, Merryl Tisch (2009–15). New York pass rates in math and English Regents exams rose dramatically to 82 and 69 per cent in 2009 and fell to 54 and 42 per cent, respectively, in revised tests the following year (Kuhn 2014, 49).

30 The size of the grants is commensurate with the state's population, smaller states receiving far less.

31 A teacher says of the observation portion of the evaluation, "The new evaluation system that was implemented in New York, the Danielson System … I never received a negative rating under it, but it created tons of work. It made the evaluation process incredibly time consuming and stressful, and it also made it feel less under my control because that rubric is … filled with language that an administrator can play with and the standard that it shoots for in terms of what you do in a classroom on a day-to-day basis with thirty-four kids, it's just not realistic … It just creates

a lot of anxiety and stress, which cumulatively is miserable for teachers" (New York Teacher 2, interview Dec. 2014).

32 Hoover Institute economists presented models that claimed to demonstrate specified dollar amounts that "great" teachers added to the earnings of their graduates. The concept received front-page coverage in the *New York Times* and an approving citation by President Obama in his 2012 State of the Union address. The responses of critics, that this modelling represented such a gross simplification of human lives as to be meaningless, received far less attention (Ravitch 2013a, 105–6). In the same speech Obama also stated, "teachers should stop teaching to the test," prompting Hursh to comment, "But RTTT, his own program, forces teachers to teach to the test. To do otherwise is to risk being publicly shamed and fired" (2013, 584).

33 Assignments designed to more closely resemble "real world" activities, for example, in an English class writing a newspaper editorial on a current event rather than simply a two-paragraph response.

34 For NYC anti-testing activists, key reasons behind the city's far lower opt out rates are the use of the 4th and 8th grade exam results as part of the school choice application for some middle and high schools; the mayoral control structure, which replaces the role of elected trustees who have vocally opposed the tests elsewhere; and the geographic dispersal of students attending schools across districts and boroughs, which makes the organization of parents more difficult (author's observations). New York Teacher 1 (2014) makes a similar argument, above, about the impact of school choice on parental activism.

35 The following exchange is extracted from a Skype interview with New York Teacher 9 in April 2015.

36 Despite a letter of endorsement from the president of my own union, the OSSTF, multiple attempts at contacting senior elected UFT officials by mail, email, and telephone were unsuccessful.

37 Personal observations at a MORE Conference, 24 October 2015, New York City.

38 Personal observations at a MORE Conference, 24 October 2015, New York City.

39 NY Teachers 2, 3, 4, 5, 7, 11, interviews Dec. 2014 – April 2015.

40 NY Teachers 1, 2, 3, 6, 11, interviews Dec. 2014 – Apr. 2015.

41 Author's personal observations at MORE meetings, socials, and conferences, 2014 to 2015.

42 Lee's story of organizing co-workers and parents to oppose and opt out from NYSED tests used for MOSL ratings is included in *More Than a Score: The New Uprising Against High-Stakes Testing* (2014), a moving anthology of writings by teachers, parents, students, administrators, and academics reflecting on fighting against high-stakes exams across the United States.

4 Mexico City

1 This vignette is a composite of interviews with Mexico City Teacher 7 in May 2015 and personal observations while visiting her school in the spring of 2016.

2 A program to convert schools to a single, lengthened shift is proceeding slowly. Most existing buildings also lack any form of cafeteria where students could eat lunch.

3 The challenges for Gordillo of ensuring that these state congresses delivered their desired results, meant that many locals, such as Sections 9 and 10 in Mexico City, simply did not have executive elections for years (Hernandez Navarro 2012, 395).

4 In a handful of states whose governors also resented Gordillo's power, these leaders succeeded in gaining legal recognition of small splinter groups from the SNTE, representing a few thousand members. The approximately 4,500 teachers of the upper high schools run directly by the Mexico City government also succeeded in gaining legal recognition for the independent SITEM union (Hernandez Navarro 2012, 395; Leyva Piña and Rodriguez Lagunas 2012, 547).

5 Such influence was measured in approximately 10,000 SNTE staff (*comisionados*) assigned to electoral work and the support of Gordillo's own political vehicle, the National Alternative Party (PANAL), fully funded by the SNTE and led by her family, whose members, along with a secretary of education and the stepson of Vicente Fox, became federal senators and deputies. The PANAL alternated its endorsement of presidential and gubernatorial candidates according to Gordillo's strategy. While the numbers of PANAL's support never rose above the low single digits, its handful of deputies and senators won through Mexico's proportional representation system gave the SNTE a bargaining chip in congressional votes (Leyva Piña and Rodriguez Lagunas 2012, 552; Bensusan and Middlebrook 2013, 79–81; Hernandez 2013, 150).

6 The president of the massive entertainment conglomerate's charity arm, Carlos Gonzalez Guajardo, went on to lead Mexicanos Primero, the leading business lobby group on education policy, discussed below.

7 The SNTE created a secretary of social participation on its national executive to liaise with civil society groups such as the Associacion de Padres de Familia (Parent's Association), which were given a "corporatist" legitimacy by the Fox government through their representation in various state initiatives (Leyva and Rodriguez 2012, 557).

8 I observed an ethics class accomplished by stacking student desks and chairs in a corner of the room, in order to use rolls of thread tied to bottle caps, each held by individual students, who moved around each other

in a lesson on interdependence and cooperation. In a physical education class, students learned and practised a game devised by the teacher that involved aspects of soccer, jumping through tires, and pivoting around steel poles stuck in cement buckets.

9 I met rural teachers from Guerrero, Morelos, and Oaxaca in 2015, who noted that their schools had received regular electricity only in the year prior and in some cases still lacked indoor plumbing. This makes problematic the use of Mexico City schools as a proxy for national data in studies such as the World Bank's *Great Teachers: How to Raise Student Learning in Latin America and the Caribbean* (Bruns and Luque, 2014).

10 The tendency of schools to use much of their funds for facility improvements and the requirement that schools engage in private fundraising to access the entire 150,000 peso grant were examples of how privatization can be highly lucrative. After the first 50,000 pesos, PEC schools were obliged to obtain some funding from municipal governments, non-profits, or the private sector, this money being met 1 to 1 or 2 to 1 by the federal government, depending on the affluence of the community. Given the limited resources of most communities outside Mexico City, schools relied on business sponsorships and, where those could not be obtained, fundraising by the parents. For more affluent schools, which provided a bigger market, school supply companies gave donations in return for preferential contracts for desks, projectors, TVs, and books to be purchased with PEC funds. A fifth of the PEC magazine was typically devoted to ads for these products (Aboites 2012, 844).

11 City funding increased as its relationship with the SEP has improved over recent years, reaching a funding parity for maintenance costs of 600 million pesos each in 2016 (AFSEDF Official 1, interview Feb. 2015).

12 When asked about school fees *in other states*, a senior AFSEDF official was quick to emphasize that they were not the policy of state or federal authorities: "That was distorted … school was always free. But there were many necessities for school maintenance that were not met, that some [school] directors started to take the decision to ask for voluntary fees. Over time they became almost obligatory. Now we've returned to say no to requiring any parent to pay a fee. Other parents can ask them, not the director, so that it's not an obligation that their child, to receive their grades, must pay" (AFSEDF Official 1, interview Feb. 2015; author's translation). This official's disavowal of any role of policymakers for requiring voluntary fees would seem to contradict the requirements of the PEC in practice, if not the written letter, that parents and school staff obtain supplementary funding.

13 Most of the states, aside from the DF, with the highest rates of per pupil funding were in the north and the Yucatan peninsula. Large central states

such as Mexico State (the largest school system in Mexico, followed by the DF), Veracruz, and Puebla fared worst. States in which the CNTE controlled the union were slightly above average. The simplest explanation would be that it was in line with the north, the Yucatan and DF having the highest costs of living during this period. The northern states and some in the Yucatan were also governed by the PAN during this period in which the same party was in the national presidency.

14 Author's observations and conversations with participants.

15 Possessing the greatest institutional stability and concomitantly the most resources, the Oaxacan section had long held the most power within the CNTE. Observers believe this is a crucial reason behind the federal government's focusing of juridicial repression on this section from 2013 onwards.

16 Other axes of conflict included electoral participation with Andres Manuel Lopez Obrador, as 2012 presidential candidate for the PRD, and afterwards through his new party, Morena (Cervantes Pérez 2012).

17 It dropped in great measure as a result of extreme levels of violence and chaos in vast regions of the country caused by his government's exacerbation of conflict between drug cartels.

18 Portions of this section were originally published in "Labor Geographies of Socially Embedded Work: The Multi Scalar Resistance of Mexican Teachers," *Environment and Planning A: Economy and Space* 50 (8): 1670–87 (2018) and are reproduced here by permission of the publisher.

19 SNTE union dues, estimated at 2 billion pesos annually in 2005, were directed to the national executive, which Gordillo controlled (Leyva Piña and Rodriguez Lagunas 2012, 543). However, according to Mexican sociologist Enrique de la Garza Toledo and Hernandez Navarro, the real money and potential for corruption within the SNTE came from the large funds entrusted to it by the federal government. In 2007 Gordillo oversaw 13.5 billion pesos (equivalent to the UNAM's annual budget) for retirement programs, school technology initiatives, and teacher home-financing programs with little transparency (Enrique de la Garza Toledo, interview February 2015; Hernandez Navarro 2012, 414).

20 This view is often shared by US leftists; see, for example, Emily Keppler, "Popular Uprising Backs Striking Teachers in Southern Mexico," *Labor Notes*, 14 July 2016. www.labornotes.org [Accessed 17 July 2016].

21 Continuing the school-based management policy trajectory from the PEC, related legislation had given state governments authority to download school operations costs to families, garnering fierce opposition from organized parents where it was attempted in Chiapas, Veracruz, and elsewhere and helping broaden the struggle beyond the professional interests of teachers (Aboites 2015, 5).

22 This account is based on the conclusions of the Interdisciplinary Group of Independent Experts (2016): *Ayotzinapa Report* downloaded at http://www.oas.org/en/iachr/activities/giei.asp.

23 I visited the Ayotzinapa normale college and met with the parents of several of the vanished students in February 2015. A memorial of forty-three empty chairs and portraits of each of the abducted and presumed murdered students occupied most of the central square for the school of 500 students. I slept that night in one of the classrooms along with university students from Mexico City. The community police, independent of the government and armed with hunting rifles, guarded the gates of the college.

24 A symptom of underfunding is that only 29 per cent of instructors in normales work full time; a majority work on a variable, hourly basis (Poy Solano 2016b).

25 Remarks by Hugo Aboites at a conference of researchers and teachers critical of Mexico's education reforms, attended by the author, at Autonomous University of the City of Mexico (UACM), 29 January 2016.

26 These malfunctions led the Senate report to suggest that they were the cause of many teachers being able to complete only one section of the exam.

27 The balance were school directors.

28 The Outstanding rating would entitle them to a 35 per cent raise.

29 The similarities continue in the number of chances teachers have to improve on unsatisfactory grades in subsequent exams and the ultimate consequence of dismissal. However, all New York teachers would be required to participate in the evaluation every year, unlike successful teachers in Mexico.

30 The number of legally recognized strikes in the federally regulated sector (employees of state enterprises, most manufacturing, banking, resource extraction, interstate transportation) was an annual average of 138 between 1989 and 1994, dropping to an average of 18 a year between 2007 and 2012. To obtain legal recognition of a strike, workers must make a request before a conciliation and arbitration board comprising representatives of the state, employer associations, and unions. The latter are nearly always represented by a PRI-affiliated pro-employer union. Requests for a strike are routinely rejected (Bensusan and Middlebrook 2013, 59–60). Considering this situation and the CNTE's limited formal recognition at the state level, the movement's strikes are virtually always illegal.

31 They remain members in some provincial teachers' federations in Canada. The evolution of administrators' involvement in federations in Ontario is discussed in chapter 5.

32 He also suggests how since the Ley, though directors are appointed through a combination of exams and minimum years of service, clientelism can still work, but more in the hands of SEP administrators

than through the SNTE, by sponsors guiding prospective directors through exam preparation (CNTE Section 10 Activist, interview Feb. 2015).

33 Data are provided by the AFESDF to the author, based on the 2014–15 school year.

34 Data are based on the 2013–14 school year. See chapter 3.

35 The study used the "Stallings" method of video recording classes and analysing the proportion of time devoted to various activities. This method has been criticized by Lois Weiner and other critical education scholars as supporting deskilling by approximating the classic "scientific management" time studies that broke down work processes into discrete tasks in order that they be precisely defined (Lois Weiner, interview Dec. 2014).

36 Portions of this section were originally published in "Labor Geographies of Socially Embedded Work: The Multi Scalar Resistance of Mexican Teachers," *Environment and Planning A: Economy and Space* 50 (8): 1670–87 (2018) and are reproduced here by permission of the publisher.

37 For example, CNTE activists won an overwhelming majority of delegates to the convention of the Zacatecas state section in July 2016, but the national SNTE was still able to circumvent them and appoint their preferred executive at a secret parallel convention. The same month, the dissident slate running for the state executive of Chihuahua were simply removed from the ballot by the national SNTE (Valadez Rodríguez 2016).

38 After the *charrazo*, the SNTE temporarily reoccupied the Section 9 building and destroyed most of the electrical wiring. CNTE supporters soon forced their way back in. Mexico City police did not intervene in either case (Hernandez Navarro 2012, 446–8). As of 2018, much of the large five-storey building remains dark and unrepaired (author's personal notes).

39 A teacher gave an example: the students from her school came from a working-class neighbourhood with a lively music culture that has produced famous cumbia bands; yet the school offered neither music classes, nor music clubs or activities, nor even the use of its space after hours for community groups (Mexico City Teacher 6, interview Feb. 2015).

40 The CNTE did have a more positive relationship with a PRD governorship in Michoacan in the 2000s. However, it was under the same party banner in Guerrero in 2014 that the forty-three students of the Ayotzinapa Teachers' College were abducted and presumed murdered with the complicity of the authorities.

41 Email correspondence with member of the Trinational Coalition in Defence of Public Education, 19 July 2016.

42 Conversation with Professor Maria de la Luz Arriaga Lemus, October 2016, Mexico City.

43 The SNTE and other major unions in Mexico may face growing pressure to democratize in the near future, following the passage of legislation in April

2019 under Lopez Obrador that mandates transparent internal elections (Alma Muñoz, "Insta AMLO a líderes sindicales a respetar la ley y dejar simulaciones," *La Jornada*, 5 May 2019. https://www.jornada.com.mx/ultimas/2019/05/02/insta-amlo-a-lideres-sindicales-a-respetar-la-ley-y-dejar-simulaciones-1025.html [Accessed 2 May 2019].

5 Toronto

1 Most rural Ontario electoral districts outside the far north and the southwest consistently voted PC.
2 Suffering in part from a popular backlash against the Harris era, the PCs were frozen out from winning any of Toronto's provincial electoral districts in the four general elections during this period.
3 "Director" is used in Ontario to describe the "chief executive officer" or chief superintendent of a school district.
4 The chair of the board resigned over a controversial contract with the Chinese government for language programs and a scheme to staff private schools in Vietnam with TDSB teachers. Others were implicated in forms of influence peddling (Wilson 2015).
5 He has authored dozens of books, many published by the Ontario Principals' Council and marketed in an airport bookstore business empowerment style, including *Change Forces: Probing the Depths of Educational Reform*, *Change Forces: The Sequel*, *Change Forces with a Vengeance*, *Leading in a Culture of Change*, *The Six Secrets of Change*, *The Challenge of Change*, *Change Wars*, *Freedom to Change*, *Motion Leadership in Action*, *Professional Capital*, and *The New Meaning of Educational Change*.
6 A strong parallel can be drawn here with the creation of the Mexican National Institute for the Evaluation of Education (INEE) in 2002 (described in chapter 4), which was similarly autonomous from the main education administration, also with the rationale that formal separation would increase the testing agency's objectivity.
7 Students must pass this test to eventually graduate from high school. In the case of failure, they must take the test again the following year. If again unsuccessful, they are enrolled in a "Literacy" course, which from my personal experience as a teacher has a very high pass rate.
8 Pinto (2012) critiqued the outsourcing of provincial curriculum development under the Harris government to non-profit and for-profit consultants for its lack of accountability to both the educators who would be required to follow their guidelines and the broader public. She found a loss of internal capacity through privatization under the PCs to accommodate the rapid rewriting of the high school subjects curriculum. Teachers were hired through external companies and given limited

autonomy, owing to hierarchy, tight timelines, and the government's prioritization of input from business lobby groups.

9 Development was outsourced by the PCs to a US testing agency (Fullan and Boyle 2014, 62).

10 According to OSSTF president Paul Elliot, publicized government statistics on graduation rates and EQAO test scores always use 2003 as the base year, which is when the Liberals entered office (interview Sept. 2016).

11 Where this approach fit into their austerity agenda is seen in the next section, "How to Do More When Money Is Tight." It is explained that by increasing class sizes, close to half a billion dollars could be cut by having fewer teachers. The platform also recommended cutting 10,000 jobs dismissed as "non-teaching" positions, primarily educational assistants, youth workers, custodians, and school secretaries. The PCs earned the fervent opposition of teachers, education workers, and their unions, helping the Liberals return to power in 2014 with a majority government, despite the latter's attack on collective bargaining rights in 2012.

12 Most grades 9 and 10 Ontario courses are streamed into two levels of difficulty: applied and academic.

13 The rate at which students pass courses.

14 Along with family income, the index also considers parental education levels and the proportion of single-parent families.

15 Wolfe did mention a secondary school in a low-income community in Toronto whose principal eliminated applied courses. She believed that the principal did so to artificially boost the academic profile of his school. She notes that it will actually have an immediate adverse effect on the students, regardless of how struggling students will navigate a more rigorous curriculum, as applied classes are provincially mandated to have a lower student/teacher ratio.

16 I worked at an average-sized Toronto high school with students from predominantly low-income and racialized families, where the ostensibly parent-led school council consisted of one parent. Attendance at parent-teacher interview nights was also sparse.

17 Ontario's public post-secondary education system is far more equitable than that of the United States or Mexico, possessing little substantive difference between similar undergraduate degrees offered by different universities.

18 Aside from competing with the Catholic school board and private schools for higher enrolment, another way of compensating has been to recruit tuition-paying international (mostly secondary) students. Their enrolment has increased by over 200 per cent since 2001 to over 1,400 students by 2015–16 (TDSB 2016, 6). It has also been selling properties, because of declining enrolment, for more revenue, with 59 sold (often parcels of land,

such as part of a schoolyard, not completed schools) from 2009 to 2016, netting over $412 million (ibid., 35).

19 Interestingly, two other specialty programs oriented towards academically successful students, Advanced Placement and International Baccalaureate, were much more racially diverse, drawing disproportionate numbers of south and east Asian students, whose parents were nearly as likely to be university educated as those attending Gifted and French Immersion programs, but with lower incomes (Parekh 2013, 75, 80–1).

20 Academic subjects in the Ontario curriculum stream grades 9 and 10 students into academic and applied versions and, in grades 11 and 12, into workplace, college, and university-bound courses.

21 Personal notes from conversations with school staff, September 2016.

22 As the focus of my research is limited to secondary school teachers, the effect of standardized testing on elementary schools is mentioned only to provide context.

23 Quebec has perhaps the most complex structure. Salary and pensions are negotiated at a third level, between a coalition of public sector unions and the provincial government (Sweeney, McWilliams, and Hickey 2012, 251).

24 "Two tier" is the term most often used in official government and journalistic reports on provincial/local collective bargaining in Ontario. It is not related to its usage elsewhere in labour studies research to refer to union contracts where new workers are placed on an inferior salary and benefits scale.

25 Over 300 local teacher and occasional teacher bargaining units existed in Ontario, with each board having four units unless the locals had amalgamated (Shilton 2012, 224, 226).

26 The Liberals could also be punitive, rescinding part of a salary increase for Elementary Teachers already accepted by the other unions, when they held out in 2009 for parity in prep time with OSSTF. The federations were frequently feuding at this time, for instance, in a battle over representation between OSSTF and ETFO for early-childhood educators and a squabble over dues owed by OSSTF to the Ontario Teachers Federation. This conflict likely diminished solidarity when the Elementary Teachers attempted to buck the trend (Shilton 2012, 236, 239).

27 The decline in tax revenue was primarily due to the economic downturn, but also because of a decision by the provincial government to reduce the corporate tax rate.

28 Lay-offs of thousands of custodians, school secretaries, and educational assistants and the intensification of work for those who remained were subsequently carried out with little media attention (personal notes, 2014).

29 The latter benefit had high symbolic value. A year earlier it was the focus of Toronto mayor Rob Ford's drive for concessions from municipal employees.

30 In addition to this conflict, his government was embroiled in a scandal over the cost of cancelling the building of gas-powered electrical generators to help win several electoral districts in the 2011 election.
31 Personal notes from many formal and informal discussions with OSSTF Toronto members on this topic.
32 The Wynne government did engage in limited provincial negotiations with OSSTF and ETFO in spring 2013, improving sick days allowances and partially restoring movement up the pay grid for teachers not at the top of the ten annual steps (Fullan and Boyle 2014, 85).
33 Commencing after provincial negotiations concluded, OSSTF's bargaining over workplace issues dragged on for nearly a year. Members boycotted administrative duties but not extracurricular responsibilities in order to avoid alienating parents. Eventually, the TDSB dropped a proposal to eliminate a subsidy that covered the salaries of half of the executive released from classroom duties, and the union won improvements on health and safety (Leslie Wolfe, interview Sept. 2016).
34 They include immigrant rights groups, campaigns to raise the minimum wage, a public transit riders' group, and many charities serving children and youth (personal notes).
35 After four years, the Ontario Superior Court ruled in 2016 that Bill 115 violated the Canadian constitutional right to freedom of association. The teachers' federations and the government negotiated a "remedy" whereby teachers won partial compensation for the imposed salary freeze. A deal was included that union contracts be extended by two years to avoid conflict during the 2018 provincial election, which the Liberals ultimately lost.

6 Conclusion

1 I adapt the term "Professional Learning Communities," which, following Fullan (2016) and others, is used by jurisdictions such as Ontario to mean meetings among teachers where plans are made to address specific school-level issues and subsequent progress is assessed.
2 The importance of the local scale is further exemplified when teachers broaden their targets to protest corporate actors with significant political influence, as the CNTE, the Chicago Teachers' Union, and others have done.

References

Aboites, Hugo. 2012. *La Medida de una Nación: Los primeros años de la evaluación en México*. Mexico City: Universidad Autónoma Metropolitana.

– 2015. "The Expected Crop: Social Insurgency and New Alternatives for Education in México." *Critical Education*. 6 (2): 1–8.

Addey, Camilla, and Sam Sellar. 2017. "The Rise of International Large-Scale Assessments and Rationales for Participation." *Compare: A Journal of Comparative & International Education* 47 (3): 434–52.

Aggarwal, Ujju, Edwin Mayorga, and Donna Nevel. 2012. "Slow Violence and Neoliberal Education Reform: Reflections on a School Closure." *Peace and Conflict: Journal of Peace Psychology* 18 (2): 156–64.

Ahmed, Azam, and Kirk Semple. 2016. "Clashes Draw Support for Teachers' Protest in Mexico." *New York Times*, 26 June. www.nytimes.com [Accessed 30 January 2018].

Alerta Chiapas. 2016. "'Si estamos pensando en los tres días, ya nos jodimos': CNTE." *Alerta Chiapas*, 19 May. www.alertachiapas.com [Accessed 19 May 2016].

Alter, Tom. 2013. "'It Felt Like Community': Social Movement Unionism and the Chicago Teachers Union Strike of 2012." *Labor: Studies in Working-Class History of the Americas* 10 (3): 11–25.

American Center for School Choice. 2015. "Joseph P. Viteritti." www.amcsc.org [Accessed 23 July 2015].

Amin, Reema. 2019. "New York Legislators Overhaul Teacher Evaluations, Removing Mandatory Link to State Test," Chalkbeat New York, 23 January. https://www.chalkbeat.org/posts/ny/2019/01/23/new-york-legislators-remove-mandate-linking-state-tests-to-teacher-evaluations/ [Accessed 23 January 2019].

Antonio González, Oswualdo. 2018. "La Reforma educativa no está muerta: la guerra llegó a las aulas." *Insurgencia Magisterial*, 30 January. http://insurgenciamagisterial.com/la-reforma-educativa-no-esta-muerta-la-guerra-llego-a-las-aulas/ [Accessed 30 January 2018].

Antonio Román, José. 2019. "Inicia hoy reinstalación de maestros opositores a reforma educativa," *La Jornada*, 27 June. https://www.jornada.com.mx/ultimas/2019/06/27/inicia-hoy-reinstalacion-de-maestros-opositores-a-reforma-educativa-5932.html [Accessed 27 June 2019].

Antush, John C. 2014. "Labor and 'Ed Deform.'" *Monthly Review*. www.monthlyreview.org [Accessed 25 July 2015].

Aristegui Noticias. 2014. "EPN va contra estados que se saltaron la reforma educativa." www.aristeguinoticias.com. 15 October [Accessed 17 July 2016].

Arnaut, Alberto. 2008. "La administración de los servicios educativos y el entorno político en el Distrito Federal después de la federalización de 1992." In *Descentralización y reforma educativa en la ciudad de México*, edited by Graciela *Messina*, Víctor Alejandro Espinoza Valle, Alberto Arnaut, and David Márquez Ayala, 145–52. Mexico City: Secretary of Education,

Arriaga, Maria de la Luz. 2008. "In Mexico, to Defend Education as a Social Right We Must Fight for Union Democracy." In Weiner and Compton, *The Global Assault on Teaching*, 221–6.

– 2013. *Propuesta empresarial para la mala medición y el despojo de los derechos laborales*. Mexico City: Trinacional Coalición en Defensa de la Educación Pública.

– 2015. "The Mexican Teachers' Movement: Thirty Years of Struggle for Union Democracy and the Defense of Public Education." *Social Justice*. 42 (3/4): 104–17.

Babbie, Earl, and Lucia Benaquisto. 2002. *Fundamentals of Social Research*. Toronto: Thomson Canada.

Bailey, Christopher. 2015. "Neoliberal Standardization and Its Discontents: An Interview with Diane Ravitch." In *Alternate Routes 2015: Neoliberalism and the Degradation of Education*, edited by Carlo Fanelli and Bryan Evans, 327–31. Toronto: Alternate Routes.

Bakeman, Jessica. 2015. "An Outline of Education Reform Proposals in Budget." Capital New York, 31 March. www.capitalnewyork.com [Accessed 1 April 2015].

Ball, Stephen J., and Carolina Junemann. 2012. *Networks, New Governance and Education*. Chicago: Policy Press.

Ballou, Dale. 2000. "Contractual Constraints on School Management: Principals' Perspectives on the Teacher Contract." In Ravitch and Viteritti, *City Schools*, 89–116.

Barbanel, Josh. 1993. "Cortines, Citing Litany of Failure, Plans to Close 2 Big High Schools." *New York Times*, 12 November, B2.

Barrett, Brian. 2009. "No Child Left Behind and the Assault on Teachers' Professional Practices and Identities." *Teaching and Teacher Education* 25: 1018–25.

Basu, Ranu. 2004. "The Rationalization of Neoliberalism in Ontario's Public Education System, 1995–2000." *Geoforum* 35 (5): 621–34.

Becerril, Andrea. 2016. "Persecución a maestros basta para revisar la reforma: Romero Hicks." *La Jornada*, 17 July. www.jornada.unam.mx [Accessed 17 July 2016].

Bellinghausen, Hermann. 2016. "Apoyo a maestros de Chiapas deviene en asamblea popular permanente." *La Jornada*, 13 July. www.jornada.unam.mx [Accessed 13 July 2016].

Bensusan, Graciela, and Kevin J. Middlebrook. 2013. *Sindicatos y Política en México: cambios, continuidades y contradicciones*. Mexico City: FLACSO Mexico.

Bocking, Paul. 2015a. "Why Do Governments Adopt Neoliberal Education Policies? Critical Theory on Policy Movement in the Context of Contemporary Reform in Mexico." In Fanelli and Evans, *Alternate Routes*, 74–100.

– 2015b. "Teachers and Parents Sustain the Struggle for Mexico's Missing Ayotzinapa Students." Waging Nonviolence, 16 March. www.wagingnonviolence.org [Accessed 26 September 2016].

– 2019. "The Mexican Teachers' Movement in the Context of Neoliberal Education Policy & Strategies for Resistance." *Journal of Labor and Society* 22 (1): 61–76.

Bracho, Teresa. 2009. *Innovación en la Política Educativa: Escuelas de Calidad*. Mexico City: FLACSO Mexico.

Bradbury, Alexandra, Jane Slaughter, Mark Brenner, Jenny Brown, and Samantha Winslow. 2014. *How to Jump-Start Your Union: Lessons From the Chicago Teachers*. Detroit: Labor Notes.

Bragg, Chris. 2014. "Groups spending heavily to push their education agenda use loopholes to keep donors anonymous." *Albany Times-Union*. www.timesunion.com [Accessed 25 July 2015].

Brambila, Aurora Loyo. 2008. "Schooling in Mexico." In *Going to School in Latin America*, edited by Silvina Gvirtz and Jason Beech, 203–28. London: Greenwood Press.

Brecher, Jeremy. 1997. *Strike!* Cambridge, MA: South End Press.

Brenner, Neil, Jamie Peck, and Nik Theodore. 2010. "Variegated Neoliberalization: Geographies, Modalities, Pathways." *Global Networks* 10 (2): 182–222.

Briseño, Héctor. 2015. Suspensión parcial de la prueba docente en Acapulco." *La Jornada*, 3 December. www.jornada.unam.mx [Accessed 3 December 2015].

Brody, Leslie. 2015. "New Evaluation Rules Set for New York Teachers." *Wall Street Journal*, 15 June. www.wsj.com [Accessed 16 June 2015].

Brogan, Peter. 2013. "Education in Global Chicago and the Remaking of Contemporary Capitalism." *Canadian Geographer* 57 (3): 303–10.

– 2014. "Getting to the CORE of the Chicago Teachers' Union Transformation." *Studies in Social Justice* 8 (2): 145–64.

Bruns, Barbara, and Javier Luque. 2014. *Great Teachers: How to Raise Student Learning in Latin America and the Caribbean*. Washington, DC: World Bank.

Buras, Kristen. 2013. "'We're not going nowhere': Race, Urban Space, and the Struggle for King Elementary School in New Orleans." *Critical Studies in Education* 54 (1): 19–32.

Caballero, Arquimedes, and Salvador Medrano. 1982. "El segundo periodo de Torres Bodet: 1958–1964." In *Historia de la Educación Pública en México,* edited by Fernando Solana, Raúl Cardiel Reyes, and Raúl Bolaños Martinez, 360–402. Mexico City: Secretaria de la Educación Publica.

Camfield, David. 2011. *Canadian Labour in Crisis: Reinventing the Workers' Movement*. Halifax: Fernwood.

Canadian Press. 2014. "Liz Sandals Calls in Outside Expert to Review TDSB." CBC, 25 November. www.cbc.ca [Accessed 2 January 2015].

Cano, Arturo. 2015. "Repudian la prueba maestros de Oaxaca." *La Jornada*, 29 November. www.jornada.unam.mx [Accessed 29 November 2015].

Carlos Miranda, Juan. 2016. "CCE pide salida 'justa,' sin violar la ley, para el conflicto magisterial." *La Jornada*, 8 August. www.jornada.unam.mx [Accessed 8 August 2016].

Casco Peebles, Mariano, and Rodrigo Ocampo Merlo. 2019. "Two Forms of Syndicalism in Mexico Public Sector under an Authoritarian Government (2012–2018): Social Security Union and Oaxacan Section of Workers Education National Union." *Journal of Labor and Society* 22 (2): 477–90.

Cervantes Pérez, Felipe de Jesús. 2012. "El llamado CEND-SNTE. Un análisis crítico." Movimiento Liberación Nacional. www.mln.org.mx [Accessed 29 November 2015].

Chubb, John E., and Terry M. Moe. 1990. *Politics, Markets and America's Schools.* Washington, DC: Brookings Institution Press.

Clukey, Keshia. 2015. "Common Core Panel to Call for Teacher Evaluation Moratorium, Test Overall," *Politico New York*, 9 December. http://www.capitalnewyork.com/article/albany/2015/12/8585178/common-core-panel-call-teacher-evaluation-moratorium-test-overhaul [Accessed 10 December 2015].

Conniff, Ruth. 2014. "The Con Artistry of Charter Schools." *In These Times.* www.inthesetimes.com [Accessed 20 August 2014].

Cook, Maria Lorena. 1996. *Organizing Dissent: Unions, the State, and the Democratic Teachers' Movement in Mexico.* University Park: Pennsylvania State University Press.

Cresswell, John. 2013. *Qualitative Inquiry and Research Design: Choosing among Five Approaches.* Thousand Oaks, CA: Sage.

Cuban, Larry. 2009. *Hugging the Middle: How Teachers Teach in an Era of Testing and Accountability*. New York: Teachers College Press.

– 2013. *Inside the Black Box of Classroom Practice: Change Without Reform in American Education*. Cambridge, MA: Harvard Education Press.

Curiel Méndez, Martha Eugenia. 1982. "La Educación Normal." In *Historia de la educación pública en México*, edited by Fernando Solana, Raúl Cardiel Reyes, and Raúl Bolaños Martinez, 426–62. Mexico City: Secretaria de la Educación Publica.

Curiel Méndez, Martha Eugenia, and Geoff Decker. 2015. "City's Incoming Teach for America Class Hits Five-Year Low." Chalkbeat New York. http://ny.chalkbeat.org [Accessed 19 August 2015].

Darville, Sarah. 2014a. "As Recruitment Dips, TFA Leader Says New York Training Site to Close." Chalkbeat New York. http://ny.chalkbeat.org [Accessed 19 August 2015].

– 2014b. "Principals Applaud Fariña, de Blasio as Leaders Present a 'Tone Shift.'" Chalkbeat New York. http://ny.chalkbeat.org [Accessed 31 2014].

Decker, Geoff. 2015. "Why Is There No Teacher Shortage in New York City?" Chalkbeat New York. http://ny.chalkbeat.org [Accessed 7 October 2015].

De Jesus, Anthony. 2012. "Authentic Caring and Community Driven School Reform." In Hantzopoulos and Tyner-Mullings, *Critical Small Schools*, 63–78.

Edelman, Susan. 2015. "Principal Doesn't Want Teachers Sitting – So She Threw out All Their Desks." *New York Post*, 18 October. www.nypost.com [Accessed 9 November 2015].

EQAO. 2019. *Literature Review of the Empirical Evidence on the Connection between Compulsory Teacher Competency Testing and Student Outcomes*. Toronto: Education Quality and Accountability Office.

FAO. 2019. *Expenditure Estimates 2019–20: Ministry of Education*. Toronto: Financial Accountability Office of Ontario.

Feldman, Jay, and Anne O'Dwyer. 2012. "A Close Look at Small School Creation: Lessons Learned from the First Years of a Critical Small School." In Hantzopoulos and Tyner-Mullings, *Critical Small Schools*, 41–62.

Fine, Michelle. 2012. Foreword. "Critical Small Schools – Windows on Educational Justice in a Neoliberal Blizzard." In Hantzopoulos and Tyner-Mullings, *Critical Small Schools*, ix–xvii.

Finn Jr, Chester, and Michael Petrilli. 2013. "The Failures of US Education Governance Today." In Manna and McGuinn, *Education Governance for the Twenty-First Century*, 21–35.

Fletcher, Bill, and Fernando Gapasin. 2008. *Solidarity Divided*. Berkeley: University of California Press.

Foley, Eileen, Allan Klinge, and Elizabeth R. Reisner. 2008. *Evaluation of New Century High Schools: Profile of an Initiative to Create and Sustain Small, Successful High Schools*. New York: New Visions for Public Schools.

Foweraker, Joe (1993). *Popular Mobilization in Mexico: The Teachers' Movement, 1977–87*. New York: Cambridge University Press.

Francis, Angelyn. 2016. "TDSB Optional Attendance: Drake's High School May Close, Revealing Ugly Truth in Toronto." *Huffington Post*, 5 December. www.huffingtonpost.com [Accessed 9 December 2016].

Freeman, Joshua. 2000. *Working-Class New York: Life and Labor Since World War II*. New York: New Press.

Fullan, Michael. 2016. *The New Meaning of Educational Change*. New York: Teachers College Press.

Fullan, Michael, and Michael Barber. 2010. *Final Report of the Building Blocks for Education Summit*. Toronto: Government of Ontario.

Fullan, Michael, and Alan Doyle. 2014. *Big City School Reforms: Lessons from New York, Toronto, and London*. New York: Teachers College Press.

de la Garza Toledo, Enrique. 2012a. "La polémica acerca de la tasa de afiliación sindical revisada al 2010." In de la Garza Toledo, *La situación del trabajo en México*, 453–72.

– ed. 2012b. *La situación del trabajo en México, 2012*. Mexico City: Universidad Autonoma Metropolitana.

Gee, Marcus. 2013. "Dysfunctional TDSB Cries Out for Reform and Renewal." *Globe and Mail*, 12 January. www.theglobeandmail.com [Accessed 16 January 2013].

Gidney, R.D. 1999. *From Hope to Harris: The Reshaping of Ontario's Schools*. Toronto: University of Toronto Press.

Ginsburg, Mark. 1991a. "Educational Reform: Social Struggle, The State and the World Economic System." In *Understanding Educational Reform in Global Context: Economy, Ideology, and the State*, edited by Mark B. Ginsburg, 3–48. New York: Garland.

– 1991b. "Educational Reform, The State, and the World Economy: Understanding and Engaging in Ideological and Other Struggles." In Ginsburg, *Understanding Educational Reform*, 369–96.

Glaberman, Martin. 2002. *Punching Out & Other Writings*. Edited and introduced by Staughton Lynd. Chicago: Charles H. Kerr.

Glyn, Andrew. 2007. *Capitalism Unleashed: Finance Globalization and Welfare*. New York: Oxford University Press.

Goldman, Henry, and Freeman Klopott. 2015. "Fuel for Feud Between Cuomo and De Blasio." *Bloomberg*, 16 July. www.bloomberg.com [Accessed 18 November 2015].

Golin, Steve. 2002. *The Newark Teacher Strikes: Hopes on the Line*. New Brunswick, NJ: Rutgers University Press.

Gonzalez, Juan. 2015. "Hedge Fund Execs' Money for Charter Schools May Pay Off." *New York Daily News*, 12 March. www.nydailynews.com [Accessed 12 March 2015].

González, Roberto, Lucía Rivera, and Marcelino Guerra. 2017. *Anatomía política de la reforma educativa*. Mexico City: Universidad Pedagógica Nacional.

Gordon, Andrea. 2017. "Annie Kidder and People for Education Have Made a Mark on Ontario Schools, but Have They Become Part of the System?" *Toronto Star*, 2 September. www.thestar.com/news/insight/2017/09/02/annie-kidder-and-people-for-education-have-made-a-mark-on-ontario-schools-but-have-they-become-part-of-the-system.html [Accessed 2 September 2017].

Greene M. (2014) "On the Inside Looking In: Methodological Insights and Challenges in Conducting Qualitative Insider Research." *The Qualitative Report* 19 (29): 1–13.

Hagopian, Jesse, ed. 2014a. *More Than a Score: The New Uprising Against High-Stakes Testing*. Chicago: Haymarket Books.

– 2014b. "'It was the right thing to do': Interview with Carol Burris." In Hagopian, *More Than a Score*, 269–78.

Haimson, Leonie, and Shino Tanikawa. 2015. "Time to Reform Mayoral Control," *Gotham Gazette*. 28 May. www.gothamgazette.com [Accessed 28 May 2015].

Hantzopoulos, Maria, and Alia R. Tyner-Mullings, eds. 2012. *Critical Small Schools: Beyond Privatization in New York City Urban Educational Reform*. Charlotte, NC: Information Age Publishing.

Haraway, Donna. 1991. "Situated Knowledges. The Science Question in Feminism and the Privilege of Partial Perspective," In *Simians, Cyborgs and Women: The Reinvention of Nature*, edited by Donna Haraway. London: Routledge.

Harris, Elizabeth. 2015. "20% of New York State Students Opted Out of Standardized Tests This Year." *New York Times*, 12 August. www.nytimes.com [Accessed 19 August 2015].

Harris, Elizabeth, and Ford Fessenden. 2015. "'Opt Out' Becomes Anti-Test Rallying Cry in New York State." *New York Times*, 20 May. www.nytimes.com [Accessed 23 May 2015].

Harvey, David. 2007. "Neoliberalism as Creative Destruction." *Annals of the American Academy of Political and Social Science* 610: 22–44.

Head, Jim, and Jack Hutton. 2005. *The Union Makes Us Strong: OSSTF, 1964–2004*. Toronto: Ontario Secondary School Teachers' Federation.

Hecock, R. Douglas. 2014. "Democratization, Education Reform, and the Mexican Teachers' Union." *Latin American Research Review* 49 (1): 62–82.

Hemphill, Clara. 2000. "Public Schools That Work." In Ravitch and Viteritti, *City Schools*, 45–64.

– 2009. "Parent Power and Mayoral Control: Parent and Community Involvement in New York City Schools." In Viteritti, *When Mayors Take Charge*, 187–205.

Hemphill, Clara, and Kim Nauer. 2009. *The New Marketplace: How Small-School Reforms and School Choice Have Reshaped New York City's High Schools*.

New York: Center for New York City Affairs, Milano, the New School for Management and Urban Policy.

Henig, Jeffrey. 2009. "Mayoral Control: What We Can and Cannot Learn from Other Cities." In Viteritti, *When Mayors Take Charge*, 19–46.

Hennessy, Peter. 1975. *Teacher Militancy: A Comparative Study of Ontario, Quebec and New York Teachers*. Ottawa: Canadian Teachers' Federation.

Hennessy, Rosemary. 2013. *Fires on the Border: The Passionate Politics of Labor Organizing on the Mexican Frontera*. Minneapolis: University of Minnesota Press.

Henríquez, Elio. 2016a. "Padres marchan junto a maestros chiapanecos." *La Jornada*, 23 May. www.jornada.unam.mx [Accessed 23 May 2016].

– 2016b. "Miles de padres de familia y pobladores marchan en 80 municipios de Chiapas," *La Jornada*, 28 May. www.jornada.unam.mx [Accessed 28 May 2016].

Hernandez, Javier, and Susanne Craig. 2014. "Cuomo Played Pivotal Role in Charter School Push." *New York Times*, 3 April. www.nytimes.com [Accessed 3 April 2014].

Hernández, Juan Manuel, Ignacio Llamas, and Nora Garro. 2012. "El mercado de trabajo de los trabajadores de la educación." In de la Garza Toledo, *La Situación del trabajo en México*, 313–44.

Hernandez Navarro, Luis. 2012. *Cero en Conducta: Crónicas de la resistencia magisterial*. Mexico City: Rosa Luxemburg Stiftung.

– 2013. *No habra recreo: contra-reforma constitucional y disobediencia magisterial*. Mexico City: Rosa Luxemburg Stiftung.

– 2016. "La masacre de Nochixtlán y la reforma educativa." *La Jornada*, 5 July. www.jornada.unam.mx [Accessed 30 January 2018].

Herod, Andrew. 2001. *Labor Geographies: Workers and the Landscapes of Capitalism*. New York: Guilford Press.

– 2010. "Labour Geography: Where Have We Been? Where Should We Go?" In *Missing Links in Labour Geography*, edited by Anne C. Bergene, Sylvi B. Endresen, and Hege M. Knutsen, 15–28. Burlington, VT: Ashgate.

Herszenhorn, David. 2005. "In Push for Small Schools, Other Schools Suffer." *New York Times*, 14 January. www.nytimes.com [Accessed 24 July 2015].

Hess, Frederick, and Olivia Meeks. 2013. "Rethinking District Governance." In Manna and McGuinn, *Education Governance for the Twenty-First Century*, 107–29.

Hewitt-White, Caitlin. 2015. "The OSSTF Anti-Bill 115 Campaign: An Assessment from a Social Movement Unionism Perspective." *Alternate Routes* 26: 170–99.

Hursh, David. 2007. "Assessing No Child Left Behind and the Rise of Neoliberal Education Policies." *American Educational Research Journal* 44 (3): 493–518.

– 2013. "Raising the Stakes: High-Stakes Testing and the Attack on Public Education in New York." *Journal of Education Policy* 28 (5): 574–88.

IEESA. 2013. "Desvalorización de la labor docente." Instituto de Estudios Educativos y Sindicales de América. www.ieesa.org [Accessed 10 October 2015].

INEE. 2015. *Los docentes en México: Informe 2015.* Mexico City: INEE.

Jensen, Kari, and Amy Glasmeier (2010). "Policy, Research Design and the Socially Situated Researcher." In *The SAGE Handbook of Qualitative Geography*, edited by Dydia DeLyser, Steve Herbert, Stuart Aitken, Mike Crang, and Linda McDowell, 82–93. London: SAGE.

Jiménez, Isabel Mayoral. 2012. "La OCDE 'lee la cartilla' a Peña Nieto.'" CNN Expansión. www.expansion.mx [Accessed 17 July 2016].

Jones, Allison. 2016. "Teachers' Near-'Perpetual State of Bargaining' Costing Ontario Millions," *Toronto Star*, 4 September. www.thestar.com [Accessed 4 September 2016].

Jornada, La. 2019. "Maestros inician paros en cinco estados; repudian nueva reforma." *La Jornada*. 16 May. https://www.jornada.com.mx/2019/05/16/estados/027n1est? [Accessed 16 May 2019].

Kearns, Robin. 2004. "Being There: Research through Observing and Participating." In *Qualitative Research Methods in Human Geography*, edited by Iain Hay, 103–21. Oxford: Oxford University Press.

Kerchner, Charles, Julia Koppich, and Joseph Weeres. 1997. *United Mind Workers: Unions and Teaching in the Knowledge Society*. San Francisco: Jossey-Bass.

Kerr, Lindsay. 2006. *Between Caring and Counting: Teachers Take on Education Reform*. Toronto: University of Toronto Press.

Kirst, Michael. 2009. "Mayoral Control of Schools: Politics, Trade-offs, and Outcomes." In Viteritti, *When Mayors Take Charge*, 46–64.

Klees, Steven. 2008. "A Quarter Century of Neoliberal Thinking in Education: Misleading Analyses and Failed Policies." *Globalisation, Societies and Education* 6 (4): 311–48.

Klein, Naomi. 2007. *The Shock Doctrine: The Rise of Disaster Capitalism*. New York: Picador.

Kozol, Jonathan (2009). *On Being a Teacher*. Oxford: One World Press.

Kretchmar, Kerry. 2014. "Democracy (In)Action: A Critical Policy Analysis of New York City Public School Closings by Teachers, Students, Administrators, and Community Members." *Education and Urban Society* 46 (1): 3–29.

Kuehn, Larry. 2006. "Intercambio – Social Justice Union Internationalism in the BC Teachers' Federation." PhD diss., University of British Columbia.

– 2008. "The Education World Is Not Flat: Neoliberalism's Global Project and Teachers Unions' Transnational Resistance." In Weiner and Compton, *The Global Assault on Teaching*, 53–74.

Kuhn, John. 2014. *Fear and Learning in America: Bad Data, Good Teachers, and the Attack on Public Education.* New York: Teachers College Press.

Kunin, Jason. 2016. "Optional Attendance Is Killing Neighbourhood Schools." *Toronto Star,* 9 December. www.thestar.com [Accessed 12 December 2016].

Kurek, Dominik. 2016. "Racial Segregation Blamed for Possible Closure of Vaughan Road Academy." *York Guardian,* 19 October. www.insidetoronto.com [Accessed 19 October 2016].

La Jornada. 2015. "Reconocen organizaciones internacionales al SNTE." 11 May. www.jornada.unam.mx [Accessed 11 October 2016].

Larnar, Wendy, and Nina Laurie. 2010. "Travelling Technocrats, Embodied Knowledges: Globalizing Privatisation in Telecoms and Water." *Geoforum* 41: 218–26.

Leithwood, Kenneth, Michael Fullan, and Nancy Watson. 2003. *The Schools We Need: Recent Education Policy in Ontario & Recommendations for Moving Forward.* Toronto: Ontario Institute for Studies in Education.

Lessard, Claude, and André Brassard. 2009. "Education Governance in Canada, 1990–2003: Trends and Significance." In Levine-Rasky, *Canadian Perspectives on the Sociology of Education,* 255–74.

Levine, Murray, and Adeline Levine. 2014. "Follow the Money: There's No Business Like the Ed. Business." *American Journal of Orthopsychiatry* 84 (4): 377–86.

Levine-Rasky, Cynthia, ed. 2009. *Canadian Perspectives on the Sociology of Education.* Toronto: Oxford University Press.

Levinson, Bradley. 2001. *We Are All Equal: Student Culture and Identity at a Mexican Secondary School.* Durham, NC: Duke University Press.

Leyva Piña, Marco Antonio, and Javier Rodriguez Lagunas. 2012. "La construcción conflictiva del SNTE." In de la Garza Toledo, *La Situación del trabajo en México,* 529–67.

Lipman, Pauline. 2011. *The New Political Economy of Urban Education: Neoliberalism, Race, and the Right to the City.* New York: Routledge.

– 2017. "The Landscape of Education 'Reform' in Chicago: Neoliberalism Meets a Grassroots Movement." *Education Policy Analysis Archives* 25 (54): 1–26.

Lorinc, John. 2014. "Toronto, Queen's Park, and the Circus at the School Board." *Spacing Magazine,* 24 November. www.spacing.ca [Accessed 24 November 2014].

MacLellan, Duncan. 2009. "Neoliberalism and Ontario Teachers' Unions: A 'Not-So' Common Sense Revolution." *Socialist Studies,* 51–74.

MacNeil, Michael. 2014. "Collective Bargaining between Teachers and the Province of Ontario, 2012–2013: A Study in Charter Politics." *Education and Law Journal* 23: 121–47.

Manna, Paul, and Patrick McGuinn, eds. 2013. *Education Governance for the Twenty-First Century: Overcoming the Structural Barriers to School Reform.* Washington, DC: Brookings Institution Press.

Manzer, Roland. 2003. *Educational Regimes and Anglo-American Democracy.* Toronto: University of Toronto Press.

Marquez Ayala, David. 2008. "Análisis económico de la descentralización educativa en México. La situación del Distrito Federal." In *Decentralización y reforma educativa en la ciudad de México*, edited by Graciela Messina, Víctor Alejandro Espinoza Valle, Alberto Arnaut, and David Márquez Ayala, 153–216. Mexico City: Secretaría de Educación del Distrito Federal.

Martin, Christopher. 1994. *Schooling in Mexico: Staying In or Dropping Out*. Aldershot, UK: Avery.

McAlevey, Jane. 2016. *No Shortcuts: Organizing for Power in the New Gilded Age*. Oxford: Oxford University Press.

McCann, James. 2016. *2015 Global Go To Think Tank Index Report*. University of Pennsylvania. www.repository.upenn.edu/think_tanks/10 [Accessed 14 September 2016].

McDonnell, Patrick. 2016. "Protesters Say a Massacre Took Place in This Mexican Town. Now It's Become a Rallying Cry against the Government." *Los Angeles Times*, 6 August. http://www.latimes.com [Accessed 30 January 2018].

McDowell, Linda. 2010. "Interviewing: Fear and Liking in the Field." In *The SAGE Handbook of Qualitative Geography*, edited by Dydia DeLyser, Steve Herbert, Stuart Aitken, Mike Crang, and Linda McDowell, 156–71. London: Sage.

McGuinn, Patrick, and Paul Manna. 2013. "Education Governance in America: Who Leads When Everyone Is in Charge?" In Manna and McGuinn, *Education Governance for the Twenty-First Century*, 1–20.

McKenna, Laura. 2015. "Why Don't Suburbanites Want Charter Schools?" *The Atlantic*, 1 October. https://www.theatlantic.com/education/archive/2015/10/why-dont-suburbanites-want-charter-schools/408307/ [Accessed 1 October 2015].

Merriam, Sharan B., Juanita Johnson-Bailey, Ming-Yeh Lee, Youngwha Kee, Gabo Ntseane, and Mazanah Muhamad. 2010. "Power and Positionality: Negotiating Insider/Outsider Status Within and Across Cultures." *International Journal of Lifelong Education* 20 (5): 405–16.

Messina, Graciela. 2008. "Análisis comparado sobre experiencias de descentralización y gestión educativa municipal." In *Descentralización y reforma educativa en la ciudad de México*, edited by Graciela Messina, Víctor Alejandro Espinoza Valle, Alberto Arnaut, and David Márquez Ayala, 15–106. Mexico City: Gobierno del Distrito Federal.

Mindzak, Michael. 2015. "What Happened to Charter Schools in Canada?" *Equity & Excellence in Education* 48 (1): 105–17.

Moe, Terry M. 2011. *Special Interest: Teachers Unions and America's Public Schools*. Washington, DC: Brookings Institution Press.

Monsiváis, Carlos. 1987. *Entrada Libre: crónicas de la sociedad que se organiza*. Mexico City: Ediciones Era.

MORE. 2016. "MORE/New Action Wins the UFT HS Executive Board." Email correspondence, 28 May.

Murphy, Marjorie. 1992. *Blackboard Unions: The AFT and the NEA, 1900–1980*. Ithaca, NY: Cornell University Press.

Navarro, César. 2016. "Maestros sustituibles y suplantados: nueva estrategia de la reforma." *La Jornada*, 22 May. www.jornada.unam.mx [Accessed 22 May 2016].

NEPC. 2016. "Manhattan Institute Website Grades Schools Based on Mirage of Poorly Linked Computations." National Education Policy Centre, 10 March. www.nepc.colorado.edu [Accessed 10 March 2016].

Nuñez, Isabel, Gregory Michie, and Pamela Konkol. 2015. *Worth Striking For: Why Education Policy Is Every Teacher's Concern (Lessons from Chicago)*. New York: Teachers College Press.

NYC DOE. 2015. *Advance Guide for Educators*. New York: New York City Department of Education.

NYC Kids PAC. 2015. *Mayor de Blasio's Education Report Card*. New York City: NYC Kids PAC.

OECD. 2013. *Getting It Right: Strategic Agenda for Reforms in Mexico*. Paris: OECD.

– 2016. *Education at a Glance 2016*. Paris: OECD.

O'Neil, Peter, and Tracy Sherlock. 2016. "Court Ruling to Force Hiring of Hundreds of Teachers in B.C." *Vancouver Sun*, 10 November. www.vancouversun.com [Accessed 10 November 2016].

Ontario Ministry of Education. 2008. *Energizing Ontario Education*. Toronto: Queen's Printer for Ontario.

– 2010. *Growing Success: Assessment, Evaluation, and Reporting in Ontario Schools*. Toronto: Queen's Printer for Ontario.

Ontario Government. 2012a. *Commission on the Reform of Ontario's Public Services*. Drummond Report. Toronto: Queen's Printer for Ontario.

– 2012b. *Government of Ontario Parameters for the 2012 PDT Discussions – February 22, 2012*. Toronto: Government of Ontario.

OSSTF. 2015a. *Understanding Professional Judgement*. Toronto: OSSTF.

– 2015b. *Collective Bargaining Bulletin* 22 (8 April). Toronto: OSSTF.

– 2015c. *Teacher/Occasional Teacher Central Ratification Results*. 18 September. Toronto: OSSTF.

– 2016. "Professionalism = Autonomy," OSSTF. www.osstf.on.ca [Accessed 20 February 2016].

OTF. 2019. *A Recipe for Failure: The Math Proficiency Test for Beginning Teachers*. Toronto: Ontario Teachers' Federation.

Owen, David. 2005. *My Confession: The Making of a Militant*. Toronto: On Edge Press.

Padilla, Tanalis. 2013. "Espionage and Education: Reporting on Student Protest in Mexico's Normales Rurales, 1960–1980." *Journal of Iberian and Latin American Research* 19 (1): 20–9.

Panitch, Leo, and Sam Gindin. 2012. *The Making of Global Capitalism: The Political Economy of American Empire*. New York: Verso.

Parekh, Gillian. 2013. *Structured Pathways: An Exploration of Programs of Study, School-Wide and In-School Programs, As Well As Promotion and Transference*

Across Secondary Schools in the Toronto District School Board. Toronto: Toronto District School Board.

PC Party of Ontario. 2013. *Paths to Prosperity: Preparing Students for the Challenges of the Twenty-first Century*. Toronto: Progressive Conservative Party of Ontario.

Peck, Jamie. 2010. *Constructions of Neoliberal Reason*. New York: Oxford University Press.

Peck, Jamie, and Nik Theodore. 2010. "Recombinant Workfare, across the Americas: Transnationalizing 'Fast' Social Policy." *Geoforum* 41: 195–208.

– 2015. *Fast Policy: Experimental Statecraft at the Thresholds of Neoliberalism*. Minneapolis: University of Minnesota Press.

Peck, Jamie, and Adam Tickell. 2002. "Neoliberalizing Space." *Antipode* 34 (3): 380–404.

Peterson, Bob. 1999. "Survival & Justice: Rethinking Teacher Union Strategy." In *Transforming Teacher Unions: Fighting for Better Schools and Social Justice*, edited by Bob Peterson, 11–19. Milwaukee, WI: Rethinking Schools.

Pinto, Laura. 2012. *Curriculum Reform in Ontario: "Common Sense" Policy Processes and Democratic Possibilities*. Toronto: University of Toronto Press.

– 2015. "Fear and Loathing in Neoliberalism: School Leader Responses to Policy Layers." *Journal of Educational Administration and History* 47 (2): 140–54.

Pinto, Laura, John P. Portelli, Cindy Rottmann, Karen Pashby, Sarah Elizabeth Barrett, and Donatille Mujawamarya. 2012. "Charismatic, Competent, or Transformative? Ontario School Administrators' Perceptions of 'Good Teachers.'" *Journal of Teaching and Learning* 8 (1): 73–90.

Postman, Neil, and Charles Weingartner. 1969. *Teaching as a Subversive Activity*. New York: Dell.

Potter, Jackson. 2016. "CTU Joins Canadian, Mexican Teachers in Solidarity with Colleagues Facing Severe Repression." Chicago Teachers Union, 19 May. www.ctunet.com [Accessed 19 May 2016].

Poy Solano, Laura. 2014. "Inicia examen para ingresar al Servicio Profesional Docente." *La Jornada*, 12 July. www.jornada.unam.mx [Accessed 14 October 2014].

– 2016a. "La reforma educativa, como se aplica, puede no ser la que se requiere, reconoce el INEE." *La Jornada*, 16 July. www.jornada.unam.mx [Accessed 31 July 2016].

– 2016b. "Escuelas normales, en el abandono oficial." *La Jornada*, 14 March. www.jornada.unam.mx [Accessed 14 March 2016].

– 2016c. "Expertos: acuerdos SEP-SNTE no tocan el carácter punitivo de la evaluación." *La Jornada*, 17 July. www.jornada.unam.mx [Accessed 17 July 2016].

– 2017. "Maestros de la CNTE entregan al Senado iniciativa en educación." *La Jornada*, 10 February. www.jornada.unam.mx [Accessed 10 February 2017].

– 2018. "El magisterio disidente tendrá un papel determinante en las elecciones." *La Jornada*, 21 January. www.jornada.unam.mx [Accessed 21 January 2018].

Poy Solano, Laura, Diana Manzo, Jorge A. Pérez Alfonso, y Sergio Ocampo Arista. 2014. "Suspenden en Michoacán y Oaxaca aplicación de examen para maestros." *La Jornada*, 12 July. www.jornada.unam.mx [Accessed 17 October 2014].

Ravitch, Diane. 2000. *The Great School Wars: A History of the New York City Public Schools*. Baltimore: Johns Hopkins University Press.

– 2010. *The Death and Life of the Great American School System*. New York: Basic Books.

– 2013a. *Reign of Error: The Hoax of the Privatization Movement and the Danger to America's Public Schools*. New York: Alfred A. Knopf.

– 2013b. "The de Blasio Mandate for Education." *Huffington Post*. www.huffingtonpost.com [Accessed 10 October 2015].

Ravitch, Diane, and Joseph Viteritti, eds. 2000. *City Schools: Lessons from New York*. Baltimore: Johns Hopkins University Press.

– 2000. Introduction. In *City Schools*, 1–18.

Rethinking Schools. 2014. Editorial: "The Gathering Resistance to Standardized Tests." www.rethinkingschools.org, 28 (3) [Accessed 26 May 2016].

Rezai-Rashti, Goli. 2009. "The Neo-liberal Assault on Ontario's Secondary Schools." In Cynthia Levine-Rasky, *Canadian Perspectives on the Sociology of Education*, 307–22.

Rich, Motoko. 2015. "Teacher Shortages Spur a Nationwide Hiring Scramble (Credentials Optional)." *New York Times*, 9 August 2015. www.nytimes.com [Accessed October 2015].

Riegel, Sarah, 2003. "Teachers' Unions and the Politics of Neoliberal Educational Restructuring: Explaining Teachers' Union Responses in Cincinnati, Ohio and Kitchener-Waterloo, Ontario." Doctoral thesis. Queen's University.

Rincones, Rodolfo, 2008. "The Context of Teachers' Democratic Movements in Mexico." In Weiner and Compton, *The Global Assault on Teaching*, 217–20.

Rivera-McCutchen, Rosa. 2012. "Considering Context: Exploring a Small School's Struggle to Maintain Its Educational Vision." In Hantzopoulos and Tyner-Mullings, *Critical Small Schools*, 21–40.

Robles, Jorge, and Luís Angel Gómez. 1997. *De la Autonomía al Corporativismo: Memoria Cronológica del Movimiento Obrero en México*. Mexico City: El Atajo Ediciones.

Robertson, Susan. 2000. *A Class Act: Changing Teachers' Work, Globalisation and the State*. New York: Falmer Press.

– 2008. "'Remaking the World': Neoliberalism and the Transformation of Education and Teachers' Labor." In Weiner and Compton, *The Global Assault on Teaching*, 11–30.

Rodriguez, Sabrina. 2015. "The City's Opt Out Movement, by the Numbers." Chalkbeat New York, 12 August. www.ny.chalkbeat.org [Accessed 19 August 2015].

Roman, Richard, and Edur Velasco Arregui. 2015. *Continental Crucible: Big Business, Workers and Unions in the Transformation of North America*. Halifax, NS: Fernwood.

Rose, Joseph. 2002. "The Assault on School Teacher Bargaining in Ontario." *Industrial Relations* 57 (1): 100–28.

– 2012. "The Evolution of Teacher Bargaining in Ontario." In Slinn and Sweetman, *Dynamic Negotiations*, 199–220.

Ross, Stephanie. 2012. "Business Unionism and Social Unionism in Theory and Practice." In *Rethinking the Politics of Labour in Canada*. edited by Stephanie Ross and Larry Savage, 75–87. Halifax, NS: Fernwood.

Sandals, Liz. 2015. Letter to TDSB trustees, 15 January. Toronto: Ontario Ministry of Education.

Santiago, Paulo, Isobel McGregor, Deborah Nusche, Pedro Ravela, and Diana Toledo. 2014. *Revisiones de la OCDE sobre la Evaluación en Educación: México 2012*. Mexico City: Instituto Nacional para la Evaluación de la Educación.

Sassen, Saskia. 2012. *Cities in a World Economy*. 4th ed. Thousand Oaks, CA: SAGE/Pine Forge.

Schucher, Karen, and Sara Slinn. 2012. "Crosscurrents: Comparative Review of Elementary and Secondary Teacher Collective Bargaining Structures in Canada." In Slinn and Sweetman, *Dynamic Negotiations*, 13–49.

Sears, Alan, and James Cairns. 2019. "Schooling Goes to Market: The Consolidation of Lean Education in Ontario." In Greg Albo and Bryan M. Evans, *Divided Province: Ontario Politics in the Age of Neoliberalism*, 415–40. Kingston and Montreal: McGill-Queen's University Press.

Sellar, Sam, and Bob Lingard. 2013. "The OECD and Global Governance in Education." *Journal of Education Policy* 28 (5): 710–25.

Senate of Mexico. 2016. *La evaluación del desempeño docente: de lo comprometido a lo realizado*. Mexico City: Instituto Belisario Domínguez, Senate of Mexico.

SEP. 2015. *Secundaria por Dirección, Sostenimiento y Modalidad Inicio de Ciclo 2014–2015*. Mexico City: Secretaria de la Educación Publica.

Shapiro, Eliza. 2015a. "City, State Teachers' Unions Take Different Tacks on Exam Scores." *Politico New York*. www.capitalnewyork.com [Accessed 19 August 2015].

– 2015b. "Cuomo Says de Blasio Must Earn Mayoral Control." Politico New York. www.capitalnewyork.com [Accessed 10 November 2015].

Shiller, Jessica. 2007. "Educational Reform in the Global City: The Case of the Quality Schools for the Poor Initiative in New York City." *Diaspora, Indigenous, and Minority Education* 1 (2): 127–34.

– 2009. "'These Are Our Children!' An Examination of Relationship-Building Practices in Urban High Schools." *Urban Rev* 41: 461–85.

– 2010. "It's Only Part of the Story: The Fallacy of Improved Outcomes Data in New York City's Effort to Make its High Schools Small." *Education and Urban Society* 42 (3): 247–68.

– 2011. "Marketing Small Schools in New York City: A Critique of Neoliberal School Reform." *Educational Studies* 47: 160–73.

– 2012. "City Prep: A Culture of Care in an Era of Data-Driven Reform." In Hantzopoulos and Tyner-Mullings, *Critical Small Schools*, 3–20.

Shilton, Elizabeth. 2012. "Collective Bargaining for Teachers in Ontario: Central Power, Local Responsibility." In Slinn and Sweetman, *Dynamic Negotiations*, 221–46.

Shipps, Dorothy. 2009. "Updating Tradition: The Institutional Underpinnings of Modern Mayoral Control in Chicago's Public Schools." In Viteritti, *When Mayors Take Charge*, 117–47.

Singer, Alan. 2014. "Big Profits in Not-for-Profit Charter Schools." *Huffington Post.* www.huffingtonpost.com [Accessed 20 November 2015].

Slinn, Sarah, and Arthur Sweetman, eds. 2012. *Dynamic Negotiations: Teacher Labour Relations in Canadian Elementary and Secondary Education.* Queen's School of Policy Studies No. 163. Montreal: McGill-Queen's University Press.

Smith, Rex. 2015. "Next, Blame Teachers for Draft Picks." *Albany Times Union*, 14 February. www.timesunion.com [Accessed 1 December 2015].

SNTE. 2014a. "SNTE refuerza colaboración con la American Federation of Teachers, en beneficio de sus agremiados." Sindicato Nacional de los Trabajadores de la Educación, 9 July. www.snte.org.mx [Accessed 2 May 2015].

– 2014b. "El SNTE y la American Federation of Teachers amplían colaboración en beneficio de sus afiliados." Sindicato Nacional de los Trabajadores de la Educación, 14 July. www.snte.org.mx [Accessed 2 May 2015].

– 2014c. "Internacional de la Educación reconoce liderazgo del SNTE." Sindicato Nacional de los Trabajadores de la Educación, 17 July. www.snte.org.mx [Accessed 2 May 2015].

– 2014d. "El SNTE asiste a reunión anual de la American Federation of Teachers (AFT)," Sindicato Nacional de los Trabajadores de la Educación, 10 November. www.snte.org.mx [Accessed 2 May 2015].

– 2015a. "Maestros mexicanos comparten experiencias con docentes estadounidenses." Sindicato Nacional de los Trabajadores de la Educación, 22 April. www.snte.org.mx [Accessed 27 April 2015].

– 2015b. "La UNESCO reconoce al SNTE, por su compromiso con la educación." Sindicato Nacional de los Trabajadores de la Educación, 2 December. www.snte.org.mx [Accessed 10 January 2016].

– 2016a. "Posicionamiento del SNTE ante los hechos ocurridos en Nochixtlán y Hacienda Blanca, Oaxaca." Sindicato Nacional de los Trabajadores de la Educación, 22 June. www.snte.org.mx [Accessed 8 August 2016].

– 2016b. "Reconoce la UNESCO al SNTE por su Trabajo a Favor del Magisterio." Sindicato Nacional de los Trabajadores de la Educación, 8 April. www.snte.org.mx [Accessed 8 August 2016].

– 2016c. "Reconoce la OCDE al SNTE por el apoyo brindado a los maestros en su proceso de evaluación." Sindicato Nacional de los Trabajadores de la Educación, 4 January. www.snte.org.mx [Accessed 10 January 2016].

– 2016d. "El SNTE y la OCDE coordinan acciones por una mejor educación." Sindicato Nacional de los Trabajadores de la Educación, 11 October. www.snte.org.mx [Accessed 11 October 2016].

Spagnuolo, Mario, and Larry Glassford. 2008. "Feminism in Transition: The Margaret Tomen Membership Case and the Demise of the Federation of Women Teachers' Associations of Ontario." *Historical Studies in Education* 20 (Fall): 55–72.

Spencer, Brenda. 2012. "Counting In, Counting Out, and Accounting For." In *Canadian Education: Governing Practices & Producing Subjects*, edited by Brenda L. Spencer, Kenneth D. Gariepy, Kari Dehli, and James Ryan, 131–44. Rotterdam: Sense Publishing.

Strauss, Valerie. 2015. "Teacher Evaluation: Going from Bad to Worse?" *Washington Post*, 1 January. www.washingtonpost.com [Accessed 1 January 2015].

Strong, Luman, and Roland Yoshida. 2014. "Teachers' Autonomy in Today's Educational Climate: Current Perceptions From an Acceptable Instrument." *Educational Studies* 50: 123–45.

Steiner-Khamsi, Gita, Margaret Appleton, and Shezleen Vellani. 2018. "Understanding Business Interests in International Large-Scale Student Assessments: A Media Analysis of *The Economist*, *Financial Times*, and *Wall Street Journal*." *Oxford Review of Education* 44 (2): 190–203.

Sweeney, Brendan. 2013. "The Labour Geographies of Education: The Centralization of Governance and Collective Bargaining in Ontario, Canada." *Geoforum* 44: 120–8.

Sweeney, Brendan, Susan McWilliams, and Robert Hickey. 2012. "The Centralization of Collective Bargaining in Ontario's Public Education Sector and the Need to Balance Stakeholder Interests." In Slinn and Sweetman, *Dynamic Negotiations*, 247–63.

Sweetman, Mick. 2012. "Why Ontario's High School Student Walkouts Give Me Hope." *Rabble*, 26 September. www.rabble.ca [Accessed 30 November 2016].

Tayor, Kate. 2015. "Como, in Shift, Is Said to Back Reducing Test Scores' Role in Teacher Reviews." *New York Times*, 25 November. http://www.nytimes.com/2015/11/26/nyregion/cuomo-in-shift-is-said-to-back-reducing-test-scores-role-in-teacher-reviews.html?_r=1 [Accessed 25 November 2015].

TDSB. 2004. *Policy P.013 SCH: Optional Attendance.* Toronto: Toronto District School Board.

– 2006. *Fresh AER.* Toronto: Toronto District School Board.

– 2016. *Toronto District School Board Financial Facts: Revenue & Expenditure Trends.* Toronto: Toronto District School Board.

Tilly, Charles, and Sidney G. Tarrow. 2007. *Contentious Politics.* Boulder, CO: Paradigm.

Tisch, Merryl, and Elizabeth Berlin. 2014. *Correspondence with Jim Malatras, Director of State Operations.* Albany: New York State Education Department.

Toronto Star. 2013. Editorial: "Toronto Teachers' Union Plays Cynical Game." 4 February. www.thestar.com [Accessed 30 November 2016].

Torres, Carlos. 1991. "State Corporatism, Educational Policies, and Students' and Teachers' Movements in Mexico." In Ginsburg, *Understanding Educational Reform,* 115–50.

Traver, Amy. 2006. "Institutions and Organizational Change: Reforming New York City's Public School System." *Journal of Education Policy* 21 (5): 497–514.

Turati, Marcela. 2014. "Ayotzinapa: Las huellas de los militares." *Proceso,* 23 December. www.proceso.com.mx [Accessed 26 September 2016].

UFT. 2014. "Frequently Asked Questions." United Federation of Teachers. www.uft.org [Accessed 1 December 2015].

Universal, El. 2015. "Organiza SNTE Coloquio Internacional por la Educación Pública." *El Universal,* 9 February. www.eluniversal.com.mx [Accessed 11 October 2016].

Valadez Rodríguez, Alfredo. 2016. "De madrugada, el SNTE aplica charrazo en sección 34 de Zacatecas." *La Jornada,* 16 July. www.jornada.unam.mx [Accessed 1 August 2016].

Vangrieken, Katrien, Ilke Grosemans, Fiip Dochy, and Eva Kyndt. 2017. "Teacher Autonomy and Collaboration: A Paradox? Conceptualising and Measuring Teachers' Autonomy and Collaborative Attitude." *Teaching and Teacher Education* 67: 302–15.

Vaughan, Mary Kay. 1982. *The State, Education, and Social Class in Mexico, 1880–1928.* Decal: Northern Illinois University Press.

Vergari, Sandra. 2013. "Education Governance in Canada and the United States." In Manna and McGuinn, *Education Governance for the Twenty-First Century,* 231–51.

Verger, Antoni. 2009. "The Merchants of Education: Global Politics and the Uneven Education Liberalization Process within the WTO." *Comparative Education Review* 53 (3): 379–401.

Verger, Antoni, Hula Altinyelken, and Mireille de Konig. 2013. *Global Managerial Education Reforms and Teachers: Emerging Policies, Controversies and Issues in Developing Contexts*. Amsterdam: Education International.

Vibert, Ann. 2009. "Painting the Mountain Green: Discourse of Accountability and Critical Practice." In Levine-Rasky, *Canadian Perspectives on the Sociology of Education*, 293–306.

Viteritti, Joseph P. 2009a. "Why Governance Matters." In Viteritti, *When Mayors Take Charge*, 1–18.

– ed. 2009b. *When Mayors Take Charge: School Governance in the City*. Washington, DC: Brookings Institution Press.

Wallner, Jennifer. 2014. *Learning to School: Federalism and Public Schooling in Canada*. Toronto: University of Toronto Press.

Weiner, Lois. 2012. *The Future of Our Schools: Teachers Unions and Social Justice*. Chicago: Haymarket Books.

Weiner, Lois, and Mary Compton. 2008. *The Global Assault on Teaching, Teachers, and their Unions*. New York: Palgrave Macmillan.

Winerip, Michael. 2012. "In Race to the Top, the Dirty Work Is Left to Those on the Bottom." *New York Times*, 23 January. A15.

Willen, Liz. 2014. "New NYC Schools Chancellor Carmen Fariña Wants Joyful Departure from Bloomberg Era." *Washington Monthly*. www.washingtonmonthly.com [Accessed 18 November 2015].

Wilson, Margaret. 2015. *Review of the Toronto District School Board*. Toronto: Government of Ontario.

Winton, Sue, and Curtis Brewer. 2014. "People for Education: A Critical Policy History." *International Journal of Qualitative Studies in Education* 27 (9): 1091–109.

Winton, Sue, and Katina Pollock. 2016. "Meanings of Success and Successful Leadership in Ontario, Canada, in Neo-Liberal Times." *Journal of Educational Administration and History* 48 (1): 19–34.

Wong, Kenneth. 2009. "Does Mayoral Control Improve Performance in Urban Districts?" In Viteritti, *When Mayors Take Charge*, 64–90.

World Bank. 2016. "Mexico." www.worldbank.org [Accessed 7 October 2016].

Zernike, Kate. 2015. "Obama Administration Calls for Limits on Testing in Schools." *New York Times*. http://www.nytimes.com/2015/10/25/us/obama-administration-calls-for-limits-on-testing-in-schools.html [Accessed 25 November 2015].

Zimmerman, Alex. 2016. "Exclusive: Teacher Tenure Approvals Tick up, Continuing a de Blasio-Era Shift." Chalkbeat New York. www.chalkbeat.org [Accessed 17 February 2017].

Zimmerman, Alex, and Monica Disare. 2016. "In a Win for the UFT, City Reaches Deal That Moves Further Away from Evaluating Teachers Based on Multiple-Choice Tests." Chalkbeat New York, 21 December. http://www.chalkbeat.org/posts/ny/2016/12/21/in-a-win-for-the-uft-city-reaches-deal-that-moves-further-away-from-evaluating-teachers-based-on-multiple-choice-tests/ [Accessed 21 December 2016].

Zionts, Arielle. 2015. "Charter Schools Unions Are Spreading: Teachers at Elite Chicago Charter Network Vote to Unionize." In These Times, 4 June. http://inthesetimes.com/working/entry/18013/teachers_at_elite_charter_school_network_vote_to_unionize [Accessed 5 June 2015].

Index

Absent Teacher Reserve (ATR), 93–5
Acuerdo Nacional para la Modernización de la Educación Basica (National Accord for the Modernization of Basic Education; ANMEB), 129
Administración Federal de Servicios Educativos en el DF (Federal Administration of Education Services in the Federal District; AFSEDF), 130, 134, 136, 141, 149–50, 156–7
African Americans, 16–17, 45, 48, 68, 72, 75, 83, 85–6, 123–4, 253–4n6, 259n8
Alberta, 15, 60, 191, 218, 222, 244
Alianza Por la Calidad Educativa (Alliance for Quality Education; ACE), 128–9, 133, 143–5, 147–8, 150–1, 153, 179, 243
American Federation of Teachers (AFT), 19, 24, 35, 39–40, 62–4, 97, 257n23
American Legislation Exchange Council (ALEC), 101
AMLO. *See* López Obrador, Andrés Manuel
Annual Professional Performance Review (New York State) (APPR), 109, 111, 159
austerity, fiscal, 25, 29, 45, 49, 67, 77, 97, 103, 114, 137, 185, 200, 222–3, 225–8, 233, 244, 256n18, 270n11
Australia, 189
Ayotzinapa College, 35, 64–5, 154–5, 177, 267nn22, 23, 268n40

Bill 115 (Putting Students First Act), 227–8, 230–2, 272n35
Bill and Melinda Gates Foundation, 85
Blair, Tony, 194
Bloomberg, Michael, 6, 9, 23, 27, 47, 69, 73, 76, 78–82, 84, 88–9, 93, 97–8, 101–3, 106, 108, 110–11, 115, 116, 217, 236, 238–9, 241, 258n2, 261n16
Brazil, 56
British Columbia Teachers Federation (BCTF), 12, 64, 66, 222, 257nn21, 23, 258n26
Bronx, The, 18, 70, 75, 84–6, 101, 115
Brookings Institution, 20, 47, 54–5
Brooklyn, 16, 75, 85, 112, 115, 122
Bush, George W., 6, 60, 101, 124, 238, 243
business interest groups, 13, 28, 55, 58, 60, 62, 77–8, 128, 142, 144–5, 150–1, 179, 259n9, 264n6, 269–70n8. *See also* Mexicanos Primero
business unionism, 120

Calderon, Felipe, 27–8, 52, 131, 134–5, 143–5, 147, 150–2, 238
California, 40, 63, 97, 189
Canadian Teachers Federation (CTF), 36, 41, 257n23
capitalism, 114
Caucus of Rank and File Educators (CORE), 65–6, 115, 123, 258n28
charter schools, 10, 17, 27, 47–8, 55, 59–60, 72–3, 76, 96, 100–3, 105, 108, 112, 114–16, 120, 125, 235, 246–7, 257n19, 258–9n4, 261n20
Chicago Teachers Union, 26, 35, 64–6, 123, 247, 260n15, 272n2
Chile, 56
civil rights movement, 17, 74
civil society, 9, 55, 58, 264n7
class size, 29, 45, 49, 80, 89, 102, 185–6, 192, 222–5, 227, 229–30, 237, 257n21, 270n11
classroom management, 7, 146, 157
clientelism. *See* patronage
Cold War, 39, 257n23
collective bargaining, 9–10, 25, 29, 36, 40, 42, 49, 100, 104, 114, 116, 158, 184–5, 201, 222–4, 228–9, 233, 239, 242, 245, 247, 259n8, 270n11, 271n24
Colombia, 56
Common Core State Standards (United States), 79, 106, 113, 261n25
Community School District (New York City) (CSD), 74–5, 79
Confederación de Educadores Americanos (Confederation of American Educators; CEA), 61–2, 257n23
Coordinadora Nacional de los Trabajadores de la Educación (National Coordination of Education Workers; CNTE), 11, 13, 22, 28, 42–4, 48, 51–3, 62, 64–7, 128–9, 131–5, 137, 143–5, 147–50, 152–5, 157, 159–62, 164–5, 171–80, 240, 242, 249, 255n4, 256nn15, 16, 265–6n13, 266n15, 267–8n32, 268nn37, 38, 40, 272n2; of Chiapas, 9, 13, 29–30, 43–4, 48, 52, 147–8, 155, 159, 162, 175–6, 180, 242, 255n4; of Guerrero, 13, 22, 30, 43–4, 52, 148, 154–5, 162, 176; of Mexico City (primary teachers Section 9), 52–3, 130, 147–9, 155, 157, 164, 173–4, 177–8, 256n16, 268n38; of Mexico City (secondary teachers Section 10), 53, 132, 144, 160–2, 165, 171–5, 178, 267–8n32; of Michoacán, 22, 30, 52, 133, 148–9, 155, 159, 268n40; of Oaxaca, 9, 13, 22, 29–30, 43–4, 48, 52, 148–9, 155, 159–60, 162, 176–7, 180, 242, 255n4, 265n9; of Veracruz, 30, 153, 171
Cuba, 43
Cuomo, Andrew, 6, 23, 73, 97, 99–100, 102–4, 110–14, 125, 135, 159, 190, 236, 243
curriculum, 4–5, 16, 18, 21, 27, 39, 42, 49, 67, 69, 73, 79, 81–2, 90, 106, 123–4, 130, 143, 145, 185, 192–3, 199, 201, 203–5, 207–8, 212–14, 220, 232, 240, 245–6, 261n25, 262nn27, 28, 269n8, 270n15, 271n20

de Blasio, Bill, 6, 23, 73, 95, 98, 100–3, 104, 238, 261n16
declining enrolment, 29, 93, 186, 188, 218–19, 230, 241, 270n18
Democratic Party, 77, 81, 100–1, 103, 124
deskilling of teachers, 3, 79, 139, 157, 204, 268n35
deprofessionalization of teaching, 146–7
DeVos, Betsy, 124
Dewey, John, 33

DF. *See* Distrito Federal
Distrito Federal (Federal District), 130–1, 148, 165, 172, 176, 265–6n13
Duncan, Arne, 17, 47, 78, 101, 189

Education International, 62–4, 177
Education Quality and Accountability Office (EQAO), 49–50, 189–91, 194–6, 198–9, 202, 206–8, 212–14, 218, 221, 232, 236–7, 243, 270n10
Elementary Teachers' Federation of Ontario (ETFO), 11, 227, 228, 271n26, 272n32
English as a Second Language (ESL), 74, 85, 123
ethnicity. *See* race

Finland, 56, 59, 189
Ford, Doug, 234–6
Fox, Vicente, 27, 52, 128, 131, 133–5, 139–40, 143, 150–2, 238, 264nn5, 7
Fraser Institute, 218
French Immersion, 219–20, 271n19

gender, 16, 21–3, 121, 255n5
Giuliani, Rudy, 46, 68, 75, 93, 258nn2, 3
globalization, 105, 246
Gordillo, Elba Esther, 27, 39, 52–3, 61–2, 67, 128, 131, 133–5, 142–5, 147–8, 151, 164, 171–3, 255n4, 256n15, 264n3, 266n19
grievance, 39, 42, 116–18, 124, 249
Gross Domestic Product (GDP), 37, 256–7n18

Harlem, 18, 48, 75, 83, 107, 115
Harris, Mike, 28–9, 49–50, 183, 186–90, 192–5, 197, 201, 203–4, 212–13, 215, 221–6, 230, 232, 234, 237, 255n5, 269n2

Hispanic. *See* Latinx
Hoover Institute, 47, 55, 110, 263n32

Indigenous peoples, 12, 16, 35, 43–4, 142, 152, 155, 196, 255n4
inner city schools, 23, 45, 48, 184
Instituto de Seguro Social de Trabajadores al Servicio del Estado (Public Sector Social Security Institute; ISSSTE), 134, 144
Instituto Nacional por la Evaluación Educativa (National Institute for the Evaluation of Education; INEE), 28, 58, 127, 135–6, 140, 142–3, 149, 158, 160–2, 166–8, 257n24, 269n6
International Labour Organization, 144
International Monetary Fund, 45
Iztapalapa, 22, 31, 126, 130, 137, 160, 174–5, 177, 179

Janus Supreme Court decision, 124

Klein, Joel, 78, 80, 82, 84–6, 110, 258n3

Labor Notes conferences, 23, 65, 258n27, 266n20
Latin America, 56, 129
Latinx, 17–18, 45, 68, 75, 83, 85, 123–4
lesson plans, 5, 8, 98, 246
Liberal Party of Ontario, 28, 33, 50, 183–4, 186–9, 194, 200, 215, 221, 226–8, 232, 235–6, 239, 241
López Obrador, Andrés Manuel (AMLO), 180, 236, 266n16, 268–9n43

Manhattan Institute, 46–7
McGuinty, Dalton, 28, 33, 50, 184, 186, 188–90, 193–5, 197, 199–202, 204, 213–15, 221–2, 226, 228, 230–3, 236, 239, 245

Measures of Student Learning (New York State) (MOSL), 109, 111, 263n42
merit pay, 131–2, 142, 189–90
Mexicanos Primero, 28, 60, 144–5, 150–2, 164, 179, 264n6
MORE. *See* Movement of Rank and File Educators
Morena. *See* Movimento Regeneración Nacional
Movement of Rank and File Educators (MORE), 14, 23, 27, 65, 74, 85, 99, 102, 107, 115–16, 118–20, 121–5, 128, 261n19, 263nn37, 38, 41
Movimento Regeneración Nacional (National Regeneration Movement; Morena), 177–8, 180, 242–3, 266n16

Nation at Risk, A, 53, 77, 105, 256n17
National Assessment of Education Progress, 46
National Education Association (NEA), 19, 24, 35, 40, 64, 257n23
National Education Policy Centre, 46
NCLB. *See* No Child Left Behind
NEA. *See* National Education Association
neighbourhood school, 27, 68, 73
nepotism, 146. *See also* patronage
New Democratic Party (NDP), 42, 49, 66, 190, 226, 228, 235, 243
New Jersey, 40
New Teacher Induction Program (Ontario) (NTIP), 191–3
New York City Department of Education (NYC DOE), 6, 70, 78–9, 85, 87, 90–7, 101–2, 104, 109, 116–17, 122
New York State Education Department (NYSED), 97, 104, 113, 262n29, 263n42
New York State United Teachers (NYSUT), 40, 104, 110, 112
No Child Left Behind (NCLB), 6, 14, 50, 60, 73, 82, 105–6, 144, 183, 191, 195, 238, 241, 243, 261n23
normale (Mexican teacher training school), 7, 39, 67, 130, 146, 154–7, 267n27. *See also* Ayotzinapa
North American Free Trade Agreement (NAFTA), 54, 64, 152

Obama, Barack, 6, 60, 98, 108, 113, 124, 238, 243, 263n32
OECD. *See* Organization for Economic Cooperation and Development
Ontario College of Teachers (OCT), 49, 191
Ontario English Catholic Teachers' Association (OECTA), 36, 227
Ontario Institute for Studies in Education (OISE), 33, 39, 50–1, 183, 186, 189, 235
Ontario Ministry of Education, 7, 21, 29, 33, 42, 50, 184–5, 187–9, 194, 196, 198, 214–15, 218, 221, 229–30, 233, 239, 254n10
Ontario Public School Boards Association (OPSBA), 222–3, 225, 229–30
Ontario Secondary School Teachers Federation (OSSTF), 5, 6, 11, 13, 21, 23–4, 29, 36, 42, 64, 181–2, 184, 193, 200–1, 203, 207–9, 212, 214–15, 223–33, 235, 244, 249, 255nn8, 9, 258nn25, 26, 263n36, 270n10, 271n26, 272nn31, 32
Opt Out movement, 14, 17, 27, 74, 104, 112–14, 122–3, 125, 243, 263nn34, 42
Organisation for Economic Cooperation and Development

(OECD), 13–14, 20, 23, 28, 33, 56–60, 63, 66, 128, 136, 142, 150–2, 164, 169–70, 248
OSSTF. *See* Ontario Secondary School Teachers Federation

Panel for Education Policy (New York City) (PEP), 78
Partido de la Acción Nacional (National Action Party; PAN), 27, 52, 131, 134–5, 144, 150–2, 178–9, 242, 265–6n13
Partido Revolucionario Institucional (Institutional Revolutionary Party; PRI), 28, 36, 38–9, 42, 44, 52, 128, 131, 134, 150–2, 176, 242, 267n30
Partido de la Revolución Democratica (Party of the Democratic Revolution; PRD), 130–1, 137, 151, 176–8, 180, 242, 266n16, 268n40
patronage (corruption), 44, 75, 124, 133–4, 146, 168, 253n5, 258n4
pedagogy, 4, 7–8, 29, 33, 37, 83, 90, 106, 133, 135, 143, 146, 149, 156–7, 171, 192, 205, 232, 240, 244–5, 249
Peña Nieto, Enrique, 28, 30, 56, 62–6, 128, 135, 142, 144, 150–4, 157–8, 160–1, 164, 171–2, 175–80, 190, 236, 238, 240, 242, 258n25
pensions, 36, 99, 134, 144, 148, 222, 256n11, 271n23
People for Education, 50, 220, 256n14
PISA. *See* Program for International Student Assessment
policy mobility, 11, 26, 32, 56, 60–1, 115, 123, 183, 247
poverty, 4, 16, 51, 64, 76, 83, 195, 200
precarious employment, 89, 114, 128, 163, 167
PRI. *See* Partido Revolucionario Institucional
privatization, 19, 26, 29, 46, 51, 57, 60, 64, 101, 116, 135, 137, 151, 175, 186, 190, 218, 245, 248, 260n12, 265n10, 269n8
preparation time, 49, 84, 170–1, 185, 223, 230
professional development, 19, 56, 132, 137–8, 165, 185, 195–6, 202, 249, 257n19, 262n27
Programa de Escuelas de Calidad (Quality Schools Program; PEC), 128–30, 135–40, 142–3, 164, 199, 265nn10, 12, 266n21
professionalism, teacher, 5, 15, 19, 29, 34, 47, 50–1, 61, 66, 73, 79, 129–30, 146, 157, 190–1, 207, 214, 216, 232–3, 244–5, 260n13
Program for International Student Assessment (PISA), 46, 58–60, 147, 152, 189, 243, 247
Progressive Conservative Party of Ontario (PC), 16, 28, 33, 49, 182–4, 186, 188, 190, 200–1, 215, 221, 223, 227, 235, 269n1

Quebec, 41, 64, 257n21, 271n23

race, 17, 55, 72, 80, 82–3, 86, 114–15, 121, 125, 213, 216, 218–19, 214, 261n25, 270n16
Race to the Top (RTTT), 6, 60, 74, 98, 108–9, 111, 144, 189, 238, 261–2n25, 263n32
Regents exams, 27, 69–70, 73, 82, 86, 94, 98, 105–6, 108–10, 124, 135, 191, 254n13, 260n13, 262nn27, 29
religious schools, 186
Republican Party, 77, 103
rote learning, 17, 19, 34, 110

salaries, teachers', 8, 29, 41, 49, 52–3, 92–5, 129, 132–3, 142, 149, 168, 191, 222, 224–5, 227, 230–2, 249, 271nn23, 24, 26, 272n35
Salinas, Carlos, 51–2, 54, 131, 134, 152, 256nn15, 18
Scarborough (Toronto), 21, 220, 235–6
School Autonomy, 128, 164, 176, 200, 212, 239
School Based Management (SBM), 7, 136–7
school choice, 8, 10, 19, 27, 29, 47, 53, 55, 59, 67–8, 73, 80–1, 85–6, 88, 101–2, 114, 125, 138, 143, 184, 186, 188, 202, 213–14, 217–18, 220–1, 233, 236, 241, 245, 247, 263n34
school fundraising, 137, 164, 265n10
school vouchers, 54–5, 236, 256n12
Secretaria de la Educación Publica (Secretary of Public Education; SEP), 6, 14, 25, 37–9, 43, 48, 52, 56–8, 96, 130–6, 138–42, 144–5, 147, 149–50, 154–61, 164–5, 168, 170, 177–8, 242, 255n7, 265n11, 267n32
segregation, 8, 27, 29, 60, 122, 214, 218–21, 233, 241
seniority, 16, 27, 73, 84, 89, 93–5, 97, 132, 146, 193, 239, 241, 255n5, 260n13
SEP. *See* Secretaria de la Educación Publica
Shanker, Albert, 17, 256n11, 257n23
Sindicato Nacional de los Trabajadores de la Educación (National Union of Education Workers; SNTE), 12–13, 19, 22–3, 25–7, 36, 38–9, 42–4, 48, 52, 61–6, 128–35, 140, 142–5, 147–9, 151, 156, 160, 162–4, 168, 171–4, 176–80, 242, 253n5, 254n9, 255n4, 256n15, 257n, 264nn4, 5, 7, 266n19, 267–8n32, 268nn37, 38, 43
Singapore, 189
small schools movement (New York), 69, 73, 81–4, 87, 93–4, 106, 110, 114, 116, 138, 260nn11, 12, 15
social democracy, 45–6, 49, 59, 122
social movement unionism, 125, 232–3
SNTE. *See* Sindicato Nacional de los Trabajadores de la Educación
Special Education, 68, 71, 74, 85, 89, 96, 123, 200, standardized testing, 8, 10, 14, 171–8, 21, 29, 35, 47, 53, 73–4, 100, 105, 108, 111–12, 122, 139, 153, 184, 189, 190, 223, 239, 243, 245, 247, 257n24, 261n25, 271n22
Spain, 56
Success Academy, 17, 102
Supreme Court (Canada), 15, 257n10
Supreme Court (Mexico), 144, 153
Supreme Court (United States), 124

taxes, 29, 36, 41, 46, 59, 77–8, 80, 108, 151, 184–6, 224, 226, 256–7n18, 271n27
TDSB. *See* Toronto District School Board
Teach for America (TFA), 59, 95–6, 120, 157, 257n19
Teacher Performance Appraisal (Ontario) (TPA), 191–2
teachers' strikes, 3, 12, 16–17, 26, 28, 39–42, 45–6, 49, 51–2, 65–6, 123, 132, 144, 147, 153–4, 161–2, 175–80, 208, 223, 227, 230, 231, 240, 242, 245, 247–8, 253–4n6, 255nn8, 9, 256n11, 258n25, 260n15
Texas, 63, 110
think-tanks, 46–7, 55, 103, 158, 218
Toronto District School Board (TDSB), 11, 29, 184–8, 195–202, 210, 211, 213–14, 217–19, 232, 254n10, 269n4, 270n18, 272n33

Trinational Coalition in Defense of Public Education, 26, 61, 64–6, 247, 258nn25, 26, 268n41
Trump, Donald, 243

UFT. *See* United Federation of Teachers
UNAM. *See* Universidad Nacional Autonoma de México
United Caucus of Rank and File Educators (UCORE), 65, 123
United Federation of Teachers (UFT), 11, 14, 17–19, 23, 27, 29, 39–40, 45–6, 74, 83–4, 87–9, 93–5, 99–105, 109–10, 112, 114–18, 120, 122, 124–5, 128, 243–4, 254n10, 261n16, 263n36
United Kingdom, 54, 136, 190, 195
United Nations Educational Scientific and Cultural Organization (UNESCO), 13, 23, 33, 37, 56–7, 63, 66, 129, 255n7
United States Department of Education (US DOE), 53–4, 60, 79, 105, 261n23
United Teachers of Los Angeles (UTLA), 64–5, 123
Universidad Nacional Autonoma de México (National Autonomous University of Mexico; UNAM), 258n26
Universidad Nacional Pedagogica (National Pedagogical University; UPN), 39

Value Added Metrics, 18
Vasconcelos, Jose, 33, 35, 255n3

working class, 17, 20, 22, 43, 46, 80, 82, 85, 114, 124, 126, 137, 141, 184, 213, 216, 246, 268n39
World Bank, 13, 20, 33, 45, 54, 56–8, 129, 136, 142, 152, 170, 248
Wynne, Kathleen, 28, 33, 50, 183, 186, 189, 194, 197, 201–2, 215, 221–2, 228, 232, 235–6, 245, 272n32

Zedillo, Ernesto, 131, 134, 151–2, 256n15

www.ingramcontent.com/pod-product-compliance
Lightning Source LLC
LaVergne TN
LVHW090151080826
844660LV00013B/767/J

* 9 7 8 1 4 8 7 5 0 6 6 0 5 *